KING OF INSTRUMENTS

Bernard Sonnaillon

KING OF INSTRUMENTS

A History of the Organ

translated by Stewart Spencer

RIZZOLI
NEW YORK

To my parents
To my teachers Jean-Jacques Grunenwald, Jacques Horneffer, Richard-Anthelme
Jeandin and Pierre Segond

c 2

French-language edtion: *L'Orgue, Instrument et musiciens*
Copyright © 1984 by Office du Livre S.A., Fribourg, Switzerland

English translation:
Copyright © 1985 by Office du Livre S.A., Fribourg, Switzerland

English translation published in 1985 in the United States of America by:

*R*IZZOLI INTERNATIONAL PUBLICATIONS, INC.
597 Fifth Avenue/New York 10017

Library of Congress Cataloging in Publication Data

Sonnaillon, Bernard.
 King of instruments.

 Translation of: L'orgue.
 Bibliography: p.
 Includes index.
 1. Organ. 2. Organ music--History and criticism.
I. Title.
ML550.S713 1985 786.5'09 84-43041
ISBN 0-8478-0582-4

Printed and bound in Switzerland

Table of Contents

Introduction		7
PART ONE: Description and History of the Instrument		9
I	Origins of the Organ	10
	Ancestors of the Organ	10
	Etymology	10
	The Ancient Organ	10
	The Principal Types of Organ	18
II	General Description of the Organ	19
	The Constituent Parts	20
	The Pipes	20

Flues Pipes 20 · Foundation Stops 21 · Mutation Stops 22 · Synthetic Tone Colors 24 · The *pleno* 24 · Flue Mutation Ranks 25 · Reed Pipes 26 · The Shape and Material of Pipes 27 · Organ Stops and their Names 28

	Mechanism	29

The Bellows and Wind Supply 29 · Development of the Bellows 30 · Modern Bellows 31 · The Wind-chests 34 · Disposition of the Pipes on the Wind-chests 37 · Tracker Action 37 · Operating the Stops 38 · Operating the Valves 38 · Keyboard Mechanisms 38 · Other Systems of Transmission 39

	The Console	42
	The Organ Case	48
	The Placing of the Organ	50
III	Organ Building and Restoration	53
	Organ Building from the Middle Ages to the Baroque	53
	Italy	56
	The Iberian Peninsula	56
	The Low Countries	57
	France	57
	German-Speaking Lands	58
	The Advent of the Romantic Organ	59
	The Modern Organ	60
	The Work of Organ Builder	64
	Restoration	67

PART TWO: A History of Organ Music   69

I   The First Organ Tablatures of the Fourteenth and Fifteenth Centuries   70

II   Organ Music in Italy   72

III   Organ Music in Germany   82
         Before Bach   82
            From the fifteenth century to the early seventeenth century 82   ·
            The Southern and Northern German Schools 85   ·   The South
            German Lands 86   ·   Northern Germany 89   ·   Central
            Germany 109
         The Organ Music of Johann Sebastian Bach   111
            The chorales 112   ·   The large-scale forms 114   ·   The trio
            sonatas and concertos 115
         Organ Music in Germany from Bach to the End of the
            Eighteenth Century   116
         German Organ Music in the Nineteenth Century   119

IV   Organ Music in the Low Countries   159

V   Organ Music in England   171

VI   Organ Music in France   185
         From Its Origins to the Beginning of the Nineteenth Century   185
            The noëlistes   192
            French Organ Music in the Nineteenth Century   193

VII   Organ Music in the Iberian Peninsula   217

VIII   Organ Music in the Twentieth Century   243
         The Organ Conquers the World   243
            Scandinavia 243   ·   Czechoslovakia and Hungary 244   ·
            Switzerland 244   ·   The United States 244   ·   Canada 245
         The Avant-Garde   246

Glossary   256
Abbreviations   259
Lexicon   260
Specifications   263
Bibliography   268
Index   271
Photo Credits   282

Introduction

Since the dawn of history men have longed to communicate with nature and her mysterious and overpowering forces. It is the same sense of longing which is expressed in the mythopoeic vision vouchsafed to the young Siegfried, who finally realizes his dream of imitating and understanding the woodbird as a symbol of human knowledge. Thus the flute, whose sounds so often accompanied the gods' first earthly epiphany, is the symbol not only of musical knowledge but also of communication and entertainment.

The organ was invented by a Greek engineer living in Alexandria. It is a distant descendant of the Pandean syrinx and of the classical *diaulos*. It is related to the Asiatic *sheng* and to the more familiar bagpipes. Ever since the birth of civilization, the organ has brought forth sounds of rejoicing, whether used to accompany Roman circus games or to afford more discreet musical pleasures to the well-to-do families of the Eastern Mediterranean. A further, less glorious, use, which we are also bound to mention here, was as a military siren in times of war. From the moment of its revival in the eighth century of the Christian era, the organ's privileged role was to mediate between men and the beyond, although in this it incurred a certain disquiet on the part of the Church Fathers. The organ learned to abandon its function as a form of entertainment and to follow medieval processions as they wound their way to holy sanctuaries. It is now a fully accepted member of both the church and the concert hall. How noble a destiny for an instrument which has continued to gain in fullness and beauty of sound: initially a simple series of pipes, the instrument developed to become the magnificent gleaming Baroque organ, subsequently adding to its voice the deep orchestral sounds typical of late Romanticism, before finally rediscovering an austere precision and vigor worthy of its master, Johann Sebastian Bach. As a result of its often monumental dimensions, and its capacity to produce at will a gentle lament or tremendous storm, the organ is seen by many as a mysterious instrument, which arouses wonderment and respect. It was described by Guillaume de Machaut as the "king of instruments," and by Franz Liszt as the "pope among instruments."

Discreetly enclosed within a modest wooden case, or else, by contrast, as elaborate and ornate as an illuminated manuscript, the organ exercises a seductive fascination by virtue of its perfection and beauty. It casts a spell of enchantment with the multiplicity of its forms and modes of expression. Every age has seen the apogee of one or another of its styles: it is this which compels us to preserve these monuments to the intelligence and sensibility of those artists who have gone before us, in the form in which they have been handed down.

I should like to thank the countless lovers of organ music who have helped me in writing this book; without their invaluable information, which they have sent me from the four corners of the world, and without their warm support, it would never have seen the light of day. They will understand that it is impossible for me to list them all by name, whether they be organists, organ builders, musicologists, experts with a

L'orgue majestueux se taisait gravement
    Dans la nef solitaire;
L'orgue, le seul concert, le seul gémissement
    Qui mêle aux cieux la terre!
(Victor Hugo, *Les chants du crépuscule: Dans l'église de ***.*)

Gravely mute the organ seemed, withal resplendent
    In the deserted nave;
The organ whose concerted sounds and soft lament
    Unite the heavens and earth!

The organ is flesh and blood. And this flesh will live in so far as it is considered as such and we learn to expose its substance.
                                                    (Jean Guillou)

specialist knowledge of organs, or churchmen. But I should like to express my warmest thanks to those who have followed the progress of my work through each of its stages, giving me the benefit of their erudition and their unfailing patience: Marinette Extermann, François Delor (who has provided the invaluable drawings which illustrate the technical section of the text), Luis Artur Esteves Pereira, Didier Godel, Dr Dieter Grossmann, Jerzy Gołos, Gerhard Grenzing, Pál Kelemen, Georges Lhôte, Thomas Murray and Luigi Ferdinando Tagliavini. I would like also to express my gratitude to Guy Bovet and Stewart Spencer for their valuable suggestions.

PART ONE:
DESCRIPTION AND HISTORY OF THE INSTRUMENT

I Origins of the Organ

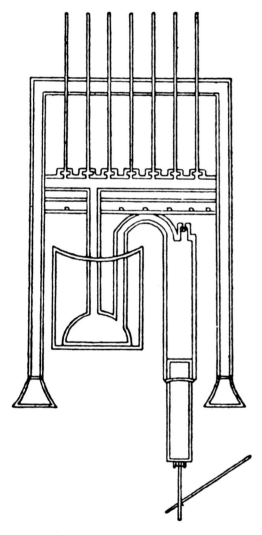

Fig. 1   Diagram of a *hydraulis* as described by Hero(n) of Alexandria, first century AD (?), from a manuscript on Pneumatics, Brit. Mus. MS. Harleianus 5589. From Sumner. p. 20
We may recall that, in his *Confessions* (Book III), Jean-Jacques Rousseau speaks of a "small and very pretty heron fountain," an allusion to a toy described by the engineer of Alexandria and particularly popular in the eighteenth century.

ANCESTORS OF THE ORGAN

From the earliest times men have known how to make a flute out of a reed, and then, by assembling a number of pipes of varying lengths, to construct an instrument which later became known as the Pandean pipe. But human ingenuity went on to harness the winds of the air. So was born an astonishing instrument consisting of a single pipe, or rather several pipes, whose mouthpiece was cut with a bevelled edge; alternatively, holes were bored in the pipes themselves at various heights. Like the Pandean pipe, these natural aerophones later developed into the ancestor of the modern organ. In this context one thinks particularly of an instrument found to this day in the Solomon Islands, where several lengths of bamboo are set up on the beach in such a way that the passing wind causes their air columns to vibrate. Aerophones of various construction may also still be seen outside various temples in South-East Asia. A similar result may be obtained by causing the instrument itself to vibrate at high speed, a method used most notably in the case of the African rhombus.

ETYMOLOGY

The word "organ" (from the Greek ὄργανον, *organon*; Latin *organum*) was originally applied to an instrument or tool. It could also be used to describe any musical instrument, though not necessarily the particular instrument which is our present concern.
    The hydraulic organ designed by Ctesibius during the third century B.C. was called ὕδραυλις (*hydraulis*, literally "water flute"). At a somewhat later date, during the first century B.C., this same instrument was described by Hero of Alexandria as ὄργανον ὕδραυλικον (*organon hydraulicon*; Latin *organum hydraulicum* or *organa hydraulica*), literally a "water-driven musical instrument." In the course of time the two words became contracted to ὕδραυλος (*hydraulos*; Latin *hydraulus*), until replaced, during the late Roman Empire, by the term *organum* or *organa*.
    In view of the various Latin uses of the word *organum* and in view, too, of the fact that from the tenth century onwards the same word was used to describe a particular type of vocal music, it is not surprising that a certain amount of confusion has arisen over the exact use of the term.

THE ANCIENT ORGAN

Ever since it was first invented (probably by Ctesibius, a Greek engineer living in Alexandria around the year 246 B.C.), the organ has led a double life, so to speak,

Fig. 2 The organ on the obelisk of Theodosius at Constantinople, end of fourth century AD; after E. de Coussemaker, *Annales Archéologiques*, 11.277, Paris, 1845.

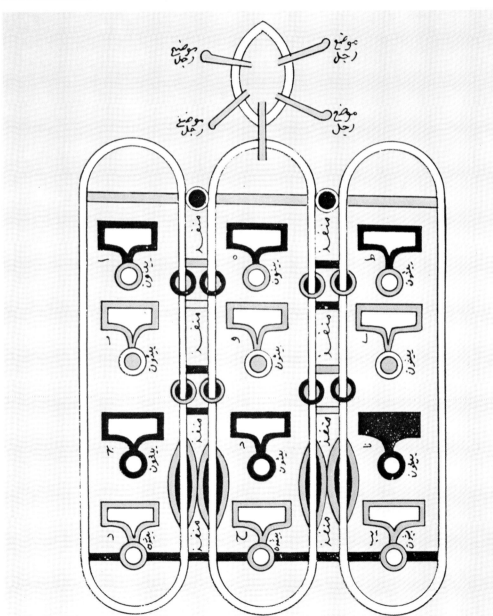

Fig. 3 Diagram of the instrument attributed to the hypothetical Muristos, as it appears in an Arab manuscript from the Greek Orthodox College of the Three Moons, Beirut. Four men, visible at the top of the picture, are to be imagined breathing into three bellows, each of which feeds four (reed) pipes. The four rows of pipes, each of which was fitted with a kind of stopper allowing the air to enter, sounded at different pitches. In the diagram, it is the third pipe, fixed over the right-hand bellows, which sounds.

The hydraulic organ disappeared from the Western Empire in the fifth century, at the time of the barbarian invasions, but when the Eastern Empire later began to adopt the religious and cultural traditions of Rome, the organ was accorded a privileged status. In the mid-tenth century, for example, there were four organs at the court of Constantine VII. From Constantinople the instrument then spread to all the Moslem countries, starting with Syria and thence to the Caliphates of Baghdad, Cairo and Córdoba. Three types of instrument developed in these regions: the traditional hydraulic organ; an instrument of considerable size whose sound could carry large distances and which was used for military purposes; and the "golden tree" with moving leaves and moving, whistling birds (see Fig. 4), inspired by similar instruments which had earlier been made in Constantinople; in Moslem countries such instruments became simple musical automata. From F. Jakob, Lausanne, 1970.

Fig. 4   Automaton in the form of a tree with whistling birds, a tradition dating back to the Hellenistic age (Ctesibius) and the Arab period; see M. Gerbert, *De cantu et musica sacra*, Sankt Blasien, 1744, Pl. 28.

successfully combining its contradictory functions as both a musical instrument and a machine. This contradiction has arisen largely because of the need to replace the human breath (which is used to produce the sound in wind instruments) by a mechanical method of compressing the wind supply. Indeed, the problem of wind supply has been one of the most persistent difficulties facing organ designers throughout the instrument's long history and has played a crucial role in its development.

Musical instrument or machine? The ingenuity of the organ's inventor commands our respect: although the basic principle of pipes having a fixed sound was already familiar to him from the Pandean pipe, he still had to invent a form of bellows comprising (as it still does today) a pump which supplied the air and a reservoir to ensure its constant flow and pressure. The ancient organ showed particular ingenuity in this respect by storing compressed air inside a bell-jar submerged in water, hence the name *hydraulis* which was given to instruments of this kind. From a technical point of view, it was an extremely efficient system, since the reservoir involved no moving mass except for the water. However, the air pressure varied in direct proportion to the amount of water in the reservoir, and operational problems soon led to the introduction of "dry" bellows or blast-bags, in which the bellows, similar to those used in forges, were made of skin or hide, serving both as a pump and as a reservoir. Since a number of surviving mosaics and medallions depict the organ being played in the open air, it seems reasonable to suppose that only hydraulically regulated reservoirs could guarantee sufficient air pressure for what were really quite modest instruments to produce an acceptable volume of sound.

Organs were introduced by the Greeks into the Roman world, but then disappeared from the Western Empire at the time of the great invasions. They continued to be built and played in the Eastern Empire, from where they spread rapidly throughout the Arab world. It was Byzantium which reintroduced the organ into the West, in the form of a present offered in 757 by the Emperor Constantine Copronymus the Fifth to Pepin the Short (714–68). Although politically motivated, this gift was to have remarkable artistic repercussions: in order that so exceptional a present might be copied, an appeal was sent out to a Venetian priest by the name of Georgius, who must have been in contact with the Eastern Empire and familiar with local methods of organ building. Transmitting his knowledge to his pupils, he was no doubt responsible for the installation of organs in a number of churches, where only a few centuries previously the instrument had been categorically banned by the Church Fathers as a symbol of paganism. From that time onwards the organ spread throughout Christendom, rapidly establishing itself in cathedrals, abbeys and churches.

1   Detail of a mosaic from Zliten, Libya, late first century or early second century AD; Archaeological Museum, Tripoli
The mosaic depicts two orchestras. In the section reproduced here (first orchestra), the sonorities of the organ are combined with those of a *tuba* (a long trumpet with a small conical bell) and two *cornua* (curved cornets), an ensemble of instruments intended to give a sense of rhythm to the exploits of the gladiators. It may be noted that the organist is a woman, and that she must have operated the pumps herself with her feet, since there are no assistants to act as blowers either here or in the Nennig mosaic.

2   Mosaic from Nennig, Federal Republic of Germany, second century AD; Rheinisches Landesmuseum, Trier, Federal Republic of Germany
This mosaic depicts an instrumental ensemble enlivening the gladiatorial games in an amphitheater, and shows that the brilliant sonorities of a hydraulic organ blended effectively with the timbre of other instruments, in this case a curved cornet or *cornu*. The Nenning mosaic differs from the usual iconographical depictions of hydraulic organs in that the treble pipes are on the organist's left; but the artist's interpretative talents are clearly more appreciable here than his sense of descriptive accuracy.

3 Sarcophagus of Julia Tyrrania, second or third century AD; Musée lapidaire d'art païen, Arles, France

Discovered in the Aliscamps Roman cemetery at Arles, this white marble sarcophagus depicts a hydraulic organ, together with a tree, some kind of quadruped and a box which may perhaps have been intended to contain a set of large Pandean pipes. Since we know that when the girl died at the age of twenty years and eight months, she was "famous for her teaching (*disciplina*)," we may surmise that she liked music and that she may even have been an accomplished organist, as were many of her educated contemporaries.

4 Contorniate from the reign of Valentinian III, fifth century AD; Cabinet des Médailles, Bibliothèque nationale, Paris

The obverse of this contorniate (a bronze medallion, talisman or commemorative medal struck to mark the occasion of gladiatorial games or musical competitions held in Roman amphitheaters) bears the likeness of the Emperor Valentinian III, son of General Constantius, who reigned from 424 to 455. On the reverse can be seen a magnificent hydraulic organ, together with an organist and two blowers. The inscription *Placeas Petri* no doubt refers to an organist who was famous at the time. We may possibly be dealing here with a example of the newer type of instrument which seems to have been built by the mid-fourth century and referred to by the historian Ammianus Marcellinus as "organa hydraulica [...] ingentes," hydraulic organs of immense size.

5 The Elect at the Last Judgement, end of the thirteenth century; Cathedral, León, Spain

The scene depicted here shows a portative organ with four short legs placed on the ground. The organist is seated on a very low stool, while a child can be seen operating the small bellows. The instrument, which is relatively tall, has a raised wind-chest. The pipes are supported by a diagonal bar attached to two uprights at either side, an arrangement reminiscent of that of Roman instruments. The fact that there is only a single pair of bellows (which, as was usually the case in the thirteenth century, were shaped like a blacksmith's bellows) is clearly due to an iconographical simplification on the part of the artist, since a positive organ of this size would require a greater wind supply than could be provided by a single set of bellows. More especially, it would require a second, compensatory pair. Positive organs of this size, which were still small enough to be transported from place to place, may be regarded as intermediaries between the portative organ on the one hand and the "great" organ on the other.

7   Gilles Binchois and Guillaume Dufay, miniature from "Le champion des dames" by Martin Le Franc, France, fifteenth century; Bibliothèque nationale, Paris, MS. fr. 12476, fol. 98

6   Tombstone of the blind composer Francesco Landini (1325?–97); Basilica of S. Lorenzo, Florence, Italy

8   Hans Memling (c. 1433–94), "Christ surrounded by Angel Musicians," detail of an organ panel, dated 1485, from the Church of Sta. Maria la Real, Nagera, Castile; now in the Musée royal des Beaux-Arts, Antwerp

This angel may well recall the famous lines from the *Roman de la Rose*: "Orgues i r'a bien maniables / A une sole main portables / Où il-méismes soufle et touche / Et chante avec à plaine bouche / Motés, ou treble ou tenéure" ("He had excellent organs that could be carried in one hand while he himself worked the bellows and played as, with open mouth, he sang motet or triplum or tenor voice") (11.21037–41). Jean de Meun[g] wrote these lines in the second half of the thirteenth century. The angel can be seen holding a portative organ on his lap. The pipework comprises two series of sixteen cylindrical pipes arranged chromatically (like the majority of portatives, this is a 2′ instrument). With his left hand the angel operates the bellows, made of two rectangular boards and four wedge-shaped folds. The keyboard is made up of two rows of "touch-buttons" mounted on short pivots extending downwards by means of a rod or sticker and used to open the pipe-chest valves when the button is depressed. The pallet valve which closes the groove, or channel, is made of wood and held in position by a spring. This system, apparently in use since the end of the fourteenth century, is found alongside the system of "touch-rods" or levers which was later to develop into the modern manual. It had itself superseded the earlier system of flat levers or note-sliders which the organist pulled towards him and then pushed back into position. There is no obvious distinction between the keys corresponding to the diatonic pipes and those corresponding to the chromatic ones. However, other fourteenth-century representations, including a fine example in the polyptych by Jan Van Eyck, "The Adoration of the Lamb," show that the chromatic keys could be distinguished from the diatonic keys either by being made shorter, by being placed back from the diatonic keys, or by being made of some other material.

9   Misericord from a choir stall in the Abbey of St. Lucien at Beauvais; now in the Musée de Cluny, Paris, France

Originally made for the Abbey of St. Lucien, this misericord has found its way into the iconography of bestiaries, a popular genre in Europe from the Middle Ages until the Age of the Baroque. Messire Porcus can be seen at the keyboard while his wife busies herself working the bellows; their offspring, insensitive to the beauties of the music, avails himself of the opportunity to partake of what appears to be a well-deserved meal. The instrument is a table positive, its pipes, crudely carved, being in the shape of a bishop's miter.

10   Organ in Amiens Cathedral, 1422–9, donated by Alphonse Le Mire
Copper engraving by Limozin of part of the tomb of the Le Mire family, Bibliothèque nationale, Paris, Ve, fol. 26

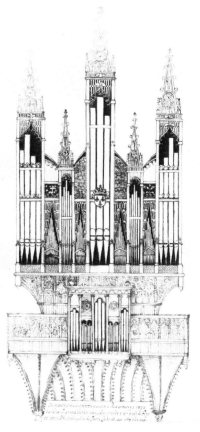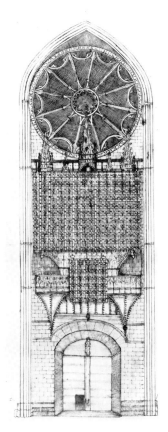

11   Cathedral, Rheims, France
Grand Orgue, 1487; *Positif*, 1570. Sixteenth-century engraving by Jacques Cellier, Bibliothèque nationale, Paris, MS. fr. 9152, fol. 75

12   Cathedral, Rheims, France
The same organ curtained off. Sixteenth-century engraving by Jacques Cellier, Bibliothèque nationale, Paris, MS. fr. 9152, fol. 74

13   Table positive. Sixteenth-century engraving by Jacques Cellier, Bibliothèque nationale, Paris, MS. fr. 9152, fol. 183

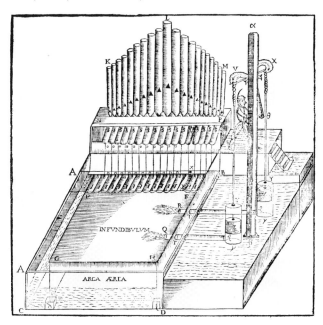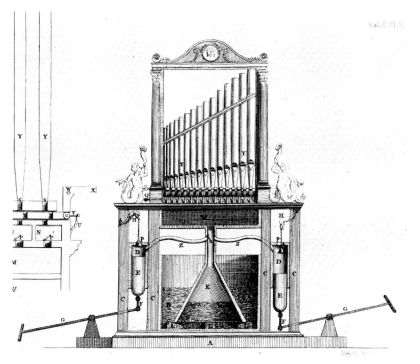

14   Athanasius Kircher, *Musurgia Universalis*, Rome, 1650
Father Kircher, failing to understand the function of the water in a classical organ, believed it gave the sound agreeable vibrations.

15   Vitruvius, *De Architectura*, from an English translation by William Newton, London, 1791
Illustration of Vitruvius' hydraulis, showing an accurate understanding of the blowing mechanism.

Fig. 5   Portative organ, fourteenth century, from a fresco under the altar canopy in the church of St. Savin (Hautes Pyrénées). From Dufourq, 1935, p. 28.

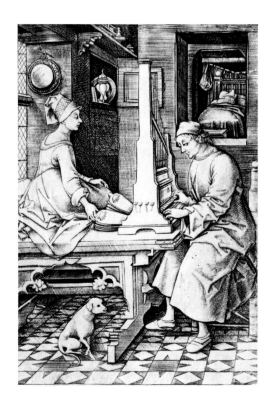

Fig. 6   Table positive: engraving of an organist and his wife by I. van Meckenem, late fifteenth century; British Museum, London.

THE PRINCIPAL TYPES OF ORGAN

It is usual to distinguish three types of organ which developed in the West: the portative, positive and great organ.

The portative organ, as its name implies, is an instrument which can easily be carried and is therefore comparatively small in size. Supported by a strap worn round the neck or simply placed on the performer's knees, the portative organ requires the presence of only one person operating the bellows with his left hand while, with his right hand, he causes the pipes to speak, initially by operating simple wooden rods (sliders) which he had to pull and then push back, and, later, by depressing the keys of a manual of limited range. The portative organ was useful for processions and, although sometimes played in church, it was regarded chiefly as a secular instrument and the preserve of strolling players. It gradually went out of fashion after the Renaissance. The positive organ is larger in size than the portative, consisting of a greater number of pipes and being more difficult to transport. Although generally placed on the ground or on some piece of furniture or other support, it could also be lifted onto a cart and, like the portative organ, be used to accompany both religious and secular processions. In the palaces of the aristocracy and the homes of rich merchants it quickly assumed a place of honor. During the Renaissance it became the favorite instrument of the middle classes and remained popular until the eighteenth century, when it was supplanted by the harpsichord and, later, by the piano. In town it was played as a solo instrument, or else was used to accompany other instruments; in church it was located in the choir, where it supported the singing of the choristers.

For a time the portative organ disappeared completely, although more and more are being built today for the performance of early music. The positive organ, meanwhile, has survived in two distinct forms: from the fifteenth century onwards it was added to or incorporated into the great organ, thus constituting the second manual of the main organ; alternatively, it was played on its own as a secular instrument and is occasionally described by writers on the subject as a "chamber organ."

Whether as a portative or as a positive organ, the regal organ is a special form of organ which has been revived in our own century following the renewal of interest in the performance of early music. Flat in shape and with concealed pipes, it was fitted with one or more reed stops without resonators, or with only short-length resonators (to which a flute register was later added); its raucous tone was to be heard accompanying royal banquets and celebrations during the later Middle Ages and adding its luster to instrumental ensembles at court. Its memory has survived in the name which it has bequeathed to certain organ stops.

The Great Organ marks an important stage in the development of the art of organ building. From the second half of the thirteenth century onwards the organ came to play a preponderant role in churches, following closely in this respect the development of polyphonic music. There was a need for instruments of a richer and more varied tone color which could imitate the choir, or even replace it, and which would support and inspire the singing of the congregation. As a result we find various places of worship striving to modify and enlarge their existing organs, or to build larger instruments. The increasing number of stops and the sonorous impact that was sought soon obliged organ builders to raise up the wind-chests and pipes, which for the first time now came to exceed a man's height, while the organist, placed on a level with the console, was given an increasing number of controls to operate. These changes represent not merely an evolution, but a revolution in the art of organ building, since the distances which were now involved required the creation of completely new methods of mechanical action, vital links between the console and the pipework of the instrument.

Originally a secular instrument of modest dimensions, the organ thus gradually assumed the role of the most important of liturgical instruments in Western Christianity, and at the same time became one of the most striking features of church architecture. It did so not only because of its often majestic size but also, and above all, because of the elaborate ornamentation which went into its design.

II General Description of the Organ

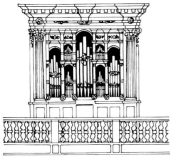

Fig. 7 Comparative diagram showing organs of differing sizes:

32' case pipes
Main organ of the Grote Kerk (St. Bavo) Haarlem, Netherlands (Christiaan Müller, 1735–8)

16' case pipes
Main organ in Auch Cathedral, France (Jean de Joyeuse, 1688–95)

8' case pipes
Organ at S. Maria del Sasso, Morcote, Switzerland (mid-seventeenth century)

4' case pipes
Organ in the Zion Lutheran church, Spring City (PA), USA (David Tannenberg, 1791)

2' case pipes
Positive organ of 1620 (Marburg Museum, Hessen, Federal Republic of Germany)

Portative organ

Person to scale

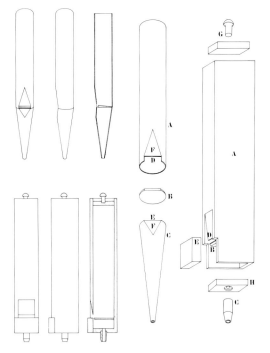

Fig. 8   Front, side view and cross section of an open flue pipe (metal) (above, left)
Front, side view and cross section of a stopped flue pipe (wood) (below, left)

Exploded view of two flue pipes: (a) open metal pipe; (b) stopped wood pipe (right)
A Body or resonator – B Languid – C Toe – D Upper lip – E Lower lip – F Flatting – G Stopper and its handle – H Block

Fig. 9   Scales of flue pipes and reed pipes; from M. Praetorius, *Syntagma musicum*, Vol. II: "De Organographia," Wolfenbüttel, 1619, Pl. 38.

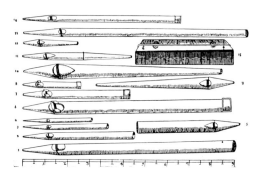

Fig. 10   Scales of flue pipes and monochord; from M. Praetorius, *Syntagma musicum*, Vol. II: "De Organographia," Wolfenbüttel, 1619, Pl. 37.

THE CONSTITUENT PARTS

In spite of the considerable modifications which the organ has undergone in the course of the centuries, its basic construction has remained the same. The organ is a wind instrument numbering one or more series of sound-producing pipes. Each pipe, in principle, produces a single note, and each series of pipes (or register) is tuned according to a precise scheme. A wind-chest receives its air supply from the bellows and in turn supplies the pipes. These various parts (the pipes, the wind-chest and often the bellows as well) are enclosed within the organ case. The console, comprising one or more manuals, pedals (where applicable) and the stops are the central controls from which all these other elements are operated, allowing the air supply to be directed towards the pipes desired.

THE PIPES

The part of the organ which produces the sound is made up principally, or essentially, of the pipes, which may be divided into two groups according to the manner in which the sound is emitted: flue pipes in which the air is the only element to vibrate, and reed pipes in which the air causes a metal tongue to beat against a metal plate or shallot.

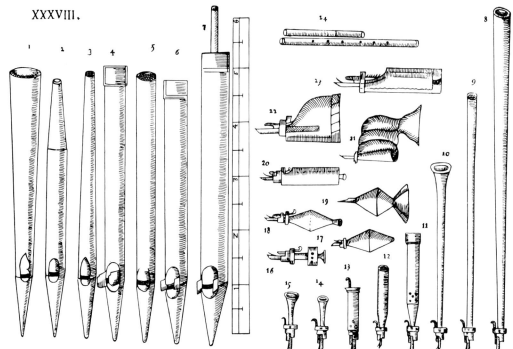

Flue Pipes

The flue pipe is made up of five separate elements (six if the pipe is stoppered at its upper end by a "cap" in the case of metal pipes or a "stopper" in the case of wood pipes): the *foot* or base of the pipe into which the air passes from the wind-chest; the actual *body* of the pipe, which is cylindrical or slightly conical in section in the case of metal pipes, and rectangular or square in section in the case of wood pipes; the *mouth* or flue, comprising an "upper lip" and "lower lip" and occasionally fitted with *ears* or "beards" to ensure a greater clarity of tonal attack; and the *languid*, a metal or wooden plate separating the foot of the pipe from the resonator. The empty space between the languid and the lower lip is known as the "windway."

The wind enters the foot-hole or bore at the foot of the pipe and is forced towards the windway between the edge of the languid and the lower lip; here it comes into violent contact with the upper lip, thus causing the air column inside the resonator to vibrate.

The frequency of the vibrations (hence the pitch of the note) is a function of the length of the resonator: the longer the column of air which is set into vibration, the deeper the note. If the pipe is stopped, the air column has to escape through the mouth of the pipe rather than through its upper end; in this way the air covers the same distance twice and the length of the column of air is accordingly doubled; the frequency of the vibrations is halved and the pitch of the note lowered by an octave (if one compares a stopped pipe with an unstopped one of the same length). The cap of a stopped pipe, which refracts the vibrating column of air, may in certain instances be lengthened by the addition of a chimney which has the effect of brightening the tonal quality: these pipes are described as being *à cheminée* or *à biberon*. Open flue pipes are tuned in one of two ways: slight adjustments may be made to the size of the opening at the upper extremity of the pipe by means of a tuning cone, a process known as *coupé sur ton*; or else a nick (or indentation) is made at the top of the resonator, which alters the height of the column of air and hence the pitch of the note. This practise was widespread during the age of the industrial organ, but is now being abandoned by most of the better organ builders, since it has been found to alter the sound quality of the pipe. Stopped pipes are tuned by altering the position of the "ears" if the cap is soldered on, or by raising or lowering the cap or stopper in the event of its not being soldered down.

The unit of measurement of the column of sound (pitch) has traditionally been the foot (about 33 cm); in Spain measurements were calculated in hands (one hand = approx. 20 cm). A stop (or register) of eight feet (abbreviated as 8′) is a row of open pipes of the same tone color whose longest pipe (the lowest note) measures 8 feet from the mouth to the top of the pipe. It is conventional to describe a stopped pipe which produces the same note as an open pipe as being 8′, although the longest pipe in the register will measure only 4′. The sound quality of pipes depends upon their scale, in other words the relationship between the length and diameter of the pipe: pipes are accordingly described as being "large scale," "moderate scale" and "small scale." The quality of a note depends not only on the scale of the pipe but also on the width of the mouth, its length, the position of the languid, the diameter of the opening in the pipe foot and the amount of air pressure involved. It is at this point that the voicer takes over, his task being to give each stop its individual character and personality.

Foundation Stops

As their name indicates, the foundation stops constitute the basis of the instrument. Four distinct families combine to form the foundation stops: the Diapasons (or Montres, as they are often called in French organs, where they function as display pipes), Flutes, Bourdons and Gambas, the last named being the latest additions to the group.

The Diapasons, open pipes of moderate scale with a wide mouthpiece, support the tonal edifice (the organ is tuned to the 4′ Diapason, since, according to Dom Bédos de Celles, "it occupies the middle ground in its range between the deeper sounds of the larger registers and the more high-pitched sounds of the smaller registers"). In length the Diapasons may measure 32′ (this stop generally being incorporated into the pedals), 16′, 8′, 4′, (known as the Principal or Octave) and 2′ (Fifteenth) and form the fundamental components of the *pleno*.

The Flutes are open pipes of large scale, tuned like the Diapasons and encompassing all the octaves from 32′ to ½′. For the most part they are cylindrical in section and of actual height, with two exceptions: the Spitzflöte, with its clear tone, and the Flûte harmonique (or Flûte octaviante) with a more intense sound; a small hole is generally pierced halfway along the speaking-length of the pipes of this register, so that the length of the vibrating column of air is doubled, the main column (from the

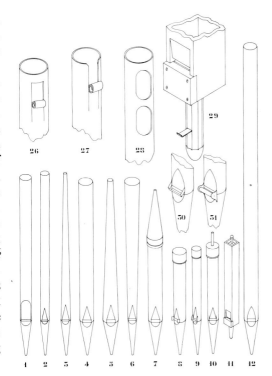

Fig. 11   Flue pipes
1 Diapason or Principal – 2 Gamba – 3 Conical Gamba – 4 Flute – 5 Conical Flute – 6 Tapered Flute – 7 Coppelflöte – 8 Bourdon – 9 Quintaton – 10 Flûte à cheminée (Chimney Flute) – 11 Wood Bourdon – 12 Flûte harmonique
Tuning apparatus:
26 by means of a tuning cone – 27 by nicking (more common nowadays)
Diagrams 1–6 show pipes which are "cut to pitch length" (*coupé sur le ton*), i.e. without any special tuning apparatus. Tuning is carried out by means of a tinned steel tuning slide which grips the top of the pipe in such a way that the opening may be enlarged or reduced, thus causing the pitch to rise or fall.
28 Holes cut in the back of a display pipe, if the body of the pipe has to be lengthened for aesthetic reasons – 29 Device for regulating the flow of wind into the foot of a wood pipe – 30 and 31 Two types of *frein harmonique*

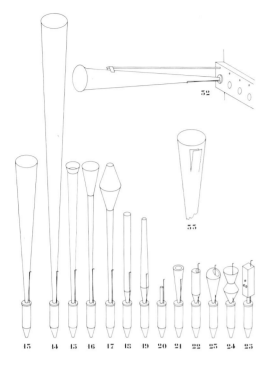

Fig. 12   Reed pipes
13 Trompette – 14 Trompette harmonique –
15 Schalmei – 16 Oboe – 17 Cor anglais –
18 Cromorne – 19 Musette – 20 Regal –
21 Trompetenregal – 22 Vox humana – 23 Vox
humana – 24 Regal (Bärpfeife) – 25 Regal (Ran-
kett) – 32 Trompette *en chamade* – 33 Resonator *à pavillon*

mouthpiece to the hole) setting off a second column (from the hole to the top of the pipe) which vibrates in sympathy with it and reinforces the sound.

The Bourdons are large-scaled stopped pipes which sound an octave lower than their actual height would suggest and are found in sizes ranging from 32′ to 2′. When incorporated into the pedals these stops may be given specific names such as the Cor de nuit or Sub-bass (16′ pedal) or Quintadena (16′, 8′ and sometimes 4′), a closed stop of narrow scale in which the fifth (i. e. 2nd overtone) can be heard as distinctly as the fundamental.

The Bourdon à cheminée (or Rohrflöte or Flûte à biberon) has a metal cap fitted with a small tube which enables it to produce a clearer sound. The wider the chimney is in cross section, the more its sound recalls an open Flute.

The Gambas are open pipes of narrow scale and recall the sonorities of string instruments, hence the names Viola da gamba, Violone, Viola, Violoncello, Contre-basse and Violonbasse which have been given to them. Attempts were made in the nineteenth century to overblow the Gambas, thus enabling them to imitate the orches-tra, but difficulties arose with the emission of the sound, and it was in order to correct this fault that the pipes were fitted with an harmonic *frein*, a metal bar or roller placed in front of the mouth of the pipe in order to stabilize the tone. Gambas are cylindrical or conical in section, and exist in lengths of 16′, 8′ and 4′. There are loud Gambas and soft Gambas such as the Salicional, the Gemshorn, the Dolce and the Dulciana. Another stop which never fails to capture the imagination is the Voix Céleste (Vox Coelestis, Unda Maris), tuned slightly sharp, so that when such pipes sound at the same time as the Gamba pipes, they produce a slight beat similar in sound to a string vibrato.

Mutation Stops

"Mutation Stops" is the term generally applied to those ranks of pipes which produce so-called "harmonics" or upper partials, but excluding those stops which sound the octave (4′, 2′ and 1′), although these, too, strictly speaking, are harmonics. In fact, every sound emitted by a vibrating mass is in reality composed of several sounds of different frequency. The lowest note – which is the one most clearly heard – is called the fundamental, while the higher notes, less easily perceived, are called harmonics, upper partials or overtones. The ear assimilates these different sounds, their number or respective intensity determining the tone quality of the fundamental.

By way of an example we may consider the upper partials of the note C (which would be the note of the first pipe of an open 8′ stop). Notes 3, 5, 6 and 7 give the fundamental a particularly rich "color." This acoustic phenomenon has been amply exploited in the case of the organ, since the organ builder has learned not only to control the emission of upper partials in constructing a pipe, but may even create registers which themselves produce the overtones of other registers, which thereby assume the role of a fundamental. The frequency of an overtone is the function of that of its fundamental according to a simple formula: in order to calculate the frequency, it is sufficient to multiply the number of vibrations of the fundamental by the number of the order in which the overtone appears in the diagram on page 24.

If, for example, we take an 8′ pipe (actual length) as the fundamental,
Note 2 is produced by a pipe twice as short as the 8′ pipe, i. e. 4′, and sounds an octave above the 8′ fundamental;
Note 3 is produced by a pipe three times as short as the 8′ pipe, i. e. 2²⁄₃′, and sounds a perfect fifth above the previous note;
Note 4, 2′ , sounds a perfect fourth above the previous note and an octave above Note 2;
Note 5, 1³⁄₅′, sounds a major third above the previous note;
Note 6, 1¹⁄₃′, sounds a perfect fifth above Note 4 and an octave above Note 3; and so on, Note 7 (1¹⁄₇′) sounding the minor seventh, Note 9 (⁸⁄₉′) the major ninth of Note 4.

A "Progressive" system

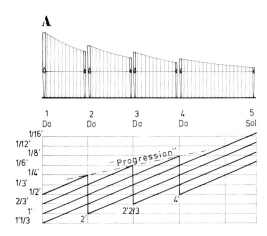

B "Ceiling" system (IV-rank Fourniture based on Dom Bédos de Celles)

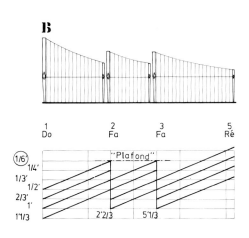

C "Ceiling" system with more frequent breaks (III-rank Cymbale based on Dom Bédos de Celles)

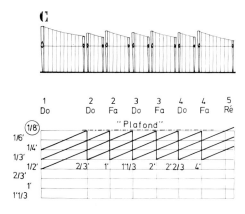

Fig. 13 Diagram showing the principal systems for breaking back in chorus Mixtures: Rank of pipes on the wind-chest, seen in profile and corresponding diagrams.

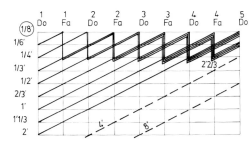

Diagram showing all the ranks of the *ripieno* of a classical Italian organ. Starting at C, the first pipes of each rank measure, respectively, 8, 4, 2, 1⅓, 1, etc. When a particular pipe in each of the ranks produces a note sufficiently high for it to measure only ⅛′, the next pipe in the rank will sound an octave lower. This process may be repeated several times ("ceiling" system).

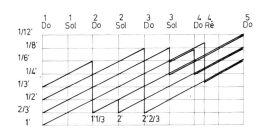

Diagram of the *Scharf* Mixture of the *Rückpositiv* at Cappel, Federal Republic of Germany (Arp Schnitger, 1680). In this "progressive" system, there is a clear imbalance between the lower registers of the keyboard (IV ranks at the outset) and the higher ones, where the treble is boosted by the presence of VI ranks and numerous duplications.

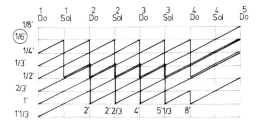

Diagram of the *Plein Jeu* (IV-rank Fourniture + III-rank Cymbale) of the main keyboard of the organ at Marmoutier, France (Andreas Silbermann, 1709–10). In this "ceiling" system, related to that of the Italian *ripieno*, the breaks occur twice every octave in each of the ranks. It will be observed that the upper limit is fixed at ⅙′.

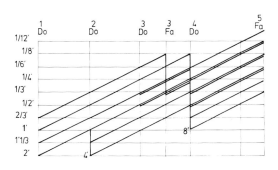

Diagram of an ensemble of "progressive" Mixtures, Notre-Dame de Paris, France, (Aristide Cavaillé-Coll, 1868). The principal is the same as that of Schnitger's organ in Cappel, but on a larger scale, with IV ranks in the lower registers and IX at the top of the keyboard.

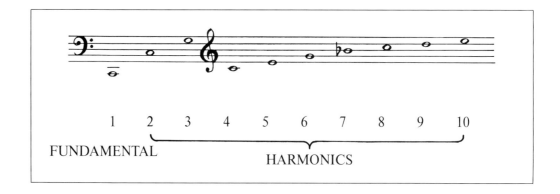

Synthetic Tone Colors

Whenever he refers to the flue pipes of his instrument, the organist traditionally uses the term "Foundation Stops" for the Diapasons, Flutes, Bourdons and Gambas of 32′, 16′ and 8′ (sometimes adding to these the 4′ pipes), and "Mutation Stops" for the pipes which sound in fifths and thirds, and also sevenths and ninths. This method of breaking down the sound mass of the organ is in fact a heritage from the nineteenth century, which favored the lower registers (from 32′ to 4′) and regarded as superfluous, if not uncivilized, the upper registers, and in particular the Mutation Stops, which of course included the Mixture Ranks.

The Middle Ages, on the other hand, and, to a very large degree, the Renaissance and the Baroque considered the sounds produced by the organ as an homogeneous whole extending from the deepest to the highest note. The divisions were rather to be found among the various families of registers: in one group were all the Diapasons, in another the Flute ranks, and, finally, there were the reeds. This "vertical" conception is now coming back into favor, the more so since it corresponds to the essential nature of the organ and is what constitutes the instrument's basic originality.

The *pleno*

The *pleno*, Plenum or *plein jeu* (in German *Mixtur-Plenum*, in Italian *ripieno* and in Spanish *lleno*) is made up of all the Diapason pipes from the lowest to the highest (i. e. from 32′ to approximately ¹/₁₂′), played on all the manuals and the pedals as well. The 32′, 16′ and 8′ Bourdons are frequently added, either to enrich the fundamentals, or to make up for an open register which would otherwise be missing. The expression *pleno* makes it clear that this particular mixture of stops is intended to produce an effect of tonal richness, and give the impression of encompassing the whole range of sound as much as of filling all the available space with sound. The *pleno* is a bold creation but to some extent an artificial one, bearing in mind the natural laws of acoustics, since it includes not only upper partials emphasizing a note which is considered as the fundamental, but also much higher notes which are in fact the upper partials of the Octave Stops, which are themselves harmonics.

We may begin by considering the general principle of the *pleno*, whose purpose is to sound not only the fundamentals but also a certain (variable) number of octaves and fifths, and sometimes of thirds, encompassing the full range of one or more of the manuals in such a way that the resultant sound falls pleasingly on the ear. Although the very high ranks may be perfectly bearable at the lower end of the keyboard, they take on an intolerable stridency in the treble, and it is at this point that the system of "breaking back" comes into operation. If a rank or a group of several ranks sounding together reaches a certain pitch, which is determined in advance according to varying criteria, its progression is interrupted and it breaks back either to the lower octave or a fourth lower (for octave ranks that become fifths), or a fifth lower (for ranks of fifths which become octaves). These small pipes are clearly visible in the inside of an organ: they are the smallest of all its pipes, and form a serrated edge when seen in profile.

The high-pitched ranks of the *pleno* may be arranged according to one of two options: the progressive option encourages the notes to ascend to a high register but, by beginning at a relatively low pitch, it restricts the number of breaks or even dispenses with them entirely; the ceiling option seeks to reproduce in each of the keyboard registers the same superposition of upper partials considered from the point of view of their absolute pitch; the lower notes on the keyboard are thus made up of higher-pitched ranks than those in the progressive system, and each time they reach a certain pitch which is considered to be the upper limit (an imaginary horizontal line), the ranks in question are subjected to a break, so that one arrives at the top of the keyboard's range with upper partials which are sometimes extremely low in pitch relative to the fundamentals. In both systems one finds two- or three-rank mixtures (in unison), above all in the upper half of the keyboard, where it is frequent practise to increase the number of pipes per key. In general the *pleno* ranks are independent up to 2′ and grouped together thereafter. Nowadays, the general term Mixture is used to describe any stop which makes up the high ranks of the *pleno*.

Organ builders have at all times shown great imagination in the composition of Mixtures: thus one finds Mixtures including the Tierce (especially in northern Europe and Spain), Mixtures composed entirely of octaves without fifths (Iberian Zimbeln), and even Mixtures of Gambas (Harmonia aetheria) and Mixtures of reeds. One stop which deserves to be mentioned for its curiosity value is the Zimbel of certain Polish, Spanish and Mexican Baroque organs, whose minute pipes are not tuned, with the result that they produce an odd sort of metallic hiss. The *pleno* is without doubt the most characteristic element in the sonorous world of the organ; rich, shimmering, deep and radiant, it is to the ear what gold leaf is to the eye. Dom Bédos describes it as follows: "In the opinion of experts and of those with a taste for true harmony, the most harmonious element of the organ is the *pleno* when mixed in just measure with the foundation stops."

Flute Mutation Ranks

Flute Mutation Stops are intended above all to give a solid base to the fundamental, and are generally, but not always, a Stopped Bourdon. They are not affected by breaks: in other words, they follow and accentuate the progression of the foundation stops. The Flute harmonic is represented in virtually every type of organ by Note 3: its speaking-length will be $2\,^2\!/\!_3′$ (Nasard) on a base of 8′, $5\,^1\!/\!_3′$ (Double Nasard) on one of 16′, and $10\,^2\!/\!_3′$ (Quinte) on a base of 32′. Note 6 is also quite common: when based on an 8′ pipe, it measures $1\,^1\!/\!_3′$ and is known as a Larigot. It is interesting to note that a Quinte added to a 16′ stop sounds like a 32′ stop. As for the Quarte de Nasard, this stop is simply a 2′ Flute mutation rank and is used in the composition of the Cornet. The Flute Tierce (Note 5) is found in several types of organ, but chiefly in the French classical organ where the builders were not slow to exploit its possibilities, whether on a foundation of 8′ ($1\,^3\!/\!_5′$ Tierce) or on one of 16′ ($3\,^1\!/\!_5′$ Double Tierce). Other examples are occasionally found on a fundamental of 32′ ($6\,^2\!/\!_5′$) and even of 4′ ($^4\!/\!_5′$). The Tierce is almost always used in combination with a Nasard and even with a Larigot, in addition to the 8′, 4′ and 2′ (and, in certain cases, 16′) foundation stops.

This combination of registers, known as the Jeu de Tierce, can be found, ready made, in the Cornet V rank, where a single stop sounds five ranks of pipes: 8′ (stopped), 4′, $2\,^2\!/\!_3′$, 2′ and $1\,^3\!/\!_5′$ (open). Intended to be used as a solo stop or to reinforce the treble reeds (upper octaves), the Cornet generally begins around middle C, and its pipes – of wide scale – are mounted on a small wind-chest placed immediately behind the front of the organ, above the other pipes. This privileged position sets it in powerful relief. The Cornet stop is by no means confined exclusively to the French

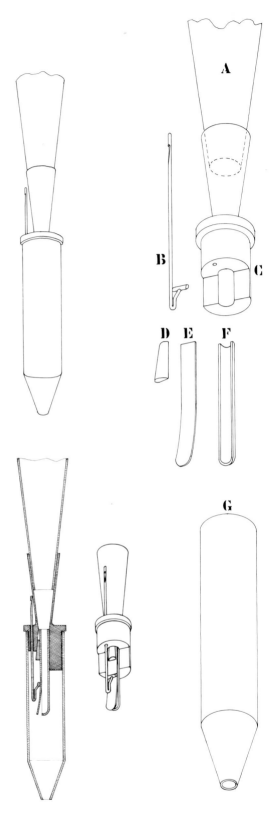

classical organ, but also occurs in English and Spanish organs (where six or seven ranks may be found, including 1⅓′ and even 1′) and in the later Italian organs (where its composition is sometimes slightly different), not to mention all the various types of modern organ.

The Sesquialtera is a stop which combines the 2⅔′ Quinte or Nasard with the 1⅗′ Tierce, and which is equally suited to solo work. Based on an 8′ Bourdon, it plays a role similar to that of the Cornet. It may be observed that the Sesquialtera is traditionally narrower in scale than the Cornet and is thus more of a Diapason, as is the Tertian, which is a kind of Sesquialtera with a Quinte of 1⅓′. The Septième or Seventh (Note 7) seems to be a relatively recent invention: Aristide Cavaillé-Coll incorporated several into the Notre-Dame organ in Paris (1868), including a pedal stop of 4⁴⁄₇′.

The Neuvième (Note 9) is occasionally found in some modern instruments.

Reed Pipes

The reed pipe is made up of seven individual parts: the *boot*, which is conical in section; the *reed-tongue* which is contained inside the boot and which beats against an opening in the side of a brass tube known as the *shallot*; the *tuning wire* (or spring), a small specially angled metal rod which holds the tongue against the shallot and whose upper end projects through the top of the block to facilitate tuning; the *block*, a lead casting which rests on and in the removable body of the boot of the pipe; the *wedge*, a small piece of wood which holds the tongue in position in the bottom of the block; and the body of the pipe which is found in various forms and is called the *resonator*.

Air under pressure enters the boot of the pipe and escapes through the opening in the shallot. The tongue is drawn towards the orifice by the eddies thus formed and produces a vibration as it returns to its former position. This phenomenon is repeated as long as air continues to enter the opening and in that way creates a number of vibrations corresponding to the frequency of a note. The sound which is emitted is amplified by the reed pipe, a simple resonating body whose shape alters the quality and timbre of the note. This system is one of "beating" or "striking" reeds, since the tongue beats against a metal plate alternately opening and covering the hole which is cut in it. But mention must also be made of the alternative system of free reeds: instead of a shallot against which the tongue beats when wind excites it, a thick oblong plate of brass is perforated with a narrow opening through which the close-fitting brass tongue vibrates. It swings freely, hence the term "free reed." It has the advantage of producing a rounder tone, but is not as bright in quality, being less rich in partials. Although free reed stops were used in certain ranks in nineteenth-century organs (the Euphone and Cor d'harmonie, for example), they are somewhat weak in volume. They continue to be used in the manufacture of harmoniums and accordions. We may also observe that, in order to dampen the sound of certain reed stops, organ builders sometimes cover the reed-tongue with skin.

The reed pipe is tuned by means of the tuning wire: the frequency of the tongue's vibrations may be altered by raising or lowering the metal wire, which is held in position against the vibrating plate.

The reed family is subdivided into two groups which may be distinguished not only on the basis of their construction but also, in a general way, by the function they fulfill within the sonorous structure of the instrument.

The first group consists most notably of the family or battery of Trumpets (reed stops of actual length): these pipes have a flared conical resonator which is of normal length, i.e. proportional to the pitch of the note emitted. In certain instances the length may be doubled, in which case one speaks of "harmonic" reeds, the note being reinforced in volume and intensity. These stops, which are as expressive in chorus work as they are as solo stops, make up a family characterized by its powerful sonorities: 32′ Contrabombardon (in the pedals), 16′ Bombardon (a reed which is most often found as a pedal stop but which also occurs as a manual stop on larger instru-

Fig. 14   Front, cross section and exploded view of a reed pipe
A Resonator – B Tuning wire – C Block – D Wedge – E Tongue – F Shallot – G Boot

ments), 8′ Trumpet and 4′ Clairon (a stop in which the final octave often breaks back or else is replaced by foundation pipes; at this pitch the pipes are too small and too awkward to build, and they would have difficulty speaking). Very rarely, the battery of reeds may be fitted with stops sounding the fifth of the note played. Horizontal or exterior Trumpets, often described as being *en chamade* (a term invented in the nineteenth century by Antoine Cavaillé-Coll) are stops whose pipes are arranged horizontally to project their voices directly out of the organ. They are a characteristic feature of Iberian organs, where their ingenious arrangement (8′, 4′ and 2′ to the left, and 16′ and 8′ to the right, although there are of course a number of overlaps and exceptions to this arrangement) gives them a role as Reed Mixture on a fundamental of an 8′ Trompette inférieure, a fact which few modern organ builders have understood.

Among this first group of reed stops of normal length, mention must also be made of the 8′ Hautbois, whose function is rather that of a solo stop. A number of other stops of this type, such as the Schalmei and the Cor anglais, were invented in the nineteenth century. These pipes are most often cylindrical or only slightly conical in section, and – in the case of the Hautbois and the Cor anglais – are surmounted by a short but very wide bell in the shape of a funnel.

The second group of reed stops are of fractional length with resonators of many varied shapes. Their function is generally as a solo stop. Their pipes are "acoustic," in other words, the pitch of the note emitted does not correspond to the length of the resonator. The Cromorne and the Clarinet, for example, have tubes which are generally half the nominal length, whereas the countless different varieties of Regals and Vox humana stops may be even shorter in length.

The Shape and Material of Pipes

The pipes are as varied in shape, and in the materials of which they are made, as are the stops we have discussed. This diversity, which is a product of the taste and of the enterprising spirit of the organ builder, may affect both the sonority and the character of the pipe.

Metal pipes are cylindrical or conical in shape. Cylindrical pipes may be open or stopped by a metal cap which may in turn be surmounted by a chimney. Alternatively, the height may be extended by an open flare, or the pipe may be pierced by one or more holes halfway along its speaking-length. Conical pipes may taper towards either the top or the bottom of the resonator. The latter is the case with the majority of stops in the reed family, where the most diversified of structures are to be found. The resonators, whether conical or cylindrical, may themselves rest on a cone of variable diameter and height, or may even be composed entirely of a series of superimposed cones, as is the case with certain Regals for example. Conical pipes of both sorts may be surmounted by a flare; this is either inverted in relation to the shape of the resonator or is the same way up as this element. Alternatively there may be a double cone or simply a stopper. It is worth repeating that the reed family is the one which, from a distance, reveals the greatest diversity of form: double cones, angled cylinders, bulblike resonating chambers and bells with side vent holes, etc.

Wood pipes are less diversified in structure than metal pipes. They are rectangular or square in section and may be open or closed. It need scarcely be added that the imagination and skill of nineteenth- and twentieth-century organ builders have produced wood pipes of every conceivable shape, although most of these have nowadays fallen into oblivion. Wood may also be used in the manufacture of low-pitched reed pipes (Bombardon, Trumpet and Bassoon). As a general rule, wood is most useful in making the largest pipes and metal more suitable for smaller ones. There are, however, a few notable exceptions, including the organ in the chapel of the Frederiksborg at Hillerød (Esaias Compenius, 1610), and the organ in the Silberne Kapelle at Innsbruck (unknown maker, *c.* 1614). Regal pipes may also be made of wood.

Not only do we find an infinite variety of shapes but also a surprising range of materials used. In this respect, however, it was earlier centuries, from the Renaissance to the High Baroque, which displayed the greatest wealth of materials. Arnolt Schlick, in his *Spiegel der Orgelmacher* [Code of Organ Builders], published in Mainz in 1511, describes pipes made of gold, silver, copper, brass, alabaster, glass, clay and paper (sized); in Provence, Spain and elsewhere some older instruments have preserved Trumpet pipes in tin; and in the second half of the eighteenth century Dom Bédos even mentions the existence of ivory flue pipes. We may also note the extremely varied characteristics of the different types of wood used north of the Alps from the end of the Middle Ages onwards, including oak, fir, mahogany, pear, cherry, cedar, maple, pine and walnut.

But all these different materials were soon to be restricted, for want of time, patience and money, to certain limited kinds of wood and the most suitable metals. The modern organ builder generally works in oak. Although oak is "the most appropriate for wood pipes" (Dom Bédos also insists that the organ builder should "choose only oak that is thoroughly dry and attractive to look at; above all there should be no knots, sapwood or cracks"), cost often compels the builder to use fir or some other more economical genus of tree. As for metal pipes, they are made of sheets of almost pure tin (up to 90%, especially if they are display pipes), of "tin metal" (a rich alloy containing between 60% and 85% tin), "spotted metal" (52% tin; this alloy has a characteristic appearance of bright irregularly shaped spots), or "plain metal" (a mixture of tin and lead containing less than 40% tin). An alloy with a high tin content (75%) gives a clearer tone, whereas an alloy rich in lead produces a more mellow sound. Although certain organ builders have recourse to copper for the beautiful sound and appearance of certain pipes (most notably display pipes, horizontal reeds and Regals), others unfortunately use zinc in the construction of the largest pipes, a metal whose tonal virtues are less than evident.

The choice of materials depends, therefore, partly on the organ builder's own preference concerning the tonal character of the pipe in question, partly on the prevailing climatic conditions, and partly of course on the amount of money available.

Organ Stops and their Names

It is impossible to conclude this chapter on the pipework of organs without including some reference to the often entertaining names of organ stops. These names can be read above, below or to the side of the old draw-stop knobs, as well as on the more recent tilting tablets made of synthetic material and distinguishable by virtue of their colors (white, pink, yellow or blue, and green).

Certain stops are content with a straightforward description which tells us all we need to know about their composition and personality: Diapason, Flute, Bourdon and Gamba. Others have names which immediately reveal their harmonic function: Septième, Neuvième, Twelfth, etc. But these self-effacing individuals are no more than a minority in a vast and often imaginative assembly. Many are guilty of self-importance in flaunting a liberal display of adjectives. The less vainglorious are by turn lovable (*lieblich, amabile*), amorous (*d'amore*) or tender (*dolce*); others arrogate to themselves more imposing adjectives such as imperial, royal, military or orchestral; and there are yet others which have cast aside all earthly concerns and describe themselves as *céleste*, aetheria or *mirabilis*. Some ranks, of a nationalistic frame of mind, are happy to proclaim their place of origin (or at least to pass themselves off as such): Cor égyptien, Cor anglais or French Horn; Flûte suisse or Wienerflöte; Spanish Trumpet, and so on – not to mention the family names with which organ builders, especially in Spain, liked to dub the stops of more suggestive sonorities: 8′ Regal stops, for example, might be called Viejas (old women's voice), Viejos (old men's voice) or Gorrinitos (piglets).

Other, more modest, ranks betray only the materials of which they are made, or the shape they have adopted, or else the sounds they imitate: Holzflöte, Holzregal;

Spitzflöte, Flûte harmonique, Open Flute, Flûte triangulaire; Bearded Gamba, Viole à pavillon, etc.

Most stops refer to the traditional instruments which they are attempting to imitate: Flûte à bec, Bombardon, Cornet, Cremona, Cymbale, Caboulet, Gemshorn, Oboe, Regal, Serpent, Trumpet, Viola da gamba, Flauto traverso, Horn, Violone, Violoncello, Clarinet, Ophicleide, Saxophone, Harmonika, etc.

Under the heading of sounds of the countryside come the Apfelregal, Bärpfeife, Bauernflöte, Baumflöte, Campana, Carillon, Cor de nuit, Kuckuck, Feldflöte, Fistula rurestris, Hunting Horn, Rossignol, Waldflöte, etc.

Last but not least there are the eccentrics hiding among the pipework, created for the most part during the nineteenth century. Their names inspire visions of Bruegel and strike terror into the hearts of all who utter them: Conoclyte, Cornopean, Dermogloste, Euphone, Heckelphone, Magnaton, Melophone, Keraulophone, Philomela, Phoneuma, Terpomela . . .

An even more splendid sense of originality is evinced by the manifold inventions which seek to imitate various sounds such as birdcalls, animal cries and the sounds of nature and of warfare: the Rossignol or Nachtigall, whose tiny pipes are suspended in water so that bubbles produced by the flow of air imitate the warbling of nightingales; a barking dog, a growling bear or a braying ass produced by untuned pipes; a storm created by a mechanism (a length of wood) which holds down the lowest notes of the pedals simultaneously; the sound of beating rain suggested by means of small pebbles rolling around inside a metal drum; military percussion (Banda militare) incorporating the big drum and cymbals, or the rolling of kettledrums (Timpani) produced by means of two untuned pipes, and, finally, the Chapeau chinois in which small spherical bells are shaken against a rod, and the Zimbelstern which consists of a revolving metal star with a set of bells attached to it. Who now will claim that the organ is a mere instrument? It is nature incarnate: human, animal, rustic and celestial. It is music; it is noise; exceptional and protean, it tells a long drawn-out love story – the story of man's love of music.

MECHANISM

To the uninformed onlooker, the organ comprises not much more than the organ case and the display pipes, a work of art which may be unpretentious or magnificent by turns. Admittedly, these visible parts of the instrument are the object of great care and attention on the part of all those involved in designing and building the organ, whether architect, cabinetmaker or organ builder, since these parts are, so to speak, the organ's sleeping partners. Indeed, there have been times when more money has been spent on decorating the organ case than on the actual pipework itself.

However, the section that is visible, no matter how impressive, is but a small part of the whole instrument, whose most important elements are concealed from public view. Its internal mechanism is made up of the bellows, which produce compressed air; wind-trunks which conduct the air supply to the wind-chests where it is distributed among the various pipes; and the action mechanism which links the manuals to the wind-chests.

The Bellows and Wind Supply

As a wind instrument, the organ requires a sufficient quantity of air to feed the whole of its pipework. The basic problem is to provide a continuous supply of air at constant pressure. This factor is so important that on many occasions during the eighteenth and nineteenth centuries organ builders indicated not only the various organ stops but also the number and capacity of the instrument's bellows. Even today there are still many instruments with the traditional system of bellows operated by hand or sometimes by foot.

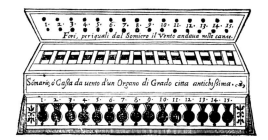

Fig. 15 Organ from Grado near Venice, before 1044 (?); wind-chest and manual; the instrument had two stops and fifteen keys; see Zarlino, *Supplementi musicali*, Venice, 1588.

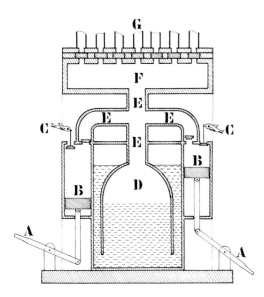

Fig. 16 Hydraulically operated, two-pump blowing mechanism, based on the description by Vitruvius, first century AD:
A Levers operating the pumps (*vectis*) – B Pump pistons (*fundi ambulatiles*) – C Counterweights in the shape of sporting dolphins (*delphini*) operating the inlet valves (*cymbala*) – D Inverted funnel (*pnigeus*) acting as a reservoir; the air inside is kept under pressure by the weight of the water – E Conduits (*fistulae*) – F Pipe-chest – G Pipes (*organa*)

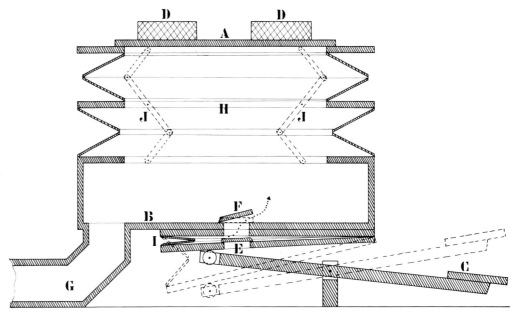

Fig. 17 Cross section of two wedge-bellows serving as pumps (operated by pedals), and a large reservoir with inverted ribs (Reservoir and Feeder-bellows)

A Upper rib – B Lower rib – C Pedal lever – D Weights – E Inlet valve – F Exhaust valve admitting air to reservoir – G Main wind-trunk – H Reservoir – I Feeder-bellows – J Frame supports

Development of the Bellows

The old idea of the *hydraulis* seems to have been abandoned in the second century because of the problems of controlling the system designed by Ctesibius. The new type of organ, whose wind supply was generated by bellows identical to those used by blacksmiths, enabled the organ builder to increase the number of pipes, which could now be fed by a larger number of bellows or by a greater volume of air. Unlike the organ of Ctesibius, in which the two pumps took turns to ensure a continuous air supply to the pipes, the first Western portative, equipped with only a single set of bellows, which the organist operated with his left hand, was incapable of maintaining a continuous and regular pressure. This problem was eliminated by increasing the number of bellows, an important development in the history of the organ, but one which now required the help of one or more organ-blowers. Various records allow us to trace this development more clearly. The organ in the St. Blaise manuscript shows some fifteen pipes fed by twelve sets of bellows (twelve, it may be added, is a symbolic number: fifteen pipes would require less air to feed them). The great organ in Winchester Cathedral (951) had twenty-six bellows supplying "an immense quantity of wind, and are worked by seventy strong men, laboring with their arms, covered in perspiration, each inciting his companions to drive the wind up with all his strength, that the full-bosomed box may speak with its four hundred pipes which the hand of the organist governs." This description, which is probably much exaggerated, is taken from a poem by Wulfstan dedicated to Bishop Elphege. According to the later description of Michael Praetorius, the Halberstadt organ of 1361 was fed by some twenty bellows which ten assistants operated using the weight of their bodies.

The earliest bellows, round in shape, were made of two pieces of wood held together by hide, which, lacking proper folds, soon wore out. Various attempts were made to overcome this major drawback, until, in the fifteenth century, an effective solution was discovered in the invention of wedge bellows constructed of small lengths of wood held together by leather hinges. This type of bellows was made up of one or more folds which could be arranged in one of two ways. German designers preferred bellows

Fig. 18 Hydraulic organ: double organ with two organists and four bellows-blowers. This is a remarkable illustration, clearly a product of the imagination of an artist who was influenced by Vitruvius's description in his *De Architectura* X, 8 of the first century AD; after the Utrecht Psalter, ninth century, NL-Uu 32, f.83ʳ, illustration to Psalm cxlix. From Buhle, 1903.

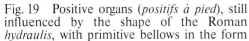

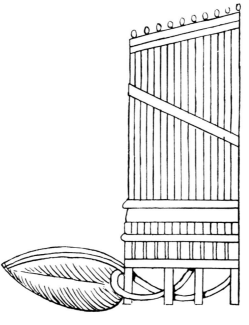

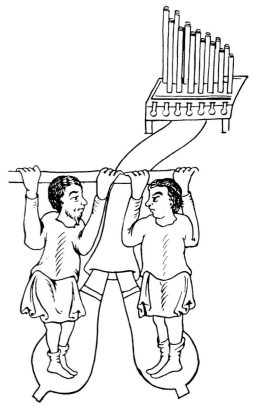

Fig. 19 Positive organs (*positifs à pied*), still influenced by the shape of the Roman *hydraulis*, with primitive bellows in the form of animal-hide blast bags; from the early tenth-century Stuttgart Psalter (Kgl. öffentl. Bibl. f. 23). From Buhle, 1903.

with a single fold closing inwards, whereas French organ builders were later to develop a bellows with several folds closing outwards.

A diagram showing the bellows of the Halberstadt organ shows us the organist's assistants, whose function was to fill the large bellows with air. But however great their skill, it was difficult for them to maintain a constant level of air pressure in the absence of any mechanism to regulate the pressure. The operators' task was considerably eased when weights were fixed to the upper part of the bellows, thus allowing the compressed air to be expelled automatically. But it was not until the end of the eighteenth century that the English clockmaker and mechanical constructor Alexander Cumming invented a set of horizontal bellows which enabled the air pressure to be maintained at any position of rise or fall. This was in 1762. The main bellows have "inverted ribs" (lower ribs closing inwards and upper ribs closing outwards) and are in effect a rectangular reservoir with an air supply coming from a second set of wedge-shaped feeder-bellows, folding inwards, placed beneath the main bellows. This large double reservoir is prevented from shifting sideways as it rises by means of metal strips fixed to the sides of the main bellows and opening and shutting in parallel. Weights are attached to the top of the reservoir in order to ensure stability of exhaust pressure.

The invention of pulleys to raise the bellows and, at a late date, the use of large wheels to reduce the strain helped to ease the organ-blower's task, until, during the closing years of the nineteenth century, came the invention of the electric motor and, with it, the disappearance of the organist's assistants. From now on there was a rapid development. Various forms of motor were devised, including some driven by mains water, petroleum, gas, hot or compressed air, and, finally, the electric motors which are still in use today.

Fig. 20 Two bellows-blowers in action: each blower in turn places the whole weight of his body on the bellows; the upper table was sprung, causing it to return to its former position once the blower moved; from the twelfth-century Cambridge Manuscript (St. John's College, B. 18). From Buhle, 1903.

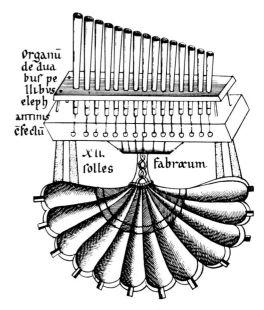

Modern Bellows

In modern bellows systems the wind is admitted and expelled by a fan which drives an electric motor varying in output from 0.2 to 2 horsepower. The air which is admitted must be taken from the area in which the pipes are enclosed, otherwise the difference

Fig. 21 Medieval organ fitted with twelve elephant-hide bellows; from Gerbert, *De cantu et musica sacra*, Sankt Blasien, 1744, Pl. 27.

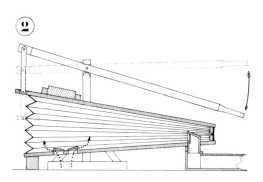

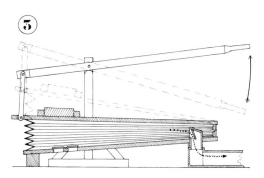

Fig. 22   How wedge-bellows work
1 Bellows at rest
A Upper board – B Lower board – C Hand-operated lever – D Lead or stone weight – E Inlet valve – F Exhaust valve – G Main wind-trunk

2 The bellows-blower has depressed the lever: the bellows are at their maximum volume, filled with air which has been admitted through the inlet valve.

3 The blower releases the lever, and the lead or stone weight forces the upper board down, expelling the wind through the exhaust valve and into the main wind-trunk.
As a general rule, the wind supply is provided by several bellows mounted in series, in order to ensure a regular supply of wind.

Fig. 23   The organ bellows of Halberstadt Cathedral; from M. Praetorius, *Syntagma musicum*, Vol. II: "De Organographia", Wolfenbüttel, 1619, Pl. 26.

in temperature between the air entering the pipes and that of the pipework itself may result in severe problems of pitch and even cause serious damage to the instrument. Ideally, the air which is driven by the fan should first enter the primary reservoirs which store the wind and hold it in reserve. These large reservoirs, square or rectangular in shape and having inverted ribs, are made up of two tables: the upper floating panel rises the moment air enters the reservoir and, thanks to the weights (lead, stones or bricks) which are fixed to it, maintains a constant pressure inside. The air is then conducted along the wind-trunks to the concussion bellows, a small lightly constructed air reservoir, having spring tensioning only, designed for low inertia and low momentum. It is a device to eliminate unsteady wind supply, cushioning the supply by instantly meeting momentary demands, and absorbing surges caused by abrupt cessation of demand. These concussion bellows are so efficient that some organ builders have dispensed with the large primary reservoirs. In recent years, however, the somewhat "mechanical" regularity with which the air is pumped to the pipes has encouraged more and more organ builders to reintroduce them and to remove the concussion bellows, in order to restore the air supply's greater individuality and flexibility, especially in those instruments inspired by the style of classical organ building.

The wind-trunks, as their name indicates, are the pipes which carry the air from the bellows to the various parts of the instrument. The large wind-trunks which lead from the main bellows to the wind-chest reservoirs are automatically cut off, as soon as the latter have been inflated, by means of a regulator valve. The conveyances are made of wood and are square or rectangular in section, although occasionally (especially during the nineteenth and early twentieth centuries) they were made of zinc and were round in cross section. Cylindrical in shape and made of lead, alloy, wood, cardboard or plastic, the wind-trunks take the air supply from the wind-chests to the various individual pipes located either on the sides of the instrument (bass pipes which, because of their size, cannot be planted on the wind-chest itself) or on the front of the organ case (display pipes for example). In order to distinguish them from those pipes which are located on the wind-chest and are said to be "on the note," the isolated pipes are described as "off the note." They are planted on a hollow or grooved wooden board and fed by small wind-trunks.

The fan has to supply enough wind at constant pressure to be able to meet the often considerable demands placed upon the system by the player. The average discharge of an 8′ Diapason, for example, is over 10,000 cubic inches per minute for the note C. As a general rule the wind pressure varies between 2 in. and 4½ in. water gauge, depending upon the volume of sound, the desired "mélanges" and the chosen means

Fig. 24 Cross section of an organ and its *Positif*, showing the route taken by the wind supply on its way from the bellows to the windchests of the *Grand Orgue* and the *Positif*; from Dom Bédos de Celles, *L'art du facteur d'orgues*, 4 vols., Paris, 1766–78, Pt. I. Chap. VI, Sec. VI. Pl. 52.

Fig. 25 The *Balgmaschine* or bellows machine of Friedrich Haas, which produced a constant wind supply; from J.G. Töpfer, *Lehrbuch der Orgelbaukunst*, Weimar, 1888.

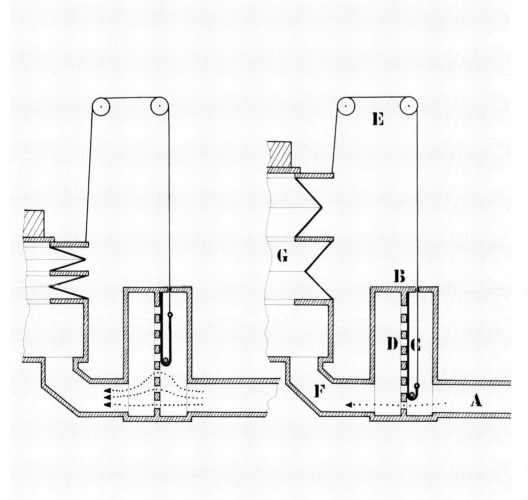

Fig. 26 Wind-pressure regulator
This is a system which allows the wind supply to be regulated on its way from the fan to the reservoir.
The wind is propelled by the fan along conduit A, and is more or less interrupted by the roller-blind C sliding against gate D, before passing along conduit F and entering the reservoir G. Inside the regulator B, the roller-blind is connected up to the reservoir by means of a cord E mounted on pulleys. The fuller the reservoir, the less wind is supplied by the fan.

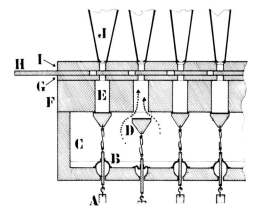

Front view

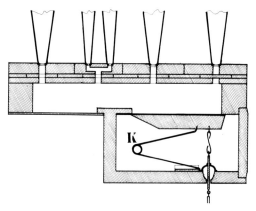

Cross section, pallet valve closed

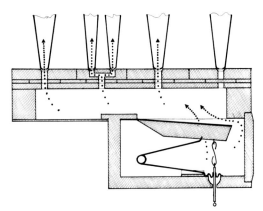

Cross section, pallet valve open

Fig. 27   Cross section of a slider-chest:
A Trackers – B Buttons or leather nuts –
C Pallet box – D Pallet valve – E Groove or
channel – F Soundboard bar – G Table –
H Slider – I Upper board – J Pipes – K Spring

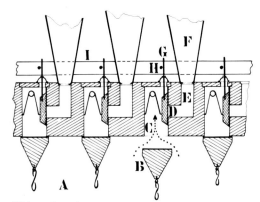

Slider closed

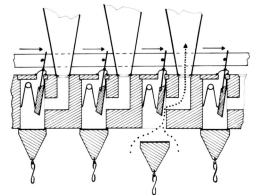

Slider open

Fig. 28   Longitudinal and partial cross section
of an Italian-type spring-chest:

A Pallet box – B Pallet valve – C Groove – D
Groove valve for each individual pipe, held
closed by a spring – E Conduit channeling the
wind from the groove to the pipe – F Pipe – G
Metal rod to open groove valve – H Stop-pin
to hold rod G – I Stop lever bar to open all the
pallets of a single rank of pipes

of harmonization. Although fairground organs, for example, require very high pressures (which may exceed 8 in. wg.), house organs are normally content with between 0.8 in. and 2 in. wg. Antique organs were driven by a wind supply whose pressure was as varied as that of modern instruments. The pressure of the Italian organ, for example, was around 1.4 in. wg., while that of Schnitger's organ was 4 in. wg.

Wind pressure is normally measured by means of a water manometer or wind gauge, said to have been invented in 1667 by the German organ builder Christian Förner. It is a simple system consisting of a U-tube half-filled with water, which operates on the principle of communicating vessels and allows one to calculate the distance of the total water displacement measured in inches. Nowadays, air pressure may be measured by an anemometer.

Before concluding this discussion of the wind supply we may mention a further characteristic feature of our instrument, the tremulant or tremolo. First used during the Renaissance, this apparatus affects the passage of air in the wind-trunk, imparting a pressure wave to the air which is transferred to the sound in the pipes. The tremulant is constructed in a variety of forms but basically consists of a pallet or valve placed in the conveyance and activated by the wind, or else motor-driven. There are two types of tremulant: the *tremblant doux* or gentle tremulant, which does not allow wind to escape but acts as a sprung gate in the trunk, momentarily blocking the flow when activated; and the *tremblant fort* or strong tremulant (also known as the *tremblant à vent perdu*), consisting of a spring valve, balanced and adjustable, which allows wind to escape intermittently from the trunk, the remaining wind being admitted in uneven pulses to the pipe chests.

The Wind-chests

The wind-chests look like wooden boxes on which are planted pipes of every height and every diameter. These chests contain a large number of elements vital to the functioning of the organ, since they distribute the air under pressure among the different pipes by means of a system of selection controlled by the organist.

We shall begin by describing a wind-chest of classical format, known as a block-chest. The wind, channeled from the main bellows along a large wind-trunk, is stored in a box the same length as the wind-chest. This is the pallet box. This chamber, which is hermetically sealed although it can be opened in case of need, was for a long time described as "the organ's secret," since it is the pallet box on which devolves the task of distributing the wind to the correct pipes. This lower chamber is connected to the end of the keyboard mechanisms entering through the bottom of the chest into which holes have been drilled for that purpose. Since these holes could allow air to escape through them, they are fitted with small leather membranes or diaphragms, or else

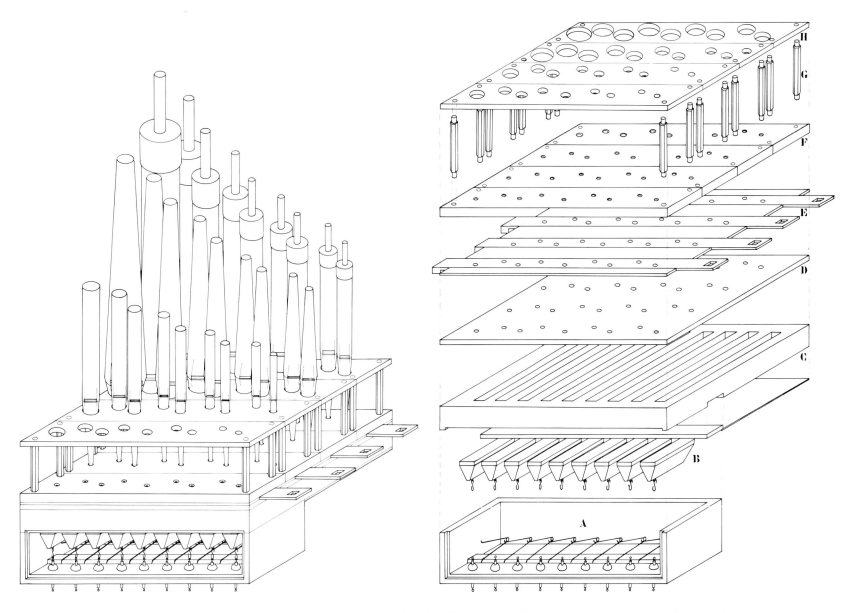

with felt buttons, which ensure that the chest remains airtight. The ends of the keyboard mechanism are in turn attached to wooden valves or pallets, rectangular in shape and covered with leather. They are kept closed in a position of rest and held against the ceiling of the pallet box by means of a spring. When the organist, seated at the console, depresses a key, the movement is transmitted to the pallet, which opens to admit air to a groove.

The grooves, which were originally carved out of the block of wood itself, are parallel channels running the length of the wind-chest and separated from each other by walls known as soundboard bars. The function of the grooves is to supply wind to all the pipes corresponding to a single note on the manuals. There is, however, a further obstacle to be overcome before the air can enter the pipes, and that is to provide some means whereby the organist can choose the ingredients of his tonal "mélanges." The most popular system is the bar-and-slider chest. A flat piece of timber or "table" is fixed on top of the grid of grooves and bars, covering the whole of the upper surface of the wind-chest and having as many holes in it as there are pipes. Over the table is placed a veneer consisting of sliders, long strips of timber which are free to move lengthwise and are perforated with holes corresponding with those in the table. Parallel to the front of the wind-chest (and at right angles to the grooves), they are held in position by guide bars known as false sliders. Finally comes the "upper board," the top section of the wind-chest, which is a board perforated with holes coinciding with those in the sliders and in the table. The pipes fit directly over these

Fig. 29   Diagram of a wind-chest and part of its pipes, with the pallet box open.

Fig. 30   Exploded view of the same chest: A Pallet box with spring and buttons – B Pallet valves – C Grooves and soundboard bars – D Table – E Sliders and false sliders – F Upper boards – G Supports for the rack boards – H Rack boards

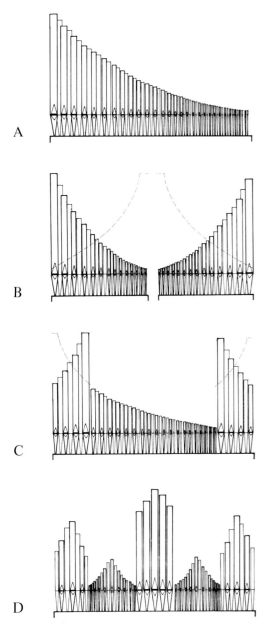

Fig. 31 Planting the pipes on the wind-chest:
A Chromatic arrangement
B Diatonic arrangement in two symmetrical groups (the dotted lines show an alternative arrangement with the bass pipes in the center)
C Diatonic arrangement of the bass pipes, which are divided into two groups; chromatic arrangement of the treble pipes
D Pipes arranged in miters

Fig. 32 The assembled organ: "perspective view of the whole of the interior of an ordinary 16′ organ"; from Dom Bédos, Paris, 1766–78, Pt. I, Chap. VI, Sec. IV, Pl. 50.

holes, each hole being countersunk in order to accommodate the shape of the boot of the pipe.

In order for a stop to speak, the holes in the slider must be aligned with those in the table and in the upper board, failing which the air supply is cut off. This occurs when the slider is moved slightly in a lateral plane, the stop then being silent, or pushed in. A suitable mechanism for drawing the stop allows the organist to open and close the stops by means of a stop knob situated near the console.

An alternative method of opening the stops is occasionally found. As a system, it is identical to the one just described, up to the level of the table, at which point the sliders are replaced by large wooden stop-lever bars arranged between the ranks of pipes. At a given command from the organist, the opened pallet admits wind to each single or multirank stop by means of a secondary pallet or groove-valve for each. A spring acting on the secondary pallet causes the stop-lever bar to return to the "off" position, hence the term "spring-chest" used to describe this type of wind-chest. Mention should also be made of the rackboard, a collection of timbers placed directly above the upper board and designed to maintain the pipes in an upright position. To this end the rackboard is perforated with as many holes as the organ has pipes.

The construction of the wind-chest requires all the skill that the organ builder commands. He must use wood which is perfectly dry and of the highest quality. Oak is generally preferred. All the individual pieces must be measured and assembled with the greatest accuracy in order to prevent serious problems arising later on. The most basic quality which one has every right to expect of a well-designed and well-constructed wind-chest is that it should be airtight. Deficiencies can occur within the slider-chest due to faults in its construction or to excessive dryness or humidity: the sliders will swell and stick or else become loose, or the table may work loose and the soundboard bars warp. As a result, air will leak from one compartment to another, or escape causing undesirable sounds and deterioration of pitch if the pipes are not receiving enough air. In this respect the spring-chest is much more reliable than the slider-chest, although it is so complicated to build that it has largely been abandoned. Nowadays, the use of stable materials such as bakelite for the sliders and the use of telescopic joints under the upper boards mean that slider-chests may be built reliably and simply. However, a rigorous code of ethics on the part of organ builders has led them to resist the introduction of these techniques, which introduce somewhat base materials into the instrument and inevitably encourage the builder to lavish less care on a task which has become oversimple. In practise it is undeniable that a wind-chest built using top-quality materials and rigorous care is every bit as reliable as an amalgam of plastic and bakelite.

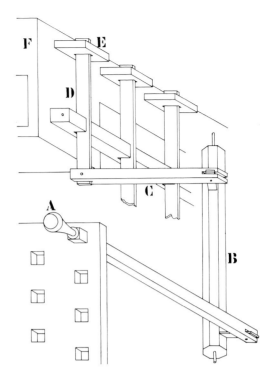

Disposition of the Pipes on the Wind-chests

In certain organs it is easy to tell the instrument's internal structure simply by looking at the arrangement of the pipes at the front of the organ. And yet even in such cases as these, it is very rare for the display pipes to adhere rigorously to the order of notes in the wind-chests. Indeed, they may be totally different. The organ builder has a choice of several different solutions for planting the pipes on the wind-chests:

a chromatic arrangement which follows the same order as the keys on the manuals (C, C sharp, D, D sharp, E, F, F sharp etc.);

a diatonic arrangement which divides the pipes into two groups, each comprising alternate notes in the chromatic scale; this would produce the following sequences with, on the one side, C, D, E, F sharp, G sharp, A sharp, c etc; on the other side, C sharp, D sharp, F, G, A, B, c sharp etc;

an arrangement in minor thirds: C, D sharp, F sharp, A, c; on the other side, c sharp, E, G, B flat, c sharp, etc.; and D, F, G sharp, B, d etc.;

an arrangement in major thirds: C, E, G sharp, c; on the other side, C sharp, F, A, c sharp and so on.

In opting for one of these solutions or in combining several such systems, the organ builder must take account of certain factors, the most important of which are the bulkiness of the large bass pipes and the organ's general symmetrical design. One very common arrangement is to have two diatonic wind-chests facing each other and corresponding to a single keyboard. The first pipe on the left will be C, with C sharp as the first pipe on the extreme right. As a result of this arrangement, which is determined in part by the need for a sense of balance in the design of the organ case, it is common practise to call the left-hand half of the instrument the "C side" and the right-hand half the "C sharp side," just as in the theater one speaks of the "prompt side" and the "off-prompt side."

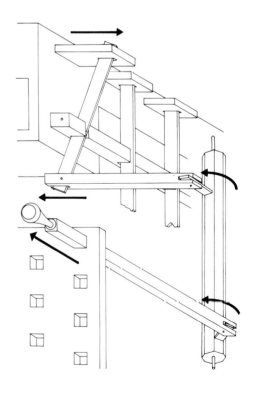

Tracker Action

The moving parts of the wind-chests are set in motion by two complementary mechanisms, one operating the stops (choice of tone colors) and the other operating the pallets (choice of notes).

Fig. 33   Draw-stop action:
A Draw-stop knob – B Roller or trundle, rotating the action of the draw-stop knob through 90° – C Sticker – D Backfall, reversing the movement of the sticker – E Slider in the wind-chest – F Wind-chest

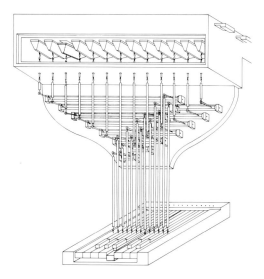

Fig. 34 Diagram of a roller board connecting the keys of the manuals to the pallet valves in the wind-chest.

Fig. 35 Recessed console of a four-manual organ, with French-style pedalboard; from Dom Bédos, Paris 1766–78, Pt. I, Chap. VI, Sec. I, Pl. 33: Description of organ cases (Fig. 7 shows a *Positif* case).

Operating the Stops

On either side of the console may be seen a greater or lesser number of knobs or levers: these are the draw-stop knobs which activate the different stops. In order to call on a particular stop, the organist generally has to pull the draw-stop knob towards him; the resultant action is transmitted to the slider, which moves lengthwise between the table and the upper board through the intermediacy of wooden or metal rods, trundles and levers which are able to negotiate long distances and awkward angles. Stops *à l'italienne* are activated by means of sideways displacement, which simplifies the mechanism, since the action involved is parallel to that of the sliders in the wind-chest.

In the case of spring-chests, the draw-stop knobs have to be fitted with a stop-lever in order to counteract the force of the return spring and to keep the stop open.

Operating the Valves

If the pipes could be planted directly above the manual keys, the key mechanism would be extremely straightforward in construction. Unfortunately, this is almost never the case since, except for the portative organ or very small positives, the wind-chest is always greater in length than the keyboard itself, a difference in size which is accentuated if there are several wind-chests for each of the manuals. Moreover, as already noted, the order of the notes in the wind-chest is not necessarily the same as that of the keyboard. And, finally, even though the wind-chests corresponding to the main keyboard are generally positioned at the front of the instrument, above the console, the other chests may be dispersed around the organ case or may even be housed independently (*Rückpositiv*, pedal pipes). The problem which the organ builder then has to face is how to connect the wind-chests to the console without the keys becoming too difficult to depress.

The essential elements of mechanical tracker action are as follows: the trackers themselves, thin rods which are used when the action is one of pulling; stickers, rigid vertical traces which transmit a thrust action; square levers which rotate on their axes, thereby turning the action through an angle of 90°; double-levers or backfalls which invert the movement; and, finally, rollers.

The roller board is a timber plank somewhat like a trapezium in shape, its longer edge equal in length to the wind-chest and its shorter edge the same length as the manual. In French the roller board is called the *abrégé*, hence the etymology of Dom Bédos de Celles: "The *abrégé* is so called because it reduces, so to speak, the length of the wind-chest, to which it is relative, to that of the keyboard." Its function in fact is to translate the order of keys on the manual – which is about 31 ½ inches (80 cm) long – to the pipes on the wind-chest – which may measure up to 20 foot (6 m), or even more if the wind-chest is a multiple one. To this block of wood is attached a series of wood or iron bars which rotate on their own axes: these are the rollers, whose function is to displace the movement laterally. Each key has its corresponding roller, which is fitted at either end with a small arm, one of which is connected to the key, the other to the pallet valve. When the organist depresses the key, the roller rotates and pivots slightly, relaying the movement to the other arm, which in turn causes the desired pallet to open. If the distance between key and pallet is too great, provision is made for several rollers interacting with each other, in order to prevent them from warping as a result of tortional stress and thereby adversely affecting the precision of the action.

The roller-board system is simple, reliable and efficient, ensuring a precise tonal attack: the organist's fingers are directly responsible for opening the pallet valves.

Keyboard Mechanisms

There are two methods of attaching the trackers to the manuals. Each key is effectively a lever having three important characteristics: the fulcrum A (the axis on which the key pivots), the weight B (the point at which the tracker is attached), and the force C (the pressure of the finger on the key). If point A is between points B and C, it is usual to speak of backfall action (pivoted at the center); if point B is located between A and C, then what we are dealing with is suspended action (pivoted at the end). This second formula produces a particularly light and sensitive touch: the player can feel the pallet valve moving inside the pallet box, assuming of course that the route of transmission does not involve too many awkward angles. It is worth noting in this respect that vertical movements, parallel to those of the organist's fingers, ensure a better touch, whereas horizontal movements (trackers or stickers) tend to slow down the response of the action.

It is impossible to include a full account here of all the ingenious devices which organ builders have employed both now and in the past in exploiting these mechanical principles, although mention may be made of the method of connecting the *Rückpositiv* to the keyboards by means of trackers passing beneath the pedals. The individual circumstances and, above all, local conditions have sometimes inspired organ builders to accomplish veritable feats of ingenuity. For instance, in the Church of San Alessandro in Colonna (at Bergamo in northern Italy), in 1781, the organ builder Giuseppe Serassi installed a system of mechanical transmission which linked together two organs on either side of the choir, the trackers beginning at the organ on the north side of the altar, where the organ console was situated, descending to ground level, crossing the choir along a channel specially excavated for the purpose, and then running up the opposite wall to the organ on the south side of the altar, a total distance of over one hundred feet.

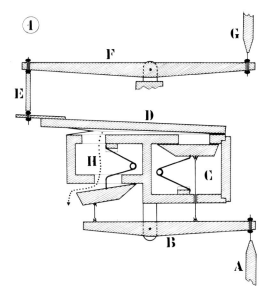

Other Systems of Transmission

In order to ease the difficulties caused by a type of action which was considered too "heavy," organ builders in the nineteenth and twentieth centuries have attempted various solutions which unfortunately lack the simplicity and sensory advantages of the system of tracker action described above. One is reminded of the saying that innovation is not always the same as progress.

The different systems which have been tried include pneumatic action, tubular-pneumatic action and electropneumatic action. But they all have their shortcomings. The removal of all physical links between the player's fingers and the pallets not only deprives the organist of any natural resistance but means that the touch of the instrument loses its personal character and precision. It renders difficult any variety of tonal attack and discourages any subtlety of phrasing. Slowness of action, attributable either to the failings inherent in certain systems or to the excessive distance between the console and the wind-chests, may cause unfortunate delays and even differences in the time taken for the individual keyboards to speak. Finally, the number and length of the conveyances increases the risk of air leaking, just as the complexity of the different types of action increases the risk of breakdowns, ciphering, silent notes and so on.

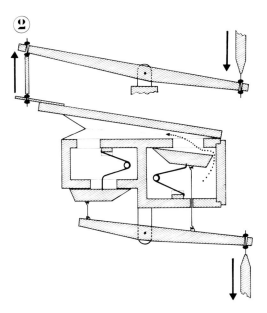

Fig. 36   Barker lever acting as a pneumatic relay in what is otherwise normal tracker action (as adapted by Aristide Cavaillé-Coll):
1 Barker lever at rest – 2 Barker lever in action
A Tracker (from the keyboard) – B Lever – C Pallet box and intake valve for pneumatic bellows D – D Pneumatic bellows operating sticker E and lever F; the latter pulls down the tracker G which leads to the wind-chest – H Pallet box and exhaust valve of bellows D

The pneumatic unit known as the Barker Lever was one of the most important inventions of nineteenth-century organ building. Invented simultaneously by David Hamilton of Edinburgh and Charles Spackman Barker (a native of Bath but for many years resident in France), the system was offered by Barker to the organ builder Aristide Cavaillé-Coll in 1837 and was used for the first time in 1841 in the organ at the Abbey Church of St. Denis near Paris. This device, which has been known ever since as the Barker Lever, overcomes the pressure of wind and of the springs on the pallets which the classic tracker action involved, while at the same time retaining the traditional concept of the tracker and wind-chest. Essentially, the system consists in the insertion of motor bellows for each key, placed between the roller board and the keyboard. The motor bellows fill with air as the key is depressed, and, in doing so, pull the trackers and rollers, which in turn open the pallet valves. As soon as pressure is removed from the key, the bellows return to their rest position, the air inside being driven out by means of an ingenious system of exhaust valves. The Barker Lever revolutionized

Fig. 37   Tubular pneumatic action:
(a) pressure-pneumatic
1 At rest – 2 In action
A Groove – B Pipe-chest pallet – C Pallet box
– D Bellows or secondary motor operating the
pipe-chest pallet B – E Exhaust valve for
secondary motor D – F Bellows or primary
motor operating valve E – G Lead tubing along
which wind travels under pressure, transmitting the action of the keys when they are
depressed (compression = action, decompression = rest) – H Touch box and exhaust pallet
admitting pressurized wind into the lead tubing
– I Exhaust pallet for the wind from primary
motor F – J Key

Fig. 38   Tubular pneumatic action:
(b) exhaust-pneumatic
1 At rest – 2 In action
A Groove – B Pipe-chest pallet – C Pallet box–
D Bellows or secondary motor operating pipe-
chest pallet B – E Exhaust valve for secondary
motor D – F Bellows or primary motor operating valve E – G Pallet box supplying air under
pressure to secondary motor D – H Return
spring on valve E – I Lead tubing transmitting
the action of the keys by a process of decompression (decompression = action; compression = rest) – J Exhaust valve for the wind
from primary motor F – K Key

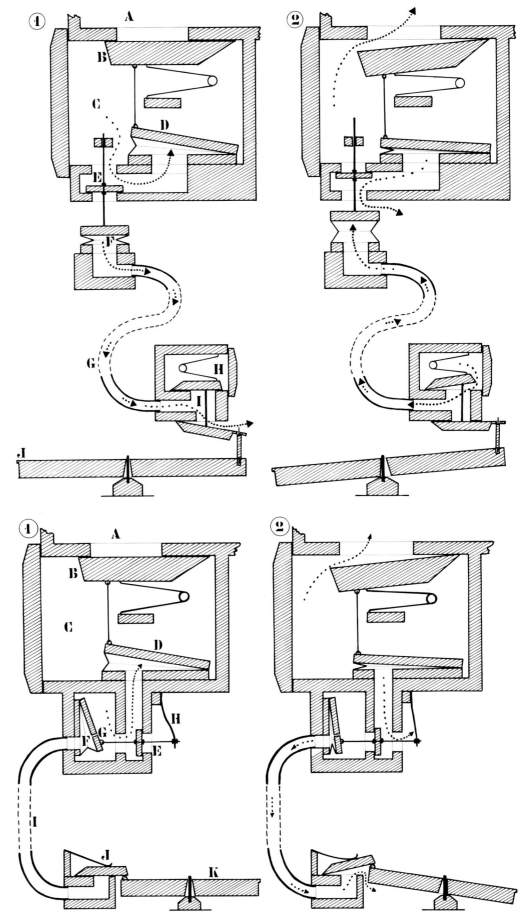

organ building: by removing the problem of heavy pressure required to depress the keys, it opened up the way to applications of its use which the classical organ of previous centuries had not needed and which the traditional system of action would not have allowed. As regards sound reproduction, the Barker Lever allowed the number of foundation stops to be increased and also allowed different pressures to be used for foundation stops and reed stops within a single wind-chest, thanks to the use of double pallet boxes. At the same time, it brought with it important changes in techniques of harmonization. Indeed, the organist's whole style of playing altered in consequence, as did his method of drawing the stops, now that he had multiple couplers at his disposal. We may finally note that this principle has also been applied to draw-stop action. Countless systems of tubular-pneumatic action were discovered and perfected during the second half of the industrial age. These new systems inevitably brought with them new technical problems, but also, and above all, a totally new concept of the function of the instrument and of the style of organ music.

The system of tubular-pneumatic action was invented in 1845 by Prosper-Antoine Moitessier of Montpellier and patented under the name of "abrégé pneumatique." When a key is depressed, air under pressure in the touchbox above the key is admitted along the lead tubing to the pneumatic motor operating the pipe-chest pallet. Such a system works by air under pressure near the key being admitted towards the mechanism operating the wind-chest main pallet valve, hence the name "pressure-pneumatic action." This system may, however, be replaced by "exhaust-pneumatic action," in which the air under pressure is contained near the pipe-chest pallet, pushing it closed when at rest; a valve near the key allows this wind to escape along the lead tubing away from the pallet, thus pulling it down. The only (relative) advantage of the exhaust system is the equalization and ease of touch, comparable to that of a piano, an advantage which becomes more appreciable when different manuals are coupled together. But the numerous drawbacks of this new type of action – most notably the sluggishness of attack in relation to the distance by which the key has to be depressed, a delay caused by the elasticity of the compressed air – forced organ builders to make various changes which, although certainly not lacking in ingenuity, continued to fall considerably short of the ideal.

An outcome of the researches of English, French and American organ builders and scientists, the system of electropneumatic action could not be applied to organ design with complete success until the twentieth century. William Sturgeon's discovery of the electromagnet in 1826 was of immediate interest to organ builders, who spent the remainder of the century attempting to adapt it to suit the action of the instrument. As early as 1852, a London organist, Dr Gauntlett, suggested that replicas of all the organs at the Crystal Palace Exhibition should be made and played by electricity from one console, and that same year he took out a patent for an electrical connection between the keys and the pallets of an organ. In 1855 the organ builder Stein built an instrument in which an electromagnet activated the opening of the pallet valves, but the system placed a greater load on the electric batteries than they were designed to take. Mention may also be made here of the fruitful experiments undertaken by the French scientists Du Moncel and Froment, by Dr Albert Peschard of Caen (who in 1861, in collaboration with Barker, devised a system whereby a solenoid was used to open a small valve which admitted wind into the pneumatic motor of the Barker-Lever system), and, during the closing decades of the nineteenth century, the researches of the Americans Schmoele and Mols of Philadelphia, together with those of the English organ builder Robert Hope-Jones. The most difficult problem involved in the application of electricity to the transmission mechanism of the organ was the load placed on the electromagnet, since the amount of current which the mechanism demanded was one which the battery-powered sources could supply only with difficulty.

Adapted first to the mechanical wind-chest and later to the pneumatic wind-chest, the new system consists of an electromagnet which, using a charge of 10–15 volts, opens the exhaust valve of a pneumatic motor filled with compressed air (a motor placed inside the pallet box and connected to the pallet valve in the note channel). The wind escapes from a pneumatic relay, causing it to collapse and thus opening the valve.

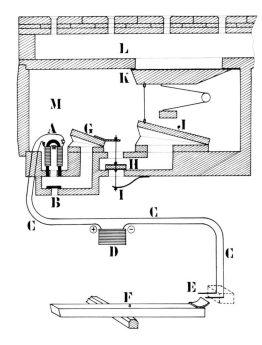

Fig. 39 Electropneumatic action applied to a slider-chest;
A Electromagnet – B Armature valve controlled by electromagnet A – C Electric circuit – D Power source – E Contact completing electric circuit – F Key. When depressed, the key completes an electric circuit which activates the electromagnet A. The armature valve B is drawn towards A, allowing wind to escape from a pneumatic relay G which in turn collapses. On collapsing, the primary motor activates the valve H which is held in position by a spring I. When opened, the valve H causes the secondary pneumatic motor J to collapse, as a result of which the pipe-chest pallet K is opened – L Groove – M Pallet box

This system was subsequently simplified and satisfactory results were obtained by the use of a single solenoid placed immediately beneath each of the organ pipes. The electromagnet then operates either as a mechanical lever which opens the pallet valve, or else as a simple valve. The keys on the manual are now reduced to the function of an electrical commutator, the end of each key being fitted with contact plates which complete a circuit and activate the electromagnet. Direct electric action – which allows the possibility of mobile keyboards irrespective of the distance between the keyboards and the instrument proper – has the advantage of instant attack and avoids the delays associated with tubular-pneumatic action, which largely failed to survive the period of its adaptation. It is, however, one of the ironies of modern technology that the console is sometimes located so far away from the organ that the organist only hears the sounds emitted after an embarrassing delay. Even the obvious advantages of this new system are counterbalanced by the drawbacks inherent in any system of electrification: apart from the problem of touch already mentioned, that of insulation is a particularly serious one, and the organ builder must make every effort to avoid oxidization, dust, humidity and induction of the solenoid.

However self-evident the technical progress of the last two centuries, it must nevertheless be said that the earlier system of mechanical transmission remains the best of all. It has stood the test of centuries, showing a remarkable solidity and reliability and remaining the surest guarantee of the organist's personal style of playing.

THE CONSOLE

There is one part of the organ – one could also say one place – which the listener would not regard as having great importance, but which the organ fanatic (the one who climbs up to the organ loft) knows well, because it is here that, enthralled, he can best appreciate the physical and intellectual labor which the organist must expend to govern his instrument. This mysterious and often invisible place is the console, the nerve center which combines, unites and controls the tonal structures of the instrument at the organist's fingertips. History has often confined the organist within the narrow space between the console and the *Rückpositiv,* only rarely granting him a proper opportunity to hear the variety of his "mélanges," to sense the balance of his world of sound, and to appreciate the precision of his phrasing. In older instruments the console was let into the substructure of the main organ case. Resting against the gallery railings or the Choir Organ case, the organist played with his back to the church. Technical developments from the eighteenth century onwards made it possible to separate the keyboards from the instrument itself, and the later pneumatic and electric systems turned the console into an independent piece of equipment, allowing the organist to face the nave. He had previously played his part in the communal act of music-making surrounded by choristers and to all intents on an equal footing with the other musicians. But technical progress has transformed him from a solitary and often invisible individual into a virtuoso performer who is frequently the center of attention, a magician in control of the multiple elements of the console – the draw-stop knobs, manuals, pedals, couplers, swell boxes, crescendo pedal, combination pistons, and even switches, control lights, pressure and power gauges and so on, all of which have turned the console into a pilot's cockpit. The draw-stop knobs of all the manuals were originally located on the jambs on either side of the console, or else above it (the stops of the Choir Organ are sometimes placed behind the organist, this unit being considered a second instrument). These knobs, wooden shanks square in cross section or occasionally simple metal rods, are frequently decorated at the end by wood or ivory pommels, which in some instances may be carved with various designs. The rank is brought into play by the organist drawing the knob towards him. The consoles of the larger instruments later assumed the shape of an amphitheater with draw-stop knobs of the most varied appearance. Initially, they were simple buttons mounted on a short wooden rod about 1 1/4 or 1 1/2 inches (3 or 4 cm) in length; then ivory tilting tablets fixed to the console, pivoting on a horizontal axis and engaged by means of downward pressure on the lower half; finally, stop-tongues or stop-keys made of synthetic materials which are depressed for the "on" position. There is no longer any precise order which the organ builder feels himself obliged to follow in the layout of the stops, except for the obvious system of grouping them by keyboard.

The console consists of between one and five manuals. Each one corresponds to the stops of a particular section of the instrument, and hence to an overall tonal structure planned in advance by the organ builder. The manuals are tiered, one above the other, the two lowest ones controlling the Choir and the Great. The third, fourth and (where applicable) the fifth rows control various ranges of tone-colors called (as the case may be) Swell, Solo, Bombarde and Echo. The keyboard compass on older instruments varied considerably, but in our own day the majority of "modern" instruments (i.e. those built since the end of the last century) are fitted with keyboards of a standard compass of between 56 and 61 notes, generally stretching from C to g^{111} (56 notes) or C to c^{1111} (61 notes). But keyboards with other compasses may also be found, especially in organs built in some historical style.

Although modern keyboards are chromatic throughout the whole of their compass, this has not always been the case. A number of notes (C sharp, D sharp, F sharp and G sharp) were removed from the first octave since they were rarely needed in the bass. This arrangement is called a short octave; and the traditional arrangement of the remaining keys was also slightly modified, so that the key normally reserved for the note E now produced a C; that of F sharp, D; and that of G sharp, E; by contrast, the keys of the notes F, G, A, B flat and B played the same notes as written. This omission of four bass notes is common to all keyboard instruments and is due to the influence of the old temperaments (traditional systems of tuning instruments) which favored those tonalities habitually used by all composers from Dietrich Buxtehude (1637–1707) to François Couperin (I, *c.* 1631–1708/12). These tonalities are direct descendants of the old church modes and have rarely more than two sharps or flats, sounding well when played on an instrument tuned according to one of these temperaments, whereas tonalities with more sharps or flats are more dissonant and generally avoided, so that the four bass notes in question are much less useful. At the same time, the short octave represents a gain in space and money for the organ builder, the larger pipes being the most expensive and unwieldy to build.

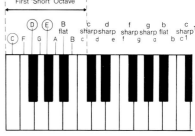

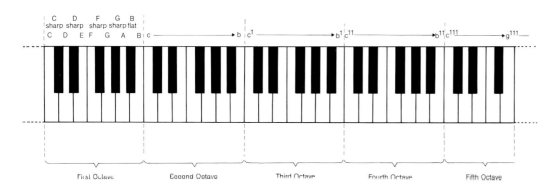

Numerous variants of this economical arrangement are to be found. The organs of Arp Schnitger, for example, have manuals with a short octave but a pedal organ whose first octave is of the usual compass, albeit lacking the note C sharp and sometimes also D sharp. In France, on the other hand, the pedals often had quite an extensive range, going as low as A^1, G^1 or even F^1.

The manual of the Great Organ or *Hauptwerk* contains the fundamental tone of the organ. Its pipes, placed at the center of the main case, are the most important and the most sonorous, with a complete range of Diapasons, including Mixtures *(pleno)*, Flute tones (sometimes accompanied by Mutation ranks), and a number of reeds.

The Positive makes its contribution to the overall tonal structure (or combination of stops) from its position either within the main case or else in a secondary case which is frequently bracketed over the gallery edge in front of the main case; it looks like a

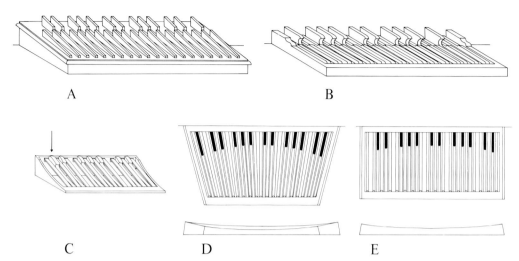

Fig. 40 A German Baroque pedalboard, such as Buxtehude will have known. Its compass extends from C to d¹ (but without the first C sharp)
B Classical French pedalboard from the time of Couperin. This is of the *petit ravalement* type, with a compass extending from A¹ to f¹. The *grand ravalement* begins at F¹
C Modern pedalboard, of a straight concave pattern. Compass: C - f¹
D Modern pedalboard, concave in shape with fan-shaped pedals, known as the "American pedalboard." Compass: C - g¹
E Italian pedalboard of the organ at L'Isle-sur-la-Sorgue, France (Le Royer, 1648; Mentasti 1825–7). Its compass appears to be C to e, but in fact the wind-chest has only eight notes; at c the keys revert to the notes of the lower octave. The note d sharp (arrowed) operates the action of the Chapeau chinois. The pedalboard is coupled to the main keyboard

A

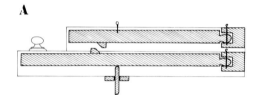

B

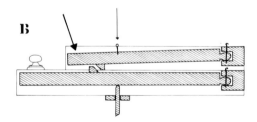

C

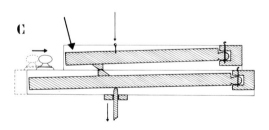

Fig. 41 Manual coupler:
A Keys at rest (not coupled) – B Keys depressed on upper keyboard (not coupled) – C Coupler engaged by moving the lower keyboard; when a key is depressed on the upper manual, it automatically depresses the corresponding key on the lower manual

modest replica of the main organ and is known as the *Rückpositiv* or, in English, occasionally as the "Choir Organ in front." The Positive contrasts with the Great Organ, repeating the latter's tonal structure but on a more modest scale; being closer to the listener, it produces a clearer, more direct sound. The harmonic pyramid of a Great Organ is based on a 16′ Diapason which normally corresponds to the 8′ Diapason on which the Positive is based. On the other hand, if the Great Organ has a 8′ Diapason (the corresponding Positive, although it, too, will have a 4′ Diapason) will acquire for itself an 8′ fundamental with the aid of a stopped pipe. The Positive is equally at home in solo writing as in chorus work.

The *Récit* manual, which might perhaps be better called simply the "third manual," was originally composed mainly of solo stops (hence its name). In fact it is difficult to translate into any other language a term which is so closely associated with the French organ of a particular period. When dealing with the small classical *Récit*, any intelligent English- or German-speaking musicologist will use the French term, the more so since there is no word in any other language to describe precisely what is meant by the term *Récit*. If, by contrast, we speak of the powerful Romantic Recit, the English organist, who knows that this manual developed in his own country at almost the same time that it appeared in France, will refer to it as the Swell, while the German organist will call it *französisches Schwellwerk*, in order to distinguish it from the German *Schwellwerk* which is more muted in tone. By the same token, it would be inaccurate to translate the latter term either as *Récit* or as *Oberwerk*, an expression used to designate either a Positive placed high up in the organ case, or even, in the case of Johann Sebastian Bach, the Great Organ itself. Its pipework, placed behind the Great Organ or above it, is limited in the classical French organ to the treble notes (upper half of the keyboard), whereas in England and Germany this third manual has witnessed considerable developments. During the nineteenth century it was fitted with a swell box, abandoning its role as a partial manual and becoming an equal partner with the Great Organ and the Positive.

If the Echo organ has a less extensive tonal range than the *Récit*, its composition and role nevertheless closely correspond to those of the *Récit*. Its pipes, frequently planted in the organ's substructure, are sometimes inserted in a niche fitted with shutters which the organist can operate in order to introduce subtle shades of tone-color into the manual's sonorities.

Large symphonic organs built in France during the nineteenth century also included a Grand Chœur, a powerful and independent tonal structure used to reinforce the Grand Orgue.

The compass of the pedals has grown only slowly in the course of the centuries but nowadays comprises some thirty notes from c¹ to f¹, or occasionally g¹. Although, historically, pedals have normally been straight and flat, English and American pedals (as defined by the organ builder Henry Willis in the middle of the nineteenth century) were arranged in the shape of a fan. Whether flat or concave in form, the wooden keys

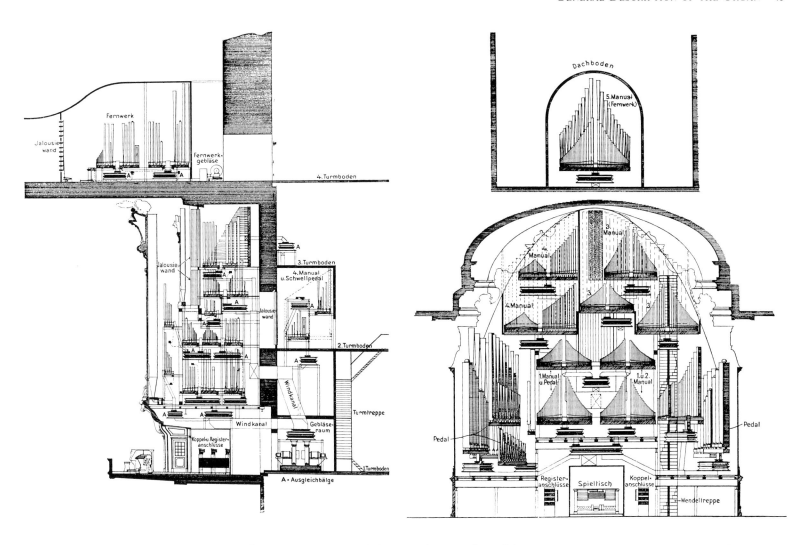

Figs. 42, 43   Cross section, and front elevation, showing the layout of the stops and
mechanism, of the huge Michaeliskirche organ
in Hamburg, built by Walcker in 1908: five
manuals and pedals, with 163 stops. Engraving
from Alfred Sitter, *Das Hauptorgelwerk und die
Hilfsorgel der grossen St. Michaelis-Kirche in
Hamburg*, Hamburg, 1912, pp. 11–12.

of today's instruments are around 27 ½ inches (70.25 cm) long and are activated by
pressure from the organist's foot (toes and heels). The pipes connected up to the
pedals nowadays constitute the harmonic base of the instrument (foundation stops, 8′,
16′ and sometimes 32′ reeds, Mutation stops, Mixtures, etc.), together with some solo
stops capable of playing in every register, especially tenor and alto. We may note,
however, that for a long time the pedals have had only certain stops at their disposal.
The height of the largest pedal pipes obliges the organ builder either to place them
behind the main case or to divide them into two groups on either side of it, in pipe
towers for example. We must also mention in this connection one of the most
astonishing – and probably the most ephemeral – inventions in the whole of nineteenth-
century organ building, namely a system of double pedals which can be found
especially in instruments built during the first half of the century. In Italy there are
examples made by Agati and Tronci in the diocese of Pistoia (Limite sull'Arno, Oratorio
della Compagnia della S. Trinità, Agati, 1821; Gavinana, Pieve di S. Maria Assunta,
Agati, 1838 and Tronci, 1852; Pistoia, S. Pier Maggiore, Tronci, 1823). In Germany five
such organs were built by Walcker (most notably St. Paul's, Frankfurt, 1833), although
none has survived, while a similar fate befell the organ of St. Eustache in Paris, built by
Daublaine & Callinet in 1854. In the pedals of the Emperor's Organ in Toledo Cathedral
(1798) there are two rows of half-keys.

    The organist may also combine these different tonal structures thanks to a method
of coupling the manuals which allows the pipes of two or more manuals to speak even
though the organist himself plays only one of them. The earliest coupling system dates
back to the beginning of the classical age of organ building, and is ingenious in its
simplicity. Like the system used to couple harpsichord manuals, it involves drawing

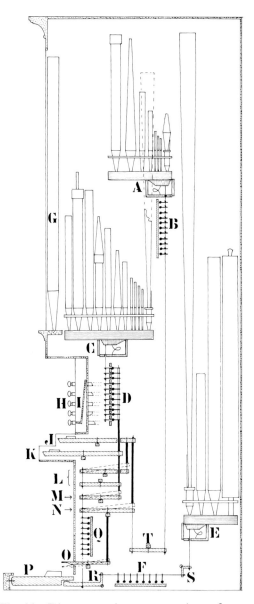

The Great Centennial Exhibition Organ, built by
HILBORNE L. ROOSEVELT.
NEW YORK.

Fig. 44 Diagrammatic cross section of an organ with two manuals and a pedalboard, showing its mechanism (the lines of the draw-stop action and distribution of the wind supply have been omitted):

A Wind-chest of the *Positif* manual – B Roller board of the *Positif* manual – C Wind-chest of the *Grand Orgue* manual – D Roller board of the *Grand Orgue* (with reverse action) – E Wind-chest of the Pedal – F Pedal roller board – G Display pipes – H Draw-stop knobs – I Music desk – J *Positif* keyboard – K *Grand Orgue* keyboard – L Coupler POS/GO – M Coupler GO/PED (L, N, N: rocking tablets) – N Coupler POS/PED – O Pedal operating the coupler POS/PED (the other pedal couplers have been omitted) – P Pedalboard – Q Roller board reducing the distance between the pedalboard keys to that of the manual keys – R Counter-keys reducing the distance by which the pedals are depressed to that of the manuals, with squares rotating the action through 90° – S Squares restoring the horizontal action of the pedal trackers to a vertical plane – T Levers reversing the action of the *Positif* trackers

Fig. 45 Centennial Exhibition Organ of 1876, Opus 15 by Hilborne L. Roosevelt, Philadelphia (PA)

It was Roosevelt's firm which did useful work in the United States with electric action, being one of the first to exploit the advantages of this form of transmission, the result of which was a freer disposition of the various tonal structures. Thus the organ at the Philadelphia Exhibition had an "Electric Suspended Organ" (Transverse Flute 8′) attached to the ceiling opposite the organ gallery, and an "Electric Echo Organ" (Stopped Diapason 8′, Vox humana 8′, Tremulant) placed in a tower and connected up to the console by over two hundred feet of cable. The power was generated by electric motors driven by six Leclanché cells. This instrument had thirty-eight stops on five keyboards (Great, Swell, Solo, Electric Echo and Electrical Suspended Organ), each with a compass of fifty-eight notes, and Pedals (thirty notes). In 1881, the organ was taken to the concert hall in Boston's Huntington Avenue, and rebuilt in its entirety by Roosevelt.

the upper manual a few centimeters forwards over the lower manual: small wooden studs fixed in the base of the keys of the upper manual are then aligned with matching studs fixed to the lower keyboard, so that as each key is depressed it automatically depresses the corresponding key on the manual coupled to it. At a later date, a new system was developed characterized by the use of small stickers, one for each key, working in a frame or register between the two manuals to be coupled: when the coupler is engaged, the sticker belonging to the note concerned will raise the back end of the key above it, thus allowing both manuals to be played together from the lower keyboard, without the upper manuals having to be pulled forwards as in the earlier system. This later system is operated either by a foot lever or a draw-stop. Finally, with the development of pneumatic and electric mechanisms came the possibility of coupling the manuals with the aid of buttons located at the same level as the manuals, while, in larger instruments, the system of coupling knobs is often replaced by "poppets," engaged simply by means of foot pressure.

From an historical point of view, the system of coupling keyboards together reflected the tonal structures of the *Werkprinzip* right up to the last century. In a general way the secondary structures could be coupled only in relation to the principal structure as defined by the Great Organ.

The nineteenth century lost this sense of spatiality in the composition of the stops and gained in its place the convenience and efficiency of increasingly brilliant Mixtures. All the manuals could be coupled to each other in descending order. In the twentieth century there are even some instruments which allow organists the facility of controlling all the stops of the instrument from a single manual of their own choice.

As the nineteenth century drew to a close, experiments on the part of organ builders brought numerous innovations to the console, including free and prepared combinations made possible by the increased provision of adjustable pistons (generally two or three of them are available, each one separately programed). Having prepared the desired combinations in advance, the organist can introduce a new registration simply by depressing a single piston. This system was later simplified with the help of electronic technology: the player prepares several different combinations which he records on a single series of setter-pistons; as long as it does not get out of order, this procedure may enable him to prepare all the combinations which he requires in the course of a single recital. Mention should also be made of fixed combinations (in France popularly known as "boutons du dimanche"), whose volume (*piano*, *mezzo forte*, *forte*, *fortissimo* or *tutti*) is fixed by the organ builder. Instruments having mechanical action occasionally included a system of free combinations (operated by small studs or diminutive stops) together with the ability to call on and return individual stops (reeds or Mixtures) by means of reversible pistons.

The swell box and crescendo pedal offer the organist the possibility of varying the intensity of sound produced by the instrument. Both mechanisms are operated by foot pressure. The swell box comprises a case containing all the stops of one manual and fitted with shutters or louvers which can be opened or closed at will. The operation was initially carried out by means of a sprung pedal which meant that the shutters had to be either completely open or completely shut, with no intermediary position. In 1863 the German organ builder Eberhard Friedrich Walcker invented a rectangular balanced pedal, without a spring, which made it possible to keep the box open in the desired position and hence maintain whatever level of sound was required. This mechanism first appeared in Spain in the final third of the seventeenth century (Ecos) and in England at the beginning of the eighteenth century (swell box first built into the organ in the Church of St. Magnus the Martyr, London Bridge, by Abraham Jordan, 1712), and then in Germany (where it was known as the *Schwellkasten*). But it was the Romantic organ which witnessed the spectacular rise of the swell box, and it was not uncommon to see instruments adorned with two or even three of them. The crescendo pedal is a by-product of electropneumatic technology: a balanced rectangular pedal or roller (German: *Rollschweller*) brings on the stops in a fixed order (predetermined by the organ builder), starting with the quietest and building up to a comprehensive full organ, from the foundation stops to the *tutti*.

These different systems are of extreme technical complexity, but have been rendered obligatory by the search for increasingly flexible tonal colors (as well as by the instrument's rapid development). They were indispensable to organists at the beginning of the present century and remain useful even today to any player who has a particularly large instrument at his command. Above all, they were responsible for a new vision of music written for the organ, an important chapter in the history of contemporary music. It is a chapter which nowadays involves a conscious choice of a particular style, since the majority of organ builders are now returning to a more classical concept of the instrument, and the organist, forgetting that he was once a one-man band, has again become the humble servant of the mightiest of instruments.

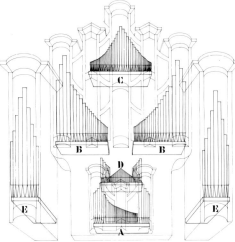

Fig. 46 The *Werkprinzip*
Diagram of an organ case showing the layout
of the different tonal structures:
A *Rückpositiv* (*Positif* or Choir Organ) –
B *Hauptwerk* (*Grand Orgue* or Great Organ) –
C *Oberwerk* or *Kronwerk* (Solo or *Récit*) –
D *Brustwerk* or *Brustpositif* (Echo) – E Pedal

THE ORGAN CASE

The organ case, a wooden housing designed to protect the organ, has more than a decorative function: it also plays an acoustic role, channeling and concentrating the sounds produced by the instrument. As the German term *Gehäuse* ("housing") suggests, it encloses and protects the pipework and mechanism.

During the early stages of its development the organ was often simply covered by cloths which served as a kind of dust sheet: thus, for example, the organ described by the monk Theophilus in the eleventh century was protected by a sort of tent which covered the entire instrument when it was not in use. Before beginning to play, the organist would raise the cover by means of a rope running over a pulley. At the close of the Middle Ages organ builders erected curtains, or screens, in front of the display pipes, often decorating them with various designs. An engraving by Jacques Cellier of the organ in Rheims Cathedral, dating from the end of the sixteenth century, shows a screen decorated with a fleur-de-lis pattern.

In the field of organ-case decoration, changing tastes have brought about numerous and constant transformations, and even resulted in the wholesale destruction of instruments thought no longer fashionable. In this way each organ has developed within the bosom, so to speak, of the same aesthetic family, but acquired personal characteristics in keeping with the individual creative abilities of the architect or wood-carver. This latter aspect, it is true, can only rarely be appreciated today since almost all organs have undergone later alterations, with the addition of a separate Choir Organ or pedal towers, the raising up of part of the structure, additional decorations, new paintings, and so on.

Originally the organ case opened and closed like a cupboard, having doors or shutters at the front. These panels, which were made of solid wood or fabric, were very soon painted and ornamented, while the empty spaces at the foot and at the top of the display pipes were overloaded with wood carvings, which were frequently gilt. The acoustic function of the case became increasingly evident: the chest gathers together the sounds, reflecting them and directing them towards the listener. As for the doors, in addition to their protective and decorative function, they could be used to shut off the instrument from view, during Lent, for example, from the Gloria of Good Friday to the Gloria of Easter Day, thus presenting the congregation with the sight of their ornamental displays and the paintings decorating their outer surface. On other occasions the organ was simply shrouded from view by means of its curtain or screen. As both a musical instrument and a work of decorative art, the organ became an integral part of the church, enhancing the building by virtue of its overall design and its wood carvings. As a veritable jewel of church architecture, it came to be considered a counterpart of the Gothic or Baroque altar.

The medieval organ is basically rectangular in outline, comprising elements which may be arranged parallel or in tiers. The facework is interrupted only by the formal arrangement of the pipes and the bulk of the pipe towers. The result is an austere image enlivened by simple decorations (generally leaf patterns) masking the top and bottom of the pipes. Decorated panels, bell turrets, square or triangular pinnacles and crenellations completed the design.

As the instrument itself evolved, the organ case too became more complex. The flamboyant style of decorative art, dating from the end of the fifteenth century, left a profound mark on the history of organ-case design: openwork wood carvings were added, and mouldings decorated with foliated scrolls enlivened the overall picture, while finely wrought decorations (floral garlands, lancet, arches, quadrifoliate and trefoiled arches, arabesques, statuettes and lantern turrets) gave the organ a detailed intricacy comparable to the work of a goldsmith.

The Renaissance witnessed the consolidation of different national types in both the acoustic and visual conception of the instrument. Reacting against the excessive concern for geometrical patterns which Gothic art had evinced, the Renaissance introduced new elements inspired by classical models. If the pedal towers of northern Europe lost their austerity of design and grew increasingly diversified in form with the adoption of triangular, semicircular or semihexagonal structures, they nevertheless threw into relief a more sober facework which was later framed by pilasters and abutments modelled on the classical Greek orders. The degree of detail is often astounding: friezes consisting of triglyphs alternating with bucranes; cusps; apses; paterae; basins; *pots-à-feu*; corbels; *culs-de-lampe*; colonnettes supporting candelabra, etc.; the panels of the lower part of the case (like the gallery balusters) were later carved with *trompe-l'œil* designs intended to give a sense of perspective.

With the exception of a handful of large instruments built during the Middle Ages, it was not until the sixteenth century that the organ case generally assumed noble proportions and a more complicated architectural design. Until the beginning of the nineteenth century, the *Werkprinzip*, which in England and Germany divided the pipework into separate groups, each corresponding to a particular manual, made it possible to tell at a glance the number of keyboards simply by looking at the organ case. But this splendidly logical and Germanic arrangement should not allow us to forget those Latin countries in which the case, for all its magnificence, did not reflect the instrument's internal structure, being a mere decorative facework, an ornamental fantasy designed to ravish the eye.

The Baroque style, a product of the revitalization of the senses inspired by the Counter-Reformation, continued this development without a break, conferring an increasingly sumptuous appearance on the organ case, which now became the repository of the most diverse ornaments, testimonies to the aesthetic taste of the moment: flora and fauna (from nature and from legend), pagan mythology (chimeras, dragons, satyrs, caryatids, episodes from the lives of classical heroes), Christian imagery (angels, devils, allegories, representations of saints, prophets and kings of Israel). It was also decorated with representations of numerous other musical instruments. Nor was this lavish ornamentation limited merely to the organ case and gallery: it extended to the display pipes themselves, which were sometimes decorated with brightly colored designs or geometrical patterns carved in relief or bas-relief (chequered designs, lozenges, cable moldings and tracery); and if the metal of the display pipes was deemed insufficient to enliven the design, the artist could paint the flattened edges of the pipe-mouths. This extreme degree of ornamentation in pipework flourished above all in Spain, Germany and England and can still be seen in English, Australian and American instruments built during the nineteenth century, and even during the present century.

Various accessories were invented to regale the eye of the worshiper, such as mechanisms which allowed angels to beat their wings, to blow trumpets and even to beat time. We may further mention, to the greater glory of their waggish inventors, the grotesque masks capable of moving their jaws (the famous "Gossip" in the Church of Notre-Dame d'Avesnières in Anjou, dating from the sixteenth century, or the *Roraffe* in Strasbourg Cathedral in Alsace), the presence of an ox on the two notes of the Kuckuck (Abbey Church of Ochsenhausen in southern Germany, 1729–33), an eagle beating its wings (Cistercian convent at Lezajsk, Poland, 1680–93), or the remarkable sight of a fox's brush striking the face of the wretch who dared draw the stop marked *Noli me tangere* (Do not touch me), found in a number of Polish and German organs.

Renaissance and Baroque cases both maintained and developed the grand tradition of medieval illuminators. They were often decorated with works by famous artists, such as Hans Holbein the Younger, to whom we owe the two panels of the organ in Basle Cathedral, or Paolo Veronese, who in 1560 decorated the organ in the Church of San Sebastiano in Venice.

For almost three centuries the organ was a visual centerpiece appreciated by all who saw it, in the same way as they appreciated a painting: the gilt of the carvings and friezes and the silver of the display pipes harmonized with the natural colors of the different types of wood; the lavishness of the decorations and the delicate blend of the various colors turned the organ case into a finely crafted object and made the organ the most perfect of the church's works of art.

The nineteenth century, which witnessed the advent of large-scale industries, gradually abandoned the personal creations of master organ builders. Architects were

Fig. 47   Sta. Maria della Scala, 1516–18, Giovanni di Antonio Piffero, Siena, Italy, Organ case by Baldassarre Peruzzi. Engraving from A.G. Hill, London, 1883–91
The original stoplist reveals a feature typical of this transitional period of Italian organ building at the beginning of the sixteenth century: certain of the upper ranks of the *ripieno* are collected together on one slider (Principale, Ottava, XV + XXIX, XIX + XXVI, XXII + XV, Flauto in quintadecima). The organ had a spring-chest ("a vento"), and a single manual with a compass of forty-seven notes (F^1 - f^{11}); a reed stop was added in the eighteenth century. The instrument, which has been preserved almost intact with its original stops, was restored by Tamburini in 1975–6.

inspired by the various styles of the period (Empire, Louis-Philippe and so on) until the middle of the century, when the lack of appeal of any new style gave way to designs which derived from a renewed infatuation with the Middle Ages, creations of Gothic inspiration modeled on cathedral architecture. Parallel to this formal revolution was the nineteenth century's renunciation of color, resulting in a somber and often monotonous handling of the available choice of polished woods. Even in Germany, the organ case was merely a pretext for concealing an often erroneous layout of the internal mechanism and of noisy machinery intended to facilitate the organist's control over these musical monsters.

Our own century, finally, has seen the disappearance of these artificial façades and the development of instruments whose architectural design is content with the idea of free-standing pipes, a concept which unfortunately robs the instrument of the case's acoustic and protective properties. Following attempts to adapt this new vision to the idea of the *Werkprinzip*, contemporary organ builders are finally rediscovering the advantages of the organ case and of the classical arrangement of the different tonal structures.

From the point of view of the organ case's general development, it is interesting to see how the architect has progressively freed the instrument from the severe two-dimensionality of the Gothic case, a process of emancipation which culminated in the eighteenth century's emphasis upon the disparate structure of the instrument. Having subsequently abandoned this emphasis in the nineteenth century, the architect now finds himself returning to the most basic form of Western organ design, and rediscovering the acoustic and aesthetic qualities of the classical organ case. Increasing numbers of organ builders have given a new lease of life to the organ case in the twentieth century. Whether the result is an individual creation or a copy of some earlier organ case is a question which cannot be settled in any peremptory fashion but depends, as is now generally agreed, upon the particular instrument's tonal style. If the adherents of contemporary art frequently have occasion to reproach today's organ builders for the conservatism of their approach, they would do well to adopt an historical point of view and recall, with due modesty, that our own century will no doubt form a chapter in the history of organ building notable for its indispensable awareness of the merit of instruments from past centuries and for the desire of many organ builders and musicologists to understand their centuries-old heritage and to penetrate its secrets.

The Placing of the Organ

Ideally, the best place for the organ is the one which allows the sound waves the greatest freedom to travel. Yet it is a sad but true fact that organ builders have often had to content themselves with a compromise solution and to take account of other considerations of a practical, aesthetic or liturgical nature. We may also draw attention to the more specific fate which the organ has suffered in the different Reformed churches (most notably in England and Germany), where the instrument not only accompanies the parish choir but above all provides a musical backing for congregational hymn-singing, whereas in Catholic countries the organ is essentially a solo instrument in dialog with the choir.

The most usual position for the organ in the majority of churches is still the gallery above the west door, the sonorities of the instrument being heard to best advantage when it is positioned here. Although these are acoustic considerations, there are also architectural reasons for placing the instrument here, since this part of the church has almost always been the most spacious. The major drawback associated with this site is that the organ blocks off the stained glass of the west window, but organ builders have learned to overcome this problem by dividing the organ case into several separate units. One of the most extreme examples of this arrangement is that of the Rococo organ in the Abbey Church of Weingarten (1737–50) in southern Germany, where the layout of the instrument respects the six windows in the west wall of the building. If

Fig. 48 Different positions of the organ:

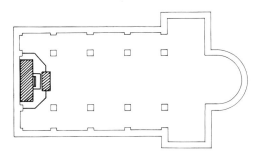

Traditional position of church organ on a gallery above the west door at the far end of the principal nave

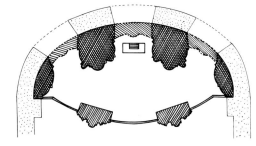

Diagram showing the layout of the organ in Weingarten Abbey, Federal Republic of Germany (Joseph Gabler, 1737–50), divided into several cases sited between the six windows of the principal façade

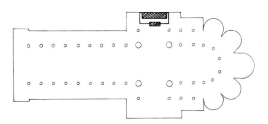

Site of the organ in Rheims Cathedral, France, in the north transept (Oudin Hestre, 1487; Denis Collet, 1570)

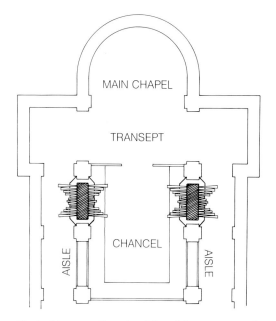

Typical layout of a pair of Spanish organs, positioned symmetrically on either side of the chancel (double cases with four fronts)

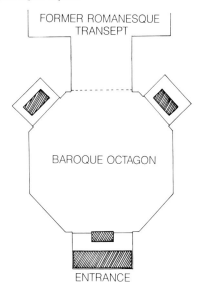

Diagram of the octagon of the abbey church at Muri, Switzerland, showing its three organs, a main organ (Thomas Schott, 1619–30) and two *Chororgeln* (Josef and Victor Ferdinand Bossard, 1743–4)

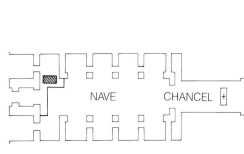

Typical Portuguese organ: layout of the instrument in the monastery church of St. Martin at Tibães (Francisco António Solha, 1785)

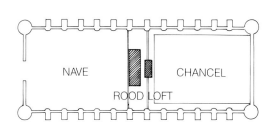

Organ of King's College Chapel, Cambridge, England (Thomas Dallam, 1605–6; Lancelot Pease [?], 1661), positioned on the rood loft, with one of its fronts facing the nave, the other facing the chancel

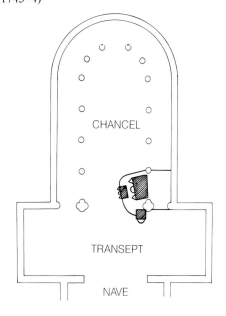

Organ of St. Ludgeri, Norden, Federal Republic of Germany (Arp Schnitger, 1686–8), sited in a most unusual position, at an angle in the first bay of the chancel. A single pedal tower is orientated towards the transept, giving the instrument an asymmetrical aspect unique among Baroque instruments.

this position generally confers the greatest acoustic advantages, having been adopted for this reason from the end of the Middle Ages onwards, there are nonetheless other positions which have been favored in different periods and above all in different regions.

The positive organ of the Middle Ages, being small in size, was placed in the chancel or at the side of the choir, a choice determined by its role as an accompanist. In consequence, the chancel continues to house the main organ even today, in some churches, where it is suspended above the choir stalls. This arrangement is regularly found in England, Spain and Italy. In Italy the organ's privileged position is the cantoria, a small gallery where the choristers sat and whose austere rectangular form, decorated by the great artists of the time, harmonized well with the pure lines of the Latin basilica.

In the Hispanic countries of Spain, Portugal and South America, and in Italy, two separate organs are frequently placed on either side of the chancel, the epistle organ on the south side and the gospel organ on the north side, mirroring each other with their often identical facework. This layout is found only rarely in other countries, although there are some notable exceptions (Abbey Church at Ottobeuren (1754–66) in southern Germany and the Benedictine Abbey (1743–4) at Muri in Switzerland). Another site which was frequently used during the Middle Ages to enhance the instrument's visual and aural appeal was the rood loft or screen separating the chancel from the nave. This was an excellent site from the point of view of the diffusion of sound, since it allowed the organ to fulfil its role both in chorus work and as a solo instrument. Occasionally the instrument comprised two frontages, one facing the choir, the other the nave. The intransigence of the Reformation, the changes in the Catholic liturgy and, at a later date, the evolution in taste during the eighteenth century led to the disappearance of these marvelous structures and often of the instruments themselves. Such an arrangement was encouraged particularly in Flanders and England and still exists to this day in the latter country, especially in Protestant churches.

These sites, although frequently adopted, are not, however, the only ones found: the organ may be hidden behind the altar, raised up above one of the transept doors or bracketed to one of the transept walls close to the chancel. The last mentioned position, which was popular above all at the time of the Renaissance, enables the organ to forge an excellent aural link between the chancel and the main nave, allowing a dialog to develop between the Great Organ and the Choir Organ. The instrument has also been sited in one of the naves or in a side-chapel, in the ambulatory or attached, like a swallow's nest, to the *cul-de-lampe* of one of the walls in the central nave, a position characteristic of the end of the Middle Ages. But, in the final analysis, is it not the taste and intelligence of the organ builder which determines where the organ should be positioned? There are instruments so well concealed beneath a vault, so well enclosed within tiny niches that the observer views them with condescension, only to discover that, thanks to the organ builder's skill, they are capable of producing the most magnificent sounds.

III Organ Building and Restoration

ORGAN BUILDING FROM THE MIDDLE AGES TO THE BAROQUE

As described by the monk Theophilus in the early eleventh century and by the anonymous writer of the Berne Codex in the late eleventh century, the organ of the High Middle Ages was a modest instrument, fairly rough in construction. The wind-chest, made of wood or metal, was fed by a greater or lesser number of bellows using alternate action, which must have compensated to some extent for the lack of a reservoir. We may note that the organ depicted in the Utrecht Psalter of around 830, which is shown operated by hydraulic bellows, appears to be an anachronism inspired by Byzantine tradition, for such organs were unknown in the West at this period.

The medieval wind-chest did not contain any device for controlling the stops, but only one for operating the notes by means of sliders similar to those of a modern slider-chest, which had to be pulled out and then pushed back by hand. The writer of the Berne Codex suggests a primitive keyboard, since the hand-sliders were operated by means of a pivoted square which allowed the player to move his hands and fingers vertically, the "keys" returning automatically by means of a spring.

The pipes were of equal scale, in other words their diameter remained the same no matter what their length. This also limited the compass of the keyboard since pipes which are too long or too short cannot sound correctly. The layout of the keys (or sliders) on the keyboard was the same as that of the pipes, and precluded both virtuosity and the sounding of several stops at once.

It appears that the pipes were doubled at a quite early date (and in any case by the eleventh century) in order to obtain not so much a louder noise as a more ample tone, necessary to fill the vast buildings in which the instrument was now to be found. This process was to be the point of departure for a remarkable development which ultimately led to the *plein jeu* or *pleno*. First it was essential, however, to discover the technical means which would enable it to be put into practise. This came when organ builders abandoned the idea of a fixed diameter to the pipes and adopted progressive scaling in order to be able to take advantage of the whole of the audible sound spectrum, from 32′ to ⅛′ and even higher. A further development that was necessary was the installation of a roller board between the wind-chest and the keyboard. The keyboard was now of a manageable size and adapted to suit the organist's hands, allowing him to play polyphonic music.

The number of keys on the manual continued to vary greatly, although by the fifteenth century it was increasingly common to find a compass of 38 notes (from F to a¹¹, but lacking the first two sharp keys, F sharp and G sharp, together with the last sharp key, g sharp¹¹). But the most important advantage of progressive scaling was less the increase in the number of keys than a radical change in the tonal quality of the sound produced by the organ, since, in addition to the existing two pipes sounding the unison and representing the fundamental tone of the stop, there now appeared octave and super-octave doublings and, later, the twelfth and even the fifth. The space available in the treble, as well as acoustic requirements, permitted numerous doublings at the upper end of the keyboard, thereby giving rise to the medieval Fourniture, where the number of pipes per note could be increased to a quite disproportionate degree (e.g. Amiens, 1422: 19 to 91 ranks). These ranks, however, could not be isolated and as a result it was impossible to vary the tonal color. The invention of slider-chests and spring-chests towards the end of the fifteenth century left organ builders with the task of devising some way of enabling the pipes to speak separately, either by means of a keyboard controlling a double row of pallets, each one in a pallet box fitted with a separate intake valve *(Sperrventil)*, or else by means of different manuals each governing a different sonority, and playable together. The Halberstadt organ, described by Michael Praetorius in 1619, must have been a particularly impressive example of these fourteenth-century organs in which the increased number of manuals (three manuals plus a pedalboard) seemed intended rather to produce different sonorities than to be used in *alternatim* music. But organ music was still in its infancy, and if the earliest text that has been rediscovered and recognized as keyboard music (the Robertsbridge Codex) dates from the fourteenth century, like the Halberstadt organ, not all keyboards lent themselves to polyphonic music. The treble keyboards of the Halberstadt instrument had fourteen notes each, the bass keyboard and the pedals only twelve. But the "old organs of Notre-Dame in Dijon," dating from 1350 and described in 1425 by Henri Arnaut de Zwolle, already had a modern keyboard comprising 47 notes (B to a^{111}). Apart from the variety of different keyboards, we may also mention the inconsistencies of pitch, which could vary in practise by as much as an octave.

Although, as we have seen, the fourteenth century was a decisive period in the history of the organ, the instrument continued to defy all attempts at standardization both as regards scale (32′ organs are known to have existed at this time), the composition of the *pleno* and the technical ingenuity displayed by its one or more keyboards. Throughout the whole of Europe, however, it maintained the principle of its fundamental tone, together with a stylistic unity in organ-case decoration, the case now having become a necessary item of church furniture required to frame the display pipes, protect the other pipework and ensure their tonal cohesion. Even today the cases of the organs at Salamanca and Sion (Valère) attest to the elegance and richness of these precious objects.

A new technical revolution came with the invention of the double chest in the fifteenth century, effectively the only mechanical advance until the technical innovations of the nineteenth century. In this way the organ, having developed abruptly, rapidly acquired the essential features of its classical format, which each country and each school would later adapt to suit its own personality and its own potential. It would not be an oversimplification to say that the Renaissance made all the discoveries, and that, at least until the Romantic era, only minor modifications of detail followed. Around the middle of the fifteenth century there developed out of the indivisible medieval *Blockwerk*, roughly speaking, two distinct types of organ; in the south an instrument with one stop for each rank of the Fourniture, an arrangement which gave rise to the Italian *ripieno* organ; in the north an instrument in which the Fourniture ranks remained grouped together but were immediately divided into Fourniture and Cymbale. This latter system was already capable of a variety of registrations besides the Foundation Stops, which could be called up in isolation (Principal and Octave). The Cymbale, a high Mixture of octaves and fifths, may have been intended to imitate the cymbalum or bell-stop found in many organs. This was the first of the mutation stops which, together with the Mixtures, was to enjoy a brilliant future.

The increased number of keyboards, which had already been used previously as a technical device (bass and treble manuals, or else mutation stops and Fourniture, and pedals operated by a pedal coupler), could now be put to a new use in the combination of the Great Organ and the accompanying Choir Organ. The same device could also be implemented whenever an older organ with an indivisible Fourniture needed the addition of a modern keyboard with separate stops. The pedals, intended either to operate the bass notes of the manuals by means of a coupler or to sound the

Fig. 49 *Positif à pied*, single manual with six hand-sliders; after the eleventh-century Pommersfelden Psalter (Gräfl. Schönbornsche Bibl. Cod. 2776). From Buhle, 1903.

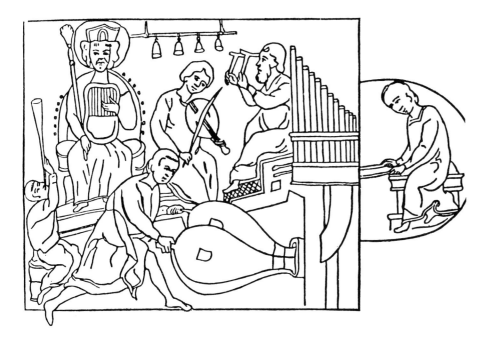

Fig. 50 Detail from a miniature depicting King David and his musicians. The organist, apparently installed in an adjoining room, is seen operating two of the four hand-sliders. The two large bellows are worked by a single assistant. From *St. Elisabeth's Prayerbook* in the museum at Cividale del Friuli, first third of thirteenth century. From Buhle, 1903.

independent bass notes of the Trompes (Haarlem or Chartres, for example), were later given their own stops, mostly in the bass and tenor registers. The Trompes themselves led an ephemeral existence and were quickly incorporated into the modern keyboards, whose compass was extended from B down to A in the fifteenth century, and then to C^1, resulting in a relatively uniform compass of four chromatic octaves for the manuals, the absence of the first sharp semitones recalling the diatonic scale of the Trompes. The invention of the double chest made it possible to divide the harmonic pyramid, but it was first necessary to reorganize its composition, since it is difficult to plant a progressive number of pipes on a wind-chest constructed in this manner. The desire to furnish the bass notes in the tonal spectrum with higher-pitched harmonics requires the ranks to break each time they reach a certain pitch ($\frac{1}{6}'$ or $\frac{1}{8}'$, for example). Organs of the *ripieno* type break back an octave, as do those with the newer Fourniture mixtures (which may have an increasing number of ranks towards the top of the compass, although fewer than in medieval instruments). The Cymbale breaks back twice by a fifth or a fourth, frequently dispensing with a Tierce rank which is normally housed elsewhere or as a separate stop. Doubling of the fundamental continued to be found in the highest ranks of the *pleno*. In northern organs we occasionally find the fundamental doubled above a certain pitch, the pipes appearing *en façade*; in southern organs these doublings may be housed under a separate register.

The Diapasons having been divided up among separate registers, it was the Flutes and reed voices which were to become the object of organ builders' researches: 8′, 4′, 2′ and 1′ Flutes, together with $2\frac{2}{3}'$ and $1\frac{1}{3}'$ Quints first appeared during the early sixteenth century, as did reeds in the form of Regals and, later, Trumpets. At the same time we begin to find various Tierce stops (Sesquialtera, Nasard, Toulousaine and Cornet) making their way across the whole of Europe, due to the movements of the various organ builders of the time and the close political relations between states. It could be said that until 1600 the organ continued to combine a number of common attributes, which national or regional schools would strive to differentiate from the seventeenth century onwards, once they had at their disposal all the necessary technical expertise and the entire range of sonorities needed to fashion a new world of sound. Theoreticians such as Mersenne in France (1627), Praetorius in Germany (1619) and Antegnati in Italy (1608) took it upon themselves to describe this new world.

We may mention finally a number of additional technical details including the invention of the wedge bellows, which improved the wind supply until such time as the nineteenth century triumphantly produced parallel bellows; and the almost simultaneous invention of the slider-chest and spring-chest at the end of the fifteenth

Fig. 51 King David playing a positive organ, depressing the large keys with both hands; miniature from the Rutland (Belvoir Castle) Psalter (f.97^v), thirteenth century. From Buhle, 1903.

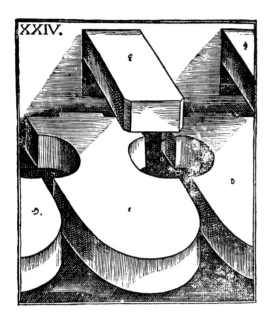

Fig. 52 Detail of the organ keyboard in Halberstadt Cathedral, German Democratic Republic; from Michael Praetorius, *Syntagma musicum*, Vol. II: "De Organographia," Wolfenbüttel, 1619, Pl. 24.

Fig. 53 The organ keyboards in Halberstadt Cathedral, German Democratic Republic, showing the treble and bass manuals and the pedals; from Michael Praetorius, *Syntagma musicum*, Vol. II: "De Organographia," Wolfenbüttel, 1619, Pl. 25.

century. After a certain amount of hesitation, the spring-chest came to be the preferred type in Italy, the Low Countries and northern Germany, the slider-chest being the general rule in France, Spain and the Alpine lands. We may also draw attention to various accessories such as trumpet-blowing angels, the Kuckuck and Rossignol, and the Tremulant, all of them not only amusing toys but valuable aids for the organist, as were pedal couplers, pistons and intake valves admitting wind to the pallet box.

ITALY

In comparison with those in other European countries, the Italian organ was one of the most traditional in its adherence to medieval organ design, equipped as it was with stops for each rank of the family of Diapasons which together made up the *ripieno* (the Italian equivalent of the French *plein jeu* or *pleno*). The highest ranks would break back an octave as soon as they reached some predetermined ceiling ($\frac{1}{8}$' or sometimes $\frac{1}{6}$'), combining numerous characteristic doublings in the treble. Among the original features of the Italian organ, the following are worth mentioning:

The Italian organ normally had only one manual; if there was a second one, it was customarily an echo manual placed in the substructure, rarely a *Rückpositiv*. The pedals were normally coupled to the first notes of the keyboard, only occasionally having their own stops.

The organ case was often rectangular in shape, crowned by an imposing fronton. In the Venetian tradition it was positioned in the axis of the church, above the altar; in the rest of the peninsula it was most often to be found at one side of the chancel, facing a second case (with speaking or dummy pipes), as also in Spain. The case was often fitted with wings painted by well-known artists of the time.

At certain periods and in certain regions the stops were divided into treble and bass, a device which later encouraged the development of "concert stops" (which were not part of the *ripieno*) such as various Flutes, Nasards, Cornets, and other solo stops. Reed voices, although they had existed from the outset and were developed during the nineteenth century, were relatively few in number in comparison with French or Iberian organs.

The chests were generally of the slider type. Mechanical devices such as the Tiratutti, which allowed the organist to draw all the *pleno* ranks at once, or an extremely ingenious system of mechanical combinations sometimes called *polisire*, or an octave coupler known as *terza mano*, together with paramusical accessories such as bells, big drum, Kuckuck and so on, progressively adorned an instrument which nevertheless remained relatively simple in structure.

In order to increase the available combinations, the keyboards were often given supplementary notes *en ravalement* at the bottom of their compass (as low as F^1 or C^{11}), or else in the treble. One stop typical of Italian organs was the Voce umana, a Principal-scaled pipe mistuned with the 8' Principale and thus producing an undulating effect reminiscent of the human voice. This stop was exported to the north in the seventeenth and eighteenth centuries and may be found, Gamba-scaled, in Romantic organs where it forms one of the most characteristic sonorities, the Voix céleste.

THE IBERIAN PENINSULA

Starting out from what, in the fifteenth century, had been a common European model, the Spanish organ developed into a highly individual instrument whose chief characteristic from the 1560s onwards was divided stops which enabled a solo to be played prominently with the right hand and a soft accompaniment with the left. The Iberian organ, like the Italian one, generally had only a single manual; if there was a second keyboard it was either an echo manual or, less frequently, a Choir Organ variously positioned. As for the pedals, apart from rare exceptions such as the Emperor's Organ at Toledo, they normally consisted of only a few foundation voices

Cantus.   Organum.   Saltus.   Gaudium.   Verecundia.   Ira.   Litargyrum.

Fig. 54 Abul Hasan El-Muchtar ben El-Hasan, *Tacuini Sanitatis* (1531) or the beneficent effects of the organ.

(16′ and 8′) and/or a pedal coupler, having a common compass of one octave. In the large cathedrals, two instruments were placed on either side of the *côro*, each one having a double frontage, one front facing the nave, the other the side-aisle. This layout made it possible to furnish these organs with two tonal structures on the same level, one directed towards the nave, the other towards the side-aisle. A further characteristic of these organs was the horizontal reeds *en chamade* first seen in the second half of the seventeenth century and often added to earlier cases. Some technical details follow:

The slider-chests were chromatically designed, and divided into bass (on the left) and treble (on the right); this often necessitated a complicated chest layout to feed the display pipes (Montres and horizontal reeds), which were generally arranged in a symmetrical design.

These wind-chests were often made of several sections connected by wind-trunks. Some stops might be isolated in an echo box fitted with a lid which the organist could operate at will. This was the forerunner of the swell box.

As for the sumptuous architecture of Spanish organs, their display-pipe compartments, boldly superimposed upon each other, were generally only decorative, the internal structure remaining very simple, in spite of the extraordinary ingenuity shown in its realization. The Spanish organ spread to South America and to other Spanish mission stations and colonies; its horizontal reeds continued to exercise the imagination of foreign organ builders for centuries to come.

THE LOW COUNTRIES

It was in the Low Countries in the sixteenth century that the organ appears to have undergone its most significant developments, thanks to the Brabantine school most notably represented by the Niehoff family of 's-Hertogenbosch. They retained the archaic function of the main keyboard as the *Blockwerk*, adapting the double chest for the other manuals and thus giving the instrument the richest possible sonorities. In addition to the tonal structure of the now traditional *Rückpositiv*, they installed a further collection of stops in the main case, called either the *Brustwerk* if the limited size of the pipes allowed them to be housed immediately above the console window, or the *Oberwerk* if their bulk required them to be planted in the upper part of the main case. Thus the Brabantine organ contained a potential for future development as the classical organ of the later period, in respect of both its design and its sonorities (most notably its pedals, which were richly furnished by the most varied of national schools).

FRANCE

It was, however, from a more southerly region, Liège, that the French classical organ drew its inspiration, since a unique type of instrument was imported from that area.

The first complete organ of this type is attested at Gisors in 1580. It spread rapidly, due to the influence of the Rouen composer Jehan Titelouze, among others. The characteristics of the French organ may be summarized as follows: it was an organ with two main keyboards, the *Grand Orgue* and the *Positif* (behind the player). The *Récit* and *Echo* short-compass manuals (treble only), and the *Bombarde* (a subdivision of the

Grand Orgue intended to ensure an independent wind supply for the reed voices) were technical gimmicks rather than independent tonal structures. The pedals remained undeveloped: an 8′ Flute (to play the bass line in trios), and a Trumpet (to declaim a plainchant melody accompanied by the full *pleno*, or to mark cadences in pieces played on the *Grand Orgue*, in which case the instrument may occasionally have included some additional reed voices). The pedal pipes were generally located in the main case, but sometimes behind it. All the chests were slider-chests.

The *Grand Orgue* manual was both the main keyboard and the bass keyboard (for duos, trios etc.). It was this manual which included the 32′ Montre or Bourdon in all the biggest instruments, and, as a general rule, the 16′ Double Tierce or Acoustic Bass Fournitures. The *Positif* was always based on an 8′ Montre or Bourdon. These two tonal structures each had a complete keyboard spanning four octaves, whereas the compass of the other manuals and pedals was variable. The classical French organ had three basic tonal "mélanges":

1) The *plein jeu*, comprising all the Principals, Bourdons, Fournitures (breaking back an octave) and Cymbales (breaking back a fifth and a fourth). It was a "mélange" for the manuals only (*Grand Orgue* and *Positif*). Since the *plein jeu* was not suitable for polyphony, it was used in harmonic writing, lighter in character when played on the *Positif*, more majestic on the *Grand Orgue*.

2) The *grand jeu* comprised the reed voices of the Trumpet and Clairon family, together with the Cornets (to reinforce the treble), and a 4′ Prestant. On the *Positif*, the Trumpets might be replaced by the Cromorne, and on the *Récit* by the Cornet. The *Echo* might also be represented by a Cornet or reed voice, and the pedals by their Trumpet stop. This "mélange" could be used either in dialogs, the different tonal structures contrasting with each other, in embellished solos in the bass or treble (on the *Grand Orgue* accompanied by the *Positif*), in echo effects, or else in fugal writing of a more rigorous nature.

3) The *Jeu de tierce*, comprising the Bourdons or Flutes, Nasards, Larigot and Tierces, was played on the main manuals (*Grand Orgue*, *Positif* and sometimes even the *Echo* manual), being used for the bass or treble (or both) of a polyphonic piece (duo, trio or quatuor). Each of two manuals might include a Tierce in its registration (Duo sur les Tierces); alternatively the Tierce was often combined with reed stops. The large-scale Tierce – which replaced a more archaic narrow Tierce which could be combined with the *plein jeu* – is one of the most striking elements in the tonal world of the classical French organ. It later found its way to Spain, Italy and central Germany.

GERMAN-SPEAKING LANDS

One of the characteristics of the Germanic organ was its increased number of independent tonal structures: to the Great Organ and *Rückpositiv* were added the *Brustwerk* (above the console window) or *Oberwerk* (high up in the main case), or both. The pedals acquired a real independence not only in the number of their stops and their positioning (in the wings of the main case or, from the end of the sixteenth century onwards, in independent pipe towers), but also by virtue of their considerable compass. Every structural permutation now became feasible thanks to these diverse possibilities, which the more impressive instruments could exploit simultaneously. A similar variety characterizes the number of stops which were available, whether it was a question of the foundation voices (various kinds of Flutes, Quintadena, Diapason, sometimes a Gamba stop, and so on), reed voices (in particular, a very wide range of Regals) or mutation stops (Sesquialtera, Terzzimbel, Rauschpfeife, Tertian). Nonetheless, the large-scale separate Tierce remained unknown, and the reeds did not have the same brilliance as in French or Spanish organs. Although the finest examples were to be found in the well-to-do Hanseatic towns, the "Germanic" organ was a familiar instrument throughout the whole region north of the Alps, from the French border in the west to Russia and the frontiers of Orthodox Christianity in the east. It is not possible to list in detail all the numerous variant forms which existed, although it is certainly true that organs in those countries to the east, such as Austria, Poland and the Czech lands, had fewer reed voices, but a greater variety and number, by contrast, of 8′ foundation stops. On the other hand, foreign influences – such as those of Eugen Casparini at Görlitz (now Zgorzelec) around 1700 or of Gottfried Silbermann in Saxony, following his apprenticeship in Paris – enriched this type of organ, bringing to it new sonorities, including the undulating stops of the Italians and the large-scale Tierces of the French.

Being less schematized than the French or Italian organ, for example, the Germanic organ is more awkward to define. We may, however, draw attention to its fidelity to the *Werkprinzip*, with its facework reflecting the internal structure of the instrument. Although the pedals normally assumed the role of bass register, they also included higher-pitched voices (4′, 2′ and even 1′), which were used to emphasize a *cantus firmus*. We may add, finally, that throughout the period in question German organ builders sometimes preferred slider-chests, and at other times spring-chests.

The Advent of the Romantic Organ

As a result of the technical advances of the late fifteenth century, the organ developed and spread in ever increasing diversity across the whole of Europe, although its basic conception and function remained largely unaltered. Its multiple keyboards and their division into treble and bass stops enabled the instrument to survive the revolution which took place in music at the beginning of the seventeenth century, when accompanied melody replaced the old polyphonic style. The two types of writing, it must be admitted, coexisted for a time and pursued a parallel course. During this period organ music remained somewhat apart, and even lagged behind the general direction which music was now taking. By the beginning of the nineteenth century, various tendencies which had been latent during the preceding century made their presence clearly felt, encouraging the instrument to adapt itself to the musical taste of the age. These tendencies included, for example, the search for a new dynamic potential made possible by a greater flexibility of tonal nuance, a more convenient method of operating the console, and new sonorities.

In order to realize these new ideas, it was first necessary for a technical rejuvenation of the instrument's structure to be taken in hand. The invention of reservoirs with inverted ribs at the end of the eighteenth century made it possible to maintain a sufficient and regular air supply, so ending the chief worry which had beset all organ builders from the time of Ctesibius onwards. In order to ensure a proper distribution of the wind supply, the French organ builder Cavaillé-Coll had the idea of fitting two pallets to each groove, whereas Eberhard Walcker invented the cone-valve chest (*Kegellade*) which ensured an individual supply to each pipe. These double pallets increased the pressure necessary to depress the keys, and it was to overcome this problem that the Barker-Lever system was devised by the English organ builder Charles Spackman Barker. Thus freed of its problems of wind supply and mechanical action, the Romantic organ could pursue its course, which it proceeded to do with a certain amount of initial hesitation and a number of wrong turnings.

However, as long as the majority of organ builders continued to prefer classical technology, the only area in which the Romantic organ could prove innovative was in the type of sounds it produced. The sonorities which were appropriate only to certain anachronistic genres were now abandoned (*Jeux de tierce* and high-pitched stops in general), and in their place "new" sonorities were added (8′ foundation voices, powerful or bucolic reeds, etc.). The possibility of simultaneously drawing every stop on the same manual had been virtually unknown before this era but was now made feasible by the improved wind supply. At the same time, the opportunity was taken to rebalance the different reed families and generally to reduce the number of Mixtures, which very often disappeared entirely. The search for a progressive range of tonal nuances led not only to a more widespread use of the swell box but also encouraged the disappearance of the *Rückpositiv*, which was incorporated into the main organ case. Pistons, couplers and other accessories made the organist's task easier, granting him a more fluent mastery over his instrument.

In France and, at a later date, in Anglo-Saxon countries, there was one characteristic in particular which determined the style of the Romantic organ and its neo-Romantic successor, and that was the so-called *Récit expressif*. Initially modest in size and composed chiefly of solo stops (small reed voices and Cornet), it was later enlarged to become a self-contained tonal structure, powerful but controllable, and used as much for its characteristic stops (Hautbois, Voix humaine and Voix céleste) as for its *tutti* which, thanks to its swell box, allowed the most spectacular dynamic effects to be produced. The Great Organ manual was fitted with powerful reeds and with a wide variety of foundation voices, while the *Positif*, whose function until then had been somewhat ill defined (it was a sort of reduced Great Organ or second *Récit* deprived of the latter's facilities of expression), was given a number of additional solo stops. The pedals included only low-pitched stops, their indispensable high-pitched complement being provided by the multiple couplers.

This type of instrument was adopted in numerous countries either through the direct agency of its inventor, Cavaillé-Coll, who himself exported the instruments he built, or else through his influence which, for a century or more, continued to permeate those countries which had previously been subject to other traditions. Among these first and foremost were the Germanic nations, which even today frequently ignore the great French *Récit* and which tend to produce their dynamic effects by progressively adding (or subtracting) stops. It is a different aesthetic which is reflected, moreover, in the Romantic and contemporary music written in these countries. We may also mention in this context Italy and Spain, each of which later developed a highly individual and fascinating instrument, combining centuries-old stylistic traditions with technical and tonal innovations of the greatest ingenuity. But in general the Romantic organ became an instrument for massive symphonic effects and dynamic contrasts. It is a style whose ideal is undoubtedly an instrument with a certain breadth and volume but one which remains attractive in its half-tone effects.

THE MODERN ORGAN

At the end of the nineteenth century, organ builders fell into the trap of what has been called technical progress (electric or pneumatic action, which removed all limitations, standardization of the stops and their scaling; industrial manufacture of pipes; illogical layouts made possible by the modern types of action, and so on) and built standardized instruments betraying an increasing degree of negligent workmanship. Lacking in style, these instruments no longer allowed the classical repertory to be adequately performed on them and did not have the genius of the large Romantic organs. Other organ builders attempted to imitate the orchestra, an attempt which, for all its interest, produced neither an organ nor an orchestra.

A reaction fortunately came with the so-called *Orgelbewegung* (lit. organ movement), when the instrument rediscovered its former richness and diversity. Realizing that organ building could only regress, Albert Schweitzer concluded that what was necessary was a return to the tonal ideal of the classical organ. This was a conviction which he advanced in 1906 in his book *Deutsche und französische Orgelbaukunst und Orgelkunst* [The Art of German and French Organ Building and Playing], which became the manifesto of the *Orgelbewegung*, a movement whose aims were defined at the Third German Organ Reform Congress held at Freiberg in 1927. Reacting against the degeneracy of the Romantic organ and its industrial production, participants in the congress spoke out in favor of a return to a classical aesthetic, which was that of the polyphonic organ; in this way each work could be performed on the instrument for which it had been conceived. Hence the need to investigate the principles of organ building in past centuries, especially the century of Bach – principles which were rediscovered in organs preserved in Germany, most notably in Hamburg and Lübeck.

16 Former console from the Domkirche organ, Sankt-Annen-Museum, Lübeck, Federal Republic of Germany, Arp Schnitger, 1696–9
Hw, *Rp*, *Bw* and *Ped* (forty-five stops), Tremulant, Drum-stop and Zimbel-stern. In their youth, Mattheson and Handel journeyed to Lübeck to inspect this instrument in 1703. Bach himself almost certainly saw it on the occasion of his meeting with Buxtehude in 1705. All that remains of this organ is the console (three manuals with a compass of forty-four notes, including a short octave). The original organ was substantially restored by Johann Christoph Kaltschmidt in 1796/7 and 1817, and by Theodor Vogt in 1833, and a new instrument was built by Walcker in 1892/3 with three manuals and *Ped* (sixty-four stops). The case of Schnitger's organ, with carvings by Johann Jakob Budde, was destroyed in 1942.

18 Console of the organ built by Joseph Riepp, 1754–66, Benediktinerabtei-kirche (Benedictine Abbey church), Ottobeuren, Federal Republic of Germany

17 Console of the Bonifaciuskirche (Neukirche) organ of 1703, rebuilt by J. F. Wender, Bachgedenkstätte, Arnstadt, German Democratic Republic
This is the organ on which Johann Sebastian Bach performed between 1703 and 1707. *Ow* and *Bw* (forty-nine notes), *Ped* (twenty-five keys), totalling twenty-four stops, plus Tremulant (*Ow*) and manual and pedal couplers. Various repairs and alterations were made in 1864–78, 1911–13 and 1938. The console was removed in 1864 and since 1934 has been on display in the Bachgedenkstätte in Arnstadt.

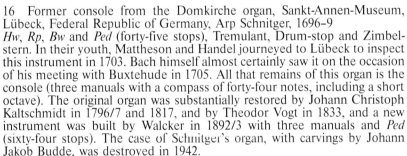
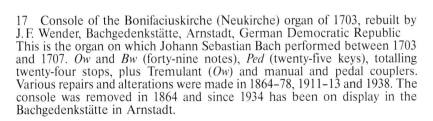

19 Bronze draw levers, Cistercian Abbey, Jedrzejów, Poland, Józef Sitarski, 1745

20 Gospel Organ, Cathedral, Lamego, Francisco António Solha, 1756-7, see caption to Pl. 238

21 Console of the "Grand Court" organ of John Wanamaker Store, Phila- ▷
delphia (PA), Los Angeles Art Organ Company, 1903-4
The task of building this organ, the largest and most famous in the world at the beginning of the century, was entrusted to the Murray M. Harris Organ Company, but they were obliged to abandon work on it, through lack of credit. The Los Angeles Art Organ Company was itself beset by financial problems and, having become the Electrolian Company, was forced to close in 1905. Transported from Los Angeles to St. Louis (MO) for the Louisiana Purchase Exposition (Festival Hall), the famous instrument was played by Alexandre Guilmant, "star guest organist." In the space of six weeks, he gave thirty-nine concerts, performing works by Scheidt, Frescobaldi, Pachelbel, Titelouze, Bach, Handel and Franck. Originally intended for the Convention Hall in Kansas City, the organ, which had been designed by George Ashdown Audsley, was erected on its present site by William B. Fleming in 1911, in accordance with the wishes of Rodman Wanamaker. A veritable workshop was set up on the twelfth floor of the store: from 1911 until 1932, forty people were employed there, working on the task of enlarging the instrument and building a second organ for the auditorium of the Wanamaker Store in New York City. Two technicians are currently employed full-time by the company to maintain the instrument. At the time it was built, the organ had 140 speaking stops and 10,059 pipes. Periodically enlarged during the period leading up to 1930, it now boasts 451 stops (469 ranks) and 30,067 pipes divided into nine departments (Orchestral, Ethereal, Solo, String, Great, Swell, Choir, Echo and Pedal). The compass of the six manuals is C - c^{1111} and that of the pedals C - g^1.

22 Part of the roller board of the *Grand Orgue*, Cathedral of St. Pierre, ▷
Poitiers, France, Francois-Henri Clicquot, 1787-90.

Fig. 55 Building a large wind-chest; from Dom Bédos, Paris, 1766–78, Pt. II, Chap. I, Sec. II, Pl. 54.

Fig. 56 Building the large wind-chest; from Dom Bédos, Paris, 1766–78, Pt. II, Chap. II, Sec. II, Pl. 55.

To begin with, Baroque stops were simply added to existing organs, but this was no more than a half-measure, and supporters of the movement soon turned their attention to building new instruments which respected "neo-Baroque" concepts. The result was an instrument operated by mechanical action and constructed according to the *Werkprinzip* (with a repertory which was confined of course to pieces written before the mid-nineteenth century), but the proponents of this instrument soon found themselves in conflict with musicians – often organ virtuosi – who were anxious to perpetuate the tradition of the concert organ and who preferred an instrument with a much wider range of possibilities, a range which had increased as a result of the comparative ease of electric action.

The synthesis of the classical organ of various schools, on the one hand, and the Romantic organ, on the other, seemed to some people to be an ideal solution – a "universal" organ which would allow all the different styles of music to be performed on it. But this proposed solution, while inventing a new style of organ with its own repertory, has not been able to achieve a synthesis of all the techniques involved which would have permitted, in turn, a synthesis of the instrument's tonal elements. As a result, contemporary organ builders are still attempting, on the basis of the different known styles, to discover the elements necessary to constitute a coherent whole. However, faced with the difficulty of such a task, and perhaps even its impossibility, many builders have turned their attention instead to analyzing and investigating historical styles. These investigations may in turn present the basis for a new style. Having rediscovered its own past, the modern organ now has a rich potential for development, which it will be left to future generations of organ builders to realize with skill and competence.

THE WORK OF THE ORGAN BUILDER

If an organ is to be successful tonally, mechanically and visually, the organ builder must possess a thorough knowledge of his trade, a craftsman's intuitive skill and experience (often inherited empirically in the great families of organ builders), a fine ear, a musical and artistic sense, and, finally, an inventive nature so that he can adapt his work to the constantly changing conditions of taste and aesthetics.

The organ builder must be able to integrate his instrument within the context of a church or concert hall, and give it a style which harmonizes with that of the building. As an architect, he draws up plans for the instrument specified; as a technician he must possess a thorough knowledge of everything from mechanics to electricity, including of course the science of acoustics. As an artist, he must use his musical sense to predict the tonal qualities of the finished instrument, while his "ear" enables him to voice and tune the organ to perfection. The builder is therefore not simply a conscientious and versatile craftsman, but an artist capable of investing the instrument with a soul.

Creating an organ requires of an organ builder all the foregoing qualities, qualities which could be called the "gestures of his profession" and which are each special aptitudes. His studies will be devoted in turn to carpentry, the smelting of metals, mechanical fittings and, finally, to assembling the various parts of the instrument and to voicing the pipes.

As a carpenter, the organ builder must be expert in the fullest sense of the word, since the perfect working of the instrument depends on his carefully choosing the right wood, cutting the different types of wood accurately, perforating the rackboard for the pipes in exactly the right place, and meticulously assembling the various pieces which make up the instrument. Everything must be done to prevent the wood from warping when exposed to variations in temperature and humidity. If the work involves cutting and assembling the various elements of wood pipes, the task of making the organ case will rarely be the work of a single builder, and the carved sections will often be entrusted to a specialist craftsman. An additional and related task is that of cutting the leather, which must be done with equal care in order to ensure that the wind conveyances, from the reservoirs all the way to the pipes, are perfectly airtight.

Although an expert in the science of mechanics, the organ builder must be equally proficient in other areas, since the instrument which he creates is a living object whose joints and working parts are made up of multiple sections that increase in complexity the further removed the pipework is from the console. The various mechanisms of the organ operate on the lever principle, applied not only to the system of drawing the stops but also to that of opening the pallets: although a simple procedure, it requires extreme attention to detail, patience and perfectionism on the part of the organ builder. It is because of these qualities that the organist's fingers can ignore, so to speak, the various parts of the "machine" such as roller boards, square levers, stickers, trackers and springs, since they offer no resistance when he depresses the keys.

In the twentieth century the organ builder may also need to be an electrician in order to ensure that the electrical action operates correctly – assuming, that is, that he does not decide in favour of mechanical tracker action.

The organ builder ought also to be a metalworker, for the metals he handles have to be smelted, alloyed, flattened, hammered, cut up and then assembled. The pipes demand particular attention throughout the process of their construction, since each of the stages involved contributes to the beauty of their perfection. The metal has first to be smelted and mixed in the required proportions for the particular alloy of tin and lead which is desired. The molten alloy is then poured into a rectangular wooden box raised at one end to leave a narrow slot beneath it and the casting table; the box travels the length of the table, the molten metal being poured out in a layer whose thickness is determined by the size of the slot. The sheet metal is then polished (planished) or hammered while still warm and malleable, in order to avoid excessive buckling, then cut up, rolled and shaped by means of cylindrical or conical mandrels, in order to produce pipes with variously shaped resonators and of the required scaling. Finally, the various parts of each pipe are soldered together. If the organ builder's individual conception is revealed in the way he designs the overall layout of the instrument and in

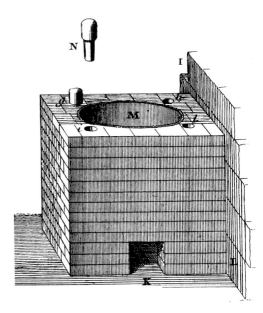

Fig. 57   The furnace and casting table; from Dom Bédos, Paris, 1766–78, Pt. II, Chap. VI, Sec. II, Pl. 64.

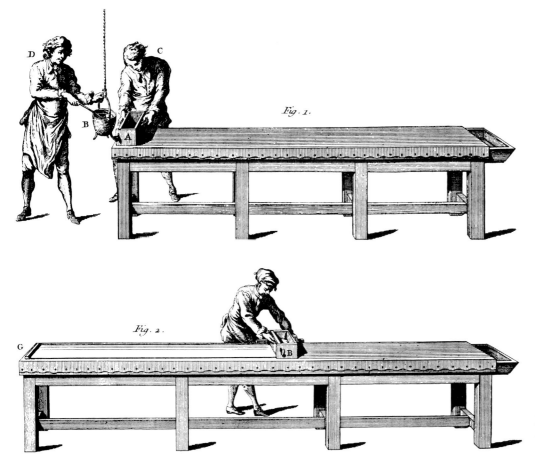

Fig. 58   The casting table and rabble; from Dom Bédos, Paris, 1766–78, Pt. II, Chap. VI, Sec. II, Pl. 66.

Fig. 59 Hammering the tin for the pipes; from Dom Bédos, Paris, 1766–78, Pt. II, Chap. VII, Sec. II, Pl. 69.

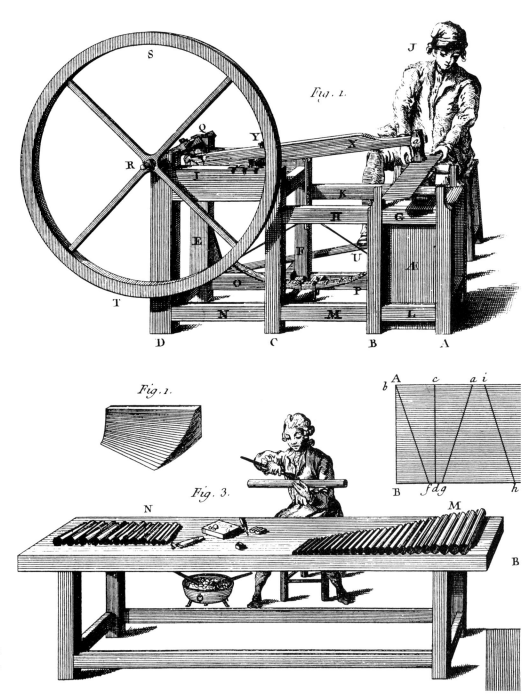

Fig. 60 Construction of flue pipes; from Dom Bédos, Paris, 1766–78, Pt. II, Chap. VIII, Sec. I, Pl. 70.

the way that he realizes that design, his individuality will be even more evident in the last creative phase (before the final assembly), which involves voicing the pipes. When complete, the pipes are placed in series (one for each stop) on a mock-up of the finished organ, a small schematic positive where the organ builder can hear the sound of each pipe for the first time, without himself having to blow into it to make it speak. He then makes final adjustments to the stop by varying its timbre, intensity, attack and mordancy, and by achieving a perfect balance of color between all the pipes of that register. Each stop must be balanced and voiced in such a way that it will fit into the future tonal edifice, while at the same time retaining its own well-defined character. Each stop is provisionally tuned while still in the workshop, prior to the final tuning which is carried out *in situ*. The voicing is also completed in the particular church or concert hall, where the voicer will take account of the acoustics of the building and the desired balance between the many different timbres of the various tonal structures.

The organ builder is equally responsible for maintaining the instrument, which must be tuned at regular intervals. A summary tuning takes place on average every six months, in the autumn and in the spring, or else before each concert. The foundation voices, although generally remaining in tune relative to each other, are very sensitive to changes in temperature which cause them to go out of tune by almost a semitone, whether the church is heated in winter or not. The reed voices, by their very nature, are much more stable as a group, although individually each pipe is more at risk because of all the movable parts which it contains. Paradoxically, then, it is the reed voices which are "put out of tune" to bring them into line with the foundation voices, since the former are fewer in number and easier to adjust.

The organ requires a general overhaul approximately once every ten years. This involves stripping it down completely and dusting it; the opportunity is taken to carry out all necessary repairs, such as remedying air-leaks. The instrument is then reassembled, and the pipes revoiced and retuned.

The transformations which may be brought about by changes in tonal aesthetics range from revoicing the stops (an operation which affects only the pipework) to constructing a whole new organ, which may be adapted to suit an older organ case preserved for its decorative value. Other, less radical, changes may include alterations to the composition of the instrument (an old stop being replaced by a new one), or increasing its size by creating a new tonal structure such as a positive manual, all of which implies of course that additional or new wind-chests have to be built. Even the whole system of transmission may be changed, as in the nineteenth century when tracker action was replaced by pneumatic action which, in the first half of the twentieth century, gave way in turn to electric action. But any changes to an organ can be justified only if the instrument has no historic or artistic value; if it has, then the changes should not be undertaken.

RESTORATION

One of the major preoccupations of the last few decades has without doubt been the conservation of early organs. Musicians have taken renewed interest in the history of their instrument and searched for as authentic an interpretation as possible of the music of the past. For a long time the options of organists and organ builders could be expressed only by means of complete transformations or "improvements" based on a lack of understanding of earlier styles and on a certain morbid hunger for technical novelty; this even involved the wholesale destruction of earlier instruments judged inadequate or badly built. Our present concern for historical objectivity has raised numerous problems of an ethical nature, made worse by the many different schools of thought among musicologists, organists, "experts," aesthetes, or quite simply amateur organ enthusiasts, who have sometimes proffered contradictory or inadequately substantiated advice.

The restorer must at all times show an unconditional respect for the work of the original builder and must refuse to allow any technical developments to intrude which are later than the date when the organ was constructed, whether his excuse be greater lightness of touch, or quite simply idleness and financial economy. It will, however, be evident that this desire to restore the original conception of an instrument can often be made extremely complicated and hazardous by the many changes which may have been made: what is the restorer to do, for example, with an instrument signed by one of the great Baroque organ builders but which has been substantially altered by an eminent master of the Romantic age? By the same token, the restorer's work is often limited by irremediable circumstances such as the disappearance of part of the pipework, or a radical change in the construction of certain stops or even of the case itself. In this instance the craftsman has to reconstruct the organ carefully, despite his ignorance of what the original instrument was like, after studying all the available documents such as contracts, other organs by the same builder and so on.

The work of restoring an organ begins with a scrupulous, detailed and precise study of all the extant parts of the instrument. The preparatory work consists of a systematic survey of all the technical details, exact measurements of the pipework and wind-chest, the elements which make up the tracker action and bellows, and even the structure of the organ case – all this even before the restorer begins to take the instrument apart.

These surveys will be supplemented by photographs of each part of the instrument. Modern recording techniques are an invaluable and indispensable means of assisting the restorer in his task. Accurate readings must be taken of the volume of sound produced, the wind pressure measured at different pitches for each stop, and observations made regarding the loss of power affecting certain stops such as the Mixtures when all the stops are drawn at once (*tutti*). Precise readings are also required of the wind pressure in the wind-trunks and bellows as well as in the chest. Finally, it may be necessary to note possible traces of earlier mechanisms.

One preoccupation which ought to be paramount is to discover the original pressure, so that the restorer may obtain an authentic tone. This depends upon the tuning pitch being reestablished if, as is often the case, the pipes have been cut up at a later date so as to make the *a* of the organ correspond in pitch with the *a* of the orchestra (organs were generally tuned lower than they are today, occasionally higher). The reconstruction of the original temperament (adjustment of the invervals of the scale) is a delicate operation, but an indispensable one. These studies should be complemented by research into archival material which may assist the restorer and throw light on his work. Inscriptions on various parts of the instrument including information on the name of the builder or the year of manufacture should be preserved.

As for the restoration work itself, it must be carried out with attention to detail and a refusal to accept any element of risk. In repairing certain parts of the instrument, the renovator must use the same techniques as those employed by the original builder. If he has to replace missing or damaged parts, he must seek out other examples of the same builder's work, designed at the same period as the organ which is being restored. This will enable him to produce an exact copy of the part in question. Restoring the pipework requires the most detailed study, involving an analysis of the metal used (the proportions and thickness of the different alloys) and the type of construction (languid, windway, resonator, and so on).

This concern for perfection will persuade some of the more scrupulous builders to undertake only a provisional restoration of certain elements and mechanisms, in the hope that further researches or the finances of the parish will some day permit a more thorough work of restoration. In the meantime, the builder should store the unused parts inside the instrument or elsewhere in the church, where they are out of the way.

Ideally, the work of restoring the organ should also involve restoring the church which houses it, a task which must be approached with care in order not to alter the acoustic properties of the place. Particular care is needed when replacing the wooden floors and pews, choir stalls and wood panelling, all of which are indispensable for correcting the bass frequencies of the instrument. The same criteria that apply to organ restoration also appertain to the restoration of buildings.

The restoration of early organs is a fascinating task which must be undertaken with respect and conscientiousness, and with an element of creativity which enables the restorer to see beyond his own ideal and grasp the essential character of the instrument he is restoring. What is involved here is a search for truth and a subservience to technical and historical imperatives. It is a profession which demands not only a good deal of culture, but, above all, a sense of affinity for the period and style of the instrument.

PART TWO:
A HISTORY OF ORGAN MUSIC

I The First Organ Tablatures of the Fourteenth and Fifteenth Centuries

Music for keyboard instruments appears at a comparatively late date in the fourteenth century. The virtual absence of written documents is not due simply to the ravages of time, nor to men's ingratitude and forgetfulness, but to the fact that, as far as we can tell, musicians generally improvised the works they performed, or else played them from memory. The organ was initially used merely to accompany or reinforce an instrumental line, generally playing the long notes in a *cantus firmus*, where their length made it difficult for the cantors to sustain the line. But the organ soon began to assert itself, to the extent that it came to be used increasingly for solo work, playing the various melodies which were collected together, for ease of reading, either in staves or in tablatures (a system in which the notes were replaced by letters, numbers or other symbols).

This music, with its mensural notation, was pressed into the service of a style whose language was international, for it was not until the sixteenth century that national and regional characteristics assumed any degree of individuality. It was a style which addressed itself indiscriminately to all keyboard instruments. The majority of texts written between the fourteenth and sixteenth centuries, and even later, could be played on the organ without necessarily having been written for that instrument.

The earliest surviving examples of keyboard writing are essentially transcriptions of polyphonic vocal pieces (especially motets and *ballate*), of compositions based on existing religious or secular themes (the *cantus firmus*), of preludes ("praeambula") and of dances, the last two being the product of melodic and rhythmic improvisation. The earliest pieces were collected together and often given the title Tabulatura or Codex. They were written for two parts only, the descant developing the upper line with short note-values, while the tenor line moved at a slower pace.

The oldest surviving keyboard collection is the Robertsbridge Codex of around 1325. Probably French in origin, the manuscript contains three transcriptions of vocal works and three estampies. In each case the upper line is written on a five-line stave, while the other lines are realized as letters placed beneath the notes. Rapid strokes, skillfully animated, are preferred to chords. This form of notation is also found in two manuscripts dating from the end of the fourteenth century and probably Italian in origin, the Codex Reina and the later Codex Faenza. The former includes two keyboard works, one of which is a tablature of a *ballata* by Landini, but it is the Faenza manuscript which is of paramount importance for our knowledge of fourteenth- and early fifteenth-century music. The notation is indicated on two staves of six lines each (a tablature known as a "keyboard score"), and includes the earliest example of the use of bar lines. The collection contains different parts of an organ mass, together with transcriptions of madrigals and Italian and French songs by Jacopo da Bologna, Bartolino da Padova, Francesco Landini, Antonio Zaccara da Teramo, Pierre de Molins and Guillaume de Machaut, with melodies which are fragments of religious themes and were apparently intended to be performed during mass. This means that the liturgical role of the organ had already been defined by the practise of alternating sections of polyphony with ones of plainchant. By replacing the former, the organ achieved a musical style in which the descant was developed in a particularly florid type of writing for the right hand, against the background of a stable plainchant melody. This style originated with the Notre-Dame school and was known as the *organum duplum*. The oldest religious music ever played on our instrument was therefore made up of liturgical phrases which the organist ornamented during alternate verses of the Psalms and the different parts of the Ordinary of the mass, namely the Kyrie, Gloria, Credo, Sanctus and Agnus Dei. The organ was probably also used to introduce the mass by short phrases or preludes, as well as certain of the priest's interjections.

II Organ Music in Italy

The history of Italian music in the sixteenth century, and especially the history of organ music, would certainly be much reduced in scope were it not for the exceptional contribution made by musicians of St. Mark's basilica in Venice to the keyboard writing of the period. The leading composers of the sixteenth and early seventeenth centuries all held appointments there, either as singers (Marco Antonio and Girolamo Cavazzoni), chapelmasters (*maestri di cappella*) (Adrian Willaert and Claudio Monteverdi) or organists, incumbents of one or other of the two instruments erected on the galleries at either side of the high altar. Whether or not it is true that the basilica had two organs as early as the second half of the fourteenth century, it is certain that two organists held office there from 1490 onwards.

The post of organist at St. Mark's was highly sought after, and candidates were required to take a test, no matter how eminent they may have been. Three test pieces were played on the very instrument which was the object of their ambitions, and in each case a considerable degree of improvisation was involved. For his first piece the postulant was required to improvise a fantasia on a specific motet, giving due prominence to the different voices. There followed an improvisation on a specified *cantus firmus*, which had to be in three parts and fugal in style. Finally, the candidate was required to provide extempore responses to the interventions of the choir. The greatest Italian organists of the day succeeded one another at the console of the two organs which were housed within the golden basilica. The first of the two instruments was entrusted, among others, to Annibale Padovano (who held the appointment from 1552 to 1566), Claudio Merulo (1566-85) and Giovanni Gabrieli (1585-1612); the most notable incumbents

Italy was the cradle of the majority of different types of musical form associated with organ music. The country also produced numerous influential musicians, and reached artistic maturity earlier than most other European countries where organ music flourished. In Italy, as elsewhere, keyboard music before 1500 essentially comprised dances, transcriptions or arrangements of vocal numbers, and liturgical compositions (parts of the mass, versets and hymns), although freer forms such as preludes are also found. This last type soon began to enjoy a wide audience, as is proved by the numerous traces visible in the pieces which Italian polyphonists took delight in composing throughout the sixteenth century. Indeed, many of the works intended for the organ were written in the toccata style. On the other hand, the evolution of the ricercare, canzone and fantasia later led to the elaboration of the fugue, that most rigorous of Baroque forms and the one most suited to the organ.

The ricercare and canzone were directly inspired by existing vocal pieces. The ricercare was generally made up of the prelude to a piece, or sometimes a postlude (*ricercare detto coda*). It was not necessarily written specifically for the organ: between 1507 and 1509, in Venice, Ottaviano dei Petrucci, the inventor of a system of printing music by means of movable metal characters, published a number of ricercari for lute, works composed by Francesco Spinacino, Ambrosio Dalza and Francescus Bossinensis. We should nonetheless remember that the word ricercare did not always indicate a contrapuntal work. With the *Recerchari motetti canzoni* [Ricercari, Motets and Canzoni], published by Marco Antonio Cavazzoni (1490-*c.* 1570) in 1523, we discover two ricercari intended expressly for the organ (in fact, they are preludes to be played before polyphonic motets), while Jacopo Fogliano (1468-1548) was instrumental in developing the style towards its definitive form.

Those musicians who attempted the ricercare style were involved in a genuine search (*ricercare* = to search), in that the chosen theme underwent numerous transformations as it evolved during the sixteenth century, the various forms including augmentation, diminution, inversion and stretto. The first composer to handle the ricercare with any real skill was Girolamo Cavazzoni (1525[?]-60), the son of Marco Antonio Cavazzoni and the author of four ricercari published in 1542 in his *Intavolatura per organo cioè recercari canzoni himni magnificati* [Tablature for Organ, viz. Ricercari, Canzoni, Hymns and Magnificats]. Andrea Gabrieli (*c.* 1515-86) wrote some twenty ricercari with a limited number of themes and sections, the earliest of which reveal extremely complex contrapuntal writing. Although the art of the ricercare was cultivated above all by Italian composers such as Girolamo Parabosco (*c.* 1520-57), Annibale Padovano (1527-75), Claudio Merulo (1533-1604), Ascanio Maione (*d.* 1627), Luzzasco Luzzaschi (*c.* 1540-1607), Costanzo Antegnati (1549-1624) and Giovanni Maria Trabaci (*c.* 1575-1647), it achieved an astonishing degree of perfection in the works of Italo-Flemish composers such as Jacob (or Jacques) Buus (*c.* 1505-65) in his *Ricercari da cantare et da sonare d'organo* [Ricercari to be Sung and Performed on the Organ] of 1547, and of course Adrian Willaert (*c.* 1490-1562).

No discussion of musical forms of the period is complete without some mention of the collection *Frottole intabulate da sonare organi* [Tablature of Frottole to be Performed on the Organ], published in Rome in 1517 by Andrea Antico (*c.* 1470–?), the first collection of keyboard music printed in Italy, in which the author uses stave notation for four-part *frottole* by Bartolomeo Tromboncini and Marchetto Cara. The *frottola*, a typically Italian three- or four-part secular song of homophonic character, enjoyed a lively success in the sixteenth century. It gave a preponderant role to the upper voice. The canzone (*canzone alla francese* or *canzone francese*) was inspired by the short strophic song of Franco-Flemish origin, as developed by Josquin Desprez and his school, and in Italy at a later date by Giovanni de Macque. Secular in character, the canzone was set to a galant text and gave rise to countless arrangements for the lute and keyboard. In contrast to the solemnity of the ricercare, the canzone was characterized by briskness of rhythm and was generally divided into sections composed in the style of imitative counterpoint, including homophonic sequences and occasionally passages which were entirely free. Although Andrea Gabrieli's *Canzoni alla francese* of 1571 and 1605 were for the most part inspired by vocal and instrumental works, composers at a very early date conceived the idea of writing pieces specifically for keyboard instruments. The chief of these were the works contained in the *Libro primo* of *Recerchari motetti canzoni* [First Book of Ricercari, Motets and Canzoni] (1523) by Cavazzoni, together with the canzoni of Merulo (*Canzoni d'intavolatura d'organo fatte alla francese* [Tablature of Canzoni Composed for the Organ in the French Style], 1592) and those of Vincenzo Pellegrini (?–1631), Giovanni (Gian) Paolo Cima (*c.* 1570–?), Ascanio Maione, Agostino Soderini (fl. 1600), Giovanni Maria Trabaci, Giovanni Gabrieli and, of course, Girolamo Frescobaldi (1583–1643). We may note, finally, that Trabaci was the first to apply the principle of varying the same theme, embellished with melodic and rhythmic variants, to each section of the canzone.

However crucial the role played by the ricercare and canzone, we must not forget other aspects of Italian keyboard music such as the *intonatio*, toccata, fantasia and capriccio, all forms which were originally based upon improvisation. The *intonatio*, inherited from the idea of "tastar de corde" (which allowed the player to test whether the strings of his instrument were in tune), was a short piece intended to introduce one of the eight tones of the mass. The most notable examples were the *Intonazioni d'organe* [Intonazioni for Organ] published in 1593 by Andrea and Giovanni Gabrieli. (The *intonatio* could also be described as a prelude, overture or even as a toccata.) The toccata was first and foremost a piece which was free in form, *agitato* virtuoso elements alternating with the calm of sustained chords. It may be noted that the term toccata comes from *toccare*, indicating that the player's fingers "touch" the keys. In much the same way, certain pieces are called cantatas (to be sung) or sonatas (to be sounded). Intended to show off the different stops of the instrument and the virtuoso technique of the performer, this form appealed to all the great composers such as Andrea and Giovanni Gabrieli, Merulo and Frescobaldi. If the toccatas of Andrea Gabrieli are still freely improvisatory in spirit, those of Merulo are more consistent in texture and characterized precisely by alternating fast and slow sections, by their development, and by the importance given to the different voices. Frescobaldi later brought the toccata to its ultimate pitch of perfection, incorporating elements from every genre, including virtuoso traits, moments of meditation, contrapuntal sections in the style of the canzone and ricercare, and, above all, *affetti* (a term for which the English word "effects" is a poor alternative); these were passages or phrases intended to move or surprise or amaze the listener. Frescobaldi explains them at length in his Prefaces (*Avertimenti*), where he suggests a parallel between such *affetti* and the new way of giving musical expression to the meaning of madrigal texts. From now on the toccata developed into a genre involving a style of writing which was moving in both the literal and emotional sense of the term. It can best be summed up by the term *stilo fantastico*.

In form, the fantasia may be compared to the ricercare; indeed, the two are often confused. As for the capriccio, its imitative style refuses to submit to any strict definition. It was based upon either a popular theme or else a simple motif such as the cuckoo, although sometimes the subject might be related to the ricercare theme,

of the second organ were Giulio Segni da Modena (1530–3), Jacob Buus (1541–51), Girolamo Parabosco (1551–7), Claudio Merulo (1557–65), Andrea Gabrieli (1566–1586), Vincenzo Bellavere (1586–88) and Giuseppe (Gioseffo) Guami (1588–95).

Local interest in the organs of St. Mark's was so great that the townspeople succeeded in imposing a fine of one ducat on any priest who dared to sing before the organist had finished playing. There is no doubt that the Venetian audience felt a genuine affection for the church's two organs, singling out for particular mention the sweetness of their tone and the skillful balance of what was admittedly a limited number of stops; and their pleasure must certainly have been enhanced when the two instruments performed together in what Diruta describes as a "duello di due organi rispondersi con tanto artificio, e leggiadria." Among the first pair of musicians to perform on the two organs in St. Mark's in this way were Padovano and Parabosco, and, after them, Merulo and Gabrieli. The origins of this custom probably went back at least a hundred years previously, but Padovano was justly famous for turning it into a display of brilliant virtuosity. It is also worth mentioning here that for important occasions such as feast days and the reception of eminent visitors a third organist might officiate from a portative organ, and that, when concerts were performed, a number of separate organs would be used to support the various groups of instrumentalists scattered around the galleries and in the chancel. Music, especially in the churches of northern Italy, played such an important role that the majority of large buildings had two organs, located either in the chancel or in the galleries of the church. One thinks, for example, of S. Antonio in Padua, S. Petronio in Bologna, the principal churches in Florence, Milan Cathedral and so on. The two instruments fulfilled a two-fold function until as late as the nineteenth century: on the one hand they supported the choirs and the priest in responsorial singing, on the other they performed as solo instruments, either accompanying the choir or alternating with them.

Encouraged by the architectural layout of these places of worship in which the chancel was overlooked by two organ lofts, the composers of northern Italy exercised their ingenuity in creating a characteristic type of polychoral music whose lengthy improvisations went far beyond the simple pretext of dialog form. The result was a new conception of choral and instrumental writing in which several groups of voices or instruments would confront each other, responding and complementing each other in a vision of dramatic intensity, typical in spirit of the Baroque. The most extreme example is undoubtedly the Mass by Orazio Benevoli, written in 1628 for the consecration of Salzburg Cathedral, in which fifty-three voices are divided among twelve choirs. Somewhat better known are the two choruses in Bach's *St. Matthew Passion*. The same idea can still be found in some of the major Romantic works whose composers set out to imitate at a considerable remove the protagonists of St. Mark's. Suffice it to mention here the four brass bands and five orchestras of Berlioz's *Requiem (Grande Messe des morts)*.

It would be futile to list here the numerous works written for two, three or four organs from the sixteenth to the nineteenth century. They are, it may be added, circumscribed works, products of the imagination of organists who for the most part held appointments in churches housing more than one instrument. It was a fashion which developed above all during the eighteenth century, not only in northern Italy but in Switzerland, Austria and southern Germany. Discounting the numerous works in which more than one organ is used to accompany the chorus and orchestra, we shall limit ourselves here to a list of those composers who have written for solo instruments. Works by Spanish composers include the *Concierto para dos organos* [Concerto for Two Organs] in G major by Petro José Blanco (*c.* 1750–1811), organist and harpist at Cuenca and Ciudad Rodrigo and, of course, the *Seis conciertos para dos organos* [Six Concertos for Two Organs] of Antonio Soler. Among works by northern Italian composers active at the end of the sixteenth century, we may single out the "Concerti" of 1587 by Andrea Gabrieli of Venice, including a *Ricercar per sonar* for two organs, the *Sacrae Symphoniae* of 1597 by Giovanni Gabrieli of Venice, including a *Canzon in Echo* for two instruments or groups of instruments, and works by Francesco Rovigo (*c.* 1530–97), who like Padovano was active at the court of Graz, and Ruggiero Trofeo (d. 1614), who held appointments in Milan and Turin. These men were followed at the beginning of the seventeenth century by Giacomo Filippo Biumi, organist in Milan. Works dating from the eighteenth century include the *Sonata a 3 organi col basso* [Sonata for Three Organs, with Bass] by Carlo Zenolini of Bologna; the *Concerto CXXX alternato col primo e secundo organo* [Concerto CXXX alternating between First & Second Organ] by Francisco Feroci of Florence; the *Sonata a due organi* [Sonata for Two Organs] by Gaetano Piazza of Florence; and a piece by Giuseppe Sarti of Milan. Nineteenth-century works include the two *Sonate a due organi* by

varied in every imaginable way and employing every conceivable rhythmic combination, with accompanying motifs which might be virtuoso in character, or even bizarre. The capriccio could be defined as a kind of display of virtuosity on the composer's part. This blossoming of new forms helped gradually to emancipate instrumental writing from the heritage of vocal models and, as a result of its variety and wealth of invention, soon overwhelmed the whole of European music. Yet, however important it may have been for the development of secular music, it should not obscure the role which the organ was now required to play during religious services. The five parts of the Ordinary gave composers both north and south of the Alps the opportunity to write music which was intended to be performed between the liturgical chants. In this context we may draw attention to the fragments of a mass composed by Buus around the middle of the sixteenth century, and to three organ masses written jointly by Merulo and Girolamo Cavazzoni. *Himni, Magnificati, Versi spirituali* [Hymns, Magnificats and Versets] and variations on the theme of the *Pange lingua* [Sing, my tongue, the glorious battle] or *Veni Creator spiritus* [Come, Holy Ghost, our souls inspire] were the most typical manifestations of church music. Frescobaldi, in his *Fiori Musicali* [Musical Garlands], sanctioned the traditional religious usage of genres which until then had often been secular in character. Thus a toccata might introduce the mass (*Toccata avanti la Messa* [Toccata before the Mass]) or encourage the congregation to mystic contemplation (*Toccata per l'Elevazione* [Toccata for the Elevation]), while the ricercare and even the secular canzone might grace certain other moments of the service (*Ricercare dopo il Credo* [Ricercare after the Creed], *Canzone dopo l'Epistola* and *dopo il Post Comune* [Canzone after the Epistle and after the Postcommunion]).

During the two centuries which followed Frescobaldi's death, the all-powerful influence of orchestral and, above all, vocal music – the oratorio in church and opera in town – did little to encourage the development of an original tradition of organ music. Numerous composers, many of them organists, were clearly anxious to shed an added luster upon religious services, but the works they produced were merely functional and modest in scale. Thereafter, the Italian organ inspired few pieces of outstanding merit.

Frescobaldi represents the culmination of Italian keyboard writing. His works remained influential throughout the peninsula for a number of decades after his death, although they only really bore fruit in southern Germany.

We may perhaps regard the modest progress of organ music in Italy not only as an outcome of its capitulation to the *éclat* of instrumental and vocal ensembles but also as a consequence of the stability of the tonal structure of the Italian organ, which had attained its definitive form before 1600 and was to remain unchanged for the next two centuries. By the time the instrument had grown more symphonic in its approach, as it did with the Serassi family, it was almost certainly too late. The dominant rhetoric of grand operatic gestures, both on stage and at the altar, left the Italian organ no alternative but to adopt a style of bravura writing which encouraged composers to transcribe and imitate fashionable operas and even military marches. They were certainly not sparing in their use of timpani, campanelli, piatti and gran cassa, to the immense delight of their audiences.

Just as instruments altered little in the years following Frescobaldi's death, so musical forms remained static. Ricercari, canzoni, toccatas, fugues, commentaries on the service (versets and hymns) continued to be the pieces composers most preferred. Elegant, detailed and rich in small-scale thematic ideas, and consisting as before of toccata effects, homophonic passages and fugal or chromatic writing, these pieces nevertheless very soon broke free of the confining influence of imitation and availed themselves of the century's melodic refinements and carefree spontaneity. Faithful to the custom that musical forms should originate in Italy and enrich the whole of European music, Italian composers of the late seventeenth and eighteenth centuries developed two expressive genres of their own, the pastorale and, especially, the sonata. Examples of the former may be found among Frescobaldi's keyboard works, and the genre enjoyed an illustrious history at the hands of numerous later musicians such as Francesco Manfredini, Giuseppe Valentini, Arcangelo Corelli, Antonio Vivaldi, Bernardo Pasquini and Domenico Zipoli. It was also imitated by Handel and Bach. The sonata, originally a piece "sounded" on an instrument, had not yet acquired the classical structure we now associate with it; originally a dance suite, it retained, in its earliest phase, the various movements and alternating tempi associated with such suites. Nevertheless, a certain confusion still exists between the newer and older meaning of the term "sonata" (canzone in several sections) and musicologists are still some distance away from establishing a precise terminology.

The following are the principal musicians and their most important works during the period between the golden age of classical Italian organ music and its nineteenth-century counterpart.

Four composers, in particular, deserve our attention, who were either contemporaries of Frescobaldi or born soon after him. Michelangelo Rossi published his *Toccate e Correnti, per organo, o Cembalo* [Toccatas and Correntes for Organ, or Harpsichord] in two editions, the second of which was dated 1657. These admirable works are inspired by the style of Frescobaldi himself and are notable above all for continuing the tradition of toccata form. Tarquinio Merula, who was *maestro di cappella* at Bergamo and in his hometown of Cremona, and organist to the Polish court, is the author not only of capricci and canzoni but also of a very fine *Sonata cromatica* [Chromatic Sonata] in which the exposition of each of the various themes is treated in the style of a fantasia. Giovanni Scipione, also from Cremona, followed Frescobaldi's example in his two collections, *Intavolatura di Cembalo, et Organo, Toccate, Capricci, Hinni sopra il Canto fermo* [Tablature for Harpsichord or Organ, consisting of Toccatas, Capriccios and Hymns on a Cantus Firmus] (1650) and *Partitura di Cembalo et Organo* [Harpsichord or Organ Score] (1652). Earlier, in 1645, Giovanni Battista Fasolo from Asti had published in Venice his *Annuale, Che contiene tutto quello che deve fare una Organista per risponder al Choro tutto l'Anno* [Annual containing All that an Organist must do in his Responses to the Choir throughout the Year]. They are functional examples of the art of organ writing, responses and preludes, short four-part works, the majority being harmonic and sometimes imitative in style. Fasolo also wrote canzoni.

At a later date, two collections of technically impressive ricercari provide us with fine examples of the complexity of a contrapuntal art which would soon be out of date: the *Ricercari a4, a5, a6, con 1, 2, 3, 4, 5, 6 soggetti* [Ricerari in 4, 5 and 6 Voices, with 5 and 6 Subjects], published in 1669 by Luigi Battiferri of Sassocorvaro near Urbino, and the *Ricercari in stile antico, e grave* [Ricercari written in a Solemn, Classical Style] by Fabrizio Fontana, a native of Turin. Both composers were probably born at the beginning of the seventeenth century.

Brief mention must also be made of the sonatas of Carlo Francesco Polaroli (1653–1722), a pupil of Legrenzi, the fugues of Giuseppe Bencini, Antonio Caldara (Venice, 1670–1736) and Nicola Antonio Porpora (Naples, 1686–1766), and the toccatas of Alessandro Scarlatti (Palermo, 1659–1725); Scarlatti's works were intended above all for the harpsichord. At the beginning of the eighteenth century four composers gradually broke free from the formal traditions of the previous century, preferring instead a transparency of style inherited from harpsichord technique and practise. Around 1700 Bernardo Pasquini of Massa da Valdinievole near Florence (1637–1710), a Rome organist and musician to the court of Prince Battista Borghese, published a number of expressive pieces for keyboard. Tackling such traditional forms as the toccata, capriccio, canzone francese, ricercare and verset, Pasquini was able to steer an intermediate course between, on the one hand, the strict polyphony of Frescobaldi, whom he considered as one of his mentors, and the ordered structures of Merulo or Rossi, and, on the other hand, the melodic appeal, harmonic richness and technical vitality of Domenico Scarlatti. Of all his works, the most noteworthy are his toccatas and a charming *Introduzione e Pastorale,* and, especially, his fourteen sonatas for two harpsichords, published in a sort of shorthand which gives only the bass or treble line and leaves the interpreter the task of completing the other parts.

A fellow Tuscan, Zipoli (born at Prato in 1688), offers us a fine collection of attractive works, the *Sonate d'Intavolatura per Organo, e Cimbalo* [Tablature Sonatas for Organ

Ferdinando Bonazzi of Milan; the *Messa in do ridotta per due organi* [Mass in C for Two Organs] by Luigi Cherubini; and the *Post communionem per due organi* [Postcommunion for Two Organs] of 1897 by Armando Galliera of Milan. Moving northwards we find occasional works by the Benedictine monk Marion Müller (b. 1724): works which are preserved in the splendid monastery library at Einsiedeln and which include a *Sonata per la festa di Pasqua* [Sonata for Easter] in C major (1772), a *Sonata pastorale per il Santa Natale* [Pastoral Sonata for Christmas] in A major (1772), and a *Sonata per la Pentecoste* in B flat major (1775), all three works written for four organs. From the same area come the *Concerto a due organi* and *Sonata a due organi* of the mid-eighteenth-century composer Giovanni Bernardo Lucchinetti. At the abbey of Petershausen near Lake Constance, the Benedictine monk Alfons Albertin wrote an astonishing *Sonata per la festa di Pasqua* (1781) for four organs, four trumpets, four horns and kettledrums. Also worthy of mention are the *Duetti* of Carl Philipp Emanuel Bach (1714–88), and the sonatas for two instruments by Franz Danzi (1763–1826) and Daniel Steibelt (1765–1823), written at the end of the eighteenth century for Milan Cathedral.

It is impossible to conclude this list without mentioning the numerous transcriptions of works for harpsichord and organ which were made during the eighteenth century by composers such as Severo Giussani and Johann Christian Bach, who studied in Bologna and who was organist at Milan Cathedral. Paraphrases for two harpsichords include the fourteen sonatas by Bernardo Pasquini (1637–1710).

GIROLAMO FRESCOBALDI

Born in Ferrara in 1583 (baptized 9 September); died in Rome on March 1, 1643.

As a boy the young Frescobaldi studied under Luzzasco Luzzaschi, the distinguished organist of Ferrara Cathedral, and enjoyed a considerable reputation both as a chorister and as an organist. In 1604 he entered the Accademia di S. Cecilia in Rome, and early in 1607 we find him performing on the organ of the church of S. Maria in Trastevere. In June of that same year he left for Flanders, a journey which took him to Brussels, Amsterdam, Antwerp and Mechlin. He returned to Italy the following year, and on November 1, 1608 succeeded Ercole Pasquini as organist of St. Peter's in Rome, an appointment which he held for the next twenty years, except for a brief stay at the court of Mantua. In 1628 he offered his services to Duke Ferdinando II de' Medici, without, however, renouncing his position in Rome. He returned to the Eternal City in 1634 and resumed his former post, which he continued to hold until his death. He is buried in the Church of the Holy Apostles in Rome.

Of all the works which Frescobaldi wrote, the most important are his keyboard compositions which he essayed in all the recognized forms, including fantasia, ricercare, capriccio, toccata, canzone, variation (partita), and hymns or versets on the Magnificat. Among the works which deserve especial mention are his *Fiori musicali* of 1635 containing three masses (*Messa della Dominica, degli Apostoli* and *della Madonna*) [Sunday Mass, Mass of the Apostles, Mass of the Madonna] in which their author seizes the opportunities offered him to write for solo organ: a liturgical toccata to introduce the mass, various settings of the Kyrie, a canzone after the Epistle, a toccata and ricercare before and after the Credo (most notably the exceptional and amusing *Ricercar con obligo di cantare la quinta parte senza toccarla* [Ricercare in which the Fifth Voice must be Sung and not Played], in which the singer has to guess his entry), a toccata for the Elevation, a canzone after the Communion, and, following the *Messa della Madonna*, a "Bergamasca" and a "Capriccio sopra la Girolmeta."

Frescobaldi not only had contact with the works of contemporaries such as Gabrieli, Luzzaschi and Gesualdo, he also had the opportunity, during his stay in Flanders, to deepen his knowledge of the works of northern European composers such as Philips, Cornet and Sweelinck. The fame of the Italian organist may strike us as surprising: even during his lifetime he was numbered among the great musicians of the period not only because of his qualities as an organist and improviser, but because of his own compositions. Indeed, he seems to have been one of the first organists to enjoy the adulation not only of the masses – it is said that his debut in Rome attracted a crowd of thirty thousand admirers – but of fellow musicians and musical theorists, too.

Mersenne cites him in 1637, and two years later André Maugars holds him up as a model for French organists to emulate. Although Frescobaldi's formal innovations are limited to the partita, he adapted existing forms to the *stilo nuovo*, sections of expressive and highly structured writing alternating with virtuoso passagework. In doing so, he opened up the way to the structural changes which organ writing was to undergo during the following two centuries. Frescobaldi astonishes us with the boldness of his style and his sense of inventive virtuosity – a virtuosity which is never indulged for its own sake alone; but what impresses us above all is his search for a personal and imaginative means of expression in which poetry, sensuality and joy are constantly present. Inspired by the works of Giovanni de Macque and Trabaci, Frescobaldi followed their example in his intelligent use of chromaticism and in his handling of the art of *durezze* (dissonances) and *ligature* (legato passages). The various forms of the canzone, capriccio and fantasia were given an increasingly clear structure comprising several sections in which the rapid binary rhythm of contrapuntal writing alternated with a more homophonic ternary rhythm, so prefiguring sonata form. Frescobaldi's awareness of the importance of treating a single theme in an exposition and development section, as in the ricercare or capriccio *sopra un soggetto solo* [on a single subject], led to his establishing the modern vision of monothematic composition. On other occasions he made it his rule to combine up to four themes, as in the ricercare or fantasia *sopra quattro soggetti* [on four subjects]. By prefacing the ricercare with a toccata, he foreshadowed the structure of the prelude and fugue.

The influence of Frescobaldi – "l'organista vero incomparabilis" [the truly incomparable organist] as Borsetti called him in 1735 – left a profound mark on his pupil Froberger, who in turn bequeathed to German musicians the sympathetic intelligence and contrapuntal art of his Italian mentor.

and Harpsichord], published in 1716 in Rome, where the composer held the post of organist at the Jesuit Church. The first part of this collection is intended specifically for the organ and adds luster to the different musical forms of the church service, notably the verset, toccata, canzone, Elevazione, Postcomunio, Offertorio and Pastorale. These are charming compositions, simply harmonized and with lines which are never less than elegant. In the same year that these works were published, Zipoli left for Seville, where he became a member of the Society of Jesus and sailed for the Americas as a missionary. He became organist of the Jesuit Church at Córdoba in the Argentine, where he died in 1726.

Among Pasquini's numerous pupils were Georg Muffat and Johann Philipp Krieger, both of whom were active in southern Germany and Austria, and Domenico Scarlatti (1685-1757) who, in addition to his hundreds of harpsichord sonatas, wrote a few works dedicated to the organ. Three of Pasquini's pupils in particular produced works that are of interest in the context of organ music. The Sienese composer Azzolino Bernardino della Ciaia (1671-1755) published his *Sonate per cembalo con alcuni Saggi, ed altri contrapunti di largo, e grave stile Ecclesiastico per grandi organi* [Harpsichord Sonatas with some Display-Pieces, and other Contrapuntal Works suitable for Performance in

Church, written for large organs in a slow and solemn style] in 1727. Although the six remarkable sonatas collected in the first part of this volume were written primarily with the harpsichord in mind, the saggi, ricercari and versets provide the organist with brief, rigorously structured commentaries in the imitative style. His Pastorale would be an impressive piece whether played on the organ or the harpsichord. The *Pensieri per l'Organo in Partitura* [Thoughts for Organ in Full Score] (1714) by the Florentine composer Giovanni Maria Casini (*c*. 1670–*c*. 1715) are characterized by their wealth of formal detail, melodic invention, chromatic writing and use of parallel thirds and sixths, two or three sections of these pieces being based on the same thematic material. The Neapolitan composer Francesco Durante (1684–1755) married the style of the fugue and that of the toccata in the beauties of his *Studii*.

In this context two important collections of organ works appeared: the *Sonate da Organo di varii autori* [Organ Sonatas by Various Composers] (1687) edited by Giulio Cesare Aresti, and the *Libro di suonate d'Organo, di diversi Autori* [Book of Organ Sonatas, by Divers Composers] (1743), edited by Giacomo Poffa. In the eighteenth century, the authority of the Franciscan "Padre" Giovanni Battista (Giambattista) Martini (Bologna, 1706–84) continued to exert an exceptional influence. Johann Christian Bach and the young Wolfgang Amadeus Mozart both benefited from his tuition. His keyboard sonatas (*XII Sonate d'Intavolatura Per l'Organo, e il Cembalo* [Twelve Sonatas in Tablature Score for Organ and Harpsichord] of 1742, and *VI Sonate per l'Organo e il Cembalo* [Six Sonatas for Organ and Harpsichord] of 1747) are certainly more suited to the harpsichord, but some of the sonatas, and particularly the slow preludes, adagios or fugues, lend themselves to the organ. Also worthy of note are the *Libro di Sonate d'Organo d'Intavolatura . . . fatto per comodo da sonare alle Messe, Vespri, Compiete, ed altro* [Tablature of Organ Sonatas well suited to being Performed at the Mass, Vespers, Compline, and so on] (1720) by Giuseppe Maria Santini; the *Versetti in tutti li Tuoni Coralli* [Versets in All the Choral Modes] by Pietro Marzola; works by Francesco Feroci and Carlo Zenolini; and, of later date, the *112 Versetti Per Organo Per rispondere al Coro in tutti i tuoni Del Canto Fermo* [112 Versets for Organ, being Responses to the Choir in All the Tones of the Cantus Firmus] by Marco Santucci (1762–1843); in the nineteenth century, the works of Felice Moretti (or Padre Davide; 1791–1863) and Vincenzo Petrali (1832–89); and an entire school based in Pistora whose works include marches, symphonies and liturgical pieces written in a style akin to Haydn and whose chief representative was Giuseppe Gerardeschi.

Vincenzo Bellini (1801–35) composed a small organ sonata, and Gioacchino Antonio Rossini (1792–1868) used a harmonium in his *Petite Messe Solennelle*. The end of the nineteenth century and beginning of the twentieth saw works by Mario Enrico Bossi (1861–1925), author of a *Metodo di studio per l'organo moderno* [The Modern Organ Primer] containing some fifty pieces written in a post-Romantic style. Ottarino Respighi (1879–1936) left to the world two chorale preludes and a free prelude in D minor reminiscent of the style of Max Reger. Alfredo Casella (1883–1947) composed a *Concerto Romano* for organ and orchestra. But with these contemporaries of the organ builders Serassi and Lingiardi, the style of organ writing had already become closely bound up with a more symphonic aesthetic.

23   Organ in *cornu epistolae* (Epistle Organ), S. Petronio, Bologna, Lorenzo di Giacomo da Prato, 1470–5

This instrument, which faces the Gospel Organ built in 1596 by Baldassarre Malamini, is one of the oldest in Italy and still possesses its original Gothic case, concealed beneath the magnificent Baroque structure of 1675. Here, as in S. Marco and Sta. Maria Gloriosa dei Frari in Venice, the right-hand Epistle Organ is calculated on a longer pipe-length than the left-hand Gospel Organ. The double case continues to display the fifty-one pipes of the *Principale* 20′ (chancel side) and *Ottava* 10′ (sacristy side). At the outset the instrument must have had ten stops (some of which had two or three ranks in the treble), nine *ripieno* ranks on a *Principale* 20′, and a Flauto in decimaquinta. The keyboard had a compass of fifty-one notes from F^1 to a^{11}, but without the first F sharp[1] and G sharp[1]. Several alterations have been made to the original instrument. In 1531 Giovanni Battista Facchetti built a new wind-chest in order to add some quarter-tones to d sharp and g sharp, as a result of which the keyboard now had a compass of fifty-four keys. In 1563 Giovanni Cipri grouped the two treble ranks of the *ripieno* on to a single slider and added a Flauto in decimanona. In 1675 Giovanni Paolo Colonna "normalized" the instrument, removing the quarter-tones and using the wind-chest grooves to extend the tonal range to c^{111} (the keyboard continuing to have fifty-four keys). Other significant alterations were made in 1798 and 1714 by Francesco Traeri, including lowering the pitch and adding a rank of *Contrabassi* 24′ to the pedals. The instrument was restored between 1974 and 1982 by Tamburini, and once more assumed the tonal aspect which Facchetti had given it in 1531.

24   Epistle Organ, SS. Annunziata, Florence, Domenico di Lorenzo, 1509–23; organ case by Giovanni d'Alessio

This instrument, on a base of 12′, includes seven *ripieno* ranks, the last three being grouped on a single slider, and a single manual of fifty keys. It still has the original spring-chest ("a vento") and pipework. It was restored in 1974/5 by Alfredo Piccinelli. The front of the case is notable for its great classical simplicity, a feature characteristic of organ building in the Florence–Lucca–Siena region. Three groups of pipes stand out beneath a large central arch, flanked on each side by two double-story miters.

25   S. Pietro, Modena, Giovanni Battista Facchetti, 1519–24; gilding by Pellegrino Munari; panels painted by Giulio and Giovanni Taraschi, 1546.

The case and the display pipes are original. A new instrument with tracker action was built in 1964/5 by Fratelli Ruffati, inspired by a number of the specifications listed in the 1519 contract. This stipulated that the organ should have a *Principale* 10′ (from F) with three ranks in the treble (*in cima*), an *Ottava*, *ripieno* ranks and two Flute stops (Flauto in ottava and Flauto in quintadecima).

26 Duomo Vecchio (Old Cathedral), Brescia, Gian Giacomo Antegnati, 1536; enlarged by Serassi in 1826 (Opus 416)

The stoplist of this organ was quoted as a model by Costanzo Antegnati (1549–1624), a fourth-generation member of this great family of organ builders, in his *L'arte organica* of 1608. (For this stoplist, see Appendix.)

Serassi's alterations of 1826 respected Antegnati's stops and tonal colors, while adding a Pedal of three stops (16′, 8′ and Timbali, a Drum-stop in which a single key causes two pipes to sound a semitone apart). To the manual he added a second *Principale* and stops of ⅓′, ¼′, ⅙′ and ⅛′. The divided keyboard further enabled him to introduce a treble Cornet and reed voices. The organ was restored by Armando Maccarinelli in 1959. The case front retains Antegnati's original design: the two side miters and the central miter, each divided into two compartments and comprising five large pipes, provide a framework for four smaller miters superimposed in pairs (*cf.* the case fronts of the organ at Sta. Maria del Carmine in Brescia and the organ in Milan Cathedral).

◁ 27 SS. Severino e Sossio, Naples, Giovanni Domenico di Martino and Sebastiano Solcito, 1690; rebuilt by Francesco Cimino, 1774

This instrument is of interest chiefly on account of the impressive structure of its case, which is typical of the Roman Baroque school. The front of the case is divided into three sections. The layout of the pipes in a curved plane gives the structure a sense of movement, a dynamism further accentuated by the attitude of the angels.

28 S. Giovanni in Laterano (St. John the Lateran), Rome, Luca Blasi, 1597–9; case by Giovanni Battista Montano, enlarged in 1731 by Annibale Traeri and Celestino Testa; unfortunate alterations in 1934
This instrument which, at the time that it was made, was the most famous and the largest in the Eternal City, originally had a single manual with twelve (?) stops, on a base of 24′. It included two reed voices (Zampogna, or Cornamusa, and Tromba). Invited to Rome by Pope Clement VIII, Luca Blasi was knighted in recognition of his work on the instrument, which was completed in time for the jubilee year 1600. In 1731 a *Positivo* was added, two manuals of fifty-nine notes, and a Pedal with twenty-six keys (thirty-two stops).

29 Sant'Anna dei Lombardi (Monteoliveto), Naples, Cesare II Catarinozzi de Affile, 1697
The last organ to be built in Naples by Catarinozzi, who was also responsible for the instruments at Montecassino (1687) and Anagni Cathedral (1702), this instrument conforms to the Roman conception of a case front made up of three miters of large pipes framed by tall Corinthian columns, arches and cornices. The two small miters at the sides give a sense of balance to the structure, which is further adorned by statues, masks and garlands. The designer was Mario Cartaro. Pre-1944 state.

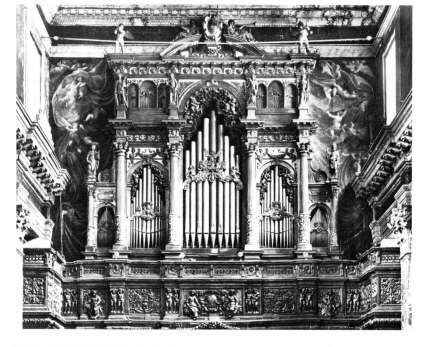

30 S. Tommaso Cantuariense, Verona, Giuseppe Bonatti, 1716
This instrument, with its twenty or so stops, is remarkable not only for its Baroque case and front consisting of two side-flats (seven pipes in the form of a miter) and four central double-story miters (eleven pipes). A unique feature is a small regal or "Pastorale" with cardboard pipes situated in a recess above the console. The organ additionally has two manuals (*Primo Organo* and a *Positivo tergale* whose case is bracketed to the parapet of the *cantoria*) and Pedal. We may also draw attention to the imitative stops (Passere, Speranza, Grillo I, Grillo II and Rossignol) which enlivened the rich sonorities of this instrument's *ripieno*, Flutes and Reeds.

31 Collegio di Spagna, Bologna, Gioacchino Pilotti, *c.* 1800
This chamber organ, with its highly distinctive case, is richly decorated with neo-classical motifs. Panels enable the keyboard and case front to be closed off. The keyboard of forty-five notes (including a short octave in the bass) comprises fourteen stops (+ *tiratutti*). The eighteen keys of the pedals are of the pull-down variety. The instrument was restored by Emilio Piccinelli in 1960.

32 Sant'Anna in Borgo Palazzo, Bergamo, Serassi (Opus 640), 1857
Discreetly enclosed beneath the arch, the instrument presents an elegant frontage. The disposition of the pipes in a single central miter flanked by two returning wings inevitably recalls the traditional design of Venetian organ building. A 16′ organ with two manuals of sixty-one notes and a pedalboard of twenty-four keys (sixteen notes), this instrument incorporates its *Organo Eco* in the case of the *Grand'Organo* rather than placing it to one side, as was usual in organs built in Lombardy and Venice in the eighteenth and nineteenth centuries. The instrument has been restored by Emilio Piccinelli and now has fifty-nine stops, including a ten-rank *ripieno*, and *timballi* in the Pedal, *griglie* and *rollante*.

III Organ Music in Germany

Fig. 61 Positive organ from the beginning of the sixteenth century; from Arnolt Schlick, *Spiegel der Orgelmacher*, Speyer, 1511.

BEFORE BACH

From the fifteenth century to the early seventeenth century

The German-speaking countries possessed a wealth of organ music in the fifteenth century. Many fragmentary tablatures dating from the first half of the century – including some from Mondsee, Sagan, Breslau (now Wrocław), Winsum, Munich, Hamburg, Erlangen and a tablature compiled in 1448 by the rector of Stendal, Adam Ileborgh – contain parts of organ masses, phrases based on popular German themes, and preludes (especially the five preludes in Ileborgh's tablature). They are remarkable for their two-part polyphony, with a third note occasionally added to complete the harmony, and for the skill, freedom and, above all, the range (up to two octaves) of a descant which is underpinned by a slow-moving tenor line ascending and descending in thirds, fifths and sixths.

From the mid-fifteenth century onwards we find a profuse growth of often didactic works, a development symptomatic of the direction which organ music was now taking. The *Nürnberger Orgelbuch* [Nuremberg Organbook] of 1452, bound together with the *Lochamer Liederbuch* [Locham Songbook] in the Berlin manuscript Deutsche Bibl. 40613, contains the *Fundamentum organisandi* [Principles of Organ-Playing] of Conrad Paumann (c. 1410–73), in addition to various pieces by other leading composers including Walther de Salice, Georg von Puteheim, Johannes Ciconia, Wilhelmus Legrant and Anton Paumgartner. The blind Nuremberg organist Paumann, who was in the service of the Bavarian court, compiled his *Fundamentum organisandi*, or "method of composition," in 1452. It is illustrated by works based on German songs as well as plainsong themes. Intended for the use of other organists, it shows how to write a florid counterpoint on a *cantus firmus*, how to write cadences, vary the rhythm or use intervals. The majority of examples include two melodic lines, although some extend to as many as five voices.

Another important manuscript, the *Buxheimer Orgelbuch* [Buxheim Organbook], a collection of organ music from the Carthusian monastery of Buxheim on the Iller, is the largest tablature of the time. Containing 258 works of sacred and profane inspiration, it was compiled around 1470. The works in question include liturgical variations on plainchant themes, *alternatim* sections of the mass, transcriptions of numerous songs and motets of German, Flemish and English provenance. Sixteen preludes, each of up to three or even four voices, give a new importance to the pedals, which are used to play the lowest notes in the harmonic line, whether these latter be part of the tenor or contratenor line. This implies the absence of a 16′ stop on the pedals, a supposition confirmed by Arnolt Schlick (before 1460–after 1527) in 1511. In addition to Paumann, who is represented by a number of pieces from his *Fundamentum*, the collection includes works by some of the major composers of the time: Johannes Ciconia,

Arnold de Lantins, Gilles de Binchois (*c.* 1400–60), Guillaume Dufay (*c.* 1400–74), Walter Frye, Hermann von Salzburg and Oswald von Wolkenstein. The fifteenth and sixteenth centuries are therefore a period of great richness in the history of organ music, not only by virtue of the number of tablatures which have been discovered but also thanks to the composers who developed its techniques of notation and execution. Certain pieces are written for three or four, and even five, six or seven voices. An extreme example of ten occurs in the *Ascendo ad Patrem meum* [I ascend to my Father] which Schlick wrote in 1520 for the coronation of the Emperor Charles V. This should no longer surprise us when we recall that, by that date, the German organ often had two manuals and a pedalboard, offering the possibility of a great number and variety of registrations. After all, had not Schlick himself already written for double pedals?

The first composer who deserves to be mentioned here is Heinrich Isaac (*c.* 1450–1517), organist to Lorenzo the Magnificent and active in Innsbruck and later at the court of the Emperor Maximilian in Vienna. His songs were transcribed for the organ by his pupils. Schlick, the blind organist of the Kurfürst of Heidelberg, published his *Tabulaturen etlicher Lobgesang und Lidlein uff die Orgeln und Lauten* [Tablatures of Hymns and Songs for the Organ and Lute] at Mainz in 1512. The collection is in two parts, the first of which comprises organ works for three or four voices based, in general, on a *cantus firmus* borrowed from plainchant. Examples include the complete cycle of the "Salve regina," the *Maria zart*, and the astonishing *Ascendo ad Patrem meum* for ten voices, four of which are on the pedals.

Paul Hofhaimer (1459–1537), known as the "Prince of the Organ," was court organist successively to Duke Sigmund of Tyrol in Innsbruck, Emperor Maximilian I and the Prince-Archbishop of Salzburg. Although better known as a virtuoso performer and as a teacher, Hofhaimer was also a great composer, a claim attested by the few works of his to have survived. His pieces are imitative in style, with a melodic motif stated in one voice before being taken up or imitated by the other voices. They include elaborate use of the appoggiatura and mordant.

The pupils and successors of Hofhaimer – the so-called Paulomines – were all active in the Alemannic part of the German-speaking South: Hans Buchner (1483–1538) in Constance, Hans (or Johann) Kotter (*c.* 1485–1541) at Fribourg in Switzerland, Fridolin Sicher (1490–1546), a pupil of Buchner's, in St. Gall, Leonhard Kleber (*c.* 1495–1556), who may have been a pupil of Schlick's, at Pforzheim, Hans Weck at Freiburg im Breisgau, and Othmar Nachtigall called Luscinius (1487–1536) at Strasbourg. Between them they wrote a large number of works which mark an essential stage in the development of organ music. For the most part they were friends or close relatives of the great thinkers and humanist artists of the German Renaissance, and their works are noteworthy as evidence of an astonishing transition from the Gothic style in music, with its flamboyant, polyphonic lines, to the newer, more harmonic conception, a conception which was able to adapt itself to the still somewhat restricted compass of the German keyboard. The manuals had a range of between three and three-and-a-half octaves, from B to a^{11}, f^{111} or g^{111}, while the pedals had a compass of about one-and-a-half octaves from F to b flat, or c^1. The pedals in fact assumed a remarkable importance, composers occasionally requiring organists to play two notes at once.

Buchner's *Fundamentum*, compiled around 1525, requires a section to itself, since it contains the principal forms which had been treated in the earliest tablatures. Against a *cantus firmus* of long note-values of equal length, the composer develops an imitative counterpoint following the Italian example, which he himself appears to have introduced into the southern German-speaking lands. The theoretical section of the text shows a particular concern for playing and fingering, and illustrates the numerous ways an organist can treat a plainchant theme in response to the choir.

The first third of the sixteenth century is noteworthy for the two collections which Kotter presented to the Basle humanist Bonifacius Amerbach, and also for the collection of Leonhard Kleber. These works give special emphasis to transcriptions of German, Italian and French songs, whether written by the compilers themselves or by other composers. Kotter's anthologies also include numerous dances written on themes or basse-danses popular at the time.

Fig. 62   Cart of the organist Paul Hofhaimer, musician to the Emperor Maximilian I. Engraving by Hans Burgkmaier in *The Triumphs of the Emperor Maximilian I*, 1526.

Side by side with these transcriptions and dances we also find more freely improvisatory pieces entitled Praeludium, Proemium, Anabole, Fantasia or Finale in which solid chords alternate with sections of a more florid character. The latter include the *Praeambulum sex vocum* [Prelude in Six Voices] by the Swiss composer Ludwig Senfl (or Sänfli, *c.* 1486–1543), and Kotter's *Fantasia in C* of 1513, the oldest known keyboard fantasia. We also find here the earliest variations on hymn-tunes, including "Aus tiefer Not schrei ich zu Dir" [In deepest need I cry to thee], "Maria zart von edler Art" [Gentle Mary, nobly born], "Christ ist erstanden von der Marter allen" [Christ is now risen again from his death and all his pain], "Komm Heiliger Geist" [Come, Holy Ghost] and "Herre Gott" [Lord God].

The influence not only of German composers but of Italian and French masters as well spread as far as the neighboring regions to the east. The two most important Polish tablatures, compiled between 1540 and 1550, are the tablatures of Jan z Lublina, canon of the monastery at Kraśnik, and one from the Monastery of the Holy Ghost at Cracow. In addition to a treatise on counterpoint which, following the example of Buchner's *Fundamentum*, elaborates the rules of imitative counterpoint and liturgical treatment of a *cantus firmus*, these collections include transcriptions of both sacred and profane works, and dances by all the leading Western composers from Germany, France and Italy, as well as others by Polish composers, most notably Mikolaj z Krakowa, and possibly also Jakub Sowa. Also included are organ preludes requiring the use of the pedals. It is worth underlining the preeminent position occupied by the city of Cracow in the history of Polish music. The orchestra and choir created by King Sigismund I at Wawel in 1543 was enhanced by contributions from the greatest Polish composers, while the king's orchestra attracted countless foreign artists, especially from Italy. In Hungary, too, Germanic influence was preponderant, as a result of links established between Buda and Vienna, the latter city being occupied between 1485 and 1490 by the forces of King Matthias Corvinus. His wife, Queen Beatrice, was unable, however, to enlist the services of Hofhaimer, who preferred to attach himself instead to the court of Archduke Maximilian. Hofhaimer's disciples, Joseph Grünpeck, who was in the service of Ulászló II in Buda, and Wolfgang Grefinger, court organist to King Lajos II at Buda and later at Brassó, in turn produced pupils such as the canon János Steck of Pécs, the Dominican Ferenc of Pécs, and János Szendi. The last-named both studied in Innsbruck and thus contributed to the spread of Hofhaimer's influence to the leading centers of music in Hungary. Nor, in this context, should we forget Willaert's seven-year appointment in Buda.

Whereas there had been a great outpouring of keyboard music in Germany throughout the fifteenth century, we have to wait until the third quarter of the sixteenth for renewed signs of activity, a delay for which the politico-religious troubles of the Reformation may be to blame. In 1571 came the publication of the tablature of Elias Nikolaus Ammerbach (1530–97), organist at the Thomaskirche in Leipzig. His three collections of 1571, 1575 and 1583 inaugurate a form of notation in which the different voices are written not as notes but as letters accompanied by indications of rhythm, a practise which survived until the second half of the eighteenth century when, for reasons of space, it was used by Johann Sebastian Bach in his *Orgelbüchlein*.

The end of the sixteenth century was a fruitful period, made richer by two collections of organ music: one by Bernhard Schmid the Elder (*c.* 1520–92), organist at the Protestant parish church of Strasbourg Cathedral (*Zwey Bücher Einer Neuen Künstlerischen Tabulatur auff Orgeln und Instrumenten* [Two Books of a New Artistic Tablature for Organs and other Instruments] (1577); and another by Johann Rühling (1550–1615) containing music for Sundays and feast days of the liturgical calendar. Rühling, who was organist near Leipzig, published his collection in 1583, the same year as the first tablature by Jacob Paix of Augsburg (1556–after 1615), who was organist in Lauingen. Paix's *Ein Schön Nutz unnd Gebreüchlich Orgel Tabulaturbuch* [A Fine and Useful Tablature for Common Use] was followed in 1589 by his *Thesaurus motetarum* [Thesaurus of Motets], and, in 1598, by the *Tabulaturbuch auff dem Instrumente* [Tablature for the Instrument] of August Nörmiger (*c.* 1560–1613), organist to the Dresden court.

These collections bring together transcriptions of famous vocal works, German, French and Italian songs and hymn-tunes, and dances such as galliards and *passamezzi*. Some of the works in question were evidently written by the great composers of the past, including Josquin, Isaac, Hofhaimer and Senfl, but others are modeled on the newer style of Orlando di Lasso, Clément Janequin, Jacobus Clemens "non Papa" and Palestrina. They are remarkable above all for their extremely florid ornamentation, in which "coloratura" and grace notes transfigure the different lines. The latter vary in number from four to six, and their compass is much greater than before. Their authors, who may fittingly be described as "colorists," played their part in disseminating the new style, which was essentially that of variation – a fact which emerges with striking clarity from the tablatures dating from the beginning of the seventeenth century. Indeed, the collections of Bernhard Schmid the Younger (1548–*c.*1625), who succeeded his father as organist in Strasbourg, and Johann Wolz of Heidelberg give particular emphasis to works which are Italianate in style and influence; they include toccatas, *intonazioni* and *canzoni alla francese*. Schmid's tablature of 1607 was entitled *Tabulatur Buch von Allerhand ausserlesnen, Schönen, Lieblichen Praeludijs, Toccaten, Motteten, Canzonetten, Madrigalien unnd Fugen von 4. 5. und 6. Stimmen: desgleichen künstlichen Passomezen und Gagliarden* [...] [Tablature of Every Kind of Rare, Beautiful & Delightful Prelude, Toccata, Motet, Canzonetta, Madrigal & Fugue in 4, 5 & 6 Voices...]; that of Wolz, published in 1617, was *Nova musices organicae tabulatura. Das ist: Eine newe art teutscher Tabulatur, etlicher ausserlesenen Latinisch: und Teutschen Motetten und Geistlichen Gesängen, auch schönen lieblichen Fugen, und Canzoni alla francese, von der berhümbtesten Musicis, und Organisten Teutsch: und Welsch Landen, mit 4.5.6.7.8.10.12. und mehr Stimmen* [...] [New Tablature of Organ Music. That is: a New Kind of German Tablature...]. A notable feature of Wolz's collection are twenty fugues by Simon Lohet of Liège (*c.* 1550–1611), organist to the court of Stuttgart. Among other important organists at the turn of the century who show clear signs of Italian influence are Adam Steigleder (1561–1633) at Ulm, Christian Erbach (*c.* 1570–1635), the organist of the Fugger family of Augsburg, Johann Klemm, who studied with Erbach prior to his appointment as organist to the Dresden court (*Partitura seu Tabulatura italica* [Full score or Italian Tablature], 1631), and the three Hassler brothers: Kaspar (1562–1618) at Nuremberg, Hans Leo (1564–1612), a pupil of Andrea Gabrieli and organist in Nuremberg, Prague and Dresden, and, finally, Jacob (1565– ?) in Prague.

The Southern and Northern German Schools

The early seventeenth century saw the emergence of two well-defined trends in the history of German organ music: the southern school, which could be considered as the logical continuation of the works we have been examining, and that of the north, which reflects the same sources, but was subjected to the powerful influence of the Dutch composer Jan Pieterszoon Sweelinck, who may well be regarded as the father of northern organists. These opposing influences complement each other in the works of central German composers, most notably Johann Sebastian Bach. This synthesis is revealed not only in their means of expression but also in their formal structures. It is a consequence of the architectural and stylistic features of the instruments concerned as much as it is of practical needs and differing forms of the liturgy. Italian influence, especially that of Frescobaldi, is frequently discernible in the writing of southern German composers. On the other hand, the musicians of the South were less organists than court musicians or harpsichordists. They were influenced by the new currents of the various national schools, in this mirroring the historical attraction exerted earlier by the courts of Vienna and Munich on Latin countries. Parallel to this development, the demands of the Catholic liturgy limited organists to expressing their ideas in brief commentaries such as versets, preludes, interludes and postludes, in which the organ became the guarantor, so to speak, of a Gregorian *cantus firmus*, rather than the unstinting and prolix commentator of the Protestant *Choral*. Whereas organists in northern Europe, following the example of the Dutch tradition, found time for organ recitals, their southern contemporaries were forced to accept the presence of other instruments in their churches, not least because of the influence of Italian opera and oratorio. As a result, the organ as a solo instrument was bound to suffer.

Without discussing in detail the characteristic differences between harpsichord writing and organ writing, we must nevertheless underline the fact that, from the mid-seventeenth century onwards, northern Germany witnessed the overwhelming superiority of the pipe organ and an almost total eclipse of works written for the harpsichord, whereas the South, by contrast, began to distinguish more and more clearly between those works intended for the harpsichord (by far the greater in number), and those written specifically for the organ and based in general upon liturgical themes.

The South German Lands

Italian influence on the South German lands is due to several factors. Numerous musicians traveled to Italy in order to study with the great musicians of the time: Hassler studied with Giovanni Gabrieli; Johann Erasmus Kindermann (1616–55) went to Venice; Johann Jakob Froberger (1616–67) studied with Frescobaldi, Johann Kaspar Kerll (1627–93) with Giacomo Carissimi, and Muffat with Pasquini; Krieger the Elder visited Venice and Rome. The presence of Italian musicians such as Alessandro Poglietti in Vienna gave rise to a style of writing whose forms (ricercare, canzone, toccata and fugue), stylistic devices (chromaticism, echo effects and *durezze e ligature*) and idiosyncrasies (among them the call of the cuckoo in imitation of Frescobaldi's *Capriccio sopra il Cucho* [Capriccio on the Cuckoo]) left a profound mark on the music of these regions. The importance of the art of the "colorists," clearly visible in the works written at the beginning of the seventeenth century, gradually receded, giving way instead to a new thematic, contrapuntal and formal clarity inherited from Italy, to a *sensibilité* in the handling of ornaments in the French manner, and, of course, to a varied melodic treatment typical of the northern German school. The composers who were active in the southern German lands need to be considered in their geographical situation, at the confluence of three major tributaries: Italy, France and northern Germany.

The great number of composers working in the South makes it impossible to consider the works and characteristic features of each of them in turn, but the most important may nevertheless be mentioned. Hans Leo Hassler, born in Nuremberg and active in Augsburg and Dresden, spent his formative years studying with Gabrieli in Venice. He bequeathed to the world a number of important organ works, including polythematic ricercari, canzoni, toccatas, introits and liturgical versets. Erbach, organist of the Fugger family of Augsburg, essayed similar forms to those treated by Hassler. Like him, he made significant use of chromaticism, but contrived, in his ricercari, to develop only a single theme. Johann Klemm, a native of Saxony, studied under Erbach in Augsburg and published the fugues of his *Partitura seu Tabulatura italica* in 1631. The two, three or four different voices here are written out on separate staves, as Scheidt had done in 1624.

The tablatures of Johann Ulrich Steigleder (1593–1635), who was organist in Lindau and Stuttgart, include a dozen ricercari of 1624 and, three years later, forty variations on a number of different themes including the "Vater unser" [Our Father], in which Steigleder is clearly at pains to highlight a *cantus firmus* which could either be played by the organist himself or sung, or even performed on another instrument. His style owes a great deal to that of Samuel Scheidt, who exercised considerable influence on all the organists of his day, not only in the use of variation but also in his harmonization of hymn-tunes.

Froberger, who spent most of his life in the service of the Habsburgs in Vienna, was born in Stuttgart and, from 1637 to 1641, studied under Frescobaldi, the chief of whose forms he later took up and developed. As a virtuoso performer on both the harpsichord and organ, he was celebrated in all the leading European centers of music including Dresden, Brussels, Paris and London. Johann Mattheson reports that, having twice been robbed on his way to the English capital, the penniless German organist was forced to accept the post of organ-blower at Westminster, offered him by Christopher Gibbons. During the ceremony marking the wedding of King Charles II, Froberger ventured to abandon his post and take the place of the enraged Gibbons. His style of playing being recognized, he was presented to the king. The anecdote may not be true, but it is not unworthy of a man described by the extremely formal William Swann as "a very rare man on the spinets." He deserves to be considered a universal artist in his synthesis of different regional styles, a synthesis which he achieved in works intended in general for the harpsichord rather than the organ (with the exception of his fantasias and ricercari). His toccatas, although marked by a wholly Italianate freedom, give pride of place to French-style ornamentation and chromaticism. They may be performed on a positive or single-manual organ. Related to the toccatas of Frescobaldi and divided into numerous sections differentiated by their rhythm, they have an ease of unity about them, a concern for harmonic progression within each movement, and fugal passages alternating with improvisatory sections. Capricci constructed after the example of Frescobaldi, canzoni elaborated according to the principle of thematic variation, fantasias with multiple rhythms and monothematic ricercari are, together with the toccatas, all part of the same richly varied repertory.

Kindermann was organist in Nuremberg. He, too, traveled to Italy, and in 1645 published his *Harmonia organica*. His *praeambula* or *intonazioni*, and his fugues, some of which are based on hymn-tunes, together with his Magnificat versets, are all clearly structured. They require the use of the pedals, although to a limited extent, as was always the case in the South and especially in the Viennese school. Their use was often confined simply to held notes or to the quotation of a theme with long note-values. We must also mention Wolfgang Ebner of Augsburg (1612–65), who made a career for himself in Vienna and whose works include variations in the form of dance suites; and the Italian Poglietti, who died in the Siege of Vienna in 1683 and who was organist at the Jesuit Church in the city, and later at the Habsburg court. A number of his works have survived which are partly post-Frescobaldian in style, partly German. Another organist from Ulm, Sebastian Anton Scherer (1631–1712), followed the Italian example with his brief *intonazioni* and toccatas published in 1664. Although these carefully wrought works never achieve the degree of development found in the major forms of the period, they deserve our attention for their bold use of chromaticism.

Kerll was organist in Munich and Vienna, both at St. Stephen's Cathedral and at the Habsburg court. He studied with Valentini in the Imperial capital and with Carissimi in Rome. His works, unlike those of Froberger, give pride of place to the organ. His *Modulatio organica*, published in Munich in 1686, comprises liturgical versets on the eight tones of the Magnificat both in toccata style and in the imitative style. In his toccatas, canzoni and capricci, Kerll pays noticeable tribute to Italian music of the time (*Toccata cromatica con Durezze e Ligature*; *Toccata Tutta di salti*; *Toccata per li Pedali* [Chromatic Toccata with Dissonances and Legato Passages; Toccata filled with Wide Intervals; Toccata for the Pedals]). As a disciple of Frescobaldi's, Kerll was also interested in the art of varied rhythms characteristic of a more modern conception. Unostentatiously virtuoso in style, his musicality expresses itself as much in its development of short motifs and brilliant elaboration of toccata passages with alternating chords and floridly impressive passagework, as in his treatment of *ostinato* themes (*Ciacona Variata* [Chaconne with Variations] and *Passacaglia Variata* [Passacaglia with Variations]) and simple musical devices of a more illustrative style (*Capriccio Cucu* [Cuckoo Capriccio], *Capriccio "Der Steyrische Hirt"* [Capriccio on "The Styrian Shepherd"] and *Battaglia* [Battle]).

The greatest representative of the Nuremberg Protestant school was the organist Johann Pachelbel (1653–1706). He studied under Kerll, deputizing for him at St. Stephen's in Vienna and subsequently holding appointments as organist in Eisenach, Stuttgart, Gotha and, from 1695, at St. Sebald's in his home town of Nuremberg. Although he felt himself to be a part of the Italianate tradition with its customary forms of toccata, fantasia, chaconne (*ciacone*) and ricercare, Pachelbel remains a notable exception in the Catholic South. He produced a large number of works based on hymn-tunes, the majority of which appeared in his 1693 collection *Erster Theil etlicher Choräle, Welche bey währendem Gottes Dienst Zum praeambuliren gebraucht werden können* [First Book of Chorales which may be Performed as Preludes in the Course of the Divine Service]. An earlier collection was the *Musicalische Sterbens-Gedancken* [Musical Thoughts on Dying] of 1683.

Pachelbel's chorale compositions are those of a simple and discreet Reformed liturgy, their chief function being to introduce the singing of the congregation. The theme, clearly announced and without ornamentation, is defined in two characteristic forms: a brief fugue (pre-imitation), generally elaborating the opening phrase of the hymn-tune; and a more detailed treatment of the entire melody in the treble or bass (sometimes on the pedals), or occasionally in the tenor. The accompaniment, while certainly not lacking in rapid passagework, respects the *cantus firmus* rhythm of the versets, whether written for two voices (*bicinium*), three (*tricinium*) or four. The combination of these two forms later produced the great chorale preludes which were to be such a striking feature of the Baroque organ repertory.

Pachelbel's works also include numerous toccatas (certain of which are followed by fugues, a development which was to have well-known consequences), fantasias, fugues (often with two subjects independently developed before being combined, as in his versets or "Magnificat fugues"), ricercari and, finally, a number of chaconnes.

The preludes, fugues and *Choräle* of Pachelbel's son Wilhelm Hieronymus (1686–1764) are more spacious and more improvisatory in style than those of Johann Pachelbel himself. The two brothers Johann Philipp Krieger the Elder (1649–1725) and Johann Krieger the Younger (1652–1735) were both organists in Bayreuth. At the end of the century, Krieger the Younger, who also held an appointment in Zittau, published a number of compositions of some merit, including ricercari, preludes, fugues, toccatas, chaconnes, *Choralfantasien* [chorale fantasies] and *Choralvariationen* [chorale variations]. The most important of these works are a *Toccata mit dem Pedal aus C* [Toccata with Pedal in C] which opens with a passage for solo pedals, a Chaconne in G minor with twenty-nine variations, and a Passacaglia in D minor.

If the period under review produced one truly cosmopolitan composer, it was without doubt Georg Muffat (1653–1704). Generally regarded as a member of the southern German school, Muffat was born at Megève in the Savoy. He studied in Paris, where he fell under the influence of Lully and other French organists. In 1671 we find him as organist in the Strasbourg chapter. Three years later he was appointed Kapellmeister in Vienna and Prague in the service of the Habsburg emperor, and in 1678 he became organist to the Archbishop of Salzburg. There followed a period of study in Rome under Pasquini, and in 1690 he was appointed organist in Passau, an office he held until his death in 1704. Published in Salzburg in 1690, his *Apparatus musico-organisticus* contains twelve organ toccatas in addition to three pieces more probably intended for the harpsichord. His toccatas are remarkable for their almost Baroque freedom of expression, particularly when they are compared with the more classical style exhibited by Pachelbel, for example. Muffat was anxious to create a synthesis of all the elements unique to each particular regional style. In doing so he drew in turn upon the grandiloquent style of the French overture; the lavish ornamentation (trills) of the Paris *clavecinistes* or the tempo of French operatic arias; the rapid treatment of a theme by means of densely written *fugato* sections and the addition of numerous melismas typical of Italian writing; and, finally, the more rigorous style of German counterpoint, the structuring of the various episodes, and the grace and spontaneity of the Viennese spirit. These works clearly leave only a limited but indispensable role to the pedals, being satisfied instead with an Italianate type of instrument, although the various sections of the pieces concerned could be performed to great effect on two alternating manuals. A near contemporary of Muffat's and a pupil of Johann Philipp Krieger the Elder, Johann Philipp Förtsch (1652–1732) published in 1680 thirty-two canons for between two and eight voices based on the hymn-tune "Christ der du bist der Helle Tag" [Christ, thou art the bright day]. Their richly contrapuntal texture sets these works apart from others written in southern Germany at this time. In Vienna we continue to find ricercari, canzoni and toccatas by Franz Mathias Techelmann (*c.* 1649–1714), and a number of brilliant works including canzoni based on hymn-tunes, toccatas, fugues and capricci by Georg Reutter the Elder (1656–1738), who was a pupil of Kerll's. He was also a theorbist and organist at St. Stephen's, among other places. Pachelbel, who was a friend of his, dedicated his *Hexachordum Apollinis* [Hexachord of Apollo] jointly to Reutter and Buxtehude.

Kapellmeister to the court of the Margraves of Baden-Schlackenwerth, Johann Kaspar Ferdinand Fischer (*c.* 1667–1746) published two collections of works intended specifically for the organ. These works, which appeared at the beginning of the eighteenth century, bore the titles *Musicalisches Blumen-Büschlein* [Musical Bouquet of Flowers] and *Ariadne Musica Neo-Organoedum*. Whereas the former contains eight cycles, each comprising a prelude, six fugues and a finale, with a tonal perspective presenting a transition between the ecclesiastical modes and modern tonalities, the second work is a collection of brief preludes and fugues in nineteen different keys, together with five ricercari on liturgical themes. Franz Xaver Anton Murschhauser (1663–1738), a pupil of Kerll active in Munich, has left us a variety of works which are often virtuoso in character and divided into cycles, as Fischer's two collections had been. They include liturgical pieces, especially preludes, toccatas, *intonazioni* and fugues, published in the *Octi-Tonium novum Organicum* of 1696 and the *Prototypon Longo-Breve Organicum* of 1703 and 1707. In 1743 Valentin Rathgeber (1682–1750) brought out his *Musicalischer Zeit-Vertreib* [Musical Pastime], in which his Pastorales for Christmastide have all the elegance and casual charm of the galant style. Gottlieb Muffat (1690–1770), son of the above-mentioned Georg and organist to the Habsburg court in Vienna, published seventy-two *Versetten Sammt 12 Toccaten* [Versets, together with Twelve Toccatas] in 1726; they include a group of twelve toccatas, each followed by six fugues. These works, with their optional use of pedals, are elegant miniatures with finely wrought melodies. His *Componimenti musicali* of 1739 contain six suites or fantasias, each consisting of an introduction which may be an overture in the French style, and fugal sections, together with a chaconne with thirty-eight variations.

Among Pachelbel's numerous pupils, two Erfurt organists deserve to be singled out for mention: Johann Heinrich Buttstedt (1666–1727) and Andreas Nicolaus Vetters (1666–1734). Other leading composers later benefited indirectly from Pachelbel's influence, which they proceeded to disseminate throughout the southern German lands, and throughout central Germany, too. They include Johann Michael Bach (1648–94), the father of Johann Sebastian's first wife, Johann Bernhard Bach (1676–1749), Georg Friedrich Kauffmann (1679–1735), a pupil of Johann Heinrich Buttstedt's (1666–1727), Johann Gottfried Walther (1684–1748), a pupil of Johann Bernhard Bach, and Gottfried Kirchhoff (1685–1746), a pupil of Friedrich Wilhelm Zachow (1663–1712). Karlmann Kolb (1703–65) wrote his *Certamen Aonium* in 1733. The composer, who was organist at the Abbey Church of Aschbach in Bavaria, has included here preludes and fugal versets written in a style reminiscent of harpsichord technique.

Northern Germany

The growth of an important tradition of organ music in northern Germany is directly attributable to the works and style of Jan Pieterszoon Sweelinck. Indeed, the earliest and most famous representatives of this school were pupils of the great Dutch master, namely Jakob Praetorius (1586–1651) and Heinrich Scheidemann (*c.* 1595–1663) in Hamburg, Melchior Schildt (1592/3–1667) in Wolfenbüttel, Copenhagen and Hanover, Paul Siefert (1586–1666) in Danzig, Andreas Düben the Younger (*c.* 1590–1662) in Stockholm, and Samuel Scheidt (1587–1654) at Halle.

One of the forms most encouraged by these writers was the prelude on a Lutheran hymn-tune (*Choralvorspiel*). As the musical basis of the Reformation liturgy, the repertoire of *Choral* themes initially comprised plainchant melodies, popular tunes

Fig. 63 Stellwagenorgel, 1467 (case front 1515), Jakobikirche, Lübeck, Federal Republic of Germany. Engraving from A.G. Hill, London, 1883–91
Small organ notable for the survival of its Prinzipal 16′ display pipes. Enlarged by Friedrich Stellwagen in 1637 (Baroque *Rp*, *Bw* and *Ped*), the instrument now boasted twenty-six stops. Following successive restorations in the eighteenth century and a series of unfortunate alterations in the nineteenth, the organ was rebuilt by Kemper (1935 and 1947), and finally by Harry Hillebrand in 1978: the *Hw*, *Rp*, *Bw* and *Ped* comprise thirty-one stops, including three Gothic ones and fourteen by Stellwagen.

SAMUEL SCHEIDT

Born in Halle on the Saale in 1587, died there on March 30, 1654.

A devoted pupil of Sweelinck's, he never left his hometown of Halle except for his visit to Amsterdam in *c.* 1605. He was organist at Halle's Moritzkirche and, from 1609, court organist to Margrave Christian Wilhelm of Brandenburg, who was administrator of the Lutheran archbishopric of Magdeburg. The composer's life was strewn with misfortune, which is reflected in the mood of his works. The Thirty Years' War witnessed the sack of Magdeburg, bringing in its wake the abdication of the margrave and the dissolution of his household. This was followed by an outbreak of the plague, and, in 1637, by a fire which destroyed the Moritzkirche's organ. Finally came the loss of his post as *director musices* at the Marienkirche, Halle's principal church. Scheidt's works may be seen as a link between the older rules of

from Latin liturgical hymns and secular melodies from songs and dances of German, French, Italian and Dutch origin. At the same time, it was a product of the German spirit and the culmination of a popular tradition. It later became the point of departure for an intensive development in music, gradually increased by original contributions in the form of new melodies composed or adapted by musicians and organists of the sixteenth and seventeenth centuries. Martin Luther (1483–1546) himself helped enrich the Protestant hymnal with some forty original or borrowed themes, which he and his friends wrote or adapted between 1523 and 1543. In this way melodies came into being on which, in the course of the seventeenth and eighteenth centuries, not only organ works came to be based, but vocal and instrumental compositions as well. It was a tradition which was to continue in German music throughout the nineteenth and twentieth centuries.

More than two hundred books of hymn-tunes were published during the second and third quarters of the sixteenth century alone. The most important was the collection which appeared in Wittenberg in 1524 under the title *Geystliche gesangk Buchleyn* [Little Book of Hymns], edited by Johann Walter and with a preface by Luther. All these various works generally include themes written by Luther himself, but there were countless other men, both musicians and poets, who made their contribution, however modest, to the art of hymn writing. They include Johann Walter (1496–1570), Nikolaus Decius (*c.* 1485–after 1546), Johannes Agricola (1492–1560), Hans Sachs (1494–1576), Matthias Greiter (*c.* 1500–50), Wolfgang Figulus (*c.* 1520–*c.* 1591), Nikolaus Selnecker (1528–92), Johann Eccard (1553–1611), Philipp Nikolai (1556–1608; Nikolai wrote the words, if not the tunes, of the hymns "Wie schön leuchtet uns der Morgenstern" [How brightly beams the morning star] and "Wachet auf, ruft uns die Stimme" [Sleepers wake, the watchman calleth]), Melchior Vulpius (1560–1615, author of the hymns "Christus, der ist mein Leben" [Christ, He is my life], "Lobt Gott, den Herrn, ihr Heiden alle" [Praise the Lord, all ye heathens] and "Gelobt sei Gott im höchsten Thron" [Praise be to God in high]), Hans Leo Hassler (1564–1612) and Michael Praetorius (1571–1621). From the seventeenth century, which witnessed the publication of around 450 hymnals, we may mention Johann Crüger (1598–1662), the composer of a number of deeply felt tunes including "Herzliebster Jesu, was hast du verbrochen" [O, dearest Jesu, how hast Thou offended?], "Nun danket alle Gott" [Now thank we all our God], "Schmücke dich, o liebe Seele" [Deck thyself, my Soul, with gladness], "Wie soll ich dich empfangen" [How shall I fitly meet Thee], "Fröhlich soll mein Herze springen" [My heart shall leap with joy] and "Jesu, meine Freude" [Jesu, my priceless treasure]; and the poets Martin Rinkart (1586–1649; "Nun danket alle Gott"), Paul Gerhardt (1607–76; "O Haupt voll Blut und Wunden" [Oh sacred head, sore wounded]); Johann Rist (1607–67; "O Traurigkeit, o Herzeleid" [Oh sadness, oh heart's sorrow] and Johann Franck (1618–77; "Jesu, meine Freude" and "Schmücke dich, o liebe Seele"). As fervent expressions of the new faith, these tunes were originally sung in unison and unaccompanied. If the theme of the hymn-tune was treated polyphonically in four- or five-part works, a time-honoured tradition demanded that it should appear in the tenor. The contrapuntal character of the composition and the allocation of the melody to the tenor line favored the choir at the expense of the congregation. It was not until the end of the century that, apparently as a result of the example of Italian melody, the theme was gradually transferred to the upper voice (descant), which encouraged the participation of the assembled worshipers. The organ was added around the middle of the seventeenth century in order to underpin the congregation. (The introduction of the figured bass or continuo, which we find most notably in Johann Hermann Schein's sacred collection of 1627, made it easier from now on for instrumentalists to accompany a tune and for organists to supply the harmony.) At this time works written on hymn-tunes (*Choralbearbeitungen*: the German word *Choral* means "hymn-tune") became an essential part of the organ repertory.

The contrapuntal elaboration of hymn-tunes produced three distinct forms. The *Choralvorspiel* or prelude was simple in structure and intended primarily as an introduction to congregational hymn-singing. It was a relatively short piece in which the *cantus firmus*, more or less unornamented, was given to the upper voice and accompanied by straightforward polyphony, sometimes on a note-for-note basis. Being purely functional, the chorale prelude departed as little as possible from the outline of the melody as sung by the congregation. The chorale fantasia was the freest and most elaborate of all the forms favored by northern German organists, and was at the same time an original reworking of the chorale prelude. Each section of the melody was treated as a distinct episode and reworked in many different ways, including toccata-like passages, sections developed along imitative lines, diminution, *stretti*, inversion of lines, changes of time signature, ornamentation, thematic fragmentation, echo effects and so on. If the *cantus firmus*, whether ornamented or not, was systematically preceded by an introduction written in the style of a fugue, then it is usual to speak of a "figural" chorale. The chorale variation or chorale fugue, in common with Dutch or English practise, delighted in exploiting the innumerable resources of variation, and included numerous figural elements. These new forms may be said to link the style of the "colorists," who had already been eclipsed by the beginning of the seventeenth century, with the new style inherited from Sweelinck and the Anglo-Dutch school. As for the freer forms, they did not follow a uniform pattern. Influenced above all by Italian models such as toccatas written in the *stilo fantastico*, they were frequently divided into different sections: fugal episodes were framed by moments of pure virtuosity in a style close to that of improvisation. A good deal of imagination is evident in the realization of these forms, in which a chaconne might replace a fugal interlude, or where a simple transition might develop into a lengthy bridge passage. But in general these forms are distinguished by their quinquepartite structure, with two fugal sections linked to three episodes in toccata style. Indeed, the works produced by the northern German school are characterized by their freedom of form, which could achieve an astonishing degree of latitude, and which gave rise to a process of formal regeneration culminating in the organ music of Johann Sebastian Bach. But it was a culmination which had grown stiff with age, and for which death lay concealed in ambush. Never was the art of organ writing so vitally alive as it was in northern Germany in the seventeenth century – an art nourished on spontaneity and its search for freedom of form and new tonal combinations.

In spirit the canzone may appear as the antithesis of the toccata. As the direct heir of the Italian canzone and of the *fugato* principle (ricercare and capriccio), it expounds an idea in an arbitrary number of separate sections which are fugal in character, the subject being varied at each of its reappearances.

As regards their form, the passacaglia and chaconne (terms which composers used interchangeably) are both based on the *ostinato* principle. This device, which had flourished during the sixteenth century, consists of a repeated harmonic bass which adopts either the triple time of a stately dance or the melodic schemes of familiar pieces such as the *passamezzo*, *romanesca* and *bergamasca*, or else motifs such as that of the pentachord. Far from limiting the composer's imagination, these motifs were easily adapted to suit the art of variation. There is no criterion which enables us to define the respective applications of the passacaglia and chaconne, forms originating in Spain, which the Italians were the first to take over into instrumental music. Normally written in triple time, these works almost always have their theme in the bass line.

To a large extent the appearance of these large-scale and often virtuoso forms in northern Europe can be explained in terms of the evolution which had taken place in organ building. While the South remained dependent upon Italian influence, contenting itself with a single-manual instrument and pedals of modest compass, the North witnessed the development of larger instruments with varied tonal colors and numerous registers divided among different tonal structures (the *Werkprinzip*). The compass of the pedals and the wealth of stops enabled them to outgrow their former supporting role and to "lead" the bass, or tenor, or alto line. As a result composers from the second half of the seventeenth century onwards began writing virtuoso and even polyphonic parts for the pedals.

Among the many composers which this period produced, we must begin by listing those members of the Praetorius family who held appointments in Hamburg in the

musical style and the formal and technical innovations of his own day. But he was also a precursor in that he was aware, as Johann Sebastian Bach was to be, of a need for solid supports which only the past could provide. At the same time he was able to give an emotional depth to the chorale themes which inspired him. A strict contrapuntalist, he invested his harmonizations of hymn-tunes with a facility of expression which the act of worship required; and, as a *coloriste*, finally, he strove for variety in performance by means of a technique borrowed from violin playing, the *imitatio violonistica*.

Although no theoretical work has survived which would allow us a clear insight into the teaching methods used by his mentor Sweelinck, the pupil by contrast has left us a work of the first importance, his *Tabulatura nova*, published in 1624. Divided into three sections and using Italian notation ("partitura"), which allocates each voice to a separate staff, the work contains "psalms/fugues, toccatas, echo, passamezzos, canons and other secular songs." Scheidt thus suggests numerous variations and canons on liturgical tunes (chorales, Latin hymns and psalms) and secular themes (the most notable a canon on the six notes of the hexachord), fantasias including one entitled "toccata," two fugues, two echo pieces and a number of dances including a passamezzo, courante and allemandes. The third section contains works based on a liturgical *cantus firmus* and intended chiefly for performance in church; they include versets and variations, in addition to two works for *organo pleno*. The secular works do not include a pedal part. The *Tabulatura nova* is a theoretical work not only by virtue of its numerous musical examples but above all in view of its "instructions on the way to play organ works and their manner of registration." It addresses itself to organists who, as Scheidt says in his preface, like to play in a manner or style that is purely musical, without too many ornaments or runs. Scheidt states that the works in question have been written for an instrument with two manuals and pedals. We may also mention that the author pays particular attention to performing chorales, stipulating the need to highlight the melody, in the descant or tenor, by playing it on the *Rückpositiv* in high-pitched registrations "in order to be able to pick out the hymn-tune all the more clearly." If the tune in question were to be in the alto, the author recommends that the player should follow the standard practise of performing it on the pedals with a 4' registration.

In 1650 Scheidt published his *Görlitz Chorale Book*, dedicating it to the civic authorities in Görlitz and setting out one hundred "sacred songs and psalms."

Fig. 64 Aegidienkirche, 1624–5, Hans Scherer the Younger, Lübeck, Federal Republic of Germany. Engraving from A.G. Hill, London, 1883–91
Hw, *Rp*, *Ow* (*Bw*) and *Ped* with thirty-seven (?) stops; case front by Michael Sommer; *Bw* added by Friedrich Stellwagen in 1648; modifications in 1795, 1808 and 1853–4 (J. F. Schulze); new instrument by Kemper in 1916, three manuals and pedals comprising fifty stops. In 1981 Johannes Klais built a new instrument in the restored case of 1625; its three manuals and pedals have forty-two stops.

Fig. 65 Main Organ, Jakobikirche, Lübeck, Federal Republic of Germany. Engraving from A.G. Hill, London, 1883–91
Of the fourteen instruments which the town of Lübeck could boast in the sixteenth century, only four cases still survive, and only two, both in the Jakobikirche, still retain their original pipes. The first main organ was built between 1464 and 1466; rebuilt in 1504 with a large Gothic case; *Rp* added by Hans Köster in 1572–3; enlarged between 1671 and 1673 by Joachim Richborn, who built a new and bigger *Rp* and added pedal towers. The instrument now comprised *Hw*, *Rp*, *Bw* and *Ped* and had fifty-two stops. The *Bw* was enlarged between 1739 and 1741 and turned into an *Ow*; rebuilt by Marcussen in 1894 in accordance with the Romantic aesthetic; and by Kemper in 1935 in accord with the principles of the *Orgelbewegung*; the organ was further rebuilt in 1958 and 1965. The instrument currently has four manuals (*Hw*, *Rp*, *Bw* and *Ow*) and pedals, with sixty-eight stops.

churches of St. James, St. Peter and St. Gertrude: Jakob Praetorius the Elder (d. 1586), Hieronymus (1560–1629) and Jakob the Younger (1586–1651), a pupil of Sweelinck's; Johann Stephanius Praetorius (d. 1616) was organist in Lüneburg, and Michael Praetorius (1571–1621), the author of the famous *Syntagma Musicum*, was organist in Frankfurt on the Oder, Groningen and Wolfenbüttel. Paul Siefert (1586–1666) worked in Danzig and Samuel Scheidt (1587–1654) in Halle. Scheidt, although strictly speaking not a member of the northern German school, may nevertheless be considered one by virtue of his influence. Other organists of note include Melchior Schildt (1592/3–1667) in Wolfenbüttel, Copenhagen and Hanover, Heinrich Scheidemann (c. 1595–1663) in Hamburg, Delphin Strungk (1601–94) in Wolfenbüttel, Celle and Brunswick, Franz Tunder (1614–67) in Lübeck, Matthias Weckmann (1621–74) in Hamburg, Jan Adam Reincken (1623–1722) in Hamburg, Christian Flor (1626–97) in Lüneburg, Peter Morhardt (d. 1695) in Lüneburg, Johann Nicolaus Hanff (1630–1706) in Schleswig, Buxtehude in Lübeck, Andreas Kneller (1649–1724) in Hamburg, Vincent Lübeck (1654/6–1740) in Stade and Hamburg, Georg Böhm (1661–1733) in Lüneburg, and Nicolaus Bruhns in Copenhagen and Husum (1665–97). We may also draw attention here to the numerous tablature works from Celle, Pelplin and Lüneburg. The Lüneburg tablature comprises free compositions such as preludes, fantasias, fugues and toccatas, variations, *Choralvorspiele*, and dances by authors who are for the most part anonymous but among whom we find Sweelinck, Scheidemann, Schildt, Weckmann and Tunder.

The genres which composers essayed during the second half of the sixteenth century and the early years of the seventeenth were still extremely diversified, belonging as they did to the earliest tradition of German organ music represented by Ileborgh, Schlick and Senfl. The genres in question included sections from the mass, hymn sequences or Magnificat sequences. However, the composers of northern Germany, encouraged by Dutch and Italian influences, supplemented their existing repertory with works based on the style of variation, together with more freely improvisatory pieces such as fantasias, short preludes, works of a fugal character using echo effects or an *ostinato* bass, canons, and so on.

The *Choral* which, in the hands of Jakob Praetorius the Younger and Samuel Scheidt, had remained austere in form, was progressively enriched by newer methods inherited from the style of secular variation. In this way the various reworkings of a particular melody assumed a style which was sometimes sober and worthy of its liturgical role (works by Praetorius the Younger, Scheidt and Strungk), sometimes more ornate (Kneller and Scheidemann), sometimes exuberantly decorated

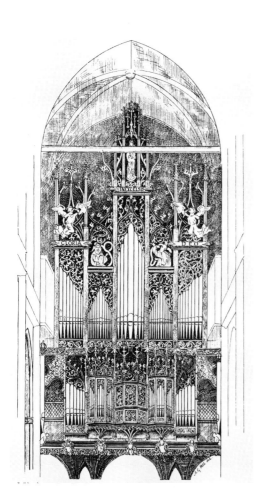

Fig. 66 Main Organ, Marienkirche, Lübeck, Federal Republic of Germany. Engraving from A. G. Hill, London, 1883–91
Among the incumbents of the Marienkirche organ are Franz Tunder (1641–67) and Dietrich Buxtehude (1668–1707). It was built by Berthold Hering between 1516 and 1518. A third keyboard was added by Jakob Scherer when he renovated the instrument in 1560–1. This instrument, which had forty-six stops, was later described by Michael Praetorius in Volume II of his *Syntagma musicum* of 1619 ("De Organographia"). The organ was restored between 1637 and 1641 by Friedrich Stellwagen (fifty-four stops); finally, at Buxtehude's request, a Vox humana and Sesquialtera were added in 1704 by Otto Dietrich Richborn. In 1968 Kemper built a 100-stop organ, comprising *Hw, Rp, Bw, Ow, Kw, Gross-Pedal* and *Klein-Pedal*, together with seven Tremulants and four Glockenspiele. (For the specification of this instrument the reader is referred to the Appendix.)

Fig. 67 Totentanzorgel, Marienkirche, Lübeck, Federal Republic of Germany. Engraving from A. G. Hill, London, 1883–91
Situated in the famous chapel of the Dance of Death, this organ was one of the oldest in Germany. It had already been restored by J. Stephani between 1475 and 1477, and was enlarged by Jakob Scherer (*Rp*, 1557–8) and Henning Kröger (*Bw*, 1621–2), before being restored by Friedrich Stellwagen between 1653 and 1655. Destroyed in an air raid on the night of March 29, 1942, the instrument was rebuilt according to the specifications listed in 1937 by the firm of Kemper: *Hw, Bw, Ow* and *Ped* (forty-two stops). (For specification, see Appendix.)

(Weckmann, Reincken and Hanff), and sometimes varied purely for pleasure (Lübeck and Böhm).

The works of Tunder, organist at St. Mary's Church in Lübeck, are both the culmination of an earlier development and the point of departure for a new and sumptuous art of which Johann Sebastian Bach would be the direct beneficiary. Tunder's seven works based on hymn-tunes (*Choralfantasien*) may surprise us with their virtuoso character, the diversity of their means, the rich and spontaneous handling of stylistic and technical possibilities and, finally, by their search for tonal colors (a search which was justified by the numerous stops which the organist had at his disposal). Notable features are the introductory passages whose rapid passagework would later be recalled by Buxtehude, the successive and varied appearance of a melody in different voices, sudden variations on the main theme or on part of it, echo effects, imitative passages and so on. This inventive richness and freedom recur in four preludes in which Tunder first introduced a tripartite structure into northern German organ music, a structure involving toccata, fugue and a coda in toccata style worked out without a break between the sections. Dietrich Buxtehude, the incumbent of three organs dedicated to the Virgin Mary at Helsingborg, Helsingør and Lübeck (where he succeeded Tunder), was not only the most prolific of northern German composers in the seventeenth century, but was also the most imaginative of contemporary organists and one whose contrapuntal talent was unrivaled throughout the period in question. Unstintingly experimental in his chorale settings, of which forty-eight have survived, written for the most part for an instrument with two manuals and pedals, he excelled at every type of chorale variation. He frequently begins his pieces with a fugal introduction (pre-imitation) based on a phrase inspired by the main theme, a procedure which is often continued throughout the piece. The use of this procedure and the rigorousness of the structure – foreshadowing the works of Johann Sebastian Bach – do not, however, limit the composer's freedom, but, on the contrary, allow him to express a

DIETRICH BUXTEHUDE

Born in 1637 at Oldesloe in the Danish province of Holstein; died in Lübeck on May 9, 1707.

Although often considered a German composer, "Diderik" Buxtehude was Danish by nationality, since at the time of his birth in 1637 the kingdom of Denmark embraced not only the part of northern Germany which includes Holstein but also the Swedish province of Skåne.

The composer's family lived initially in Hälsingborg in Skåne, where Buxtehude's father was organist at St. Mary's church, before moving around 1642 to Helsingør (Elsinore) in Zealand, where they lodged in the organists' house attached to St. Olaf's church. Dietrich later became organist in Hälsingborg, where his father continued to officiate until 1658. In 1660 he took up an appointment as organist at St.Mary's church in Helsingør, where the organ boasted two manuals and a pedal keyboard. Following a well-established tradition of musical rather than conjugal expediency (one thinks of Johann Sebastian Bach who in 1705 traveled from Arnstadt to Lübeck, tempted by Buxtehude's post there but without any affection for his daughter, Anna Margrita, who had been born in 1669 and who had already been rejected by Mattheson and Handel two years previously), Buxtehude agreed to marry the daughter of Franz Tunder (who had died in 1667) and in April 1668 he was appointed organist at St. Mary's church in Lübeck, a post considered to be one of the best and most lucrative in the whole of Germany. The town, moreover, was to play a crucial role in the musical development of northern Germany, a development which ran parallel to its growth as a commercial center.

Not content with his activities as organist and as a practising musician of exceptional influence, nor even as the composer of vocal and instrumental works including psalms, cantatas and sacred arias, not to mention his works for organ, Buxtehude revived the Abendmusiken, or evening concerts, which Tunder had founded in 1646. These concerts, which were held each year from 1673 onwards on the five Sundays preceding Christmas, consisted in performances of sacred works for chorus and orchestra and of organ works by Buxtehude himself. On important occasions he would position his musicians on the four galleries at either side of the central nave, and later, in 1699, on the two galleries at either side of the main organ. In this way Buxtehude introduced his Lübeck listeners to the polychoral tradition which had originated in Venice and which had been brought to Germany by Heinrich Schütz.

A musician of many talents, Buxtehude was not only an organist whom visitors came to hear from far afield, but a teacher whose countless pupils included Nicolaus Bruhns. He died on May 9, 1707 and was buried in St. Mary's church. A simple plaque preserves his memory.

33 Annenkirche ("Fuggerkapelle"), Augsburg, Federal Republic of Germany, Jan van Dobrau, 1518
The shutters were painted by Jörg Breu the Elder. This organ, which is typical of the Italian influence on southern Germany, is housed in a Renaissance case with a flat case front reminiscent of those at Constance, Freising and the Hofkirche at Innsbruck. The arrangement of the stops was inspired by that of Arnolt Schlick. Restored by Georg Markus Stein in 1736 and by Joseph Bohl in 1833, the instrument was rebuilt by Steinmeyer in 1902. A new instrument was built by Ekkehard Simon in 1978 inside a replica of the original case which was destroyed by enemy action in 1944 and rebuilt after the Second World War.

highly personal lyricism. He is notable for his symbolical musical realizations of keywords such as "death," "pain" and "sin," accompanied by passages of chromatic writing: the fall of Adam, for example – one of the essential ideas in the text – is mirrored by a fall of a fifteenth. Buxtehude also invented stylistic devices which set a new fashion in organ music: introductory flourishes, scales, conjunct movements, dramatic pauses, multiple rhythms, syncopation, hockets, homophony, the use of double pedal notes and so on. The chorale fantasia could therefore include, at one and the same time, stylistic and technical devices borrowed from ornamental chorales, contrapuntal chorales, echo fantasias and fugues.

The great Lübeck organist has also left us a number of more freely improvisatory pieces, three *ostinato* works (two chaconnes and the D minor Passacaglia), nine canzoni and twenty-six large-scale works comprising toccatas, or preludes and fugues. The marvelous D minor Passacaglia is from every point of view an outstanding work in the history of organ music, foreshadowing that immense cathedral of severe beauty and power, Bach's Passacaglia in C minor. The canzoni are the culmination of a development beginning with Gabrieli and imitated by countless later composers, while the toccatas and "preludes" are an austere counterpart to the toccatas of Frescobaldi. Each of these works contains between three and six sections of varied character, generally a toccata followed by a *fugato* developed in canzone form with one or more themes generally derived from the same subject, and a toccata finale. They are remarkable for their spontaneity and rigor, qualities enriched by rhythmic surprises and bold harmonies. Thus Buxtehude emerges as an exceptional figure, unique and individual in his genius.

Bruhns, a pupil of Buxtehude's and organist in Copenhagen and Husum, has left us four works of particular merit, a *Choralfantasie* and three preludes and fugues. His fugues bear witness to a style of writing in which virtuosity by no means excludes richness and elegance. They breathe the spirit and power of Buxtehude's own compositions.

The exceptional contribution of these three great musicians – one shared by Hanff, Flor, Böhm and Weckmann, to name only a few – has left its indelible mark on organ music, giving it an impetus which both revived the art and engendered future masterpieces. The High Baroque of northern Germany is found here in all its flamboyant majesty.

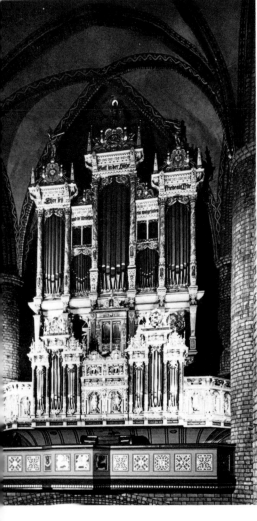

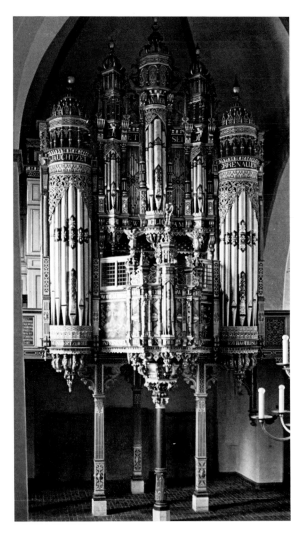

34 Nikolaikirche, Flensburg, Federal Republic of Germany, Nikolaus Maass and his pupils, Johann and Balthasar Lorentz, 1604–8

Maass was probably born in Brabant and later became organ builder to Christian IV of Denmark. His Flensburg organ has thirty-eight stops (*Hw, Rp, Bw, Ped*). The case was by Henrich Ringerink of Flensburg.

35 St. Martini, Bremen, Federal Republic of Germany, Christian Bockelmann, 1615–19

Renovated in 1707–9 by Arp Schnitger, who added fourteen new stops, bringing the total to twenty-six (*Hw, Rp, Ped*).

36 Marienkirche, Stralsund, German Democratic Republic, Friedrich Stellwagen, 1653–9

Fifty-one stops: *Hw, Rp, Bw* and *Ped*, two Tremulants (*Rp, BW*), Vogelgeschrei, Trommel and Zimbelsterne. This instrument was Stellwagen's last commission (he died at Stralsund in 1659) and is characteristic of Hanseatic organ building. Dutch influence is also evident and, as at 'sHertogenbosch (1618–38), the statues are an integral part of the case which is clearly structured according to the *Werkprinzip*. The instrument was restored by Schuke between 1946 and 1972.

37 Dom (Cathedral), Merseburg, German Democratic Republic, Zacharias Thayssner, 1666

The Merseburg organ, in its day one of the most imposing in Germany, was probably modified by Zacharias Hildebrandt at the beginning of the eighteenth century. Friedrich Ladegast rebuilt it in 1855, while respecting the magnificent case front, whose small towers of nine pipes each are a characteristic feature of organ building in this area of Germany. The design of the case gives particularly clear expression to the different tonal structures of the instrument. Liszt wrote his *Prelude and Fugue on BACH* for the inauguration of this instrument in 1855.

38 St. Cosmae, Stade, Federal Republic ▷ of Germany, Berendt Huss, 1668–73

Hw, Rp, Bw and *Ped*, with a total of forty-two stops. In 1674 the twenty-year-old Vincent Lübeck was appointed organist at St. Cosmae. At his request changes were made to the organ in 1688 and 1702 by Arp Schnitger, who was a pupil of Huss. Johann Georg Wilhelmy repaired the instrument between 1837 and 1841, and Johann Heinrich Röver made major changes to it in 1870. The display pipes were destroyed in 1917. On February 9, 1940 the instrument was formally christened the "Vincent Lübeck Organ" to mark the bicentenary of the composer's death. It was rebuilt by Paul Ott in 1948/9 and restored by Jürgen Ahrend in the years following 1972.

39 Parish church, Cappel near Cuxhaven, Federal Republic of Germany, organ originally built by Arp Schnitger for the Johanniskirche, Hamburg, using stops from a sixteenth-century organ by Jasper Johansen, 1680

The church at Cappel burnt down in 1810: following its rebuilding, Schnitger's organ was bought from the Johanniskirche in Hamburg and installed in 1816 by Johann Georg Wilhelmy. It may be noted that Schnitger inserted two keys (F sharp and G sharp) in the short octave of the first keyboard (*Hw*). The organ was restored by Paul Ott in 1937–9, and by Beckerath in 1976–7. It now has two manuals (*Hw* and *Rp*) and *Ped*, with thirty stops, Tremulant and Zimbelstern.

40 St. Ludgeri, Norden, Federal Republic of Germany, Arp Schnitger, 1686–8

Retaining a dozen of the eighteen stops from the earlier organ built by Edo Evers in 1616–18, Schnitger built a new instrument for St. Ludgeri in 1686–8, comprising *Hw*, *Ow* and *Bw* (on the same manual), *Rp* and *Ped*. There were forty-six speaking stops. The position of the instrument on a gallery at the right-hand side of the choir meant that Schnitger was limited to a single pedal tower, although there were historical precedents for this design. Schnitger, however, achieved a perfect tonal balance between the two departments, since the *Hw* and *Rp* point only indirectly into the church, whereas the pedal tower faces the congregation head-on. Various changes were made in the nineteenth century. In 1917 the display pipes were sacrificed to the war effort. Furtwängler & Hammer restored the instrument in 1929/30, reverting to the original specification. It was again restored in 1949, and in 1957–9 by Paul Ott. Fifteen of Schnitger's stops have survived, together with six by Evers; the remaining ones are by Furtwängler & Hammer. Jürgen Ahrend restored the instrument in 1981–2.

41 SS. Peter and Paul, Görlitz (Zgorzelec), German Democratic Republic, Eugenio Casparini, 1697–1703

Eugenio Casparini, or Eugen Caspar, was born at Sorau in Silesia. He was active for many years in northern Italy in the service of the Venetian Republic, and at the court of Vienna. The organ which he built at Görlitz with the help of his son Adam-Horatius and Andreas Silbermann represents a synthesis of Italian and Saxon elements. An exceptional instrument, it exercised a profound influence on other builders including Gottfried Silbermann and Johann Josua Mosengel. The case front, which is flat apart from the pedal towers at the sides, is the work of Johann Conrad Buchau and shows its indebtedness to the Italian Renaissance. The instrument is known as the *Sonnenorgel* on account of the eighteen "suns" or roundels each holding seventeen Pedal Mixture pipes and arranged as the spokes of a wheel. There were three keyboards (*Hw*, *Ow* and *Bw*) and an uncoupled *Ped* with twenty-one stops distributed among no fewer than six different chests.

42 Dom (Cathedral), Freiberg, German Democratic Republic, Gottfried Silbermann, 1710–14
Born in Saxony, Gottfried Silbermann studied with his brother Andreas in Strasbourg before returning to Saxony where he enjoyed royal patronage as organ builder to the Saxon court. He built four organs in Freiberg, of which the Cathedral organ was his first major commission. The influence of the Strasbourg school, notably evident in the absence of a *Rp*, is combined here with the northern German conception of the *Ow* and with memories of Casparini. The case was built by Elias Lindner, who was organist at the Cathedral, and the carvings are by Johann Adam Georgi. The organ remains intact with its forty-five stops, three manuals (*Hw*, *Ow* and *Bw*) and *Ped*. The case front was restored in 1967. (For the specification, in the original orthography, see Appendix.)

43 Dom (Cathedral), Freiberg, German Democratic Republic, Gottfried Silbermann, 1710–14, detail

44 Christkirche, Rendsburg, Federal Republic of Germany, Arp Schnitger, 1714–16
Hw, *Bw* and *Ped*, with twenty-nine speaking stops. Equal temperament was introduced in 1766; a Zimbelstern was added in 1775, together with a bell for the bellows-blower; changes were made by Mieck in 1820, and by Friedrich Schulze in 1827 and 1836. In 1879 Marcussen built a new instrument with thirty-three stops (*Hw*, *Ow* and *Ped*), retaining some of the old pipes. This instrument was altered by Paul Rother in 1921, and in 1927 electric action was installed. Improvements were made by Eberhard Toller in 1956 and 1960 in accordance with the spirit of the *Orgelbewegung*. A new organ was built by Karl Schuke in 1973, using five of Schnitger's stops and eleven of Marcussen's: *Hw*, *Uw*, *Bw*, *Schwellwerk* and *Ped*, with fifty-one speaking stops.

45   St. Georg, Rötha, German Democratic Republic, Gottfried Silbermann, with the assistance of his pupil Zacharias Hildebrandt, 1718–21
Inaugurated by Johann Kuhnau, the organist of St. Thomas's in Leipzig, this instrument is typical in its specification of the smaller type of organ built by Silbermann. There are twenty-three stops, two manuals (*Hw* and *Ow*) and *Ped*, Tremulant (*Hw*), and *Hw/Ow* coupler. Stephani added a *Hw/Ped* coupler in 1796; equal temperament was introduced in 1832; repairs were made by Urban Kreutzbach in 1832 and 1837; and in 1935 the Tremulant, which had been removed earlier, was replaced; further repairs were undertaken by Eule in 1979–80. (See Appendix for the specification of this instrument.)

46   Katharinenkirche, Brandenburg, German Democratic Republic, Joachim Wagner, 1725–6
Born at Karow near Genthin, Joachim Wagner settled in Berlin where he became known as the "Brandenburg Silbermann." He was one of the leading Prussian organ builders of the eighteenth century and responsible, among others, for the organ in Berlin's Garnisonkirche and the one at the Marienkirche, both of which have thirty or more stops and are close in their specification to the organs of Gottfried Silbermann. His cases are generally very ornate and enlivened by moving statues. The Katharinenkirche organ was substantially altered in 1898 by Sauer, and in 1936 by Schuke. The present instrument has forty-eight stops, three manuals and *Ped*. All that remains of Wagner's original instrument is the case front.

◁ 47   Nikolaikirche, Altenbruch near Cuxhaven, Federal Republic of Germany, Johann Heinrich Klapmeyer, 1727–30; painting by Johann August von Arnold. The first Nikolaikirche organ was built by Johannes Coci in 1497–8. It was a single-manual 12′ organ with six stops; a *Rp* was added in 1561 and a separate pedalboard in 1621. Substantial modifications were made in 1647–9 by Hans Christoph Fritzsche, son of the celebrated Gottfried Fritzsche. Further changes were made in 1697–9 by Matthias Dropa. Between 1727 and 1730 Johann Heinrich Klapmeyer, a native of Krempe near Glückstadt, moved the instrument to its present site, and enlarged it. The *Rp* remained almost unaltered, but both the *Hw* and *Bw* were new, as were the two pedal towers. Klapmeyer, it may be added, worked with his father Johann Werner Klapmeyer, who had been one of Arp Schnitger's pupils. The Altenbruch organ was restored by Karl Kemper in 1925, by Paul Ott in 1956–8 and by Rudolf von Beckerath in 1965–7. There are now three manuals (*Hw*, *Rp* and *Bw*) and *Ped*, comprising thirty-five stops, together with a Tremulant and two Zimbelsterne.

◁ 48 Benediktinerabteikirche (Benedictine Abbey church), Ochsenhausen, Federal Republic of Germany, Joseph Gabler, 1729–33
The fifty-one stops of this instrument were originally operated from four manuals (*Hw, Farbenwerk, Pos, Kw*), but this number was reduced to three in around 1750 when, for technical reasons, Gabler installed a detached console. Other important changes in the direction of greater simplicity were made at this time. We may note the existence of a Cuckoo stop which, when drawn, produces the sound of a cuckoo and causes a toy ox to emerge from its miniature stable in the central pipe tower of the *Rp*. First restored by Reiser and Walcker in 1939, the instrument only rediscovered its original potential at the time of its later restoration by Reiser in 1969–76.

49 St. Wilhadi, Stade, Federal Republic of Germany, Erasmus Bielfeldt, 1730–5
Three manuals and *Ped* with a total of forty stops. The history of St. Wilhadi's organ is one long series of disastrous fires. In 1511 lightning destroyed the church tower and organ: a new instrument, built in 1632, fell victim to the fire which ravaged the town in 1659. In 1724 lightning again struck and on this occasion destroyed the instrument which had been built between 1673 and 1678 by Berendt Huss and (later) by Arp Schnitger and which had already suffered damage during the Danish bombardment of the town in 1712. This organ was repaired in 1786 by Georg Wilhelm Wilhelmy, in 1824–5 by Johann Wilhelmy, and in 1875 by Johann Heinrich Röver. A *Rp* was added in 1937. This instrument was repaired by Paul Ott in 1963 and now has forty stops (*Hw, Rp, Bw* and *Ped*). The case and part of the pipework are original.

50 Benediktinerabteikirche (Benedictine Abbey church), Weingarten, Federal Republic of Germany, Joseph Gabler, 1737–50

The Weingarten organ has sixty-four speaking stops and five departments: *Hw*, *Ow*, *Uw* (or *Echowerk*), *Epistelpositiv* (*Bp*) and *Ped*. Additionally, there is a Tremulant (*Epistelpositiv*), Drum-stop (five pipes), Rossignol (two pipes), Cuckoo (four pipes), and a detached console necessitated by the astonishing window-embracing design of the instrument. Mention should also be made of *La Force* (forty-eight pedal pipes playing a C major triad from 4′ and perhaps intended as an alarm signal in place of a tocsin), the complexity of the (original) tracker action which allows four *Kronpositiv* stops to be played from the *Oberwerk* manual, and the existence of a pedal *Carillon* in the form of bunches of grapes above the console. A Barker lever was installed in the *Hw*, *Ow* and *Ped* in 1887 by the firm of Weigle. The instrument was restored by G. F. Steinmeyer in 1953–5, and by Kuhn in the period up to 1983.

51 St. Wenzel, Naumburg, Federal Republic of Germany, first organ built in 1613–16, rebuilt by Zacharias Thayssner (1695–1705) and again rebuilt by Zacharias Hildebrandt in 1743–6; case by Johann Goericke (1695–9)

Hildebrandt's organ, examined by Gottfried Silbermann and Johann Sebastian Bach, has fifty-three stops, three manuals (*Hw*, *Ow* and *Rp*) and *Ped*, two Tremulants (*Ow*, *Rp*) and a Zimbelstern. Modifications were made by C. F. Beyer in 1842, by Ladegast in 1915 and by Walcker in 1932–3, who restored the instrument to its original condition, while extending the compass of the keyboards and installing electropneumatic action. In 1954 H. Eule reintroduced the original sonorities.

52 Hofkirche, Dresden, German Democratic Republic, Gottfried Silbermann, 1750–5

The last of Silbermann's organs (he died in 1753), the Dresden Hofkirche organ was completed by his pupil Zacharias Hildebrandt and by his nephew Daniel Silbermann. According to Gottfried Silbermann himself, the various parts of the instrument were intended to display the following qualities: "Hauptmanual von grossen und gravitätischen Mensuren," "Brust von delicaten Mensuren," "Oberwerk von scharffen und penetranten Mensuren" and "Pedal von starken und durchdringenden Mensuren." The *Hw*, *Ow*, *Bw* and *Ped* comprised forty-seven stops. In 1944 all the pipework and the different console mechanisms were removed by Jehmlich and placed in safe keeping at the Monastery of Marienstern. The Hofkirche was destroyed, together with the organ case and blowing mechanism, on the night of February 14, 1945. Jehmlich began the task of restoration in 1962 and the new instrument was inaugurated in 1971. The case and its decorations were reproductions of the original organ case by Johann Joseph Hackl and the wood carvings by François Courdrai the Younger.

53 Prämonstratenserstiftskirche (Premonstratensian Abbey church), Roggenburg, Federal Republic of Germany, Georg Friedrich Schmahl, 1752–61; rococo case by Simpert Kramer

This organ, with its imposing case, is the most important of Schmahl's organs and worthy of being numbered among the great organs of southern Germany, including those at Ochsenhausen, Weingarten and Ottobeuren. It comprised *Hw*, *Mw*, *Ow* and *Ped*, with forty-three stops. A new instrument was built by Hindelang in 1905, with two manuals and *Ped*, and thirty-two stops; this instrument was superseded in 1955–6 by a new organ built by Leopold Nenninger, comprising *Hw*, *Ow*, *Kw*, *Rp* and *Ped*, and fifty-one stops.

54 Marienkirche, Rostock, German Democratic Republic, Paul Schmidt, 1766–70
In his day Schmidt was the greatest organ builder in Mecklenburg. The Rostock organ is an extraordinary two-story structure towering above the royal box. It had sixty stops, three manuals and *Ped.* Changes were made by E. Marx in 1791–3, and more substantial modifications were made in the course of the nineteenth century. In 1917 the metal pipes were removed and melted down for military purposes. As a result only a quarter of the original pipework remains, the display pipes having been replaced by cardboard imitations painted to look like the real thing. The instrument was rebuilt in 1938 by Sauer and now has eighty-three stops, four manuals (but five departments) and pedals. Only the lower part of the case front contains speaking pipes.

55 Former Benediktinerabteikirche (Benedictine Abbey church), Amorbach, Federal Republic of Germany, Johann Heinrich and Johann Philipp Stumm, 1774–82
This is a pre-Romantic organ behind a classico-Romantic façade, and is one of the largest of the Stumm family's organs, six generations of whom built some 340 instruments between 1722 and 1896. In 1782 the instrument had forty-six stops and three manuals (fifty-one notes) and a pedal department of twenty-five keys. It was repaired in 1838 and 1856 and rebuilt by G. F. Steinmeyer in 1865–8, when the number of stops was reduced to forty-five. Between 1934 and 1936 this number was increased to fifty-six, fourteen of which belong to the original instrument. Further restorations took place in 1964 and 1982.

56 Trinity Organ, Benediktinerabteikirche, Ottobeuren, Federal Republic of Germany, Karl Joseph Riepp, 1754–66
An admirer of Johann Andreas Silbermann, the Tyrolean-born builder Karl Joseph Riepp probably studied under Jörg Hofer in Ottobeuren and then with Merckel in Strasbourg, before settling first in Dôle and later in Dijon. He built twenty-two organs in Burgundy, in addition to the two organs at Ottobeuren and four at the Cistercian Abbey at Salem (1766–74). Built around a pillar in the chancel of the church, the two Ottobeuren organs, with their identical cases, form a unique structure in the history of organ building, a structure which demanded one of the most complex of mechanisms to be found in any instrument. The last of Riepp's instruments to have survived, these two instruments each assert their own individual personality. The Trinity or south-side organ (*Dreifaltigkeits-Orgel*) is located on the Epistle side of the altar and has sixty-three stops and four manuals (Hw, Rp, Réc [with a single Cornet half-stop] and Echo), in addition to the usual pedal department, and four Tremulants. Most of the *Rp* and Echo stops are divided. This instrument comes close in its design to the French aesthetic, with its Cornets, reeds and mutation stops. Only four Gamba stops betray its southern German provenance. The Holy Ghost Organ (*Heiliggeistorgel*) on the Gospel or north side of the altar has twenty-seven stops (Hw, Rp, Ped) and reveals an almost pre-Romantic concept of organ building. The two instruments, preserved intact, were restored in 1914, 1922, 1954 and 1978.

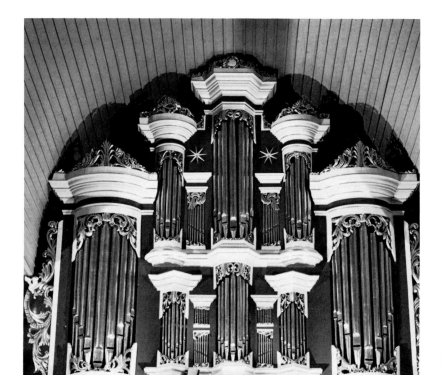

57   Church, Trebel, Federal Republic of Germany, Johann Georg Stein the Elder, 1776–7

Stein was a native of Erfurt in Thuringia. The Trebel organ had nineteen stops (*Hw*, *Uw* and *Ped*), a Tremulant, two Zimbelsterne (each of which had four very high-pitched bells known as *Krallenglöckchen*) and independent pedals. The instrument has been repaired on a handful of occasions and electric bellows were installed in 1945.

58   Neustadtkirche, Eschwege, Federal Republic of Germany, Friedrich Krebaum, 1838–9

Two manuals and *Ped*, with twenty-seven stops. An example of a neo-Gothic case front. Following various transformations in the course of the nineteenth century, a new instrument was built in 1929.

59   Stephansdom, Passau, Federal Republic of Germany, G. F. Steinmeyer, 1924–8

With its 208 speaking stops, this is a perfect example of the "outsized" organs built in Germany – and elsewhere – during the first half of the twentieth century, *cf.* Walcker's 220-stop organ in the Kongresshalle at Nuremberg (1936) and Sauer's 200-stop organ in Breslau's Jahrhunderthalle (1912). In its day the Passau organ was the biggest in Europe, spread out over four sections of the cathedral with no fewer than three consoles. A pneumatic console controlled the *Epistelorgel*, and a three-manual electric console governed the *Chororgel*, while a third console with electric action was positioned on the main gallery, its five manuals operating the *Hauptorgel*, *Chororgel*, *Evangelienorgel*, *Epistelorgel* and *Fernwerk*. The instrument is housed inside an imposing case, sixteen meters high, designed by the sculptor and architect Josef M. Götz and originally intended for the large organ built by Johann Ignaz Egedacher in 1731–3 (three manuals and *Ped*, with thirty-nine stops). The central flat was added in 1924–8. The instrument was rebuilt in 1980 by Wolfgang and Ludwig Eisenbarth, and now comprises five manuals and *Ped*, with 231 speaking stops, some of which have survived from the original instrument.

Central Germany

In their function and field of competence, the composers of central Germany may be regarded as mediators between the North and the South. They are neither confined to a state of majestic solitude as organists nor subject to customs which would obscure the distinctions between court and church by forcing them to perform as harpsichordists rather than organists. Indeed, the ascendancy of the Lutheran Reformation is more evident here in central Germany than it was in the South, and we must remember that the organist also acted as cantor. His task might extend to that of a director of music, instructing and forming both chorus and orchestra, as well as that of official and general administrator. His task of organizing the cantorate was frequently an arduous one.

The first half of the seventeenth century produced no composers of note in central Germany, with the one exception of Heinrich Schütz, whose style is clearly indebted to northern models. The later period, however, produced overtly Lutheran chorale settings of uncommon interest. M. Praetorius, a contemporary of Scheidt, has left a number of *Choralfantasien*, published in Volume VII of his *Musae Sioniae* of 1609, in addition to *cantus firmus* hymns in his *Hymnodia Sionia* of 1611. Embellished by figural writing in which the theme is the pretext for colorist treatment, his fantasias are notable for their imitative treatment of the different phases of the hymn-tune. In style, these variations remind the listener of the virginalists. By the same token, the hymn-tunes may be structured around a *cantus firmus* of long note-values in the bass, while the other voices give free rein to motifs developed in imitative style.

Composers such as Wilhelm Karges (d. 1699), organist in Berlin and harpsichordist to the Brandenburg court, Johann Rudolph Ahle (1625–73), organist at Mühlhausen, and Johann Friedrich Alberti (1642–1710), organist at Merseburg, treated the *Choral* in a great variety of different ways, composing works which were frequently intended for the manuals alone. The theme might be stated in the treble or bass ("pedaliter"). We may also mention in this context the capricci of the violinist Nicolaus Adam Strungk (1640–1700) which reveal considerable Italian influence, and the *Choralvorspiele* of Kauffmann, published in his *Harmonische Seelenlust* [The Soul's Harmonic Delight] of 1733 to 1736, a work intended as much for the organist's private pleasure as for the act of divine worship. Also noteworthy are the canzoni of Andreas Werckmeister (1645–1706), organist at Hasselfelde, Elbingerode, Quedlinburg and Halberstadt. Werckmeister was noted above all for his theoretical writings, published between 1681 and 1707, which deal with the organ, and the principles of temperament and figured bass. Nor must we forget the chorale settings of the various members of the Bach family in Thuringia: Heinrich (1615–92) at Arnstadt, Johann Christoph (1642–1703) at Eisenach, Johann Michael (1648–94) at Gehren, and Johann Bernhard (1676–1749) at Erfurt, Magdeburg and Eisenach. The majority of these works are chorale preludes, notably Johann Christoph's forty-four *Choraele welche bey währendem Gottesdienst zu Präambulieren gebraucht werden können* and Johann Michael's seventy-two *Verschiedene fugirte und figurirte Choralvorspiele* [Various fugal and figural Chorale Preludes] (including a number with variations); additionally, both Johann Michael and Johann Bernhard wrote chorale fantasias. Johann Christoph essayed the prelude and fugue as a form, while Johann Bernhard was attracted by the forms of both the fugue and the chaconne.

Zachow, organist at Halle, deserves mention, not only because he taught both Handel and Johann Philipp Krieger, but also because he wrote a number of distinguished works, including innumerable chorale settings, preludes, fantasias and variations, free preludes in the spirit of the *Toccate di Durezze e Ligature*, and various fugues. The twofold influence of Scheidt and Pachelbel is clearly evident here.

Johann Kuhnau (1660–1722), organist at Zittau and Bach's predecessor as cantor at St. Thomas's in Leipzig, is undoubtedly the first really important composer in central Germany after Scheidt. A man of vast learning, he was organist, lawyer, cantor and director of music at Leipzig University. Among his numerous works are the *Neue Clavier Übung* [New Keyboard Exercises] (1689 and 1692), *Frische Clavier Früchte*

[Fresh Fruits of the Keyboard] (1696) and *Musicalische Vorstellung einiger Biblischer Historien in 6. Sonaten* [Musical Depiction of a Number of Biblical Histories in Six Sonatas] (1700). One or two of Kuhnau's *Choräle* are intended specifically for the organ, and several other pieces may be adapted to suit the instrument. Preludes and fugues, prelude toccatas with variations (a form which inevitably recalls Froberger), toccatas (especially a Toccata in A major enhanced by a pedal part worthy of northern Germany) and fugues are found here in the company of two chaconnes which breathe the spirit of Pachelbel. The splendid biblical sonatas mentioned above are program works, including an astonishing piece describing the combat between David and Goliath which, thanks to the colorful registration, assumes a theatricality that lets us forget the work's relative poverty of inspiration.

Johann Gottfried Walther (1684–1748) was organist in his hometown of Erfurt and in Weimar, where he enjoyed a close friendship with Johann Sebastian Bach, who was his cousin and later became the godfather of Walther's eldest son. A historiographer and theoretician in addition to being a compiler and composer, Walther was also the author of a *Musikalisches Lexikon* (1732). The first dictionary of music to appear in Germany, it contained biographies and bibliographies, as well as technical information about musicians and music in general. A prolific composer, he produced almost three hundred works for the organ, the majority being a variety of different types of chorale, notably fantasias after the northern example (a novelty in central Germany), except that the melody is not divided here into separate sections. Walther also wrote chorale preludes in which the theme might or might not be embellished. The melody is generally developed in long note-values in the treble (especially in three-part works intended for the manuals only) or in the bass (for three- or four-part works with pedals), his preferred techniques being those of the bicinium and chorale fugue. Walther excelled at writing canons between upper and lower voices, and his works reveal an ingenious handling of chromaticism, ornamentation and imitation. His versets are rarely intended as independent preludes but are designed to alternate with the singing of the congregation. Particular importance is attached to the chorale partita: of his fourteen series of such variations, the most notable are his commentaries on "Jesu, meine Freude," and "Herr Jesu Christ, dich zu uns wend" [Lord Jesus Christ, turn Thou to us].

The freer forms which this contemporary of Bach's has left us include preludes, toccatas and fugues, to which may be added a concerto in five movements and fourteen transcriptions of violin concertos originally written by other composers – some evidently Italians, such as Tomaso Albinoni and Guiseppe Torelli, but others clearly Germans, such as Georg Philipp Telemann. The style which Walther adopted here is inspired by the ordered ideal of Pachelbel in his variations and freer works, but even more by the style of Böhm and Buxtehude; yet it also owes a good deal to the genius of Bach. Although we find none of the harmonic ingenuity, mystic profundity or bold symbolism of the composer of the *Art of Fugue*, Walther nevertheless reveals a sure and methodical craftsmanship, for he structured his works with elegance and skill.

We may finally draw attention to the wealth of harpsichord music written at this time by composers in both southern and central Germany, works which ought rightfully to have pride of place in any history of the instrument since they are comparable in quality to those of the great Froberger himself. The most important collections are those of Pachelbel (*Musicalische Sterbens-Gedancken*, 1683 and *Hexachordum Apollonis*, 1699), Krieger (whose *Musicalische Clavier Übung* [Musical Keyboard Exercises] of 1699 attracted Handel's attention), Zachow (*Neue Clavier Übung*, 1689–92), Kuhnau (*Frische Clavier Früchte*, 1696 and the sonatas of his *Biblische Historien*, 1700) and, of course, J. K. F. Fischer (*Musicalisches Blumen-Büschlein*, 1696 and *Musicalischer Parnassus* [Musical Parnassus], 1738). These composers are the precursors and inspired contemporaries of the great Leipzig master himself, whose harpsichord works they rival in their formal wealth and their concept of keyboard writing.

Bach's own works burst upon the scene with revelatory clarity in the first half of the eighteenth century. They were not only a revelation but a synthesis and an affirmation of the different contributions made by northern, southern and central German composers up to this time. But they were also an exception, coming as they did at a time of increasing disinterest in a style which was intrinsic to the organ. Composers now preferred to devote their attention to the sonata, a new genre which was taking on an increasingly precise form. Secular music was now the height of fashion, and was written for instrumental ensembles (symphonies, concertos and operas) or for solo instruments (sonatas). The great tradition of organ music achieved a kind of apotheosis in the works of Johann Sebastian Bach, which appear as some final, inspired swan song. A century was to elapse before the tradition was revived.

The Organ Music of Johann Sebastian Bach

Bach's organ works are without doubt the most numerous, most majestic and most magisterial ever produced by a musician. It would be futile to list, define or analyze the 260 or so organ works which the Thomascantor has bequeathed to the world.

Esteemed by his contemporaries as an artist who exercised supreme mastery over all the traditional forms, Bach was regarded above all else as an official whose task was to provide the church and court with music for special occasions. As a noted virtuoso and an admired and envied composer, he was nonetheless a subordinate member of the church's hierarchical structure. His works, and especially those written for the organ, could not withstand the aesthetic revolution which took place in the eighteenth century, any more than they could oppose the tide which inexorably turned attention away from learned music – of which Lutheranism was the final support – and directed it towards the theater and the concert hall. The galant style swept away the existing tradition, a tradition represented by the organ, which now suffered the consequences of this process of musical secularization.

Bach's works are a synthesis of all the major forms of Western music, and a culmination of traditional stylistic concepts. Even within his lifetime, Bach was the victim of his own erudition, which was that of a bygone age; yet even so, the rigorous language in which he expressed himself, with its mathematical precision, symbolism and religious mysticism, remained a prodigious and fertile source that would inspire many later composers.

For more than a century Bach's works fell into almost total oblivion, known and admired by only a few inquisitive minds who studied them with reverence. Mozart was one of the first to do so, followed by Felix Mendelssohn-Bartholdy who, encouraged by his friend and mentor Carl Friedrich Zelter, revived the *St. Matthew Passion* on Good Friday, 1829. The performance, held to mark the centenary of the work's first performance, left its Berlin audience stunned. No one doubted any longer the musical merit of Bach's works, his genius having stood the test of time. This rediscovery of Bach led to a renaissance of the organ when, on August 6, 1840, Mendelssohn gave a recital in the Thomaskirche at Leipzig, devoted exclusively to organ works by the great master. The program, which was carefully chosen to reflect the various aspects of Bach's writing, was reported by Schumann as follows: a short improvisation, the Fugue in E flat major with three subjects, the chorale "Schmücke dich, o liebe Seele," the Prelude and fugue in D minor, the Passacaglia in C minor (without the fugue), the Pastorale in F major, and an improvisation on the theme "O Haupt voll Blut und Wunden," including a fugue on Bach's initials.

If Johann Nikolaus Forkel, who was a friend of Bach's sons, forged a link, with his biography *Ueber J. S. Bachs Leben, Kunst und Kunstwerke* [On the Life, Art and Works of Johann Sebastian Bach] (1802), between the age of Bach and that of Goethe, then Mendelssohn, by dint of his ceaseless activity in the form of concerts and the first English and German editions of some sixty *Choräle*, roused the nineteenth century to an awareness of Bach and sparked off a vast movement in which Schumann and Liszt, among others, eagerly participated. Following its foundation in 1850, the Bach-Gesellschaft went on to publish a complete critical edition of the composer's works. This was followed in turn by the pioneering work of scholars such as Philipp Spitta (1873 and 1880) and Albert Schweitzer (1905 and 1908). With the passing of the

THE GREAT BACH FAMILY

In his *Ursprung der musicalisch-Bachischen Familie* [Origins of the Musical Bach Family] of 1735, Johann Sebastian Bach comments in an often somewhat caustic tone on the life and deeds of his forebears. He presents himself, above all, as continuing a family tradition in which the musician was a craftsman and a devout defender of a militant Lutheran faith. It was a family whose importance in the musical life of Erfurt was such that the town's musicians were known as the "Bachs" even after the members of that particular line had left the town.

It was also a family of which the great Johann Sebastian Bach could justifiably pride himself on being a descendant and whose line he was proud to propagate. Established in central Germany since the beginning of the sixteenth century, they continued to prosper there until the middle of the nineteenth century. Either as independent and amateur performers or as official musicians attached to a town or court, they played the cittern, violin, viol or organ, sang in church choirs or performed as strolling minstrels; they described themselves variously as Kapellmeister or Cantor, Spielmann, Hof-Musikus, Kammer-Musikus, Direktor der Raths-Musikanten or Stadtpfeifer. Disinclined to quit their native Thuringia, they concentrated their activities upon towns and villages in central Germany whose often prestigious names recur with leitmotivic regularity in the course of their biographies – Wechmar, Ohrdruf, Meiningen, Arnstadt, Eisenach, Schweinfurt, Gräfenroda, Gotha, Erfurt, Suhl, Schmalkalden and Jena.

The members of the Bach family were not only performing musicians but also composers, adding luster to their name with works of merit which bear the hallmark of the southern German style. After all, had not Johann Christoph (1671–1721) been a pupil of Pachelbel's? Among their works we may single out the chorale preludes, motets and cantatas of Heinrich Bach (1615–92) and Johann Christoph (1642–1703), the cantatas of Georg Christoph (1642–97), the cantatas and motets of Johann Michael (1648–94), the chorale settings and mass, and a Singspiel in the form of a quodlibet, *Der Jenaische Wein- und Bierrufer* [The Wine- and Beer-Crier of Jena], of Johann Nicolaus (1669–1753), the chorale settings, keyboard works and orchestral suites of Johann Bernhard (1676–1749), the cantatas and motets of Johann Ludwig, the Meiningen Bach (1677–1731), a musician particularly esteemed by Johann Sebastian, the Passion oratorio, cantatas, keyboard works, and violin and keyboard sonatas of Johann Ernst (1722–77), and, finally, the six "Concerts aisés pour le clavier," concertos for two keyboards, and cantatas of Johann Michael (1745–1820), who was also the author of a *Kurze und systematische Anleitung zum General-Bass der Tonkunst überhaupt* [Concise & Systematic Introduction to the Theory of General Bass, and Music in General]. Certain members of the family, including Johann Michael (1648–94), Johann Nicolaus (1669–1753) and Johann Michael (1685–?) were also active as instrument makers.

It was an astonishing family for a number of reasons, its members both warm personalities and characters of note: one thinks of Veit Bach (d. before 1578), the earliest member of the family to be mentioned in the *Ursprung*, a baker by trade who played the cittern to the sound of his grinding millstones; Johann Jacob (1682–1722), oboist in the Swedish army, who fought in the battle of Poltava and took flute lessons in Constantinople with P. G. Buffardin; Johann Michael (1745–1820), who traveled widely in the Netherlands, England and America; Johann Nicolaus (1669–1753) who invented and built a *Lautenklavier*, an instrument which combined the sonorities of a lute with the mechanism of a keyboard, and who was the author of a comic opera – not a work which one expects to find written by a member of the Bach family; and, finally, the twins Johann Christoph (1645–93) and Johann Ambrosius (1645–95), who could only be told apart by what they wore.

It was a family bound together by a sense of deep piety and by a Protestant faith which was both close to the soil and profoundly mystical, attractive as much for its elitism as for its communicative warmth, a sincere and living faith whose heir and propagator was Johann Sebastian Bach himself.

It was a family held together by a great sense of unity, delighting in annual reunions which took place in Eisenach, Erfurt or Arnstadt, sociable gatherings during which all those present would thank God for His blessings and catch up on events in the artistic and family lives of their numerous and prolific kinsfolk. But these occasions were also enlivened by laughter, for the Bachs were *bons viveurs* who derived pleasure from performing quodlibets in a spirit far removed from the grave and rigidly unbending aspect which might be suggested by accounts of the great Bach. Worth mentioning in this context are the thirtieth Goldberg Variation (Quodlibet) and two compositions written for his brothers, a *Capriccio in honorem Joh. Christoph Bachii, Ohrdruf* [Capriccio in Honor of Johann Christoph Bach of Ohrdruf] and a *Capriccio sopra la lontananza del suo fratello dilettissimo* [Capriccio on being Separated from his Favorite Brother], written on the

Romantic organ came a desire to return to a more classical instrument, a desire encouraged by the *Orgelbewegung* of the 1920s. These years not only witnessed a revival of the instrument but rediscovered the full scope of Bach's genius, as manifested by his works for the organ. The first instruments for which Bach wrote and to which he remained attached throughout the remainder of his life were the organ and harpsichord. From Mühlhausen to Leipzig, keyboard writing emerges as a recurrent motif, so to speak, in Bach's inspiration.

His organ works contain the distilled essence of a lifetime's thoughts, nurtured on the influences of the major aesthetic currents of the time which Bach constantly assimilated into his works. They breathe the spirit of Flemish and northern German organists such as Sweelinck, Reinken, Böhm and Buxtehude, central and southern German composers such as Scheidt, Pachelbel and Kuhnau, Italian masters such as Frescobaldi, Legrenzi and Corelli, and French composers such as Grigny and Couperin. As a synthesis of past achievements and the innovations of his own century, Bach's writing transcends all formal traditions without falling into the trap of fashionable *galanterie*. His concern was first and foremost for music as a sacred art form, a sanctity which he expressed in all its aspects, while his inspiration, which was that of a devout Lutheran, remained indebted to the idea of musical truth as defined by the great reformer himself. The key role which the chorale plays in his work, in the form of cantatas, Passions and chorale preludes, was necessarily self-evident to him. Bach's organ works may be divided into four categories: chorale settings; preludes (or toccatas or fantasias) and fugues; pieces related to chamber music (including trio sonatas, two trios and a Canzona); and transcriptions, such as the "Schübler" chorales, and concertos.

The chorales

The chorale for Bach was not simply a pretext for setting a text to music or expounding a theme, but a means of illustrating what the text in question expressed.

Of the 170 chorales which Bach wrote, the form he adopted most often was that of the contrapuntal chorale in which a fixed theme is accompanied by melodic lines treated imitatively. Occasionally Bach adds a canonic version of the tune at an interval of an octave or a fifth, the *Orgel-Büchlein* offering the best examples of this style of writing. The trio chorale, whose form is inspired by that of the Italianate sonata, enlivens the theme by means of arabesques in the other two voices. Whenever the counterpoint adopts the stricter form of a fugue, as is the case with the chorale fugue, Bach constructs architectures of vast dimensions (large-scale chorale fugues with pedals) or else fashions elegant fughettas in three or four parts written for the manuals only. As the fugue freed itself from certain constraints and left more and more scope to the composer's imagination, the figural chorale came into being, the melody giving rise to expressive writing dictated by the meaning of each phrase of the hymn ("O Lamm Gottes, unschuldig" [Oh guiltless Lamb of God; BWV 656]) When Bach describes a work as a "fantasia," he is consciously taking liberties with the traditional form of the piece. The latter may be embellished by non-thematic passages, as in "Valet will ich dir geben" [I bid thee now farewell] (BWV 735). The chorale partita is a form based on the idea of variation: the variations are not necessarily bound up with a verset of the melody, but the theme and its character will always shine through the texture of the piece. The first variation is a vertical harmonization of the hymn-tune ("Christ ist erstanden," Christ is risen; BWV 627). Another work in the same form which also deserves to be mentioned here is the canonic variations on the hymn-tune "Vom Himmel hoch da komm ich her" ([From Heaven above to us I come] (BWV 769), in which the technique adopted by Bach reveals the form's affinity with that of the canon chorale. A simpler form is the harmonized chorale in which each note of the theme is underlined by means of a single chord, the theme occasionally being embellished by linking passages between the periods which are vertically conceived. But the freedom which Bach allows himself in these linking passages is such that we can readily understand the disarray of the congregation who complained that it was impossible for them to follow the cantor.

The form which best embodies the profound and poetical lyricism of Bach's faith is that of the ornamental chorale. Here he reveals himself as Buxtehude's most responsive disciple, the subject being embellished with ornaments which highlight the meaning of the text. The most notable examples are "Das alte Jahr vergangen ist" [The old year now has passed away] (BWV 614), "O Mensch, bewein' dein' Sünde gross" [Oh man, thy grievous sin bewail] (BWV 622), "Ich ruf' zu dir, Herr Jesu Christ" [I call to Thee, Lord Jesus Christ] (BWV 639), "Schmücke dich, o liebe Seele" (BWV 654), "An Wasserflüssen Babylon" (BWV 653b) and "Herzlich tut mich verlangen" [I long with all my heart] (BWV 727).

Bach also conceived of large-scale collections grouping the chorales together according to their liturgical sequence, or else according to the spirit of the works in question. The *Orgel-Büchlein* (BWV 599–644), whose composition extended from 1713 to 1717, was originally conceived as a major compilation of 163 chorales. In the event Bach wrote only forty-five – forty-six if we distinguish the two versions of "Liebster Jesu, wir sind hier" [Dearest Jesu, we are here], intended for organists that they might "be given guidance in all sorts of ways of treating a hymn, as well as becoming competent in the use of the pedal" ("auff allerhand Arth einen Choral durchzuführen, anbey auch sich im Pedalstudio zu habilitiren"). This collection, which may be seen as a perfect distillation of the numerous technical difficulties which the organist had to overcome, includes the three principal types of chorale, namely the contrapuntal chorale, the ornamental chorale and the chorale canon. Above all, it is a marvelous commentary on the complete cycle of the liturgical year: as Couperin had done in his two masses and as Bach himself was to do in the third part of his *Clavier Übung* [Keyboard Exercises], the Leipzig composer offers organists one of the most extraordinary summations of meditative music ever intended for the act of divine worship.

As is well known, Bach published four separate volumes each bearing the title *Clavier Übung*. The first two and the last were written for the harpsichord and comprise the six Partitas of 1731 (BWV 825–830), the *Italian Concerto* (BWV 971) and *Overture in the French Style* in B minor (BWV 831), both published in 1735, and the *Goldberg Variations* of 1741-2 (BWV 988). The third volume (BWV 669–689) is devoted to the organ. Published in 1739, it was intended "for the edification of all lovers of such works, and especially of connoisseurs" ("denen Liebhabern, und besonders denen Kennern von dergleichen Arbeit, zur Gemüths Ergezung"). Bach apparently wished to give all organists, whether virtuosos or not, the possibility of adding luster to the Lutheran service with its Kyrie, Gloria, Commandments, Creed, Lord's Prayer, Baptism, De Profundis and Communion. This helps to explain the two versions contained in this volume, the one more elaborate in its style of writing and techniques, including the use of pedals (even pedal doppio in the large-scale chorale "Aus tiefer Not schrei ich zu dir" [BWV 686]), the other more modest and written for the manuals only. As a reflection of Luther's two catechisms (the so-called large catechism chorale in Latin for theologians and cultivated listeners, the small catechism chorale in German for children and the common people), this double approach has the added advantage of allowing the organist to perform the piece either on a large organ or on a more modest instrument such as a positive. This third part of the *Clavier Übung* is a regrouping of twenty-one chorales (or "Dogma in music") and four duetti, framed by the magnificent Prelude and fugue in E flat major (BWV 552).

One feature which stands out in this prodigious fresco, as it does in the majority of Bach's works, is the ease with which the composer handles numerical symbolism, the search for such mysteries being a passionate concern, most notably, of the musicologist Friedrich Smend. The figure 27, the number of works in the compilation, represents the numerical value of the initials J (9) and S (18), when added together. Above all, it is a number which exalts the Trinity, inasmuch as 27 = 3 to the power of 3. This trinitarian symbolism dominates both the prelude and the fugue. The key signature implies the existence of three flats, and the two pieces each comprise three subjects

occasion of Johann Jacob's departure for Sweden. This desire to be part of a cohesive unit is typical not only of Johann Sebastian and his attempts to research his family's origins, but also of his son Carl Philipp Emanuel (1714–88), who annotated and corrected his father's genealogy, as well as establishing and annotating a collection of works composed by various members of his family, the *Alt-Bachisches Archiv*.

It was a truly exceptional family, whose members not only propagated their faith but perpetuated their innate musical qualities, qualities which could blossom only in a region where the multiple ideas of the North and South came together. Central Germany was a melting pot in which the catalyzing influences of European music would produce an amalgam whose rich potential was soon to be discovered: and it was the genius of Johann Sebastian Bach which would take up with keen enthusiasm the options offered by his native Thuringia.

JOHANN SEBASTIAN BACH

Whether the Bach family was of Magyar or German origin – and the issue is unlikely ever to be resolved – the earliest of Bach's known forebears was *Veit* Bach, who was probably born in Moravia or Slovakia and who settled in Wechmar around 1545. A miller and baker by trade, he spent his leisure hours playing the "cythringen," a guitar-shaped cittern. One of his sons, Lips, died in 1620, and another, *Johann* or Hans (c. 1550-1626), the great-grandfather of Johann Sebastian, was apprenticed to Matz Zisecke, a *Stadtpfeifer* (town musician) in Gotha. Johann lived in Wechmar but performed as a *Spielmann* or minstrel in Gotha, Arnstadt, Erfurt, Eisenach, Schmalkalden and Suhl. He died of the plague in 1626, leaving three sons, Johann, *Christoph* and Heinrich. Christoph (1613–61) held appointments at the court of Weimar and, later, in the town of Erfurt where he joined the company of musicians under the leadership of his brother Johann, the town's "Direktor der Raths-Musikanten" (Director of the Council Musicians) and organist at the Predigerkirche. He subsequently rejoined his other brother Heinrich in Arnstadt and there became "Gräflicher Hof- und Stadt-Musikus" (Court and Town Musician). His three sons were Georg Christoph (1642–97) and the twins Johann Christoph (1645–93) and *Johann Ambrosius* (1645–95), the last of whom was the father of Johann Sebastian. Having studied the violin with his father, Johann Ambrosius became violinist in the Erfurt town music in 1667, remaining there until 1671 when he succeeded his cousin

Johann Christian, the son of Johann, as "Stadt- und Hof-Musikus" in Eisenach. Johann Christian was the first member of the Bach family to settle in Eisenach.

Johann Sebastian Bach, the fourth son (and eighth child) of Johann Ambrosius and Elisabeth Lämmerhirt, was born in Eisenach on March 21, 1685. Parallel to his musical training at the Lateinschule, he appears to have received violin lessons from his father, and also had opportunities to hear his cousin Johann Christoph (1642–1703), the son of Heinrich, perform on the organ in the St. Georgenkirche, Eisenach.

The formative years (1695–1708): Ohrdruf, Lüneburg, Weimar, Arnstadt, Mühlhausen

Following the death of his mother in 1694 and his father the following year, Johann Sebastian was taken in by his elder brother, Johann Christoph (1671–1721), a former pupil of Pachelbel's and organist at Michaeliskirche in Ohrdruf. It was from Johann Christoph that the young Johann Sebastian learned the art of keyboard technique. He left the grammar school in Ohrdruf in 1700 and proceeded to walk to Lüneburg, a distance of several hundred kilometers, in order to register at the Michaelisschule. There now began a period of fruitful discoveries for the young musician, who had a genuine thirst for knowledge and for copying out the great works of his predecessors and contemporaries. His love of learning also persuaded him to undertake a series of long and difficult journeys, often on foot and without any money, in order to hear the leading organists of his day. In addition to acquiring an indispensable grounding in the theory of music, he was also inspired by a desire to get to know the widest possible range of compositions: was it not said that at Ohrdruf, in spite of his brother's orders to the contrary, he secretly copied out pieces by Kerll, Froberger and Pachelbel, working at night by the light of a candle? At Lüneburg he stubbornly set about studying the scores in the school's well-equipped library, including works by Monteverdi, Frescobaldi, Cesti, Steffani, Carissimi, Lasso, Schütz, Hammerschmidt, Rosenmüller, Krüger and Pachelbel. It was also his wish to deepen his knowledge of the art of organ playing as it was then practised in northern Germany: in Lüneburg he listened spellbound to Georg Böhm, who had been organist at the St. Johanniskirche since 1698 and who may also have given lessons to his young admirer. He went to Hamburg, the center of Lutheran music, on a number of occasions to hear Böhm's old teacher, Reincken, who was organist at the Katharinenkirche, and he may also have heard Vincent Lübeck. And it was at the opera house in Hamburg, then under the directorship of

(the Father, a rhythmical, majestic theme; the Son, a melodic, human theme; and the Holy Ghost, a contrapuntal, aetherial theme) which remain subordinate to the first (the Father). This analysis may be taken a stage further when we turn our attention to the three large Kyries and the three small Kyries, and the three reworkings of "Allein Gott in der Höh sei Ehr" [All glory be to God on high] of the Gloria: the number 9 symbolizes the Word or Logos (which issues from the Father), but, inasmuch as $9 = 3$ to the power of 2, it also symbolizes the exaltation of the Trinity. By the same token, the six other parts of the Lutheran service are each illustrated by two chorales: $6 \times 2 = 12$, the number which symbolizes the Church; additionally, $12 = 3 \times 4$, a symbol of the bond between God (3) and the material world represented by the Cross (4). Thus the four duetti refer to the terrestrial world. Bach's works appear to us as outwardly straightforward, but beyond the melodic phrases, the harmonization and the inspiration, the composer sheds light on the ineffable mystery which only those may fathom who are initiates, in the cabalistic sense of the word. It is a vision in which the individual moment is grasped as a part of eternity: the art of the Thomascantor is a majestic link between heaven and earth. Inspiration, being a gift of God, is thus a manifestation of the structure of the divine world. Like the architects and sculptors of medieval cathedrals, the humble artist does not disdain to mark his work with a secret and fleeting imprint: the recurrence of the number 27 (= J S) has often been noted in the past, as has the fact that $14 = B A C H$, and $41 = J S B A C H$. Equally well known is the musical association of Bach's name, made possible by the alphabetical principle on which German musical notation is based (B = B flat, A, C, H = B natural). Thus Bach has placed his seal upon his life's work and upon a life that was entirely devoted to the divine.

In addition to the two large-scale compilations already discussed, Bach produced three other chorale collections: the "Schübler" Chorale Preludes (BWV 645–650), transcriptions of cantata movements which had been particularly admired by the general public, compiled at the request of the editor Johann Georg Schübler and published in about 1748/9. The *Canonic Variations* (BWV 769) were written in 1746 for admission to Mizler's Correspondirende Societät der Musicalischen Wissenschaften: these variations represent the culmination of the complex art of counterpoint, comprising five versets of three to six voices of increasingly spacious and elaborate structure. They are close in conception to the *Art of Fugue* and the *Musical Offering*. The "Eighteen" or "Leipzig" Chorale Preludes "of different kinds" (BWV 651–668), the product of many years' meditation, were assembled and copied out by Bach towards the end of his life, probably between 1744 and 1747. Vast in scope, these chorales are the final expression of Bach's creative maturity, revealing as they do his freedom of imagination, richness of polyphonic writing and delicacy of embellished melody. This list would not be complete without passing reference to all the isolated chorales, some of which are independent masterpieces.

The large-scale forms

Bach's works of a large-scale architectonic structure, originally intended for religious services, comprise in each case an introductory toccata or prelude, and a concluding fugue. They surpassed their initial limitations which brilliance and pomp imposed on this form and attained the perfection of a message addressed as much to the heart as to the mind, with arabesques and polyphonic writing in the prelude or toccata, and a hidden, intellectual *sensibilité* in the fugue. There are moments when imagination governs the virtuoso element, and others where formal constraints are all-important. Bach attempts the most varied forms, respecting their traditional structures which his instinct transcends with unfailing sureness.

In general, the prelude – as the first part of a bipartite work – may take over elements from the toccata, including its spontaneity and virtuoso character. It strikes out into space with elaborate pedal passages, drawing for its material upon broken arpeggios, scales, tremolos, and broken and staccato chords, and delighting in French-style dotted rhythms. Equally, it may abandon itself momentarily to a few bars of fugal writing or to the calm meditation of a recitative passage. It may finally grow expansive with the slow and stately progress of a rich polyphonic texture. The form of the fugue is never rigidly fixed. On the contrary, from his earliest youthful essays to the large-scale works of his Leipzig period and the theoretical summation of the *Kunst der Fuge* [Art of Fugue], Bach's mode of expression never ceased to diversify, tending towards an increasing degree of freedom – an organized, reflective and mathematical freedom which confers on the fugue the dimensions of an impressive solidity of thought and an impeccably structured progression: Bach's thoughts are fugally structured. Taking his predecessors' experiments a stage further and blending together the Italian and northern traditions, he explored the possibilities of constructing fugues of up to six voices, wrote the final *stretti* with an exuberant flourish, and concluded the work with a peroration in toccata form, embellished with numerous divertimento passages or extended by means of a da capo section borrowed from the concerto form. Thus Bach's fugues remain unpredictable in their development; they emerge as living, characterful personalities and evolve in such a way that the listener's mind is for ever kept on the alert.

Bach's large-scale works include twenty-six bipartite pieces comprising a prelude, toccata or fantasia, followed by a fugue; seven works of three, four or five sections, including the Toccata, Adagio and Fugue in C major (BMW 564), the Fantasia in G major (BWV 572) and the Pastorale in F major (BWV 590), together with a large number of individual works mostly dating from Bach's youth: *Allabreve* (possibly spurious), a Canzona, fantasias, preludes, fugues, the *Kleines harmonisches Labyrinth* [Small Maze of Harmony] (BWV 591) (probably spurious), and the *Pedal-Exercitium* [Pedal Exercise] (BWV 598).

The trio sonatas and concertos

All the works in this category are related to chamber music, and in each case it is the Italian model which is predominant. The trio sonata is inspired by the most traditional form of Baroque *musica da camera*, the sonata for two treble voices and bass, of which Corelli was one of the leading practitioners. The concertos, with their alternating sections of ripieno and concertino, are faithful adaptations of the concerto grosso. Trios occupy a relatively important place in Bach's works, whether they be pieces intended for the organ (most notably ten chorales and six sonatas) or instrumental compositions (such as sonatas for violin, flute or viola da gamba, and harpsichord obbligato). Whereas the classical trio required four instrumentalists, including a keyboard and bass for the continuo, we must marvel at the ease with which Bach has adapted this form to suit the possibilities offered by two manuals and pedals. Although the bass line retains its role as harmonic support in the slow movements of the sonatas, rapid passagework elsewhere helps it to participate as an equal member in the elaboration of the counterpoint.

Written between 1720 and 1730 for Bach's son Wilhelm Friedemann, the six Trio Sonatas appear to have been composed with a pedagogical aim in mind and intended for domestic performance on an instrument with two manuals and pedals. This traditional attribution, however, should not be considered as binding, since it will be clear from hearing the works played on an organ how much they gain from the wider range of tonal color which that instrument has to offer. In Bach's chamber music, the term "sonata" no longer has the Italian meaning of "a piece to be played on violins," but, equally clearly, it has not yet achieved the classical form of a movement with two contrasting themes. If the movements of Bach's sonatas sometimes develop two themes, they can equally well be written in the style of a three-part invention.

It was at Weimar that Bach discovered the Italian concerto and where, following the example of Johann Gottfried Walther, who himself had transcribed sixteen concertos, he wrote organ transcriptions of three concertos by Vivaldi (BWV 593, 594 and 596) and two concertos by the young Duke Johann Ernst of Saxe-Weimar (BWV 592 and

Reinhard Keiser, that Johann Sebastian discovered the Italian art of *bel canto*. He also paid a number of visits to the ducal court of Celle, where he perfected his knowledge of French music, a style to which Böhm had already introduced him. Bach studied the works of Marchand, Couperin and, especially, Grigny, whose *Livre d'orgue* he copied out almost in its entirety.

In 1703 we find Johann Sebastian as "lackey and violinist" to Johann Ernst, the brother of Duke Wilhelm Ernst of Saxe-Weimar. In July of that same year he was appointed organist of the Neukirche (formerly the Bonifaciuskirche) at Arnstadt; and it is from this period that his earliest organ compositions date – in addition to his earliest skirmishes with the church's undisciplined choristers.

The three masters whom Bach regarded as his models were Buxtehude, Reincken and Bruhns. He was never able to hear Bruhns, who had died in 1697, but he had the opportunity to admire Reincken in Hamburg. In his restless search for perfection and for a more profound understanding of the world of organ music, he owed it to himself to undertake one final pilgrimage to Lübeck to hear the great Buxtehude. Having obtained four weeks' leave of absence in October 1705, he made the journey on foot to the Marienkirche – and remained with the master for four months! Their meeting was a decisive experience and it confirmed the twenty-year-old youth in his career as an organist and organ composer. It also led to the loss of his post at Arnstadt, but the loss was soon made good by his appointment as organist at the Blasiuskirche in Mühlhausen in June 1707. The new appointment, which lasted only a year, was in succession to Johann Gottfried Ahle. On October 17, 1707 Bach married his cousin, Maria Barbara Bach, the daughter of Johann Michael. There were seven children to the marriage.

Weimar (1708–17)
Following the disappointments which he had suffered at Arnstadt, and the partisan feuding between the Pietist and orthodox faction at Mühlhausen, Bach accepted an invitation to enter the service of Duke Wilhelm Ernst in Weimar. His appointment there was as a chamber musician, playing the violin and viola – a role he found particularly congenial since he regarded the alto line as being "at the very center of the harmony." He was also court organist. These years in Weimar contributed towards his growing stature as a musician, allowing him not only to study Italian music of which the duke was a discriminating judge – Bach copied out the

works of Frescobaldi and discovered Vivaldi and his contemporaries – but also to make transcriptions of various works by the "red priest," a genre which Walther had already made his own. The results of this interest were the six organ concertos transcribed from works by Vivaldi and Duke Johann Ernst of Saxe-Weimar, and the sixteen concertos for solo harpsichord, which contain the seeds of a much later and highly personal composition published in 1735, the *Italian Concerto*. The years spent in Weimar were remarkable for the works which Bach composed for the organ, including the Passacaglia and Fugue in C minor, the great Preludes and Fugues, and the toccatas. The organist enjoyed an increasing reputation in Saxony and beyond as a great virtuoso and outstanding improviser. As an expert in organ building, he was called upon to superintend the restoration and construction of numerous instruments, including restoration of the Blasiuskirche organ in Mühlhausen (1709), and, at a later date, to submit reports on the instruments in the Liebfrauenkirche in Halle (1716) and in the Paulinerkirche in Leipzig (1717).

In August 1712 came news of the death of Friedrich Wilhelm Zachow, organist of the Liebfrauenkirche and incumbent of a post which Bach himself hoped to obtain. The salary, however, proved to be inadequate, and so he remained in Weimar where the duke had just appointed him his Konzertmeister. Although the new post required Bach to compose and perform one cantata a month, it also gave him the opportunity to conduct an orchestra, an experience which would later be of use to him when he became Kantor in Leipzig. It was in the autumn of 1717 that the notorious contest was due to take place in Dresden between the Weimar Konzertmeister and the famous French musician, Louis Marchand, the disgraced "organiste du roy." The encounter was organized by the duke in the hope of attracting the two outstanding keyboard virtuosos to his court. (It was a type of competition which was much appreciated at the time: one thinks, for example, of Scarlatti and Handel who took part in a similar contest in Rome in 1708 at the home of Cardinal Ottoboni.) But when Bach, who admired his rival's works and abilities as a performer, arrived to take up the challenge, Marchand had already left town.

Cöthen (1717–23)

Prince Leopold of Anhalt-Cöthen, the brother-in-law of Duke Ernst August of Weimar, had had an opportunity to get to know Bach personally on the occasion of his sister's marriage. An enlightened amateur

595), together with a minor work (BWV 597). Each score has been turned into a highly individual transcription that often requires considerable virtuosity, including the use of double pedals. Numerous, apparently insignificant, changes weigh down the text and make it impossible to perform these concertos at the speeds which an orchestra would adopt. In this way, the character of the work has been profoundly altered.

ORGAN MUSIC IN GERMANY FROM BACH TO THE END OF THE EIGHTEENTH CENTURY

In spite of the immense weight of Bach's authority, the music written for the organ throughout the German-speaking lands in the years following his death did little more than mark time. Having come under attack from new stylistic principles and from the fashionable idea of *sensibilité* or *Empfindsamkeit*, which asserted the claims of freedom of inspiration and hence the freedom of musical form, the polyphonic structure embodied by Bach's works – which seemed almost anachronistic – could not survive much longer. Church music began irresistibly to lose its inherent value, giving way to the new tonal ideal and, in consequence, grew increasingly impoverished. Its place was taken by orchestral music, opera and chamber music. What could organists do but adapt their art to suit the new fashion, lest they be deemed reactionary in perpetuating a style and old-fashioned forms which could only isolate them from the general course which music was now embarked upon? That is why, even in his own country, Bach's works were soon abandoned by the general public in favor of a style more in keeping with the time, namely a playful and galant lightness. It was therefore not surprising that major composers no longer wrote for the organ. Although the minor composers who did so continued to respect the older polyphonic forms and elements, they too were soon led to adopt the galant style. In this way, fewer musicians were tempted by large-scale architectonic structures, even less by learned reworkings of hymn-tunes. If they tackled such forms at all, it was with the imagination of an improvisator, so that the works they produced lacked the solidity and density of strict counterpoint and had no great sense of conviction.

Among Bach's successors who adapted hymn-tunes, either in a style close to that of Bach himself or else more in keeping with the newer fashion, were the following: Johann Tobias Krebs (1690–1762), cantor at Buttelstedt and Buttstedt, who was closer to Walther than he was to Bach; Johann Kaspar Vogler (1693–1763), organist at Stadtilm and Weimar, who wrote his *Vermischte musicalische Choral-Gedancken* [Mixed Musical Chorale Thoughts] in 1737; Johann Schneider (1702–88), organist at Leipzig's Nikolaikirche; Heinrich Nicolaus Gerber (1702–75), organist at Heringen and Sondershausen, who was not only a prolific composer but also a builder and inventor of instruments; Johann Peter Kellner (1705–72), organist and cantor at Frankenhain and Gräfenroda; Gottfried August Homilius (1714–85), organist in Dresden; Johann Friedrich Doles (1715–97), cantor in Freiberg and Bach's successor as Thomascantor in Leipzig; Johann Trier (1716–90), who worked in Zittau and who is best known for his prelude for three organs "in der heiligen Christnacht"; Johann Friedrich Agricola (1720–74), another of Quantz's pupils and organist in Berlin; Johann Philipp Kirnberger (1721–83), a leading writer on musical theory and violinist at the court of King Frederick the Great of Prussia; and, finally, Johann Gottfried Müthel (1728–88), Bach's last pupil and organist at Schwerin and Riga.

The art of chorale writing was continued in the eighteenth and early nineteenth centuries by composers too numerous to mention, but who include Johann Christoph Oley (1738–89), organist at Ascher and the composer of *Variirte Choräle für die Orgel* [Varied Chorales for the Organ]; Christian Michael Wolff (d. 1789), organist at Stettin and author of *Orgelübung-Vorspiele vor fünftzig Melodien bekannter Kirchen-Gesänge* [Organ Exercise Preludes to Fifty Melodies Based on Well-Known Hymn-Tunes]; Georg Philipp Telemann (1681–1767), the composer of *Fugirende und veränderte Choräle* [Fugal Chorales, with Variations]; Georg Andreas Sorge (1703–78), organist at

Lobenstein; Georg Heinrich Reichardt (1715–89), organist at Erfurt; Johann Georg Nicolai (1720–88), organist at Rudolstadt; Georg Michael Telemann (1748–1831), grandson of Georg Philipp and cantor at Riga; and Johann Gottfried Vierling (1750–1813), organist at Schmalkalden. Among the pupils of Johann Christian Kittel were Karl Gottlieb Umbreit (1763–1829), organist at Sonneborn near Gotha; Johann Ernst Rembt (1749–1810), organist at Suhl; and, most important of all, Michael Gotthard Fischer (1773–1829), organist at Erfurt.

Notable examples of the fugue, prelude and fugue, and toccata were produced by Bernhard Christian Weber (1712–58), organist at Tennstedt; Johann Christoph Kellner (1736–1803), organist at Cassel; Johann Wilhelm Hässler (1747–1822), organist at Erfurt; and August Alexander Klengel (1783–1852), organist in Dresden. Sonata form – often closely related to that of the trio sonata – was similarly developed by many composers, including Johann Ernst Eberlin (1702–62), organist at Salzburg Cathedral, who wrote his *IX Toccate e Fughe per l'organo* [Nine Toccatas and Fugues for the Organ] in 1747 under the influence of Bach's *Das wohltemperirte Clavier* [The Well-Tempered Clavier]; Georg Andreas Sorge; Johann Adolph Scheibe (1708–76); Johann Georg Albrechtsberger (1736–1809), who taught both Beethoven and Hummel; and Johann Wilhelm Hässler.

Bach's sons wrote very few works for the organ. Wilhelm Friedemann (1710–84), organist at the Sophienkirche in Dresden and at the Liebfrauenkirche in Halle, made his name, above all, as a brilliant improvisator whom his contemporaries thought uniquely capable of interpreting his father's works. He wrote a number of chorale preludes and fugues specifically for the organ. Less gifted as an organist, Carl Philipp Emanuel (1714–88) deserves mention for his *Preludio e 6 sonate* [Prelude and Six Sonatas]. As for the other sons and relations of the Thomascantor, they wrote only a handful of small-scale fugues and preludes for the organ.

Around the middle of the eighteenth century, there were two organists above all who merit attention, the first by virtue of the works he composed, the second by virtue of his theoretical writings. Johann Ludwig Krebs (1713–80), the son of Johann Tobias and organist at Zwickau, Zeitz and Altenburg, wrote a number of works which are without doubt among the most interesting of the entire period. His numerous compositions are related in both form and style to those of Bach, whose favorite pupil he was, and they reveal him as a musician of some talent, occasionally tempted by the idea of large-scale development sections. In his preludes and toccatas, his powerful technique gives ample scope to virtuosity and extended pedal solos. His skillful mastery of the fugue, where he delights in introducing attractive chromatic themes, and of the chorale, is surpassed only by his handling of the trio as a form, an excellence in which the example of his mentor is clearly discernible. It may be added that Krebs generally gives the melodic line to some solo instrument such as the oboe or trumpet.

One of Bach's last pupils was Johann Christian Kittel (1732–1809). Organist at Langensalza and in his home town of Erfurt, he continued his master's work both as a composer and as a practising musician. He was widely admired by his contemporaries and exercised a profound influence on other composers in Germany during the first half of the nineteenth century, notably through his pupil Christian Heinrich Rinck and through the theoretical writings he published during the final years of his life. The most important of these works were *Der angehende praktische Organist, oder Anweisung zum zweckmässigen Gebrauch der Orgel bei Gottesverehrungen in Beispielen* [The Young Practical Organist, or Instructions on the Suitable Use of the Organ during Divine Services, with Examples], published between 1801 and 1808, and his *Vierstimmige Choräle mit Vorspielen* [Four-part Chorales with Preludes].

Not only in northern and central Germany but in other countries too organ music fell increasingly under the domination of the symphony and of chamber music. Although a handful of composers attempted to remain loyal to the strictly liturgical art form, the decisive impact of the Mannheim school and Italian influence exerted an irresistible attraction, seducing musicians into thinking of the organ as a mere keyboard instrument for which they could compose sonatas, rondos and character pieces demanding pianistic and improvisatory virtuosity. In this way they abandoned the

and connoisseur of music, the prince invited Bach to settle in Cöthen where the post of Kapellmeister was waiting for him, together with the possibility of devoting himself to chamber music. Bach accepted, only too happy to be rid of the conjugate and rival demands of the two rulers, Duke Wilhelm Ernst and Duke Ernst August. The Cöthen court had paid Bach fifty thalers on August 7, 1717; but he had not counted on the refusal of Duke Wilhelm who, not wanting to lose his Konzertmeister, had him imprisoned from November 6 until his dismissal in disgrace on December 2.

Whereas the Weimar years had witnessed the realization of Bach's principal large-scale organ works, the years which were spent in Cöthen were given over to chamber music: the three sonatas and three partitas for solo violin, the six cello suites, a partita for solo flute, various sonatas for flute, violin, viola da gamba and harpsichord, the violin concertos, the six concertos "for several instruments" known as the Brandenburg Concertos, and the English and French Suites, not to mention the Inventions and first book of the *Wohltemperirtes Clavier*.

The court of Cöthen, strictly Calvinist in religious outlook, did not in fact allow Bach the opportunity to write for his instrument. He was able to perform only brief interludes in the course of the service and in that way to give an airing to the *Orgel-Büchlein* chorales. The pleasure and interest he derived from writing chamber music works throughout the whole of this period of exceptional calm in his life as a musician could not, however, satisfy him in the long run: his profoundly Lutheran soul aspired to a more intense expression of faith.

Momentarily attracted by the post of organist at Hamburg's Jacobikirche, where the organ had been built by Schnitger between 1689 and 1693, Bach played before Reincken, then in his ninety eighth year. The latter congratulated him on his improvisation on the chorale "An Wasserflüssen Babylon." But, having refused to pay the usual reception money which would have entitled him to take up the Hamburg post, Bach had to wait for the cantorate of the Leipzig Thomasschule to fall vacant before he was able to leave Cöthen. He announced his candidature following the death of Johann Kuhnau in 1722, and was finally appointed in the face of competition from a number of rivals. Bach seems to have been chosen more for his fame as an organ virtuoso than for his abilities as a composer. Having passed the obligatory theological examination, he was installed in his new post amid great pomp and ceremony on May 31, 1723.

Leipzig (1723–50)

The post which Bach had obtained was without doubt more onerous and disagreeable than the one he had left behind in Cöthen. Leipzig, however, had all the attractions of a large and prosperous town: it was not only a recognized center of music but a citadel of Lutheranism. Bach was thus free to give full expression to his profound faith, a faith which was to manifest itself not only in his major choral works but above all in the chorale settings which he wrote for the organ – and this in spite of the fact that in Leipzig he was no longer the incumbent of such an instrument. These were advantages which, at least at the outset, outweighed the crushing burden of work which the cantorate brought with it. At the Thomasschule, a boarding school for impoverished children, he had to teach Latin five hours a week and give singing lessons to the senior pupils. In his capacity as director of the town music he had to perform a cantata every Sunday and every feast day. Many of these works were of his own composition, and all were adapted to the liturgy of the day. Performances took place in one of the town's two main churches, the Thomaskirche or Nikolaikirche, a motet being sung in the church where the cantata was not being performed. Excepting the Sundays of Advent and Lent, and taking account of the exigences of the various feast days, Bach composed more than 250 sacred cantatas between 1723 and 1744. He also had to conduct a Passion each year during Holy Week, attend every service including marriages and funerals, and prepare his rebellious students – fifty-five boarders, only a third of whom he considered satisfactory – for the services which were held in the city's four churches. With the help of the eight town musicians (*Stadtpfeifer* and *Kunstgeiger*), he was required to mount performances not only in Leipzig's two main churches but at all the official functions which the town and university put on. It was a difficult task, made worse by the fact that the town musicians were not a capable and well-drilled band such as he had worked with in Cöthen, and he frequently had occasion to complain that there were so few of them, saying that ideally he needed eighteen men, and in desperation appealing to his most gifted students for extra support.

The task was exacerbated by the fact that the composer did not have the flexibility of character which might have been felt desirable by the school council and its rector, to whom he was responsible as a member of the teaching staff, and by the church consistory, to whom he was answerable as choirmaster. While recognizing his abilities, those in authority considered Bach to be incorrigi-

sonorities of the Baroque organ and its numerous tonal possibilities, and turned increasingly to colors which strove to imitate the instruments of the orchestra.

In Germany this identification with orchestral colors was largely the work of Georg Joseph Vogler ("Abt" Vogler) (1749–1814). He was a prolific composer, in addition to being a pianist, organist, "traveling virtuoso," inventor and writer on the theory of acoustics. He advocated a "simplified" organ with Principals, Flutes, Gambas and reeds but without the top notes of the Mixtures. His intention was to produce an instrument better suited to his improvisations, which fired the enthusiasm of audiences throughout the whole of Europe whenever he performed. He would unleash the most spectacular effects at his recitals by program music involving storm effects, of which Vogler was undoubtedly one of the leading innovators, sea battles such as the *Seeschlacht bei Abukir* [Battle of Aboukir Bay], pastorales (*Szene am Bach* [Beside the Brook], *Das Wetter im April* [April Weather], *Die Spazierfahrt auf dem Rhein* [Journey down the Rhine]), war music (*Geschrei der Verwundeten* [Screams of the Wounded] and *Jauchzen der Sieger* [Jubilation of the Victors]), the most terrifying events (*Der Einsturz der Mauern Jerichos* [The Walls of Jericho Come Tumbling Down]), and other exotic or African novelties or souvenirs of Vogler's distant travels. In a word, there was a hankering after sensational effects of a kind which other composers sought to emulate. One of these was Justin Heinrich Knecht (1752–1817). His most famous works were *Die Auferstehung Jesu* [The Resurrection of Christ] and *Die durch ein Donnerwetter unterbrochene Hirtenwonne* [Pastoral Idyll Interrupted by a Thunderstorm], which are particularly detailed in their account of individual emotions and atmospheres (e.g. *Sehnsuchtsvoll* [Yearningly] and *Etwas feurig und doch angenehm* [Con fuoco ma non troppo e gradevole]). This infatuation with tonal combinations and orchestral colors turned Vogler and Knecht, who wrote his *Tongemälde der Natur* [Tone Paintings of Nature] for fifteen instruments in 1784, into forerunners of Romantic expressionism, one of the best known examples of which is Beethoven's Pastoral Symphony.

Organ music in southern Germany and Austria, as well as in Bohemia, developed an increasingly melodic character, following the example of Eberlin. It delighted in figural toccata writing, a playful handling of fugal elements and simple tonal colors. This conception of course owed a great deal to Italian models. The result was a style of pure classical simplicity and works which could be adapted to the framework of the mass (where works of modest dimensions could serve as interludes) but whose worldly character made them ideally suited to grace the profane arena of public or private concerts. This development persuaded musicians to write works for solo organ such as sonatas, fantasias, toccatas and preludes, as well as compositions, including church sonatas and concertos, in which the organ was engaged in dialogs with an instrumental ensemble. Characteristic of this new but short-lived approach were the works which Wolfgang Amadeus Mozart (1756–91) wrote for the organ. These are surprisingly few in number when we recall how fond the great composer was of the instrument – "in my eyes and to my ears the organ is the king of all instruments," he wrote (1777). Nor did he ever miss an opportunity to play the instrument during his frequent travels, especially when he was in Italy. Among his works are three for mechanical organ (placed inside a clock): the Adagio and allegro in F minor (K.594) (funeral music written in memory of Field Marshal Laudon), the Fantasia also in F minor (K.608) with a polyphonic texture reminiscent of Bach, and the Andante in F major (K.616) of 1791, vacillating in spirit between melancholy, simplicity and theatricality. In addition Mozart wrote seventeen church sonatas in one movement for organ and various instrumental combinations. All these sonatas were conceived as interludes within the framework of the mass, and reflect an intense expressivity, while the organ, frequently reduced to the role of continuo, is given only a very few moments of solo writing.

Many keyboard concertos from this period breathe the same spirit of melodiousness and *galanterie*. Some were intended specifically for the organ, but in many cases could be played interchangeably on the organ, harpsichord or fortepiano. Some composers such as C. P. E. Bach even wrote alternative versions for flute, oboe or cello. Concerto writing was of course not new, having been a familiar form since as early as 1735 when Handel, a northern German composer living in England and influenced by the spirit and style of Italian models, had been one of its leading exponents. In this way the organ lost its fundamental characteristics in the course of the eighteenth century, growing increasingly indistinguishable from secular keyboard instruments of the time both in its style of writing and in its function. Besides, did not Baroque composers give our instrument the role of figured bass, encouraging performers to play short "organ phrases" (e.g. Haydn's Masses and Mozart's "Benedictus" in the C major Mass, K.259)?

Some twenty years after Handel, these concertos, which were generally conceived in three movements (fast - slow - fast), included a left-hand part whose function was often simply to support the bass, while the independent melodic lines were given to the right hand. The pedals - if they were included at all, which was rare - generally had only a supporting role to fulfill. The keyboard concertos dating from this period are legion. We can do little more than list the names of their composers, many of whom wrote several concertos. Musicians who were close to the Mannheim School include Carl Heinrich Graun (1703/4–59) and C. P. E. Bach (1714–88); among composers active in Vienna or in the southern German lands were Gregor Joseph Werner (1695–1766), Haydn's predecessor as Kapellmeister to the Esterházy family and the author of two Pastorelle for two violins, harpsichord and organ; Joseph Anton Auffmann, Kapellmeister in Kempten; Albrechtsberger; Antonio Salieri (1750–1825), an Italian by birth but from 1766 onwards a resident of Vienna; Johann Michael Haydn (1737–1806), the brother of Franz Joseph and the composer, notably, of a Concerto for keyboard and viola in C major; and, of course, Franz Joseph Haydn (1732–1809) who, in addition to thirty-two charming pieces for mechanical clocks, wrote three concertos, all in C major. Bohemian composers of this period include František Xaver Brixi (1732–71), Jiří Ignác Linek (1725–91), Jan Václav Stamic or Stamitz (1717–57), who later became one of the leading members of the Mannheim School; and Jan Křtitel Vaňhal (1739–1813).

It would be wrong to forget the Bohemian school of organ composers, a school as prolific as it was isolated. Poorly understood, because its works were long buried away in church archives and museums, Czech organ music was the product, here as elsewhere, of organists' improvisations during interludes in the mass. They drew on this "collective" fund of manuscripts and did not hesitate to appropriate and adapt the vast repertory of works which were available, comprising several hundred fugues, preludes and fugues, toccatas, pastorales and fantasias. These works reflect various stages in the development of polyphonic music in the eighteenth century. They generally consisted of more than one part and were expressive of a delicate atmosphere which was frequently elegant and occasionally refined in the art of chromaticism, and luminous in its simplicity. The founder of this school was Bohuslav Matěj Černohorský (1684–1742), a member of Prague's Minorite order, who made several visits to Italy, especially to Padua, where he was a pupil of the eminent contrapuntalist Giovanni Battista Martini. Černohorský taught numerous musicians and for the most part worked in Prague. Other Czech composers of this period include Jan Zach (1699–1773), whose works reveal a passionate and tragic nature; Josef Seger (1716–82), who was without doubt one of the most interesting contrapuntalists of this school; Brixi, the composer of *44 Sammelte Fugen für mich* [Forty-four Collected Fugues for my Own Use]; Vaňhal, a member of the Viennese nobility and, of all these musicians, the most prolific writer of fugues; Anton Zimmermann (1741–81), organist at Bratislava Cathedral; Jan Slávik (1748–1820) of Hořovice; Jan Křtitel Kuchař (1751–1829), organist in Prague and Stahov; and Antonín Reicha (1770–1836) who lived in France where he was the teacher, among others, of Liszt, Gounod, Franck, and Berlioz.

GERMAN ORGAN MUSIC IN THE NINETEENTH CENTURY

The first half of the nineteenth century is a period of transition in the German-speaking countries, at least as far as organ music is concerned. Here as elsewhere, the organ had no choice but to accept the changes in musical style which were taking place outside the church. Organ music was at best able to bask in its glorious heritage, for all

ble and work-shy. It was a situation which sorely tested the Kantor's patience and did nothing to calm his proud and often irascible temperament, still less his spirit of independence. Within seven years of his appointment he had begun to look round for another job, such as the one that had fallen vacant in Danzig.

As time passed, however, things improved: Bach handed over his strictly scholastic duties to three prefects, students chosen from among the ranks of the best choristers. He also placed a limit on the number of cantatas he was required to write, and was thus able to devote himself to the continuing exercise of copying out and studying the works of composers whom he admired, including Palestrina, Lotti and Caldara. In 1729, moreover, he assumed direction of the Collegium Musicum, which had been founded by Telemann in 1702 and was made up of professional musicians and university students. Together they performed concertos, suites and secular cantatas in one of the town's coffee shops. Bach also conducted expert surveys of newly built organs, a task in which he repeatedly showed himself to be demanding, meticulous and scrupulously fair. He gave recitals on instruments which he particularly admired, notably those of his friend Gottfried Silbermann, paid frequent visits to the courts of Weimar, Cöthen and Weissenfels, where he held the position of "Kapellmeister von Haus aus," traveled to numerous towns including Cassel, Naumburg, Hamburg, Erfurt and Dresden, where his son Wilhelm Friedemann had been appointed organist at the Sophienkirche in 1733, and twice visited the court of King Frederick II of Prussia, once at Berlin in 1741 and again at Potsdam in 1747, where another of his sons, Carl Philipp Emanuel, was harpsichordist.

As we have seen, Bach had sufficient free time in Leipzig to be able to undertake a large amount of traveling, much to the displeasure of the council and consistory, who had little interest in their Kantor's reputation, nor, it may be added, in his various titles, for which Bach himself had a particular affection: was he not called "Director Musices et Cantor," rather than simply "Cantor," and had he not in 1736 obtained the title of "Königlicher Hof-Componist" to the Chapel Royal of Dresden, at the court of Augustus III, King of Poland and Elector of Saxony? From a financial point of view, Bach was now able to live a life of ease, and his official residence, situated in the south wing of the Thomasschule, resounded with the cries of the thirteen children brought into the world by his second wife Anna Magdalena, née Wilcken, whom he married in

December 1721, five months after the death of Maria Barbara. It was at Leipzig that Bach wrote his greatest and best known works, including almost all his cantatas, the great oratorios, Passions, masses and motets, and, above all, the most highly elaborate of his works, the *Musikalisches Opfer* [Musical Offering], the Canonic Variations on the chorale "Vom Himmel hoch," a work written for L. C. Mizler's Correspondirende Societät der musicalischen Wissenschaften, and *Die Kunst der Fuge* [The Art of Fugue]. But the musician reserved his finest pages for the organ: the great Prelude and triple fugue in E flat major, the chorales of the *Dogma in Music*, the third part of his *Clavier-Übung*, the six great "Schübler" Chorales, the "Eighteen" and a number of other superb Preludes and fugues. The journey to Potsdam was the last which the Thomascantor undertook. His eyesight was growing increasingly weak, strained by long hours of copywork, of editing his own pieces and, in particular, of supervising their printing by means of copperplate engravings. Two eye operations carried out during the winter of 1749/50 by the English oculist John Taylor (who was later to operate on Handel) proved a failure. Now completely blind, Bach's general state of health continued to decline. Ten days before his death he recovered his sight, but then suffered a stroke from which he died on July 28, 1750. His final work, dictated to his son-in-law Johann Christoph Altnikol, was the chorale "Vor deinen Thron" [Before thy throne]. He was buried in the cemetery of the Johanniskirche. The body was reburied in 1950 at the Thomaskirche, Leipzig, in a stone sarcophagus which bears the simple inscription, "Johann Sebastian Bach, 1685–1750."

its attempts to assimilate the newer forms – forms born of an aesthetic based upon subjectivity and emotion, and upon greater independence of thought. It was an aesthetic forged by musicians for whom religion, and hence the organ, was no longer a central preoccupation and which logically was no longer suited to an instrument whose liturgical function restricted composers' creativity. Hence the rather unhappy marriage between the rigorous tradition of organ music on the one hand and, on the other, a modern artistic conception inspired by a more lyrical and subjectively emotional approach.

The same was true not only of organ music but of the instrument itself, now that its classical and contrastive sonorities were no longer adequate to the expressive demands of the new century: after all, had not the harpsichord suffered a similar disaffection? Musicians preferred the piano and orchestra, both of which were capable of producing shades of intensity as well as of expression. How could the organ hope to rival the drawing-room piano and the new infatuation for concerts, when it could not even manage to define its own identity either in the question of musical form or in that of its sonorities? Its conversion, however, was already in progress and, following the experiments of "Abt" Vogler and J. H. Knecht, organ builders such as Schulze and Walcker soon restored the instrument to its former youthfulness and gave it a new sense of purpose. But several decades were to elapse before composers deigned to write for the organ. In the meantime, what could organists do, in order to respond to the latest fashion in music, but borrow popular tunes from works then *à la mode*?

It follows that very few major composers addressed themselves to the organ and even fewer succeeded in renewing the language of organ music. They preferred the more spectacular forms of the oratorio and the mass. That is why, throughout the history of nineteenth-century German music, there was a large number of musicians, many of them organists, who wrote hundreds of works without ever finding an alternative either to a formalism which was wretchedly traditional or to a *sensibilité* which yielded to the tide of Romanticism but lacked the forceful vigor of that movement.

We shall simply list here the names of those musicians who stand out, among so many others, as representative of nineteenth-century organ music. The more significant composers of the period will be discussed in greater detail in due course. In the wake of the great theoreticians at the beginning of the century (one thinks in particular of Johann Christian Kittel, whose aesthetic theories reflected the heritage of Bach as seen through the mirror of nature and its vital forces, and Georg Joseph Vogler), the principal musicians who left their mark upon the leading German schools of the period by virtue of their style of writing and their teaching were the following: August Wilhelm Bach (1796–1869), director of the Institut für Kirchenmusik in Berlin, who influenced the northern German school; Friedrich Wilhelm Berner (1780–1827), organist in Breslau (now Wrocław), who was important for the Silesian school; Michael Gotthard Fischer (1773–1829), organist at Erfurt; the brothers Friedrich Schneider (1786–1853) and Johann Gottlob Schneider (1789–1864), both organists in Leipzig who, together with Fischer, influenced the Thuringian school; and Christian Heinrich Rinck (1770–1846), organist at Giessen and Darmstadt, whose influence was greatest in southern Germany. Other names include Ludwig Thiele (1816–48), organist in Berlin; Adolf Friedrich Hesse (1809–63), organist in Breslau, whose pedal playing amazed the Paris public when the organ at St. Eustache was inaugurated in 1854; Moritz Brosig (1815–87); Johann Ludwig Böhner (1787–1860), who was the Kapellmeister Kreisler of E. T. A. Hoffmann and Robert Schumann; Johann Gottlob Töpfer (1791–1870), organist in Weimar; August Gottfried Ritter (1811–85), organist in Erfurt, Merseburg and Magdeburg; Gustav Flügel (1816–87), organist at Danzig (now Gdańsk); Robert Schaab (1817–87), who studied under Mendelssohn, among others; Christian Fink (1831–1911), organist at Esslingen; Johann Nepomuk Hummel (1778–1837); Simon Sechter (1788–1867), organist in Vienna and Bruckner's teacher; Robert Führer (1807–61) and Julius André of Frankfurt (1808–80).

A pupil of August Wilhelm Bach, Felix Mendelssohn-Bartholdy (1809–47) may be regarded as a member of the northern German school inasmuch as his organ works are clearly traditional in their style of writing. They offer a perfect distillation of the German Romantic organ repertory during the first half of the nineteenth century. They include three Preludes and Fugues (Opus 37, in C minor, G major and D minor), written between 1835 and 1837 and dedicated to Thomas Attwood, and six Sonatas (Opus 65, 1844/5). We have already referred to Mendelssohn's seminal role in the rediscovery of Bach's works, most strikingly evidenced by his edition of the chorales, published by Coventry & Hollier in England and by Breitkopf & Härtel in Germany (1845), and by the numerous concerts which he devoted to Bach's major works. Mendelssohn's Preludes and fugues renew and revivify the Baroque style, while at the same time allaying its severity of expression with moments of mellifluous melody. His Sonatas, on the other hand, represent a remarkable fusion of the neo-classical and Baroque styles. Each of these six pieces is conceived according to an independent and extremely varied format and has nothing in common with the classical concept of the sonata. They are frequently enriched by chorale themes, solidly structured imitative sections, *religioso* recitative passages clearly reminiscent in spirit of the "Songs without Words," and fugues which are bold and flowing in style. The writing, it is true, remains within the pianistic tradition with its intricate passagework, arpeggios, staccato chords and lively rhythms.

In 1845 Robert Schumann (1810–56) wrote three groups of pieces for pedal pianoforte. All are the product of a marriage between the composer's traditional respect for Bachian counterpoint and a melodic sensitivity typical of the *lieder* writer. The works in question are six *Studien für den Pedal-Flügel* [Studies for the Pedal Pianoforte] in the form of a canon (Opus 56), *Skizzen für den Pedal-Flügel* [Sketches for the Pedal Pianoforte] (Opus 58), and six Fugues on the name BACH (Opus 60).

The organ works of Joseph Gabriel Rheinberger (1839–1901) must be accounted among the most impressive pieces written for the instrument in Germany during the whole of the nineteenth century. Rheinberger was organist at the Michaelskirche in Munich, and was also professor of the organ and composition at the city's Conservatory and a prolific composer of comic operas, orchestral works and religious choral music. Among the works he wrote for the organ are no fewer than twenty sonatas, dating from 1869 to 1901, twenty-two trios, twelve monologs, twenty-four fughettas, twelve meditations and twelve other pieces (Opus 174), not to mention a concertante Suite for organ, violin, cello and string orchestra (Opus 149), two suites for violin and organ (Opus 150 and 166), and two concertos for organ and orchestra, No. 1 in F major (Opus 137), and No. 2 in G minor (Opus 177). As Mendelssohn's *de facto* successor – his sonatas reveal an interesting spiritual affinity with the older composer's Opus 65 – Rheinberger adopts a traditional approach in his writing which shows an evident respect for the Baroque style; at the same time he declined to accept the nineteenth century's principal options. All his works, and especially the sonatas, are a summation of organ writing, conceived not only in the classical spirit but intended to be played on a classical organ (for example, there are no expressive markings in his scores to indicate how the piece should be performed). There are of course in these "program" works constant references to the freer style of the second half of the nineteenth century, including their harmonic writing and their construction, especially the "sonata" form. Equally typical of the period is their melodic style, inherited from Beethoven, Schumann and Brahms, and their "pathos" and range, with slow development sections, power of expressive utterance and breadth of style, together with a notable variety not only in the choice but in the number of movements. Rheinberger's style amazes the listener with its detailed handling of classical counterpoint, including canon, *ostinato* bass, passacaglia and, above all, the art of fugal writing at which Rheinberger excels. Many of his works deserve to appear in recital programs side by side with pieces by French composers of this period such as César Franck (1822–90) and Widor.

Gustav Adolf Merkel (1827–85), who studied under Schumann among others, was organist in Dresden and the composer of countless organ works in which, as in Rheinberger's, a Romantic spirit harks back to the Baroque. Merkel was able to turn his hand with equal facility to chorale preludes, fantasias, pastorales and three-movement sonatas, of which he wrote nine. Their style, now unstintingly or naively melodic, now powerfully supported by solid chords, is suited to the art of the canon, fugue and passacaglia. We may also mention here thirty pedal studies (Opus 182), in which Merkel exploits the possibilities of the pedal doppio.

The organ works of Franz Liszt (1811–86) are all exceptional examples of nineteenth-century musical style, among the most inspired and most revelatory of all the works produced during this period. With their superb combination of the instrument's orchestral power and its brilliant pianistic virtuosity, these large-scale pieces are, as it were, fantastic landscapes which the composer's imagination and profound mysticism peopled with lightning visions and sombre evocations and imbued with radiant conviction and an often fervent confession of faith. It is impossible to enumerate more than a handful of the thirty-five organ transcriptions which Liszt made of his own works, whether they be orchestral pieces (*Orpheus* or *Dante*), piano works (*Consolations, Am Grabe Richard Wagners* [At Wagner's Graveside], and the "Angelus" and "Sposalizio" from the *Années de pèlerinage* [Years of Pilgrimage]) or choral works (*Excelsior! Preludio zu den Glocken des Strassburger Münsters* [Excelsior! Prelude to the Bells of Strasbourg Minster]; *Die Legende von der heiligen Elisabeth* [The Legend of St. Elisabeth]; *Requiem* for male voice choir; *Ave Maria* and *Hosannah*). Among the original works which the Hungarian composer wrote specifically for the organ, five deserve special mention. The *Fantasie und Fuge über den Choral "Ad nos, ad salutarem undam"* [Fantasia and Fugue on the Chorale . . .] (1850) is a work in three parts, the last of which involves a fugal development of the theme. It is rhapsodical in character and enriched by pianistic arpeggios, pedal trills and virtuosic cadences reminiscent in style of a piano transcription which has taken on the dimensions of a brilliant symphonic poem. It is based on the chorale theme of the three anabaptists in *Le Prophète* [The Prophet] by Giacomo Meyerbeer, to whom the work is dedicated. The *Präludium und Fuge über den Namen BACH* [Prelude and Fugue on the Name BACH] of 1855 was originally intended for the inauguration of the organ of Merseburg Cathedral but, since the instrument had not been completed in time, the work was revised in 1870. Based on a theme formed by the four letters of Bach's name (i. e. B flat, A, C and B), it is without doubt one of the most majestic acts of homage addressed to the Thomascantor. It is written in the style of a large-scale toccata and enriched by passages of potent chromaticism. The vast tripartite structure of the "Variations on the theme of Bach" (1863) is based on the basso continuo of the first movement of Bach's cantata "Weinen, Klagen, Sorgen, Zagen" [Weeping, Lamenting, Sorrowing, Despairing] and of the "Crucifixus" of the *B minor Mass*. The work was conceived in 1862 as a piano piece following the death of Liszt's daughter, Blandine, and bears witness to a sense of profound sorrow. The *Evocation à la Chapelle Sixtine* [Evocation of the Sistine Chapel] (1862) is a large-scale fantasia transcription in four parts based on themes from a "Miserere" by Gregorio Allegri and the "Ave verum corpus" of Mozart. The final work to be mentioned here is the *Missa pro organo lectarum celebrationi missarum adjumento inserviens* [Organ Mass Serving as an Aid in Celebrating Chosen Masses], probably written in 1879.

One of Liszt's favorite pupils was Julius Reubke (1834–58), a composer who died tragically young. His legacy to the world is one of the finest works written for the Romantic organ, a sonata entitled "The Ninety-fourth Psalm," its single movement comprising three sections based on a recurrent motif made up of two elements, one rhythmic and the other chromatic. It is a brilliant and virtuosic orchestral fantasia, an example of program music which reveals an astonishing maturity on Reubke's part, although the influence of Liszt is never far away in the composer's handling of the theme, or in the harmony and figuration.

The important Austrian composer Anton Bruckner (1824–96), who was organist at the Augustinian monastery of St. Florian, was noted for his great skill at improvisation and for a profound mysticism which more readily found expression in his orchestral works, rather than in the ten or so short organ pieces which he wrote during his youth. But it is to Johannes Brahms (1833–97) that we must turn to find the most profound of interior monologs conceived for the organ towards the end of the nineteenth century. His eleven Chorale Preludes of 1896 (Opus 122) are a miraculous revelation of the composer's intense spirituality in his twilight years. Did he not twice set the chorale tune "Herzlich tut mich verlangen," and the even more poignant melody of "O Welt, ich muss dich lassen" [Oh world, I now must leave thee]? To these jewels, which are a concise encapsulation of two centuries of organ music, must be added a fugue and three preludes and fugues dating from 1855/6 which bear witness to the influence of Bach and Buxtehude, whom the young Brahms regarded as his great mentors, and two superb works written for chorus and organ, "Psalm XIII" (Opus 27), dating from 1856, and the sacred song "Lass dich nur nichts dauern" [Let nothing irk thee] (Opus 30), of 1860.

A composer who was misunderstood during his own lifetime but whose works nowadays appear on the program of almost every organ recital in Germany was Max Reger (1873–1916), who like Brahms, was faithful to the older tradition of Bach, whom he regarded as "the alpha and omega of all music." Reger succeeded where the majority of his predecessors had failed. He returned to the major classical forms without ever appearing academic. He made abundant use of the forms of the toccata, passacaglia, trio and chorale fantasia, and, even more fancifully, those of the fugue, canon and imitative style. Encouraged by the eminent cantor of the Leipzig Thomaskirche, Karl Straube, Reger subjected these forms to his overwrought *sensibilité* and intense mysticism, and to a tormented Romanticism typical of the *fin de siècle*. He produced more than two hundred works for organ notable for their compact strength, which is the result of the constant tensions between their polyphony and melodic line on the one hand, and, on the other, harmonies in which chords appear to clash in an irrational progression. The constantly shifting fabric of these pieces, woven with an intricacy of motivic detail which may at times strike the listener as mannered, nevertheless appears densely textured, while the chromatic writing of which Reger makes such frequent use may seem somewhat ponderous. However, the composer succeeds in carrying us along on the floodtide of his spellbinding virtuosity with its shifting chords and multiplicity of rhythms.

It is clearly impossible to list all of Reger's works here. A considerable number of character pieces (*Charakterstücke*, works written in older forms, such as Opus 59, 63, 65, 69, 80, 92, 129 and 145) and some of the chorale preludes (such as Opus 67, 79b and 135a) reveal a composer more restrained in his flights of fancy than in the large-scale works. Here Reger gives free rein to his imagination, which is as fertile as it is overflowing with ideas, and produces veritable symphonic poems instilled with a powerful sense of symbolism. Other works which deserve mention here are two sonatas (Opus 33 and 60), a number of chorale fantasias including "Ein' feste Burg" [A safe stronghold] (Opus 27), "Freu' dich sehr, o meine Seele" [Rejoice greatly, my soul] (Opus 30), "Alle Menschen müssen sterben" [All men must die], "Wachet auf, ruft uns die Stimme" and "Halleluja, Gott zu loben" [Hallelujah, to praise God] (Opus 52), free fantasias such as the *Fantasia and Fugue on BACH* (Opus 46), the *Symphonic Fantasia and Fugue* (Opus 57), the *Introduction, Passacaglia and Fugue* (Opus 127) and the *Fantasia and Fugue* (Opus 135b), and, above all, the variations which allow Reger a completely free hand in the art of elaboration and which clearly suit this composer best of all (*Variations and Fugue on an Original Theme* [Opus 73]). These works encapsulate the whole of Reger's strength, inventiveness and innovatory greatness. He stands at the end of a century whose inconsistencies he embodies. While adopting a classical approach, he was able to take advantage of modern chromaticism – a chromaticism which ushered in the dawn of a new era, foreshadowing atonality and even the serial music of the Second Viennese School.

The conjoint influence of Brahms and, above all, of Reger informs the works of the Austrian composer Franz Schmidt (1874–1938) and the German Sigfrid Karg-Elert (1877–1933). Schmidt wrote some fifteen works for organ, including variations, toccatas, preludes and fugues, chorale preludes and chaconnes, in a style which never strays beyond the confines of tonality but develops majestic frescos whose vastness recalls the organ writing of Anton Bruckner. Among Karg-Elert's works are a large number written for the harmonium, while those intended for the organ reveal a wide variety of different forms, including works on the *cantus firmus* of a hymn-tune or plainchant

60 Presbyteriumsorgel, Franziskanerkirche (Hofkirche), Innsbruck, Jörg Ebert, 1555–61. Fifteen stops: *Hw* (C - g^{11}a^{11}, 41 notes, short octave), *Rp* (FGA - g^{11}a^{11}, 38 notes, short octaves) and *Ped* coupled to *Hw* (C - b flat, short octave), coupler *Rp/Hw*, and Tremulant (*Zitter*) affecting every department. The case was built by Hans Perckhammer and the shutters painted by Domenico da Pozzo. The instrument was enlarged in 1770–1 by Caspar Humpel, and the number of stops was increased to twenty-six and the compass of the keyboards extended to forty-five notes. Ahrend & Brunzema restored this instrument between 1970 and 1976, reestablishing the original specification.

melody, character pieces, passacaglias, chaconnes, canzoni, partitas and fugues, together with many improvisations on chorale themes and other works redolent of a finely impressionistic atmosphere.

A number of composers such as Paul Hindemith (1895–1963) and Hugo Distler (1908–42) were influenced by the *Orgelbewegung* to write in a style traditionally described as "neo-Baroque"; and, although the principles of twelve-note music were employed by Arnold Schoenberg (1874–1951) and Ernst Křenek (b. 1900) among others, the majority of composers who wrote for the organ adopted traditional polyphony and used classical forms. The influence of the "neo-Baroque" conception, however, was crucial in allowing a style to crystallize which was more objective than had been the case hitherto. Of the countless composers committed to maintaining classical forms and the polyphonic tradition, the following are the most important: Armin Knab (1881–1951), Heinrich Kamiński (1886–1946) and, above all, Johann Nepomuk David (1895–1977), Karl Hasse (1883–1960), a pupil of Straube and Reger, who has preferred, however, the more spacious forms of the fantasia and fugue, the suite and the sonata. Hindemith made a notable contribution to the neo-Baroque movement with the works he wrote for the organ: his three Sonatas (the first two dating from 1937, the third from 1940) are an imaginative reworking of the classical form, in which spacious and sinuous melodies are treated with a rich thematic complexity. Hindemith also wrote two organ concertos, dating from 1928 and 1962, as did two other composers more prolific than Hindemith in their chorale settings, Ernst Pepping (1901–81) and Hans Friedrich Micheelsen (1902–73). Joseph Ahrens (b. 1904) recalls the neo-Baroque style in his hymn "Pange lingua" and the thirty variations of his partita "Lobe den Herren" [Praise the Lord], while the three organ sonatas of Hermann Schroeder (b. 1904) are consciously constructed on a *cantus firmus*. Helmut Bornefeld (b. 1906) and Helmut Walcha (b. 1907) have both shown a preference for chorale harmonizations.

One of the most interesting composers of the first half of the twentieth century was undoubtedly Distler, organist at the Jakobikirche in Lübeck, who appealed to a more virtuosic style in his desire to renew Baroque forms, which he reworked in complex rhythms. His organ works include two Partitas (Opus 8, "Nun komm' der Heiden Heiland" [Come now and save the heathen] and "Wachet auf"), thirty *Spielstücke* and one sonata. A similar conception informs the works of one of Distler's pupils, Siegfried Reda (1916–68), who wrote a number of chorale preludes and partitas, while a more traditional form invests the Prelude and fugue, and the Sonata, of Kurt Fiebig (b. 1908); the same is true of works by Anton Heiller (1923–79), among which we may single out his partitas, adaptations of Gregorian melodies, two sonatas and two concertos: one for organ and orchestra, the other for positive, harpsichord and orchestra.

One of the more fascinating questions concerning the future of organ music is the role of twelve-note music. It is a role which has been of only minor importance, since the advocates of serial music, with their evident aversion for the octave, have shown little enthusiasm for an instrument as fundamentally octave-orientated as the organ. Schoenberg wrote only one work for the organ, his *Variations on a Recitative* (Opus 40, 1940), composed in a style which, in spite of the work's serial treatment, is never able to break away completely from a central tonality. The piece nevertheless achieves originality by virtue of its highly compact contrapuntal writing, complexity of rhythm and constant use of dissonances. Other writers who followed Schoenberg in his handling of serial techniques include Křenek, Giselher Klebe (b. 1925) and Aribert Reimann (b. 1936).

In a later chapter we shall consider the avant-garde composers who, in their own way, have continued the Germanic tradition of organ music up to the present time.

61 Silberne Kapelle, Innsbruck, unknown builder, sixteenth century (exact date disputed)
Traditionally believed to have been a gift to the Tyrol from Pope Julius III, this Italian-built organ has no stopped pipes. The single manual (C c^{111}, 45 notes, short octave) has seven stops and the *Ped* (C - f, 14 keys, short octave) has one. There are four wedge-bellows. The ebony and gilt case displays the pipes of the *Principale* 8′ which, like the majority of the pipes, are made of cedarwood. Enlarged in 1614 (if not built at that date) and altered during the nineteenth century, the instrument was restored by Hubert Neumann in 1950-2. Electric bellows were fitted in 1956.

62 Positive, Hohenems, unknown builder from the South Tyrol, sixteenth century; Vorarlberger Landesmuseum, Bregenz
This sophisticated, Italianate positive has four stops divided into bass and treble at d^1 / d sharp^1. There are, accordingly, eight draw-stops. The 41-note compass includes a short octave of a somewhat unusual structure, in that the first three black notes are C, D and B flat. The bagpipes held by the figure at the very top of the case sound two Zimbel pipes. The instrument was restored by Walcker in 1956. (Photograph: pre-1980 state.)

63 Regal, Lambach, *c.* 1580; Kunsthistorisches Museum, Vienna   ▷
Table positive with an 8′ stop. Beneath the single keyboard (CE - g^{11}a^{11}, 41 notes) is an ebony panel ornately carved with cherubs and female musicians.

64 Augustinerchorherrenstiftskirche (Augustinian Monastery church), Klosterneuburg, Johann Georg Freundt, 1636–42
Freundt took over much of the pipework from an earlier organ built by Jonas Scherer in 1556 which had twenty-one stops, three manuals and *Ped*. He also used part of another smaller instrument from the same period with eighteen stops, two manuals and *Ped*. Both these organs had previously been repaired by Leonhard Marckhstainer in 1629–30. Freundt's *Festorgel* was made of tin pipes of exceptional quality and thickness, and had thirty-five stops on *Hw*, *Bw*, *Rp* (C - c^{111}, 45 notes, short octave) and *Ped* (C - b flat, 19 keys, short octave). The case, which was originally fitted with shutters, is the work of Jakob Khoffler, Konrad and Michael Schmidt, Georg Gemmelich and Max Peyer. The keyboards are of ebony, the draw-stops being wrought-iron levers. The instrument was repaired in 1716, 1821, 1832, 1885 and 1905; it was restored between 1942 and 1949 by Wilhelm Zika and his son, Kuhn, Johann M. Kauffmann and Rieger.

65 Wallfahrtskirche (Pilgrimage church), Frauenberg near Admont, unknown builder, 1680–5
A second keyboard was added in 1823 by Peter Hötzel (?), a pupil of Franz Xaver Chrismann. The organ was restored in 1978 by Krenn and now comprises eighteen stops, *Hw*, *Ow* (C - f^{111}, short octave) and *Ped* (C - g sharp, short octave). The pedal department includes a Bombardon 16', typical of the Admont region.

66 Kajetanerkirche (Konvent der barmherzigen Brüder), Salzburg, Johann Christoph Egedacher, 1696
This instrument, on which Mozart is known to have played on a number of occasions, is still in its original condition with the exception of a Salicional 8' added by Mauracher in 1930. It has a single manual of eight stops and *Ped* (including a *Sub-bass* 16') permanently coupled to the manual. The instrument was repaired after the Second World War. Worthy of note is the exceptional construction of this organ, in the balustrade above the chancel.

67 Pfarrkirche (Parish church), Scheibbs, Johann Moyse, 1724
Originally built for the Minoritenkirche in Stein by the privileged organ builder Johann Moyse, this organ was transported to Scheibbs by Ignaz Gatto in 1796, and it is from that time that the case decorations by Karl Stilpp must date. Drastic alterations were made by Josef Breinbauer in 1874, and further changes were made in 1938, when pneumatic action was installed. Josef Mauracher made additional changes in 1946–7. About a third of the original stops have survived. There are two manuals (*Hw* and *Pos*) and *Ped*, with a total of twenty-three speaking stops.

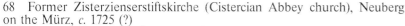

68 Former Zisterzienserstiftskirche (Cistercian Abbey church), Neuberg on the Mürz, *c.* 1725 (?)
Built around elements of an older instrument probably made by Georg Bredthaimer in 1598, this organ is characterized by its semi-elliptical structure. It was repaired in 1727 and 1734, and in 1754 was removed from the north gallery to the west gallery and enlarged. It now had two manuals and *Ped.* In 1897 Matthäus Mauracher transformed this instrument, bringing the total number of stops to thirty. In 1971–80 a new instrument was built by Gebrüder Krenn of Graz. It has twenty-seven stops, two manuals (*Hw* and *Schwellwerk*) and *Ped.*

69 Cistercian Abbey church, Zwettl, Johann Ignaz Egedacher, 1728–32
Egedacher was a member of the celebrated Salzburg family of organ builders, chief of whom were his father Joseph Christoph who built the organ at Salzburg Cathedral in 1703, and his brother Johann Christoph who enlarged the Salzburg instrument in 1705–6. The Zwettl instrument comprises twenty-seven stops, *Hw*, *Pos*, *Ped* (including a Pompardon in 32 Schueh, a rarity in Austria) and a third manual with eight half-stops. The case, which was decorated by Josef Matthias Götz, confines the three manual keyboards to a central section framed by two pedal cases. Repaired by Ignaz Gatto in 1755/6 and adapted to the Romantic aesthetic by Josef Breinbauer in 1880, the instrument was restored by Gerhard Hradetzky in 1983 and the original specification reinstated. There are currently thirty-five stops (including twenty from the original instrument), distributed among three manuals (47 notes, short octave) and *Ped* (18 keys).

70 Organ in the choir, Zisterzienserstifts-kirche (Cistercian Abbey church), Stams, unknown builder from Bavaria or Swabia, 1756–7
Blending harmoniously with the overall design of the choir stalls, this original instrument has a single manual (C - c^{111}, short octave) with eleven stops, and a Sub-bass 16′ in the *Ped* (C - g sharp, short octave), permanently coupled to the manual. The illustration shows only a third of the case front (*Prinzipal 8′*). Restored by Johann Pirchner in 1951.

71 "Brucknerorgel," Augustinerchorherren-stiftskirche (Augustininan Monastery church), Sankt Florian, Franz Xaver Chrismann, 1770–4. Chrismann, who was of Slovenian extraction, traveled in Italy, where he was inspired by peninsular ideas of organ building. The St. Florian organ originally had two (later three) manuals and a pedal department, with a total of seventy-four stops. The 32′ case makes it the biggest organ in Austria. It was restored in 1839 by Matthäus Höfer, who effectively completed Chrismann's work for him. Bruckner held the post of "Stiftsorganist" from 1848 to 1855, and it was on his instructions that Matthäus Mauracher rebuilt the instrument in 1873–5. There were now seventy-eight stops and four manuals. The majority of the old stops were retained, but they lost their pre-Romantic and Italianate character. The central case was raised at this time. Having been trans-formed by Gebrüder Mauracher in 1932, when electropneumatic action was installed and the number of stops increased to ninety-two, this instrument was rebuilt between 1945 and 1951 by Wilhelm Zika. There are now four manuals and *Ped*, with a total of 103 speaking stops.

72 Augustinerchorherrenstiftskirche (Augu- [stinian Monastery church), Herzogenburg, Johann Hencke, 1749–52
Vienna's "bürgerlicher Orgelmacher" was born in Westphalia. His 39-stop organ for Herzog-enburg has three manuals (*Hw*, *Rp*, *Kleinpos-itiv*, C - c^{111}, 45 notes, short octave) and *Ped* (C - a, 18 keys but only twelve real notes, short octave). The case – one of the most beautiful in Europe – frames a painted *trompe l'œil* depicting King David in a niche. It was com-pleted by Ferdinand Maurer in 1780. Trans-formed by Leopold Breinbauer in 1894, the organ was restored in 1964 by Gregor Hradetzky.

73   Benediktinerstiftskirche (Benedictine Abbey church), Altenburg, Anton Pfliegler, a pupil of Johann Hencke, 1772–3
Hw, *Pos* and *Ped* with twenty-five stops. Important changes were made in the nineteenth century, notably by Matthias Metall in 1847 and by Johann M. Kauffmann in 1880. Damaged during the Second World War, the organ was restored by Rieger in 1951 and again in 1977. Most of Pfliegler's pipework has survived. The black and gold case, with the *Positiv* positioned between the two large cases, is typical of this builder.

74   Pfarrkirche (Parish church), Bartholomäberg, Johann Michael Grass, 1792
French influence was clearly at work in the building of this instrument, which for a long time was attributed to Josef Bergöntzle, a representative of the Silbermann tradition in the Vorarlberg region of western Austria. Apparently built over an older structure, the instrument was "repaired and improved" by Alois Schönach in 1861, and in 1929 enlarged by Franz Gattringer who removed the short octave and extended the pedalboard to twenty-seven notes. The instrument was restored to its original state by Georges Lhôte in 1973. The single manual (forty-five notes) and *Ped* (18 keys) control a total of sixteen stops.

75   Piaristenkirche (Basilika Maria Treu), Vienna, Carl-Friedrich Ferdinand Buckow (Opus 50), 1856–8
Three manuals and *Ped*, with thirty-four stops. An unexaggerated representative of the Romantic tradition, Buckow's organ was transformed by Brauner in 1895/6. Electric bellows were installed in 1934 by Karl Soukup. In spite of these changes Buckow's organ has retained its personality intact. It was played by Liszt while still unfinished, and in 1859 and 1861 was chosen by Anton Bruckner for the test pieces he was required to play as part of his passing out examination to qualify as a teacher.

76 Detail of the display pipes and draw-stop knobs, Slotskirke (Castle church), Frederiksborg, Hillerød, Esaias Compenius, 1610

77 Slotskirke (Castle church), Frederiksborg, Hillerød, Esaias Compenius, 1610
Built for Heinrich Julius Duke of Brunswick-Wolfenbüttel, this chamber organ was bequeathed by the late duke to King Christian IV of Denmark in 1617, and placed on a gallery in the castle church at Frederiksborg. The instrument, which is a masterpiece of metalwork, cabinetmaking, marquetry and organ building, contains 1,001 pipes, the majority of which are made of different types of wood. The display pipes are of ebony and ivory, the pedals are of ivory, and the draw-stop knobs are of solid silver. Described by Michael Praetorius in Part II of his *Syntagma musicum* of 1619 ("De Organographia"), the instrument has two manuals and a pedalboard (short octave), with a total of twenty-seven stops. It has unequal temperament. Restored by Félix Reinburg, a pupil of Cavaillé-Coll, in 1895, the organ remains intact. (For its specification, see Appendix.)

78   Slotskapel (Castle chapel), Clausholm, Nikolaus Maass (?), early seventeenth century
Resited, restored and partly rebuilt around 1700 by the brothers Johann and Peter Petersen Botzen, the Slotskapel organ is a single-manual instrument with a compass of four octaves (with a short octave in the bass) and eight stops; the pedals are coupled to the manual. Originally fitted with shutters, the instrument was restored by Th. Frobenius & Sønner in 1963.

79   Sct. Mariae Kirke, Helsingør (Elsinore), Johann Lorentz, 1636
Following improvements carried out by Hans Christophensen Fritzsche in 1662–3, this organ boasted a *Hw*, *Rp*, *Ped* and twenty-four stops. It was in this form that Buxtehude knew the instrument during his period as organist at St. Mary's from 1660 to 1668. It was renovated in 1854 and rebuilt by Frobenius in 1960. It now has three manuals (*Hw*, *Rp*, *Bw*) and *Ped*, and twenty-nine stops. The *Rp* display pipes are from Lorentz's original instrument.

80   Kristkirke, Tønder
The *Rp* dates from the time of the first instrument at Tønder, built by Mathias Mahns (Meister Matze) in 1596. This instrument was enlarged by Johann Heide in 1630 and by Johann Heinrich Wernitzky in 1684–5, by which date it comprised *Rp*, *Hw*, *Bw* and *Ped*, with thirty speaking stops. This instrument was repaired by Johann Dietrich Busch in 1741, by Johann Daniel Busch in 1754, by Jürgen Hinrichsen Angel in 1786–8 and by Boye Lorentzen in about 1790. Major changes were made in 1894, and in 1927 by Marcussen & Søn. Th. Frobenius rebuilt the instrument in 1946, and it now comprises *Rp*, *Hw*, *Bw* and *Ped*, and thirty-seven stops.

81 Domkirke, Ribe, Johann Heide, 1634–5
The thirty-stop Domkirke organ was repaired in 1683–4 by Hans Heinrich Cahman. In 1845 the *Rp* was dismantled and rebuilt in 1856 at the church in Hostrup (Sønderjylland). The instrument was restored in 1937 by Th. Frobenius, and rebuilt in 1973 by the same firm. A copy of the original *Rp* was incorporated, with the result that the instrument now comprises *Rp*, *Hw*, *Bw* and *Ped*, with forty stops.

82 Domkirke, Roskilde, Johann Lorentz, Gregor Mülisch and Peter Karstensen, 1654
The first Roskilde organ was built by Hermann Raphaëlis (Raphaelssen) Rottensteen-Pock in 1555 and repaired by Nikolaus Maass in 1612. It was rebuilt by Lorentz, Mülisch and Karstensen in 1654, when a new case front was added. The original *Pos* of 1555 was subjected to a Baroque reworking. The organ now comprised *Rp*, *Hw*, *Ow* and *Ped*, and had twenty-seven stops. It was restored in 1833 by Marcussen & Reuter, in 1877 by A.H. Busch & Søn, in 1926 and 1952–7 by Th. Frobenius, and, finally, in 1975 by Jensen & Thomsen. There are now fifty stops, some of which date back to the original instrument. The three manuals (*Rp*, *Hw*, *Ow*) have a compass of C - g^{111}; the *Ped* compass is C -f^1.

83   Domkirke (Vor Frue Kirke), Haderslev, Peter Karstensen, 1652

Karstensen's organ comprised *Rp*, *Hw*, *Ped*, with twenty-four stops, in addition to a Vogelgesang and Trommel. Repaired by Jürgen Hinrichsen in 1732 and rebuilt by Amdi Worm in 1782, the instrument was again repaired by Jürgen Hinrichsen in 1792, and by Jürgen Marcussen in 1813. This instrument was replaced in 1893 by the thirty-nine-stop, two-manual organ built in 1863 by Furtwängler & Söhne for Hamburg's Nikolaikirche; the case was altered by Emil Hansen. Marcussen rebuilt this instrument in 1932, incorporating twenty-nine of Furtwängler's stops in his fifty-two-stop organ, which now comprised *Rp*, *Hw*, *Schwellwerk* and *Ped*. Marcussen and Poul-Gerhard Andersen were responsible for the 1951 rebuild, when the case fronts were restored and the number of stops increased to sixty-nine. This instrument was in turn rebuilt by Marcussen & Søn in 1977, and now comprises *Rp*, *Hw*, *Bw*, *Schwellwerk* and *Ped*, with a total of seventy-three stops. There are two consoles, one for the whole organ, the other for two manuals and *Ped*.

84   Parish church, Møgeltønder, probably built by Joachim Richborn, 1679

Richborn's instrument had nine or ten stops, a single manual and pull-down pedals. Repaired by Reinerus Caspary in 1730, it was restored between 1954 and 1957 by von Beckerath, who added an eight-stop *Rp* and seven independent *Ped* stops. This instrument, the oldest playable organ in Denmark, currently has twenty-five stops, of which eight (*Hw*) date from 1679. The illustration shows the instrument before it was restored by von Beckerath.

85   Domkirke (Budolfikirke), Ålborg, Hartvig Jochum Müller, 1750

Restored by Th. Frobenius in 1959, when a new *Rp* was added, the organ now comprises *Rp*, *Hw*, *Bw* and *Ped*, and has forty speaking stops.

86 Sct. Knudskirke (Domkirke), Odense, Amdi Worm, 1752
Hw, *Rp*, *Bw* and *Ped*, with forty-two stops. Rebuilt in 1862, and again in 1935 by Marcussen & Søn, the organ was radically altered and repaired by the same firm in 1965. It now has a *Hw*, *Rp*, *Bw*, *Crescendowerk* and *Ped*, with a total of fifty-six stops.

87 Organ case of *c.* 1370, made by the master organ builder Werner of Brandenburg; Statens Historiska Museet, Stockholm
The inscription on this case reads, "Hoc opus est Sundris per Vernerum fabricatum / In Brandborgh natum subtilior arte magistrum." Made in Sundre (Gotland), this case is the oldest surviving evidence of organ building not only in Sweden, but in Europe generally. It probably housed a Principal 4′ as a display pipe, and a *Blockwerk*. It is possible to make out the slots for the manual keys (eighteen keys in two rows), as well as those for the eight pedal keys.

88 Kyrka (church), Övertorneå
Originally built for the German Church of St. Gertrud in Stockholm by Paul Müller in 1608, this instrument was rebuilt by George Herman and Philip Eisenmenger in 1625, when a *Rp* was added, and by George Herman in 1647–51, when an *Ow* was added. At this stage the organ must have had a *Hw*, *Rp*, *Ow* and *Ped*, with thirty-five stops in addition to a Vogelgesang and Zimbelstern. It was altered on numerous occasions, most notably in 1780, when Mathias Swahlberg transported it to Övertorneå and removed the *Rp*. Restored by Grönlunds in 1969–71, the organ currently comprises *Hw*, *Ow* and *Ped*, and has twenty-five stops.

89 Kyrka, Torrlösa, unknown builder, 1628 (?)
Built for St. Mary's Church at Hälsingborg, Skåne, where the organists included Johann Buxtehude (from 1641) and his son Dietrich (1657–60), this instrument was transported to Torrlösa in 1849–50 and rebuilt there by Sven Fogelberg. It was later rebuilt in 1962 by Th. Frobenius, who added a modern *Rp*. It now comprises *Hw*, *Rp* and *Ped*, and has twenty-four stops, of which six are original, the remaining ones dating from 1850. The original *Pos* case has survived, as has its pipework.

90   Virestad, Hans Heinrich Cahman, 1690–1700; Smålands Museet, Växjö
Cahman was a pupil and son-in-law of Hans Christoph Fritzsche. The present organ was built for the church at Virestad, and transported to the church at Uråsa by Söderling in 1855, before being donated to Småland Museum in 1895. Restored by the Moberg Brothers in 1952, this single-manual organ (C - c^{111}, short octave) has eight stops.

91   Folkströms Kapell (chapel), Hallestad, Johan Agerwall, 1700
This single-manual organ (C - c^{111}, short octave) has a pedalboard (C - e) coupled to the manual, and six stops. Built for St. Lars's Church in Linköping, it was restored by Jonas Wistenius in 1741 and transported to the church at Vinnerstad in 1767. Repaired by C. Rylander in 1823 and by Becker in 1845, it was taken to its present site in 1870, and restored in 1953 by the firm of Moberg.

92   Kyrka, Fresta, Eric Mansson German, c. 1720
German was a pupil of Arp Schnitger's in Hamburg in 1712. This single-manual instrument with six stops and a Tremulant was built for Stockholm's Barnhuskyrka, and was transported to Fresta in 1788 by Jonas Ekengren. Restored by J. Grönvall in 1961, it currently has five stops.

93   Kyrka, Lövstabruk (Leufsta Bruk), Johan Niclas Cahman, 1725–8
The son of Hans Heinrich Cahman, this German builder kept alive the Nordic tradition of separate cases. The Lövstabruk organ was repaired in 1773 by Olof Schwan, in 1858, in 1933 by John Vesterlund, in 1946 by Bo Wedrup and Eric Dalin and in 1963–4, when Marcussen & Søn restored the instrument: it now comprises *Hw*, *Rp* and *Ped* and has twenty-eight stops.

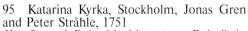

94   Kapell, Bingsjö, Daniel Stråhle, 1738
This eleven-stop instrument was built for Svärdjö Church; it was repaired by Mathias Swahlberg in 1770 and by Frederic Salling in 1774, when a pedalboard was added, coupled to the manual. It was modified by Salling in 1807, and by Gustaf W. Becker in 1870. In 1908 the instrument was transported to Bingsjö and rebuilt by Jonas Nylander. Restored by Harry Noberg in 1968, it now has seven stops.

95   Katarina Kyrka, Stockholm, Jonas Gren and Peter Stråhle, 1751
Hw, *Ow* and *Ped*, with thirty stops. Rebuilt in 1863 by Per Larsson Åkerman and Carl Johan Lund, who reduced the number of stops to twenty-five. A new forty-five-stop instrument was built in 1909, and rebuilt in 1938 and 1975–6. In each case the builders were Åkerman & Lund. The instrument now has fifty-six stops, including seven from the original instrument, distributed among *Hw*, *Ow*, *Schwellwerk* and *Ped*.

96   Kyrka, Järlåsa, Jonas Gren and Peter Stråhle, 1754
Built for the church at Västerlövsta, this instrument originally had ten stops and a pedal coupled to the single manual. It was transported to Järlåsa in 1882 by Daniel Wallenström, who had previously rebuilt it in 1855. Rebuilt by C.R. Löfvander in 1929, it currently has nine stops. The compass of the manual is C - c[111], while the pedal compass is C - g.

97   Kyrka, Hökhuvud, Olof Schwan and Mathias Swahlberg, 1783
Transformed by C. Granlund in 1857 and by Nils Hammarberg in 1936, this instrument was restored by Rolf Larsson in 1973–4. The single manual has a compass of C - d[111]; that of the pedal, which is coupled to the manual, is C - g. There are ten stops.

98   Kyrka, Västra Eneby, Sven Nordström, 1850
This instrument has survived almost intact. Restored by C. A. Lund in 1925, it comprises a *Hw* and *Ow* (C - f^{111}) and *Ped* (C - b) coupled to the manuals. There are seventeen stops. The dummy display pipes are original.

99 Sw. Jana Chrzciciela i Bartłomieja, Kazimierz Dolny, unknown builder, 1607–20
Restored in 1781 and 1883, this instrument retains its original specification, with thirty-five stops distributed among *Hw*, *Rp* and *Ped*. It is currently being restored.

100 Sw. Jakuba, Toruń (Thorn), Johann Hellwig, 1611
All that remains of Hellwig's organ is its case. It originally had two manuals, pedal, and twenty-three stops. It was rebuilt by W. Sauer at the end of the nineteenth century, and by M. Wybrański between 1920 and 1930, and now has two manuals, pedal, and twenty-seven stops.

101 Old Cistercian Abbey church, Chełmno, Christian Heymann (or Neumann), 1613–19; case by Anus and Hans Krüger
This instrument originally had three manuals, pedal, and thirty-three stops. A new instrument was built in the nineteenth century with two manuals, pedal, and eleven stops.

102 Cistercian Abbey church, Pelplin, Johann Georg Wolff and Daniel Nitrowski, 1677–80; case by Maciej Szoller
The original instrument had around forty-five stops distributed among three manuals and pedal. Rebuilt in 1870 by the Tertletzki brothers and repaired in 1898 by Julius Witt, the instrument was again rebuilt by B. Goebel and currently comprises two manuals and pedal, with a total of twenty-one stops.

103 Bernardine Abbey church, Leżajsk, Stanislav Studziński and Jan
Głowiński, 1680–93
Taking over where Studziński left off, Jan Głowiński completed an instrument
which is unique for the disposition of its eight cases: the *Hw* and *Schwellwerk*
occupy the center of the gallery, with the *Rp* in front; there are two independent side *Positive* with pedal pipes, two *Positive* in the side aisles and two
decorative cases against the side pillars containing the Vogelgesang stops. The
work of decorating the cases was completed in 1729; further work was carried out on them in 1904–6. The instrument was repaired in 1729 and in
1776–8, when the display pipes were replaced; it was restored by Roman
Duchenski in 1852–4, and rebuilt by Schlag and Aleksander Zebrowski, who
added Barker levers and adapted the organ to meet the demands of the
Romantic aesthetic. Repaired by Hasse in 1926, and again in 1958, the Leżajsk organ was enlarged and partly rebuilt between 1965 and 1967 by Robert
Polcyn of Organoton. At this stage the organ comprised forty-one stops –
fifteen of them new – distributed among three manuals and pedal; the toy-
stops included Timpanum, Cuculus and Avicula. Between 1968 and 1970 the
same builder restored and enlarged the north *Pos* (twenty-one stops, two
manuals and pedal), and rebuilt the south *Pos* (thirteen stops, one manual
and pedal). The manual compass is C - f^{111}, that of the pedal C - d^1.

104 Cathedral, Frombork, Daniel Nitrowski, 1683–4
Hw, *Rp* and *Ped*, with twenty-six stops, plus Totentrommel and Zimbelstern. The instrument was restored by Jana Staniszewski in 1702, by Mietke in 1804, by Scherweit in 1830 and by Terletzky in 1855–7; it was rebuilt by Emanuel Kemper in 1934–5, and by Dominik Biernacki and Zygmunt Kamiński in 1966–70.

105 Jesuit Church, Swieta Lipka, J. J. Mosengel, 1719–21
Two manuals and pedal, with forty stops. The case was completed in 1751 and is decorated with moving figures, while the central tower of the main case contains a carillon. Altered by Max Terlecki and B. Goebel in 1905, the instrument was rebuilt in 1945 and again in 1965 by Czesla Kruszewski.

106 Sw. Anny, Cracow, Szymon Sadkowski, 1724
This instrument was altered by Blazej Głowacki in 1816, by Sapatski during the second half of the nineteenth century, and by Aleksander Zebrowski in 1908; it was rebuilt in 1958–63 by Robert Polcyn, and now has twenty-six stops distributed among *Hw*, *Pos* and *Ped*.

107 Old Cistercian Abbey, Oliwa (part of Gdańsk), Jan Wulf (Michael of Orneta) and Friedrich Rudolf Dalitz, a pupil of Gottfried Silbermann, 1791–3. Dalitz completed the Oliwa organ, which had a total of eighty-three stops, including five at 32′ (four of which are in the pedal). There are three manuals (*Hw*, *Ow* and *Fw*) and a thirty-two-stop *Ped*, in addition to Zimbelsterne and twenty-five moving statues of musical angels operated by the Angelica stop. The case, designed by Wulf, was built between 1763 and 1788. Repaired by J. B. Wisniewski in around 1831, and by K. F. Schuricht in 1840, the organ was rebuilt in 1863–5 by F. W. Kaltschmidt; it was further rebuilt by J. Goebel in 1938 and by Dominik Biernacki and Zygmunt Kamiński in 1955. It now has 101 stops.

108 Týnskem chrámu (Týn Church), Prague, Johannes Mundt, 1670–3
This instrument, the oldest in Prague, has never been restored, although it was rebuilt by Josef Gartner in 1823. It has twenty-nine stops distributed among *Hw*, *Rp* and *Ped*, together with two Zimbelsterne.

109 Church of St. John of the Minorites, Brno, Anton Richter, 1732; case by Anton Riga
Repaired by Franz Seibler in 1847, the organ was "Romanticized" in 1928 by Jan Mudroch and now has twenty-four stops, two manuals (*Hw* and *Rp*) and *Ped*.

110   So-called Charles Church, Prague, Bedřich Semrád, 1733–40
Repaired by Vocelka in 1873, the organ was rebuilt in 1969 by the firm of
Igra, who more or less retained the original specification of sixteen stops
distributed among *Hw*, *Rp* (45 notes, short octave) and *Ped* (C - d^1).

111   Old Premonstratensian Abbey church, Teplá, Antonín Gartner, 1754–6
Hw, *Rp* (described by Gartner as *Brustpositiv*), *Tischpositiv* (C - c^{111}) and *Ped*
(C - c^1), with thirty-four stops. Altered slightly in the nineteenth century –
notably by Christoph Müller in 1891 – the organ was repaired by the firm of
Igra in 1960–1, and now has thirty-three stops.

112   Portative Organ, Györ, builder unknown, beginning of the eighteenth century; Xantus János Múzeum
Single-manual instrument (C - c^{111}, 45 notes, short octave), with four stops.

113   St. George, Sopron, perhaps built by Johann Wöckherl, 1633
Transported from Vienna to Sopron, this organ was restored in 1734, when it is possible that the pedalboard was added. Restored and enlarged in 1957 by a firm of organ builders (Johann Seidl) in Budapest, it now has two manuals and pedal, with eighteen stops, including those from the original instrument.

114   Roman Catholic Church, Fertörákos, Josef and Johann Wiest, 1784
This ten-stop instrument had one manual and *Ped*. It was restored in 1957–8 by a firm of organ builders in Budapest, who added two stops to the *Ped*.

115   Roman Catholic Church, Császár, unknown builder, end of the eighteenth century
Single manual and *Ped*, with ten stops.

116 Old Cathedral, Vilnius (formerly Vilna), Lithuania, probably from the workshop or school of Casparini, eighteenth century
Rebuilt by Juozapas Radavičius at the end of the nineteenth century, and by A. Schuke in 1969, this instrument has three manuals (*Hw*, *Schwellwerk* and *Ow*) and *Ped*, with a total of forty-nine stops.

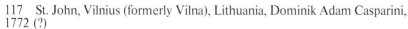

117 St. John, Vilnius (formerly Vilna), Lithuania, Dominik Adam Casparini, 1772 (?)
Built for the Jesuit Church at Polotsk, this instrument was transported to Vilnius in 1837, when a third manual was added by Tytman. It has thirty-nine stops.

118 Church, Tytuvėnai, Lithuania, Eugenio Casparini or one of his pupils, 1780
This instrument bears similarities to the organ in the Dominican Church at Vilnius, built by Dominik Adam Casparini in 1776. It has two manuals and twenty-four stops, in addition to a Zimbelstern, Paukenton and Glockenspiel.

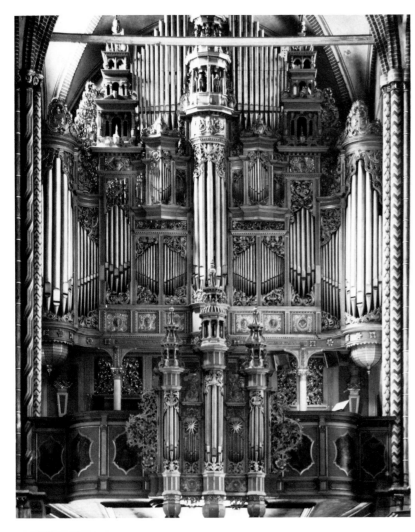

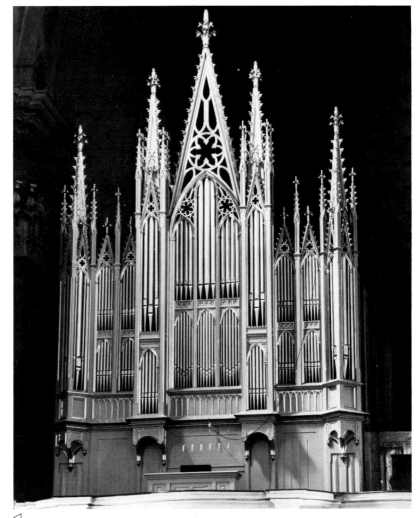

◁
119 Cathedral, Riga, Latvia, Eberhard Friedrich Walcker & Co, 1881–4 (Opus 413)
It was for the inauguration of this instrument – in its day the largest and most modern in the world – that Franz Liszt composed his chorale *Nun danket alle Gott*. There were 124 stops, four manuals (C - f^{111}) and *Ped* (C - d^1: *Haupt-Pedal* and *Schwell-Pedal*). This instrument has survived largely intact, although substantial changes were made in 1907 by Emil Martin, who removed the *Rp* and replaced it by a fourth, pneumatic keyboard, using part of the *Rp* mechanisms. The pipes of this new manual surmount and disfigure the original case front. Further changes were made in 1961 by Hermann Eule, who rebuilt the seven hundred or so tin pipes which had been stolen during the last war. The firm of Flentrop began a further restoration of the instrument in 1981.

121 Great Hall of the Conservatory, Moscow, Aristide Cavaillé-Coll and Charles Mutin, 1900; case by the architect Simil
GO, *Swell* and *Réc* (C - g^{111}) and *Ped* (C - g^1), with fifty stops. Commissioned at the instigation of Charles-Marie Widor a few months before the death of Aristide Cavaillé-Coll in October 1899, this instrument was the last ever to be designed by the French builder. It was first seen at the World Exhibition held in Paris in 1900. Transported to Moscow in 1901, it was soon to serve as a hiding-place for Bolshevik arms during the Revolution. It was not until 1958 that it was repaired, and modified, by Hermann Lamann and Sauer. Additional work was undertaken by Ladegast in 1965; and between 1974 and 1976 the old firm of Merklin began work on restoring the instrument, a task continued by Merklin's successors, Michel, Merklin & Kuhn. Thirty-six of Cavaillé-Coll's stops have survived.

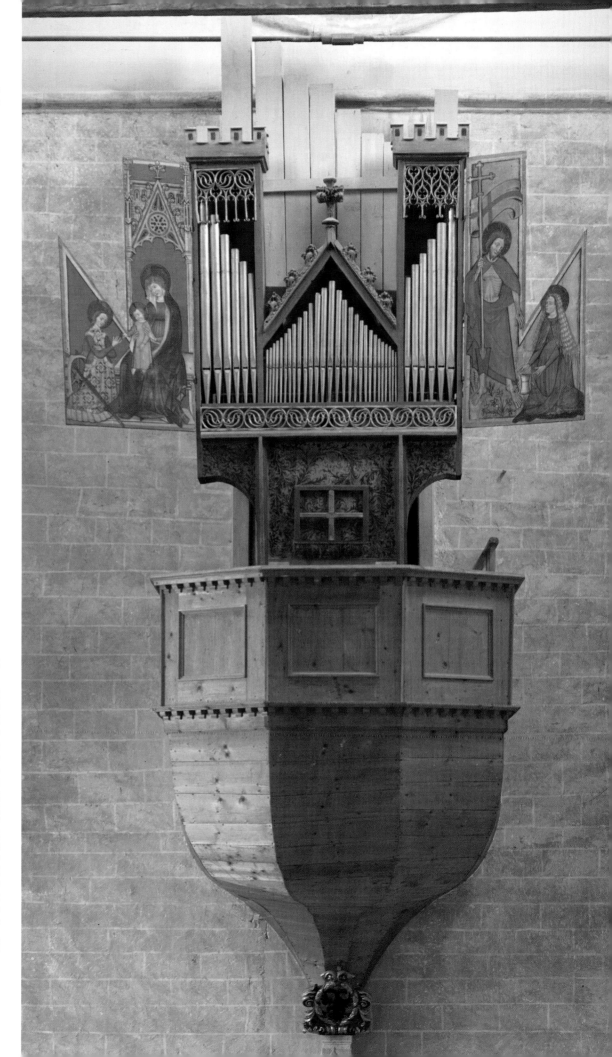

◁ 120 Cathedral, Kaunas (Kovno), Lithuania, Juozapaz Radavičius (Lithuanian builder), 1882
Three manuals and *Ped*, with sixty-two stops.

122 Cathedral of Notre-Dame de Valère, Sion (Sitten), Switzerland, 1390–1420, builder unknown
Wings painted by Pierre Maggenberg between 1434 and 1437. This instrument, which may be regarded as the oldest extant playing organ in the world, is inspired by the Franco-Burgundian school of organ building. In the fifteenth century it was a small *Positif* based on a Montre 4′. Three stops from this original instrument have survived: they are Gothic pipes made of lead and comprise a Fifteenth 2′, a Quint minor 1⅓′ and a Mixtur 1′. The organ was skillfully rebuilt in 1687 by Christopher Aebi, who added the Koppelflöte 4′, the Quint major 2⅔′, the Tierce rank (added to the Mixtur 1′) and most probably also the Oktav 4′. From now on the tonal pyramid was based on a Prinzipal 8′ (case pipe), and reinforced by a pull-down pedal comprising nine keys (short octave: Bass 16′ + 8′). The manual originally had a compass of three octaves, but was now extended to four (C - c[III], with a short octave), and had seven stops. This organ was preserved intact and repaired in 1954 by T. Kuhn.

123 Sta. Maria del Sasso, Morcote, unknown builder, mid-seventeenth century
This Italian-built instrument is housed in a priceless case typical of the Lombardy region. The single manual (C - f^{111}; originally probably C - c^{111}) has twenty-one stops, while the Pedal (C - g sharp) has one stop of Contrabassi 16' + 8', possibly added in 1797. The instrument was restored by Hans-J. Füglister in 1967.

124 Table organ, unknown builder, seventeenth century (or *c.* 1700); Historisches Museum, Basle, Inv. 1870. 886
Unusual in its design, this three-stop instrument has a single manual with a compass of C - c^{111}.

125 Positive organ, unknown builder, six- ▷ teenth century; Historisches Museum, Basle, Inv. 1927. 258
This table positive, from the Ab-Yberg family chapel in Schwyz, has four stops operated by iron draw-stops. Their modern specification would be *Prinzipal* 2' (case-pipe), *Quinte* 1 ⅓', *Gedackt* 4' and I-rank *Zimbel* ½'

126 *Chororgel* in the form of a sarcophagus, former Stiftskirche, Rheinau, Johann Christoph Albrecht, 1709–10; case by Joseph Anton Tschupp
This single-manual instrument (C - c^{111}, short octave) originally had six stops. It was repaired in 1727 by Maurus Briol, who added a two-stop *Ped*, and rebuilt in 1746 by Johann Conrad Speisegger, who increased the number of stops to twelve, including a treble Suavial. Repaired by Maucher in 1808 and altered by Friedrich Haas in 1840/1, the positive was restored by Th. Kuhn in 1944 in accordance with the specification of 1746.

127 Former Benediktinerstiftskirche (Benedictine Abbey church), Rheinau, Johann Christoph Leu, 1711–15
The main Klosterkirche organ originally included a *Glockenwerk*, but this was replaced by a six-stop *Ow/Flötenwerk* following representations by the local clergy who objected to the immorality of the stop. The result was a forty-one-stop instrument with *Hw*, *Rp*, *Ow* and *Ped*, together with a Vogelgesang and Zimbelstern. This instrument was repaired and altered by Johann Conrad Speisegger in 1745, when two more stops were added, by Bihler in 1756, when three were added, by Lang in 1780 and by Maucher in 1808. It was rebuilt in 1840–1 by Friedrich Haas and now had thirty-nine stops, fourteen of them new. There was a further rebuild in 1941–2, this time by Th. Kuhn who removed the Romantic stops and the short octave.

128 Former Zisterzienserklosterkirche (Cistercian Monastery church), Sankt Urban, Joseph Bossard, 1716–21
This thirty-nine-stop instrument has three manuals (C - c^{111}, short octave) and an eighteen-key *Ped* (C - a, short octave). The *Bw* stops are on either side of the console, those of the *Hw* and *Ow* are behind the triple cross above the *Hw*. The specification of this exceptional instrument reveals a variety of different national styles, including Italian (V-rank Mixture), French (V-rank mounted Cornet) and German. With its strikingly individual case front, the St. Urban organ is the oldest of Bossard's instruments to have survived. Drastically altered in the nineteenth century, it was repaired by Th. Kuhn in 1944.

129 Pfarrkirche (Parish church), St. Georg, Ernen, Christopher Aebi, 1679. This instrument, which originally had eleven stops, was altered by an unknown builder in 1745, by Felix Karlen in 1791, by Eduard Konopka in 1871 and by Th. Kuhn in 1896. Restored by Hans-J. Füglister in 1968, it now has a single manual with thirteen stops (including seven from Aebi's organ) and a pedal department with three. The *Ped* specification is typical of the Valais region.

130 Former Dominikanerinnenklosterkirche (Dominican Convent church), Sankt Katharinenthal, Johann Jakob Bommer, 1735–41; *Rp* case 1705
All that remains of the original Klosterkirche organ are the cases, display pipes and mechanical blowing apparatus with five foot-operated bellows. Having suffered frequent repairs between 1754 and 1864, the organ was twice restored by Th. Kuhn in 1941–3, and in 1965–9. It now has nineteen stops distributed among a *Rp* and *Hw* (C - c^{111}, short octave) and *Ped* (C - a, short octave).

131 Main organ, former Benediktinerklosterkirche (Benedictine Monastery church), Muri, Joseph and Victor Ferdinand Bossard, 1743–4
Bossards' thirty-three-stop organ (*Rp*, *Hw* and *Ped*) was a rebuild of a twenty-eight-stop instrument built by Thomas Schott between 1619 and 1630. Schott's instrument had been renovated by P. Jodokus Schnyder in 1662, and dismantled and restored by Hans Melcher during alterations to the structure of the church in 1695–8. The instrument underwent numerous repairs between 1778 and 1832. In 1833 it was restored by Konrad Bloch, who rebuilt the *Rp* as a *Hw* and positioned it between the pedal towers. Further repairs were carried out by Friedrich Haas in 1851–2, and by Friedrich Goll in 1920/1, when pneumatic action was installed and drastic changes made to the instrument. Following O. Metzler's rebuild of 1965–70, the organ comprised thirty-four stops (including seventeen from Bossards' instrument) distributed among a *Rp* and *Hw* (C - f^{111}) and *Ped* (C - f^1); a Vogelgesang stop completed the specification. Joseph Bossard and his son built three instruments for the Klosterkirche, the main organ and two *Chororgeln*: together, they form an exceptional group, with a disposition which is unique in the history of organ building.

132 Gospel Organ, Klosterkirche, Muri, Joseph and Victor Ferdinand Bossard, 1743/4
The Gospel Organ at Muri is a single-manual instrument (c - c^{111}, short octave) with seven stops, and a pedal division (C - a) comprising a Sub-bass 16′. The organ – which is unaltered – was restored by the firm of O. Metzler in 1961/2, at the same time as its big brother, the sixteen-stop Epistle Organ.

133 House Organ, Toggenburg, Wendelin Looser and his son Joseph Looser, 1754; Heimatmuseum der Albert-Edelmann-Stiftung, Ebnat-Kappel
The case of this single-manual (CD - c^{111}, 48 notes), six-stop instrument is made of pinewood, painted in oils. Throughout the eighteenth and early part of the nineteenth centuries small instruments like this were built in the the Emmental and Toggenburg regions, and the cantons of Zurich, Appenzell and Graubünden, intended for domestic use in rural dwellings. The Zwinglian tradition excluded music from church services, a tradition which for centuries considered the organ as *Teufels Trompeten*; instead, it encouraged the singing of hymns and musical evenings in private homes. Among the organ builders who built chamber organs we may cite Caspar Bärtschi, Melchior Grob, Ulrich and Heinrich Ammann, Johann Conrad Speisegger and Johann Jakob Bommer.

134 Dom (Cathedral), Arlesheim, Johann Andreas Silbermann, 1759–61
Hw, Rp, Réc and *Ped*, with thirty-two stops, of which five were divided into treble and bass, two were treble only and one bass only. This instrument was rebuilt by Carl Weigle in 1888 in accord with the Romantic aesthetic, leaving only nineteen stops (including the *Rp* display pipes) and the cases intact. Weigle's instrument was rebuilt in 1959–62 by the firm of O. Metzler, who reinstated the stops which Weigle had removed and added five more stops to the *Ped*. The instrument now comprises a *Rp, Hw, Réc* and *Echo* (C-c^{111}) and *Ped* (C-d^1), with a total of thirty-seven stops.

135 Peterskirche (Chorherrenstift St. Peter), Basle, Johann Andreas Silbermann, 1770
This instrument was built for the Theodorskirche in Basle and spent some time in the town's Historical Museum before being transferred to its present site. Restored by Neidhart and Lhôte in 1968, it has retained its original specification, with thirty stops distributed among three manuals and a pedal.

136   Reformed church, Samedan, Graubünden, unknown builder, 1772
The case of this instrument is inspired by Italian models. Rebuilt by Th. Kuhn in 1969, it comprises two manuals and *Ped*, with seventeen stops.

137   Cathedral of St. Nicolas, Fribourg, Aloys Mooser, 1824–34
The Fribourg organ is the largest and best preserved of all the instruments built by Aloys Mooser, who worked with the sons of Andreas Silbermann before moving to Germany and finally to Vienna. It represents a synthesis of the classical and Romantic traditions in organ building, having sixty-one stops distributed among a *Petit Positif, GO, Grand Positif* and *Echo* (54 notes) and *Péd* (C–c^1); there are, additionally, two Tremulants (*Petit Positif* and *Echo*) and a *GO/Péd* coupler. Modified and transformed by Friedrich Haas in 1852, by Louis Kyburz in 1858–61, by Joseph Merklin in 1872, and by Th. Kuhn in

1900, the instrument underwent its most important changes in 1911–12 when Henri Wolf-Giusto increased the number of stops to ninety. Further changes were made by Heinrich Pürro in 1960. Between 1974 and 1983 Neidhart and Lhôte restored this instrument, reverting to the specification of Mooser's organ, of which some fifty stops have survived.

Mooser's instrument was famous for *L'Orage*, performed by its first incumbent, the organist Jacques Vogt, who enthralled Romantic travelers with his "imitation of a storm in which one can hear the whistling of the winds and the roar of thunder." His performance was admired by George Sand, whose only regret was that "lightning alone, rebellious lightning [. . .] is missing from Mooser's storm." The novelist visited the cathedral in 1836 in the company of the Comtesse Marie d'Agoult and Franz Liszt, who improvised on Mozart's *Dies Irae*.

IV Organ Music in the Low Countries

The earliest contribution which the Low Countries made to the history of organ music dates back to the fifteenth century, when it took the form of transcriptions in the *Buxheimer Orgelbuch* of works by Dufay and de Binchois, certain other works such as the three-part "Salve regina" of Jacob Obrecht (*c.* 1450–1505) and, of course, all the motets whose influence is so clearly visible in the *praeambula* which Paumann published in his *Fundamentum organisandi*.

But the first real evidence of a new maturity of approach in organ writing is provided by two leading Flemish composers who were active in Venice: Willaert and Buus. As indicated earlier, both these men were noted for their skill in handling the ricercare, a form whose origins are in some dispute. Certain writers consider it typically Italian, others believe that it was in fact these two Flemish composers who introduced their own local tradition into Italy. In discussing the term, we should remember, however, that ricercare does not always refer to a contrapuntal work. Indeed, the term includes pieces of every generic description, and even glosses on dance themes. Worth mentioning in this context are Willaert's *Ricercari per sonar con tre stromenti (organo)* [Ricercari to be Performed on Three Instruments (Organ)], published in Venice around the middle of the sixteenth century (not in tablature form but in separate voices), and Jacob Buus's *Recercari da cantare e sonare d'organo et altri stromenti* [Ricercari to be Sung and Performed on the Organ and Other Instruments] (1547; second tablature compilation, 1549). The structure of his works is often more spacious than that of Willaert's ricercari and their conception more scholastic. His psalm settings exploit the device of *cori spezzati*, i.e. "broken" or antiphonal choirs, which he and many Italian composers used at St. Mark's in Venice. Here, no doubt, lie the origins of the echo effects which we find in Sweelinck's celebrated fantasias.

We must also mention Jean (or "Giovanni") de Macque (*c.* 1551–1614) and his canzoni, written in a style rather more Italianate than that of his two predecessors. The art of writing variations, introduced into the Low Countries by the exiled English composers John Bull (1562/3–1628) and Peter Philips (*c.* 1560–*c.* 1628), left a profound mark on Dutch organ music and influenced the country's two leading organ composers, Jan Pieterszoon Sweelinck (1562–1621) and Peeter Cornet (? – 1633).

Sweelinck's organ music comprises, essentially, fantasias, echo fantasias, toccatas, chorale preludes and variations on popular melodies. His most important contribution to the organ repertory was his structural reworking of the fantasia so as to produce a totally new structure transcending the pieces previously conceived under that name. These large-scale fantasias are monothematic pieces, generally divided into three sections. The first section defines the theme, which is stated in all the voices in a continuous manner; in the second section the theme is repeated in long note-values

Fig. 68   St. Jan, 's-Hertogenbosch, Netherlands, 1618–38, Floris II Hocqué, Hans Gottfuss, Galtus and Germer van Hagerbeer. Engraving from A.G. Hill, London, 1883–91. The instrument originally comprised thirty-seven stops and three manuals (Hoofdwerk, Rugwerk and Bovenwerk), plus pedals. Designed by Frans Simons and Gregor Schysler, a native of the Tyrol who settled in Cologne, the case is without doubt one of the finest examples of Brabantine organ building, a superb reflection of the diverse parts of the instrument. The display pipes, sometimes reversed, are chased. Substantial alterations were made by Heinemann in 1787, and an inept attempt at rebuilding was carried out by Léon Verschueren in 1953. Restored by Flentrop in 1984, the instrument now comprises forty-eight stops, distributed among three manuals (C-f^{11}) and *Ped* (C - f^1).

interwoven with a rapid and highly varied counterpoint; and the third section treats the theme in diminution. The work may end with a "coda" written in toccata form. Sweelinck's popularity during his lifetime owes a great deal to the originality of his echo fantasias, divided into two or three sections. The first is treated imitatively, while the second exploits the possibilities of echo effects produced by the repetition of short motifs or melodic fragments. (The effect is achieved in a variety of ways, notably by repeating the motif at a lower octave or else at the same pitch, a device which presupposes the availability of a second manual.) The third section of the fantasia may combine imitative passages with yet more echo effects, or else assume the form of a toccata *à l'italienne*, or passages reminiscent in style of the *clavecinistes*.

The use of chromaticism, culminating in the *Fantasia cromatica*, was an additional device which allowed the Netherlands composer to express his sense of fanciful imagination. All the various forms essayed by Sweelinck, including the fantasia, are notable for their brilliant originality, warmth of spirit and astonishing purity. His toccatas avoid the pitfalls of monotony and of virtuosity for its own sake, while his variations on secular themes, written in a style already familiar in the Low Countries, and enhanced by a facility of writing typical of the *clavecinistes*, are masterpieces of varied tone color. Sweelinck excelled in infusing the different sections with a very real sense of individuality: the theme may appear in each voice, binary rhythm may alternate with ternary rhythm, and so on. The most eloquent example of Sweelinck's style is perhaps the variations on "Mein junges Leben hat ein Endt" [Now my young life is at an end]. All his works, whether they be chromatic fantasias, toccatas or variations on secular themes, may be played interchangeably on the harpsichord or organ.

The chorale preludes (variations on hymn-tunes), which are divided into two, three or four variations, reveal Sweelinck's indebtedness to his predecessor Isaac, with their ornamentation of the melody, subtle art of harmonization and use of imitative writing. This treatment was to leave its profound mark on chorale writing in northern Germany.

The Spanish Netherlands are notable for the organ works of Cornet and of the English composers Bull and Philips. Cornet, who was appointed organist to the Catholic archduke's court in Brussels in about 1603, has left only a handful of works, virtually all of which were written for the Church. His surviving organ works consist of five fantasias on different modes, a *toccada*, a chorale prelude and five versets on the "Salve regina." Although less elaborate in concept than the works of his great contemporary Jan Sweelinck, Cornet's organ writing is by no means lacking in interest, since it represents a fusion of the Anglo-Dutch style with Italian and Spanish influences (Cornet probably visited Portugal and Spain), and includes a number of striking features such as the exposition of a subject and its countersubject, and an intensification of the work's concluding section by means of passages of virtuosic writing.

Many of the works of Dr John Bull, organist at the archduke's court in Brussels from 1613 onwards and later at Antwerp Cathedral, figure in the *Fitzwilliam Virginal Book*. His skill at writing variations, best exemplified by the fantasias on the "Salvator mundi" and "Miserere" and by his hexachord fantasias, left a profound mark on Sweelinck. We may also mention here Bull's two fantasias on old Flemish carols, written at Antwerp.

The organ works of Philips (*c.* 1560–*c.* 1628), who was also organist at the Brussels court and a colleague of Cornet's, are more traditional in style, if only because of the marked Italian influence which characterizes his fantasias.

Other notable contributions to the organ music of the Low Countries were made by Charles (or Carl) Luython (*c.* 1556–1620), a native of Antwerp, who became leading organist at the Imperial court in Prague; Samuel Mareschall of Tournai (1554–*c.* 1640), organist at Basle Cathedral; Simon Lohet (*c.* 1550–1611), organist to the Stuttgart court; and Charles Guillet of Bruges (?–1654). Guillet is the author of "Twenty-four Fantasias in Four Voices arranged according to the Order of the Twelve Modes (in accordance with the recommendations of Gioseffo Zarlino)," a collection published in 1610 by Ballard of Paris.

Organ music in the Spanish Netherlands drew on the tradition of Cornet, whose style was reflected in the works of Abraham van den Kerckhoven (1627–1701). One of

JAN PIETERSZOON SWEELINCK

Born in Deventer (or Amsterdam) in May 1562; died in Amsterdam on October 16, 1621.

He was organist in Amsterdam, an appointment which he took up at the age of fifteen and retained until his death. He was nominated for the post, around 1577, in what was then the Roman Catholic church of St. Nicholas, renamed the Oude Kerk following the town's conversion to Calvinism in 1578. Thereafter he rarely left the town for more than a few days at a time, and then only in connection with his work, which took him to Antwerp, Rotterdam and Deventer. His predecessors as organist of the Oude Kerk were his father Pieter Swybbertszoon (d. 1573) and Cornelis Boscoop. Brought up by Jacob Buyck, the parish's learned curate, Sweelinck, who had probably received his earliest musical education from his father, continued his studies with Jan Willemszoon Lossy in Haarlem. It was in Amsterdam, and not as long supposed during a visit to Venice, that Sweelinck studied the works of Gioseffo Zarlino, Claudio Merulo and Andrea and Giovanni Gabrieli. At the same time he was in contact with two English virginalists who had settled in the southern Netherlands, John Bull and Peter Philips. He is buried in the Oude Kerk.

In the Catholic liturgy, the organ introduced the service and the singing of the congregation, as well as accompanying the choir and performing *alternatim* music with the latter. It was a liturgical function which totally eschewed the idea of music as a form of entertainment. The Reformation brought with it the first in a series of puritanical prohibitions, the fathers of the Dutch Reformed Church arguing that the organ was a papist instrument and agreeing with Erasmus that only the devil could play it. The Protestant authorities in the towns limited the organist's role to performing before and after the service, a decree which, while limiting, also liberated the organist's function by allowing him to improvise liturgical works at certain hours for the edification of the passers-by – a typically Dutch tradition which has survived to this day. Although the organist's repertory is virtually unknown to us, it appears to have consisted in improvisations and variations on religious tunes, and of course on melodies contained in the important Genevan Psalter. The organist, being employed by the town, was in the service of the parish and could not absent himself from his instrument without the permission of the civic authorities. In addition to the functions listed above, Sweelinck was required to perform every morning of the weeks when he was not required for Sunday services, his hour-long improvisations taking place even on the coldest days in the depths of winter. He was also placed in charge of vocal music and conducted the Collegium Musicum of Amsterdam, a commitment which enabled him to perform his own works alongside those of other composers.

In the absence of a printed repertory of organ music in the Netherlands, it is perhaps not surprising to find that none of the keyboard compositions of a man whom his contemporaries regarded as "the Prince of Musicians" was published during his lifetime, although manuscripts of his works have been found in all the principal centers of music, from Oxford to Bártfa in Hungary, and from Uppsala to Padua and Paris. The main impact which the great Amsterdam organist was to have on his contemporaries was that of a teacher: he was first and foremost a pedagog, his fame being such that many musicians traveled to Amsterdam to hear him and to profit from his instruction, coming not only from the Netherlands but, more especially, from northern Germany where he was dubbed the "Deutscher" or "Hamburger Organistenmacher." Among his pupils may be numbered Heinrich Scheidemann, Johannes Praetorius and his friend Samuel Scheidt, with whom he published a number of sets of variations. He was also the head of a school which was to have a crucial influence on the future of organ music by virtue of the new dimensions which he gave to the forms of the fantasia and of monothematic variation writing.

Heir to all the different Western schools, Sweelinck was to assimilate their multiple options and to combine, on the one hand, the brilliance and virtuosic greatness of the Venetians and the consummate art of chromatic writing and dissonances whose most skillful exponents lived south of the Alps, and on the other, the virginalists' intimate refinement of style and conception of freer rhythms.

a large family of musicians and organists, van den Kerckhoven was organist of the Chapelle Royale and at Ste. Catherine's church in Brussels. His numerous works include more than one hundred versets on the church modes, the "Missa duplex" and the "Salve regina," as well as fugues, fantasias, and preludes and fugues. All of them are bound up with the Catholic liturgy in which the organ had only a limited role to perform, a fact attested by the brevity of his versets. Written for three or four voices, his works are all straightforward pieces involving brief imitations and using a prominent solo voice in the versets (in the form of a prelude or fugato). They generally develop only a single theme in the fugues and in eight rather more elaborate fantasias, which are sometimes boldly and sinuously embellished, and enriched by countersubjects, imitations and numerous ornaments. Notable for its echo effects in the tradition of Sweelinck, the Fantasia in D "pro duplici organo" specifies the use of two manuals (*boven* = above, or upper; *onder* = below, or lower).

Two other composers from the area around Liège are notable for the French orientation of their style. The abbé Lambert Chaumont (*c.* 1635–1712) published his *Pieces D'orgue sur les 8 Tons Avec leurs variété leurs agreemens leurs Mouvemens et le Mélange des Jeux propres à chaque espèce de Verset* [Organ Works in Eight Modes, with Variations, Ornaments, Movements and Specifications appropriate to each Kind of Verset] in 1695, containing around one hundred works, with twelve to fifteen pieces to each tone. In addition to works indebted to the French school of organ writing,

Chaumont's compilation also contains allemandes and chaconnes. A similar spirit informs the preludes and allemandes of Henry Du Mont (1610–84), organist at the collegiate church of Notre-Dame in Maastricht before he settled in Paris in 1638.

Surprisingly, Sweelinck's works had a greater influence in Germany than in his own country, where his numerous pupils, including Jan Pieters van Rijnsburch, Michael Utrecht and Sweelinck's son, Plemp or Dirck Sweelinck, produced only highly formal works. Perhaps this is the fate which the history of music reserves for all composers such as Sweelinck and Bach who are able to abstract, distill and transcend the various trends of a particular era? The only one of Sweelinck's followers to publish organ music was Anthoni van Noordt (?–1675), organist at the Nieuwe Kerk in Amsterdam. His *Tabulatuur-Boek van Psalmen en Fantasyen* [Tablature of Psalms and Fantasias] of 1659 combines Italianate notation with the system of letters traditionally found in German tablatures of this period. In addition to six fantasias, the collection contains ten psalms of between three and eight variations each, which may readily be compared with Sweelinck's chorale preludes and works by Scheidt.

The Low Countries, however, were soon to lose their cultural autonomy, as the works they produced became increasingly indistinguishable from those written in more influential neighboring countries such as Germany. It is impossible to do more than cite the names of later organists who continued the local tradition. The most important of them were Gijsbert van Steenwijck (d. 1679), organist at Arnhem and Kampen; Quirinus van Blankenburg (1654–1739), organist at The Hague, and a theoretician and advocate of the new system of "equal temperament"; Matthias van den Gheyn (1721–85), organist and bell ringer at Louvain; and Conrad Frederik Hurlebusch (1696–1765), a native of Brunswick and organist in Amsterdam, who edited harmonizations of Calvinist psalms, as did the majority of organists in the North of the country. But these musicians, many of them bell ringers by profession, soon gave up writing organ music and contented themselves with the conscientious discharge of their liturgical function, in the course of which they gave free rein to a degree of virtuosity whose excesses occasionally provoked the anger of the church authorities. Thus we find eighteenth-century Dutch organists preferring the art of improvisation and moving in the direction of a more naturalistic style involving the imitation of storms, tempests, shipwrecks, birdcalls and pastorals, and, in due course, a simulated reenactment of the battle of Waterloo. If, however, we consider the historical contribution which the Low Countries (including Flanders, which is now a part of Belgium) have made to organ music, certain names emerge which we shall rediscover in the chapters devoted to the regions where they were influential. We should not forget that Belgium has always claimed as her own the great composer and organist César Franck.

We shall later mention the profound influence of Nicolas Jacques Lemmens (1823–81) on the French school of organ music, an influence which is particularly noticeable in the works of Lemmens's pupils Joseph Callaerts (1838–1901), Alphonse Mailly and Joseph Jongen (1873–1953). Jongen's *Sonata eroica* is additionally indebted to the heritage of Reubke and Liszt, while his *Toccata* is written in the virtuosic tradition of Widor. Paul de Maleingreau (1887–1956) conceived vast compositions of a religious character, close in spirit to the world of Marcel Dupré. Examples of his work include a *Symphonie de la Passion* [Symphony of the Passion], Opus 20, and a *Symphonie de l'Agneau mystique* [Symphony of the Mystical Lamb], Opus 24. Similar influences are found in the two symphonies of Guy Weitz (1883–1970), a Belgian composer resident in England.

Flor Peeters (b. 1903) is a composer who has been equally active in editing early music texts and in teaching. His compositions, which are among the most perfect syntheses of French and Flemish influences, are frequently based upon plainchant themes or Flemish melodies. In addition to works notable for their rich and seductive harmonies, Peeters has also written a Concerto for organ and orchestra (Opus 52). Of the many Dutch composers who have written organ works based on popular songs or Calvinist hymns, we may mention Hendrik Andriessen the Elder (1892–1981), whose harmonic style is closely related to that of Louis Vierne; Marius Monnikendam (b.

1896); Anthon van der Horst (1899–1965), whose large-scale works involve a considerable element of virtuosity; Cor Kee (b. 1900), whose psalm settings were tonal in character but who has subsequently shown considerable interest in serial music, with a variety of rhythms and tempi, and dissonant chords; and Jacob Bijster (b. 1902), who remains more traditional, as do Henk Badings (b. 1907), Jan Koetsier (b. 1911), Hermann Strategier (b. 1912) and Albert de Klerk (b. 1917). The organ works of Piet Kee (b. 1917) reveal a splendid freedom in their handling of rhythm and counterpoint. The contribution which Netherlands composers have made to contemporary music will be considered below.

138 Koorkerk, Middelburg, organ originally built for St. Nicolaas in Utrecht; *GO* by Peter Gerritsz, 1478–80; *Bw* (spring-chest) by Cornelius Gerritsz, 1547; *Rw* (slider-chest), 1580; *Ped* with Trompette 8′, 1600
The upper keyboard of forty-two notes controlled the *Blokwerk* (sliderless chest), together with the seven stops planted on the two spring-chests, while the second manual controlled eight stops.

139 Small organ in the north ambulatory, Sint Laurens (Grote Kerk), Alkmaar; *Hw* by Jan van Covelens (Johann von Koblenz), 1511; *BW* and *Ped* by Allaert Claesz, 1555
Numerous repairs, including modifications in 1625 by Jan Jacobsz, in 1651 by Jacobus Galtus van Hagerbeer, in 1703–4 by Jan Duyschot, in 1779 by Pieter Müller, in 1781 by M. Körnelein, in 1854 by. C.F.A. Naber and in 1894–5 by L. Ypma. Restored by Flentrop in 1939, the organ now has two manuals and dependent pedals, with fourteen stops, of which nine belonged to the original instrument.

141 Sint Bavo (Grote Kerk), Haarlem, Christian Müller, 1735–8
Using part of the metal from the pipes of the earlier organ built by Galtus &
Germer Hagerbeer in 1630–3, Müller designed an instrument with three
manuals (*Hw, Rw* and *Bw*) and *Ped* (two 32′ pedal towers), comprising a total
of sixty stops. Built by Jan van Logteren, the monumental case, which
measures twenty-three meters from the foot of the *Rw* decorations to the top
of the main structure, presents a classically Dutch arrangement of the various
parts of the instrument. The organ has undergone frequent transformations,
most notably in 1761 by J. Schmidt and, in the nineteenth century, by Friedrichs, Bätz, Gabry and, above all, C. G. F. Witte who made radical changes to
the instrument in 1866. A Barker lever system was added to the *Hw* in 1905.
Between 1959 and 1961 the organ was completely rebuilt by Marcussen, who
more or less reverted to Müller's original scheme, adding two stops and
some pedal notes, as well as three pedal couplers; equal temperament, however, was retained.

140 Nieuwe Kerk (Abbey Church), Middelburg, Jan Duyschot, 1690–2
This organ, a masterpiece of South Belgian Baroque and built for Amsterdam's Lutherse Oudekerk, originally had two manuals (*Hw* and *Rw*) and *Ped*,
comprising thirty stops. The case was by Jan Albertsz Schut, carvings by
Jasper Wagenaar and panels painted by Filip Tideman (?). A new instrument
was built by W. van Leeuwen in 1954 with three manuals (*Hw, Rw* and *Bw*)
and *Ped*, and a total of thirty-nine speaking stops.

142 Nieuwe Kerk, The Hague, Jan Duyschot, 1700–2
Hw, Rw, Bw and pull-down pedals (thirty-five stops). Shutters painted by Theodorus van der Schuer. Following several restorations in 1727, 1736, 1793 and 1842, the builder C. G. F. Witte adapted the instrument in 1867 to conform to the Romantic aesthetic; it now has twenty-six speaking stops.

143 Sint Martini (Grote Kerk), Sneek, Arp Schnitger and Rudolph Garrels, 1710–11
Hw, Rp, Bp and *Ped* (thirty-six stops). Clearly North German in structure, this instrument was repaired by Christian (or Christiaan) Müller in 1726 and by Lambertus van Dam in 1779. Alterations were made in 1896–7 and in 1925 such that all that now remains of the original instrument are eight stops and the display pipes.

144   Console of the organ built in 1733–6 by
Jean (or Jacob) François Moreau, Sint Jans
(Grote Kerk), Gouda
Hw, Rp, Ow and *Ped* (fifty-two stops). Organ
case designed by Hendrik Carré. The instrument was restored by Flentrop between 1958
and 1960 and now has fifty-three stops.

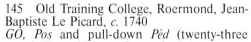

145 Old Training College, Roermond, Jean-Baptiste Le Picard, *c.* 1740
GO, Pos and pull-down *Péd* (twenty-three stops). The wide case front of this instrument is a common feature of the southern Netherlands. The organ was modified in 1888 by Vermeulen, in 1927 by Pereboom and in 1953 by Verschueren. It now comprises *GO, Rp, Bw* and *Ped*, and has thirty-four stops, some of which date back to the eighteenth century.

146 Reformed church, Nijkerk, Matthijs van Deventer, 1756
The case of this two-manual organ presents a typically Dutch formal structure, enlivened in this instance by rococo carvings.

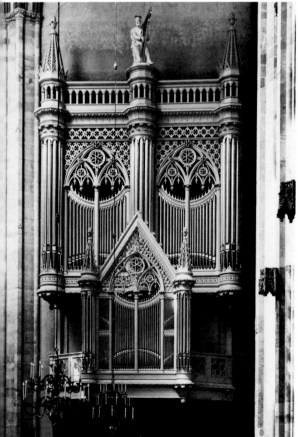

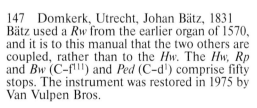

147 Domkerk, Utrecht, Johan Bätz, 1831
Bätz used a *Rw* from the earlier organ of 1570, and it is to this manual that the two others are coupled, rather than to the *Hw*. The *Hw, Rp* and *Bw* (C–f¹¹¹) and *Ped* (C–d¹) comprise fifty stops. The instrument was restored in 1975 by Van Vulpen Bros.

148 St. Peter's Church, Boxtel, Franciscus Cornelius Smits, 1842
The Baroque case of this instrument may come as something of a surprise in the mid-nineteenth century. The instrument itself remains unaltered with its original twenty-eight stops: three manuals of fifty-four notes coupled to the *Ped* (twenty-seven keys). In 1956 J.F. Clercx provided the pedals with eight stops of their own.

149   St. Jacques, Liège, organ attributed to Nicolaas Niehoff or Floris (Florent) Hocqué the Elder, both of Brabantine extraction, 1600–1
The case of this instrument, designed in a style which is widespread in the Meuse region, is typically *liégeois*. The organ has undergone many modifications, including alterations by André Severijn in 1669. Further, less substantial, changes were made by Arnold Graindorge between 1815 and 1829, by Arnold Clérinx in 1854, when the shutters were destroyed, and by Charles Anneessens in 1888–9. The instrument was dismantled in 1965. Etienne Schumacher is planning to build a new instrument with fifty-three stops.

150   St. Paul-des-Dominicains, Antwerp, Nicolaes van Haeghen, 1648–58
Case designed by Erasmus II (Artus l'Ancien) Quellin and built by Peter Verbruggen the Elder. Its northern German design is exceptional in the Spanish Netherlands. The organ must originally have had three manuals and forty-seven stops. It was transformed in 1732–6 by Jean-Baptiste Forceville and his pupil Pieter van Peteghem the Elder, who added the two pedal towers; in the nineteenth century, modifications were made by Jean-Joseph Delhaye in 1824, by François Bernard Loret-Vermeersch in 1842–6, by Geurts the Elder in 1870 and by Veuve Geurts in 1885. The instrument is currently not in use. *GO, Pos, Réc* and *Péd* with forty-nine stops.

151   Notre-Dame, Lissewege, Boudewijn Ledou, 1651–2
Perhaps designed by Walram Rombaut, the case of this single-manual instrument is structurally akin to that of the two-manual organ built by Ledou in
1643 for Notre-Dame de Watervliet.

152   Ste. Anne, Bruges, Jacob van Eynde, 1707–9
GO and *Pos* (nineteen stops), Rossignol and Tremulant. The keyboards of this
instrument had a compass of forty-eight notes. In 1876–7 a new instrument
was built by Louis Hooghuys: it had two manuals (fifty-six notes) and thirteen stops. A two-stop *Péd* (twenty-seven keys) was added at the beginning of
the twentieth century by Aimé Hooghuys or Jules Anneessens.

153   Basilican Church, Saint-Hubert, Antoine Le Picard (whose family came
from Noyon and settled in a Walloon district of Belgium), 1685
GO, Pos, Echo and *Péd* (thirty-seven stops). This instrument is typically
French in the separation of its cases and the richness of its Mixtures and
Reeds. It was the first and most important of its kind to be built in the
Walloon region. It was restored in 1772 and 1842 (by Louis and Jacques
Möller), and adapted to the Romantic aesthetic in 1934 by Jules Annesseens:
GO, Pos, Réc and *Péd* (forty-four stops).

154   St. Charles-Borromée, Antwerp, Jean-Baptiste Forceville (probably a
native of Lille who had settled in Antwerp) or Karel Dillens, 1720–2
Conceived on the grand scale, the organ case by Jan Pieter van Baurscheit
and his son divides the *GO* into two sections in order to provide a framework
for the case front of the *Pos*. A similar design may be seen in the Church of
St. Pierre at Malines (1713) and at St. Jacques in Antwerp (1726). Forceville
has striven to produce a synthesis of French and German Baroque art and
designed a two-manual instrument with twenty-two speaking stops. It was
transformed in 1808–10 by Jean-Joseph Delhaye, in 1858 by the addition of a
pedal coupled to the *GO*, in 1866 by new bellows and additional ornaments
to the case and in 1877–8 by work undertaken by H. Vermeersch. In 1928
Geurts added an electric motor and some new stops, and in 1958 G. D'Hondt
raised the pitch of the instrument. It currently has two manuals of fifty-four
notes each and a pedal department of thirty keys; there are twenty-three
speaking stops.

V Organ Music in England

Organ music in England – unlike its vocal counterpart – was long considered to be of only secondary importance. Nevertheless, religious music accorded the organ pride of place, as is clear from the fact that the majority of large churches, at least until such time as they were dismantled or destroyed during the Wars of Religion, had two organs, one of which was located in the chancel and the other placed on the rood-screen. The English organist, like his continental colleague, was called upon to perform *alternatim* with the choir, or to play parts of the Ordinary of the mass.

Very few manuscripts (and no printed texts) have survived from this period, so that our knowledge of the works performed on these occasions is extremely limited. With the exception of the *Robertsbridge Codex*, probably of foreign provenance, and the influence exercised in an indirect way by Dunstable and his school on certain compilations such as the *Buxheimer Orgelbuch*, the works which may be regarded as having been composed specifically for the organ remain relatively few in number until the middle of the sixteenth century. The only two keyboard works which we may ascribe to the fifteenth are a three-part piece attributed to John Dunstable (*c*. 1385–1453) and a version of the "Felix namque," which was to remain a favorite theme of English composers until around 1650. A second melody dear to English musicians was that of the mass *Gloria tibi Trinitas*; John Taverner (*c*. 1490–1545) was the first composer to adapt the section "In nomine Domini." This segment of plainsong served generations of English composers as *cantus firmus* for contrapuntal "fancies," a musical form known from that time onward as an "In nomine."

The Tudor period witnessed a flowering of keyboard works written on plainchant themes. They included pieces by Taverner, who was organist at Cardinal College (now Christ Church), Oxford, and subsequently at Boston in Lincolnshire, where he died; Philip ap Rhys, a Welsh composer active in London in the mid-sixteenth century; John Redford (*c*. 1480–1547), vicar-choral at St. Paul's Cathedral in London; Christopher Tye (1500–*c*. 1572); Richard Alwood; Thomas Preston (d. *c*. 1564); John Thorne (d. 1573) and Robert Coxsun, not to mention the numerous anonymous works which have survived from this period.

Although the organ mass was as yet relatively undeveloped (its chief exponents being Taverner, ap Rhys and Preston), hymn-tunes and plainchant melodies comprise the majority of organ works dating from this time. They are relatively close stylistically to certain pieces published in Paris by Pierre Attaingnant and are generally treated as large-scale fantasias based on the technique of variation, with three voices elaborated in constantly changing and often highly complex rhythms. Our most important insight into the art of organ writing in England at the beginning of the sixteenth century is given by the *Mulliner Book*, a collection made around 1560 by Thomas Mulliner. It contains some 120 works for organ and virginal by composers such as Taverner, Redford, Alwood, Tye and Thomas Tallis (*c*. 1505–85). Two specific musical forms which appear here, apart from dances, are voluntaries (a term which here implies a free

Fig. 69   The organ which was offered as a present by Queen Elizabeth I of England to the Turkish Sultan Mahommed III in 1599. Engraving from the *Illustrated London News*, October 20, 1860.

prelude, although it later came to include any piece written for organ) and points, short monothematic pieces treated imitatively. John Redford wrote fifty or so organ fantasias for the manuals. They are based on liturgical *cantus firmi* and comprise two, three and even four voices. Although similar in many respects to the style of Dutch organ writing of the fifteenth century, they are notable for their bold melodic sense. The second half of the sixteenth century and the first thirty years of the seventeenth witnessed a flowering of the art of variation writing which was to reach its apogee in the hands of English composers, while the virginal rapidly established its supremacy as the leading keyboard instrument of the time. It is difficult to determine exactly which pieces, though written for the virginal, may equally well be performed on the organ; but there is no doubt that many keyboard works dating from this period lend themselves to be played on the organ. This is scarcely surprising when we recall that the majority of the great virginal-players were organists: Tallis, William Byrd (1543–1623), Bull, William Blitheman (c. 1525–91), Orlando Gibbons (1583–1625), Thomas Tomkins (1572–1656) and Thomas Warwick (d. 1660). All of them were appointed to the Chapel Royal; Thomas Morley (1557–1602) was at St. Paul's, and Philips at the Chapelle royale in Brussels.

This later period is often regarded as the golden age of English music on the basis of the six hundred or so works which have survived. They are contained for the most part in manuscript collections typical of the years around 1600 and known as Virginal Books. In addition to *My Ladye Nevells Booke* of around 1585/90, *Benjamin Cosyn's Virginal Book*, and *Parthenia, or the Maydenhead of the First Musicke that ever was printed for the Virginalls* of 1612/13 (the only virginal book to be printed), the most famous collection is undoubtedly the *Fitzwilliam Virginal Book*, compiled by Francis Tregian probably between 1609 and 1619, and containing nearly three hundred pieces. The intimate style of the virginalists – in all probability inherited from Antonio de Cabezón (c. 1500–1566) – is expressed above all in variations notable for their extreme degree of imaginative virtuosity. They comprise variations on liturgical hymns and on the notes of the hexachord, fantasias, fancies, pavanes, galliards, transcriptions of chansons, preludes and so on. Although the writing may appear straightforward, it involves ornamentation of the original melody, embellishments and triplets, while the variation technique includes skillful changes of rhythm, harmony and counterpoint. In addition to variation, there are numerous *cantus firmus* works clearly written with the organ in mind: one thinks especially of the works by practising composers of the generation preceding these compilations, including Blitheman, Bull, Redford, Preston, Tallis and Tomkins.

English musical life at the end of the sixteenth century suffered from the violent repercussions of the country's politico-religious troubles. The authoritarian policies of King James I and his successor, their conservative outlook as head of the Anglican Church and their desire to rule without troubling themselves with a Parliament jealous of its own prerogatives were soon to lead to a profound crisis in a country where, since 1534, politics and religion had been inextricably linked. It was a crisis which led to the execution of King Charles I, the victory of Cromwell, and the triumph of a severe and rigid brand of Puritanism. Between 1649 and 1660 musical activity in England, especially in places of worship, was subject to the dictates of an intransigent religion: church music was restricted and even banned; the majority of the country's organs fell victim to iconoclastic zeal or were dismantled and sold for the price of the metal which they contained; musicians, especially organists, were reduced to inactivity. Many preferred a life of exile, while others attempted to survive but, deprived of work, died of starvation.

Following the Restoration in 1660, music regained its former status, both at court and in church. Organ building similarly took on a new lease of life, encouraged by inventive local builders such as Renatus Harris and Abraham Jordan, and by others of German extraction such as Bernhard Schmidt ("Father Smith") and Johann Snetzler. But there had been a long interruption, and the great tradition of the virginalists was by now little more than a distant memory. This break in the development of organ writing in England was, moreover, aggravated by the continuing importance which the singing of hymns and psalms continued to enjoy in the Anglican service: the organ's principal role was that of an accompanying instrument, only infrequently was it allowed to express itself in solo writing. Organist-composers rarely seized the opportunity to write liturgical melodies with skillful variations, but instead produced pieces intended merely to entertain. In doing so they reflected a style of writing which had been suborned by the aesthetic options of the day.

English music of the first two thirds of the seventeenth century continued to bear the imprint of the virginalists' style. This was a transitional period enlivened by a handful of works by Edward Gibbons (1568–c.1650) and Christopher Gibbons (1615/16–76), respectively the elder brother and son of Orlando Gibbons, as well as works by Benjamin Rogers (1614–98) and Matthew Locke (c. 1630–77). Locke wrote a number of interesting preludes and voluntaries, published in his *Melothesia, or, Certain General Rules for Playing upon a Continued-Bass* (London, 1673). Another composer who deserves to be mentioned here is John Blow (1649–1708) who, from 1668 to 1679 and again, following the death of Henry Purcell, from 1695 to 1708, was organist at Westminster Abbey and St. Paul's Cathedral, in addition to being Master of the Children and Composer to the Chapel Royal. Among his versets, preludes and voluntaries we may single out a *Voluntary for Full Organ* remarkable for its rapid toccatalike passagework, a *Voluntary for the two Diapasons and Flute*, a *Voluntary for the Cornett Stop* and a *Verse for the Cornett and Single Organ*. The titles, which are still a rarity at the end of the seventeenth century, are an indication of the sonorities to be used.

Henry Purcell (1659–95), who studied under Blow, among others, and who, like his mentor, was one of England's leading composers, was likewise organist at Westminster Abbey, although his surviving works for the instrument number no more than ten highly ornamented verses and voluntaries. The *Voluntary on the Old 100th Psalm Tune*, attributed to Purcell, although possibly by Blow, is probably intended to be performed on a keyboard divided between C and C sharp: opening with a fugal introduction, this fine composition goes on to state the complete chorale theme in the left hand before taking it up in the treble. The *Voluntary for Double Organ* is remarkable for its dazzling passagework. From its beginnings in the sixteenth-century works of Redford and Alwood, the voluntary remained ill defined as a musical form. Musicians described their compositions indiscriminately as voluntaries, fancies, verses, "In nomines," fantasias or preludes. Initially, a voluntary was a continuous piece of moderate length. However, it soon developed a broader structure, culminating in a bipartite form with a slow opening section comparable to a prelude, generally played on the Diapasons or full organ, and a second, fast section, involving a Cornet or Trumpet solo or, more rarely, some other stop suited to fugal writing. The voluntary further benefited from the various possibilities afforded by the newer types of organ: while the single-manual organ may have had the advantage of stops divided into treble and bass, the addition of a second manual (Double Organ) and later a third (Echo Organ) brought with it a greater choice of registrations, and the possibility of more solo passages and echo effects. Towards the end of the seventeenth and during the eighteenth century, the voluntary came close in structure to the Baroque suite or sonata in four or five sections, or to the prelude and fugue. We may recall that when Mendelssohn was commissioned by the publishers Coventry & Hollier to write three voluntaries, he preferred to call them "sonatas," adding that he did not know precisely what was meant by the term "voluntary." Before considering Handel's remarkable contribution to the genre, we may recall the psalm settings "with their interludes of great variety" by Daniel Purcell (c. 1660–1717), brother of Henry Purcell, together with the voluntaries – generally in two sections – by William Croft (1678–1727), Blow's pupil and successor at Westminster.

Heir to the great northern German tradition, George Frideric Handel (1685–1759) was a pupil of Zachow and a friend of Mattheson, the famous virtuoso organist with whom he visited Lübeck in 1703 to hear Buxtehude perform in the town's Marienkirche. At the same time, he was a convinced disciple of the Italian style whose models he occasionally followed to excess – *il caro Sassone* (the dear Saxon) was how

Fig. 70   St. Paul's Cathedral, London 1694–7, Bernard Smith
Designed by Sir Christopher Wren and built by Grinling Gibbons, the original organ case was situated in the rood loft, its two frontages facing east and west. This instrument had three manuals and twenty-seven stops. The rood loft having been removed in 1859, the two façades were resited in their present position, to the north and south of the chancel. This was in 1872, and the builder was Henry Willis, who made a replica of the Choir Organ from the east façade for the second case, which now faced north. Willis's organ, which had four manuals and fifty-two stops, was further enlarged in 1897–1900, 1930–9 and 1960. Noël Mander rebuilt the instrument between 1973 and 1977, imitating Willis's composition for the chancel organs. There were now 105 stops, divided into three separate sections: Chancel section (Great, Swell, South Choir, Solo and Pedal), Dome section (Fifth manual, and Pedal) and West section.

Domenico Scarlatti described his fellow organist. Handel was born in Halle, where he was deputy organist at the Domkirche (Schlosskirche) from 1702 to 1703. He paid his first visit to England in 1710, settling there two years later. In 1714 his patron, the Elector of Hanover, became King George I of England. It was in London that Handel died in 1759. Already valued and celebrated for his improvisations on the "chamber organs," Handel brought a breath of fresh air to a country whose musical style had lost its sense of direction. The whole of eighteenth-century English music owes Handel an enormous debt as a result. We will not mention here the composer's remarkable career, except to say that in the summer of 1717 he was appointed resident composer of the Duke of Chandos. The duke's household already included an equally famous German musician, the Berlin master Johann Christoph Pepusch (1667–1752), who may be regarded as the mentor of an entire generation of English organists, including William Babell (*c.* 1690–1723), William Boyce (1710–79), John Keeble (*c.* 1711–86), John Travers (*c.* 1703–58), James Nares (1715–83) and Benjamin Cooke (1734–93).

Handel essayed the forms of the fugue and voluntary "for the organ or harpsichord," respecting the rhythmical opposition of their two movements as well as their essential spirit, using Cornet, Trumpet or Flute solos, and echo passages. But he is best known as the innovator of the concerto for organ and orchestra, a genre which rapidly became one of the most important both in quality and quantity in England and the German-speaking lands, most notably in Vienna and Prague. Historically, these works of Handel had very few predecessors: three works by Vivaldi, including two for organ and violin, and one for two organs and two violins; the keyboard concertos of the Nuremberg organist Johann Matthias Leffloth (d. 1733); the concertos transcribed for organ by Walther or Bach; and, finally, Bach's *sinfonie*, written for his cantatas BWV 29, 35, 49, 146 and 169.

Handel's sixteen concertos were in general conceived as interludes in oratorios – one thinks, for example, of the ninth concerto (Opus 7, No. 3), whose first movement takes up the initial cell of the "Hallelujah" chorus from *Messiah*. Performed by the master himself, they were intended to show off his brilliant virtuosity, after an introductory prelude performed *extempore* and designed to loosen the performer's fingers. The concertos were published in four sets: the first six appeared in 1738 as Opus 4; Nos 13 and 14 followed in 1740, together with four organ transcriptions of the *Concerti Grossi* (Opus 6, Nos 10, 1, 5 and 6); a further six concertos, Nos 7–12 (Opus 7) were published posthumously in 1761, and Nos 15 and 16 followed in 1797. Handel also planned a concerto for two organs adapted from the first movement of Opus 7, No. 4.

It was in 1735 that he first performed one of his own works in public. Towards the end of his life, notwithstanding a road accident in the United Provinces which he suffered during his last visit to Halle in 1750, and the loss of his sight in 1753, Handel continued to perform his own concertos in benefit concerts, or else to direct the orchestra from the keyboard in performances of *Messiah*.

Although some of these works were written for the harpsichord, the majority were intended for the English organ of the period, an instrument with a limited number of stops and no pedals. Examples of this type of organ are the instrument built by Abraham Jordan at Handel's request for the Covent Garden Theatre, and one built by Richard Bridge, now at Great Packington, and again designed by Handel: its single manual has a compass of fifty-six notes from G to d^{1111}, without a short octave, and with seven stops: Open Diapason 8′, Stopped Diapason 8′, Principal 4′, Twelfth (Quinte 2^{2}/$_{3}$′), Fifteenth (Doublette 2′), Great Tierce (1^{3}/$_{5}$′) and a Trumpet 8′ (Jordan) or Flute (Bridge). Only the seventh concerto (Opus 7, No. 1) demands an independent pedal part, and was probably written for one of the concerts which Handel gave on the continent. In addition to strings and harpsichord for the continuo, these works are scored for an orchestra whose sonorities are enriched by two oboes and, in the case of Opus 7, Nos 1 and 4, by bassoons. Two concertos provide notable exceptions to this rule, namely the sixth (Opus 4, No. 6), in which flutes replace the oboes, while violins play *con sordino* and the remaining strings *pizzicato*; and the sixteenth in F major, in which two horns complement the normal instrumentation. Although indebted to the *sonata da camera*, *sonata da chiesa* and *concerto grosso* (in which the organ or *concertino* instruments alternate with the *ripieno* of the full orchestra), these sixteen concertos eclipse their Italian models in their inventive facility and rhythmic ease, while drawing additionally on German polyphony (especially the passacaglia), on the elegance, vivacity and ideas of composers such as Purcell and Blow and, finally, on the rhythmic brilliance of the French-style overture. There are normally four movements, as in the *sonata da camera*, comprising an introduction, allegro, adagio and final allegro, often dancelike in character, but this number may vary between two and seven, as in the case of the astonishing sixteenth concerto. The soloist is occasionally required to improvise a movement in these works.

These concertos are original pieces, with an intimacy and distinction reminiscent of the incisiveness of harpsichord technique; but Handel is not afraid to exploit other composers' ideas or even those which he himself had used in earlier works: according to Romain Rolland, "not only did [Handel] create his own music, he also created that of other composers." We may add that in matters of both style and form Handel remained a model for later English composers, acting as their guide and mentor long after his death in 1759.

Evidence of the interest evoked by the works of this impulsive German, whom the English finally adopted as one of their own, are countless keyboard concertos written from the 1740s until well into the nineteenth century. The most important of these were the thirty-two *Concertos for the Organ or Harpsichord with Instrumental Parts* which the Reverend William Felton of Hereford (1715-69) published in London from 1744 onwards. (There were four collections, each containing six concertos: Opus 1, 1744; Opus 2, 1747; Opus 4, 1752; and Opus 5, 1755; plus the eight concertos of Opus 7, 1759[?].) Also of note are the *Six Favourite Concertos for the Organ, Harpsichord or Piano Forte: with Instrumental Parts* by Thomas Augustine Arne (1710-78). These works, by the celebrated author of "Rule, Britannia," flirt with the galant style and foreshadow the later classical structure. The concertos of Charles Avison (1709-70) of Newcastle upon Tyne, a pupil of Francesco Geminiani, Philip Hayes (1738-97) of Oxford, and Henry Burgess the Younger remain largely dependent on their formal model. This is also true of the six concertos by (Charles) John Stanley (1712-86), the blind London organist. He was a pupil of John Reading and Maurice Greene and, following the death of Handel (whom he knew personally), continued his tradition of performing during the breaks in oratorios. The organ or pianoforte concertos of Thomas Sanders Dupuis (1733-96) offer increasing scope to a new dimension of virtuosity in their solo writing. Dupuis, it may be added, was probably the first composer to die of opium poisoning. In addition to the works of two musicians born in Norwich, William Crotch (1775-1847), organist in Cambridge and Oxford, and John Charles Beckwith (1788-1819), we may refer here to the *Six Concertos for the Organ or Harpsichord* (Opus 1, 1781) by Charles Wesley (1757-1834) and to the eleven concertos by his brother Samuel Wesley (1766-1837). One of these is a variation on the theme of "Rule, Britannia."

The fascination exerted at this time by the concerto form, which had removed the organ from its liturgical framework and subjected it to the secular influence of the orchestra, should not blind us to the numerous works written for the organ as a solo instrument. As noted above, these works were no longer limited to the traditional forms. At most, there are a number of attempts at fugal writing, mostly in three voices, which achieve a richer texture by multiplying the thematic entries and by introducing passages in a freer style.

The majority of these works were written interchangeably for the organ, the harpsichord and, later, the piano. English composers remained faithful to a tradition dating back to the Elizabethan age. They produced vast numbers of works whose elegant freedom and simple, direct beauty illuminate more eloquently than any liturgical designation could have done the pleasure of playing chamber organs. Cultivated bourgeois liked to have such organs in their music rooms. They were built by the leading craftsmen of the day, such as Father Smith, Snetzler, Samuel Green, Robert Adam, Thomas Chippendale and John Linnell. Music which had been

Fig. 71 Design for a chamber organ by the eighteenth-century cabinetmaker John Linnell. Chamber organs achieved their greatest glory in England in the eighteenth century. London, Victoria and Albert Museum, GC 5961.

intended primarily to entertain gave way increasingly to character pieces describing emotions and states of mind and recreating trivial events – works which in the nineteenth century were to assume a preponderant role in organ music. The organist's repertory also included large-scale (and sometimes highly skillful) transcriptions of orchestral or vocal works.

A large number of English composers of the eighteenth and nineteenth centuries wrote only a handful of works for the organ (generally voluntaries, fugues, interludes, "select pieces" and so on). Again, we can consider only the most notable names of the period. In the first three quarters of the eighteenth century six musicians who had the opportunity of appreciating Handel's music, if not of knowing him personally, were the following. Thomas Roseingrave (1688–1766), of Winchester, studied in Italy, where he had contact with Alessandro and Domenico Scarlatti. Admired above all as an improvisator, he left two collections of organ works, *Voluntaries and Fugues made on purpose for the organ or harpsichord* and *Six double fugues for the organ or harpsichord*. Maurice Greene (1695–1755) of London was organist, most notably, at St. Paul's and a friend of Handel's. His twenty or so voluntaries are all bipartite in structure, and respect the *cantabile* and often sober lines of the different voices. A pupil of Greene and Pepusch, William Boyce (1710–79) wrote ten voluntaries, the chief qualities of which are their freshness, liveliness and rhythmic facility; bipartite in form, these pieces are not unrelated structurally to the prelude and fugue. (Charles) John Stanley is the author of a number of concertos and three collections of ten voluntaries, published in 1742 (Opus 5, 6 and 7). Clearly inspired by the style of Handel, these pieces are written for three voices and are generally in two sections; more melodic than contrapuntal, they comprise, like Boyce's works, alternating sections of solo writing and echo effects. William Walond (1725–70), organist at Oxford, and John Bennett (1735–84), in London, wrote voluntaries stylistically and structurally related to the Baroque sonata.

Less obvious in the authentic domain of religious music, the new stylistic attainments of continental Europe, and especially those of the great German school, may be found in organ works written in England during the second half of the eighteenth century. It was a century in search of its own identity, if we are to judge from the few pieces by Charles Burney (1726–1814) and John Marsh (1752–1828), whose works reflect a galant style designed to satisfy public taste. Burney, who played the violin in Handel's orchestra, has left us *Six Cornet Pieces with an Introduction for the Diapasons, and a Fugue. Proper for young Organists and Practitioners on the Harpsichord* (1751), and *Preludes, Fugues, and Interludes for the Organ* [. . .] *for Young Organists* [. . .] (1787); but his musical compositions are of secondary importance when set beside his intellectual curiosity: attracted from an early age by astronomy, he even went so far as to publish an essay on the principal comets. He is remembered above all as the leading witness of the musical life of his time, a man who, having frequented the cultural centers of Europe and gathered a vast amount of information, proceeded to publish a number of standard works on the subject. The most important of these remains his *General History of Music*, which appeared in London in four volumes between 1776 and 1789. As for John Marsh, the composer of five collections of *Voluntaries for Young Practitioners,* his passion for acoustical researches led him to construct a harpsichord with quarter tones (*nihil novi sub sole*: there was also one at Padua) – this in addition to his lively interest in astronomy and military strategy!

By the beginning of the nineteenth century, English organ writing, while continuing to hanker after Handel, was also alive to the spirit of the moment, and ready to respond to the advances of early German Romanticism. It continued to draw extensively upon the resources of the art of the fugue and sonata, but remained somewhat vague about the direction it intended to take. Thomas Attwood (1765–1838) was one of Mozart's favorite pupils and the first to recognize the talents of his future friend Felix Mendelssohn (who later dedicated his three Preludes and Fugues, Opus 37, to Attwood); George Guest (1771–1831), Crotch and William Russell (1777–1813) were other notable composers of the period. But it was two members of the Wesley family who gave English organ music its particular freedom of expression and contributed a splendid chapter to musical history. Natives of Bristol, the two brothers were sons of the Reverend Charles Wesley and nephews of the celebrated preacher and founder of the Methodist movement, John Wesley. Charles (1757–1834) and, above all, Samuel (1766–1837) wrote pieces which remain clearly indebted to the eighteenth century in their outlook (concertos, short character pieces, voluntaries, variations, fugues, interludes and independent movements), but their aesthetic, particularly in their formal structure (fugues, and preludes and fugues) reflects the profound admiration which the two brothers felt for the works of Johann Sebastian Bach. Samuel Wesley, one of the greatest organists of his generation, was largely responsible for the rediscovery in England of Bach's genius, not only through his concert performances of Bach's works, but also through his editions (in collaboration with Karl Friedrich Horn) of the *Wohltemperirtes Clavier*, published between 1810 and 1813, and of the trio sonatas in a version for two pianos. He also encouraged an English translation of Forkel's biography of Bach (1820). In this context, the meeting which took place between Samuel Wesley and Felix Mendelssohn at a concert given by Mendelssohn at Christ Church in Newgate Street, London, on September 12, 1837, a month before the death of the English organist, assumes a symbolic importance.

Although the nineteenth century did not produce any large-scale organ works in England, it remains an outstanding period thanks to the contributions of such eminent organist-interpreters as Thomas Adams (1785–1858), the "Thalberg of the organ," Samuel Sebastian Wesley (1810–76), the son of Samuel, Thomas (Attwood) Walmisley (1814–56), a great admirer of Bach and a friend of Mendelssohn's, and, above all, William Thomas Best (1826–97). Best, who was organist in Liverpool, transcribed and adapted for the organ a large number of orchestral works, just as the celebrated music publisher Vincent Novello (1781–1861) was to do for numerous vocal works by older English composers. Best also compiled *The Modern School for the Organ* (1853) and *The Art of Organ Playing* (from 1869), and edited works by some of the great masters of the past. He may be seen as the first significant advocate in England of the "secular" and symphonic organ, at a time when the study of works from previous centuries made up perhaps for the loss of any genuinely national sense of creativity, a sense which had already grown somewhat insipid even by the beginning of the century. It was a time, too, when organ building in England was growing increasingly responsive to a more generous aesthetic, embodied in the Great Exhibition of 1851 and developed, under the influence of Aristide Cavaillé-Coll, by William Hill, Henry John Gauntlett and Father Henry Willis. All of them created luxurious instruments in which the heritage of classicism coexists harmoniously with the orchestral ambitions of Romanticism.

England remained faithful to this aesthetic at least until the 1950s. It had been given a solid basis by the tradition of liturgical music which flourished in the great Anglican cathedrals. The style of writing of composers of this period – the majority of whom wrote only a few works for the organ – likewise remains indebted to this same perspective. In 1895 Sir Edward Elgar (1857–1934) wrote his imposing Sonata in G major (Opus 28). Basil Harwood (1859–1949) is the composer of two sonatas and a concerto that were influenced by the German Romanticism of Rheinberger. Celebrated in Great Britain are Sir Charles Villiers Stanford (1852–1924), an Irish composer noted especially for his Anglican church music, and Sir Hubert Parry (1848–1918), who was deeply influenced by Bach. Finally, brief mention may be made of Charles Wood (1866–1926), Walford Davies (1869–1941), Martin Shaw (1875–1958), Geoffrey Shaw (1879–1943), Herbert Murrill (1909–52), Richard Arnell (b. 1917), and above all Frank Bridge (1879–1941), Herbert Howells (1892–1983) and Benjamin Britten (1913–76), whose only piece for the organ is his *Prelude and Fugue on a theme by Victoria* (1947).

155 St. Stephen, Old Radnor, Wales
The case of this instrument is typical in style of the transitional period in art between Late Gothic and Early Renaissance. In spite of doubts as to its authenticity, it appears to date from the first half of the sixteenth century, which would make it the oldest case in the British Isles. Originally boasting five or seven stops (five for the Great Organ and perhaps two for the Choir Organ), the instrument was rebuilt in 1872 by J.W. Walker & Sons. It now has fifteen stops, two manuals (Great and Swell) and Pedal.

156 Adlington Hall, Cheshire, Bernard Smith, c. 1670
This instrument, which includes some of the pipework and perhaps also part of the case of an earlier instrument, must have been played on by Handel when he stayed at Adlington Hall in 1741 and 1751. In 1958 it was restored by Noël Mander, who rescued the instrument from a long period of total neglect and almost irreversible decay. It now comprises a Great Organ (twelve stops) and Choir Organ (three stops). The hall dates from around 1475, the organ having been built between two oak trees which are still rooted in the ground on either side of it.

157 King's College Chapel, Cambridge, Thomas Dallam, 1605–6
Perched on the screen in King's College Chapel, this case is one of only ten pre-Restoration English organ cases to have survived the political and religious troubles of the seventeenth century. Made of oak, it was designed and built by Chapman and Hartop of Cambridge. A Positive or Choir Organ was added in 1661 by Lancelot Pease, who also built the present Positive organ case, and may also have been responsible for the east case of the Great Organ. It was repaired and enlarged in 1640 by Henry Jennings; in 1677 by Thomas Thamar; in 1688 by Renatus Harris; in 1804 by John Avery; and in 1859 and 1906 by William Hill. It was rebuilt by Harrison & Harrison in 1934, 1950 and 1968, and now comprises four manuals and *Ped* with a total of seventy-eight stops.

159   St. James's Church, Piccadilly, London, Renatus Harris, 1685–8; originally in Queen's Chapel, Whitehall (known as the "Popish Chapel"), the organ was rebuilt in its present position by "Father" Smith in 1691, albeit without its Choir Organ; wood carvings by Grinling Gibbons

The instrument on which Henry Purcell and John Blow performed in July 1692 had twenty stops and three manuals, a Great and Swell Organ of forty-nine notes each, and an Echo Organ with a compass of twenty-five notes. The organ has been restored and altered on numerous occasions – by England in 1803; by Davis in 1821 when a pedalboard was added; by Bishop in 1831, 1852 and 1866 when the organ was converted to the German model and a new Swell Organ and Pedal were added, producing a total of thirty-nine stops of which eleven were part of the original instrument; and by Rothwell in 1914 and 1954 when electropneumatic action was installed. The organ is at present silent.

158   St. Michael's Church, Framlingham, Thomas Thamar, 1674; built for Pembroke College Chapel, Cambridge, and moved to its present site in 1708. Six stops and two half-stops, all of which still exist. The case dates from around 1630. The instrument was repaired in 1741 by John Byfield who added (or enlarged) the Swell Organ, and radically rebuilt by Alfred Hunter in 1898. It was restored in 1970 by Bishop & Son of Ipswich, and now comprises two manuals (Great and Swell) and a Pedal division, with a total of twenty speaking stops.

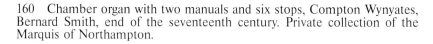

160   Chamber organ with two manuals and six stops, Compton Wynyates, Bernard Smith, end of the seventeenth century. Private collection of the Marquis of Northampton.

161   Trinity College Chapel, Cambridge, Bernard Smith, 1708
In 1686 Smith repaired an organ which Thomas Thamar had rebuilt in 1660, before himself building a new instrument for Trinity College Chapel in 1694. This was followed by a further instrument – the present organ – in 1708. Left incomplete on the death of the builder, it was finished by Christopher Schreider (or Shrider). Although the double case dates from 1708, the Choir Organ appears to be part of the 1694 instrument. Frequently modified, most notably in 1870 when Sir Arthur Blomfield added a pedal tower and pipe-flats to each side of the main case, the instrument was rebuilt by Harrison & Harrison in 1912–13. In 1975 the Swiss firm of Metzler built a new instrument in the tradition of "Father" Smith with four manuals and Pedal division, comprising forty-two speaking stops, of which seven are those of Smith's original instrument.

162 St. Magnus the Martyr, London Bridge, London, Abraham Jordan, 1712
This four-manual organ is the first to have been fitted with a swell box, an invention of the organ builders Abraham Jordan and his son (also called Abraham). They were presumably familiar with the echo boxes found in Iberian organs of the period. Still somewhat precarious, the system consisted of a panel which slid up and down on a cord which was passed over a pulley; one end of the cord was fixed to a pedal operated by the organist, whose chief task was to ensure that the board did not fall down with a bang. The instrument was rebuilt in the present century by R. Spurden Rutt & Company.

163 Parish Church of St. James, Great Packington, Thomas Parker, after 1749
This chamber organ, formerly at Gopsall Hall, Leicestershire, was built to Handel's specifications (see his letter to Charles Jennens of September 30, 1749). The Great Organ (seven stops) was built by Thomas Parker, and the three-stop Choir Organ by Johann Snetzler, still (it seems) in consultation with Handel.

164 Eton College, Eton, Johann Snetzler, 1760
This chamber organ, built for King George III, has eight stops. At the foot of the case were two pedals, the one on the left enabling the organist to cut out the Principal 4′ and all the higher stops, the one on the right (since removed) allowing him to open the shutters of a swell box.

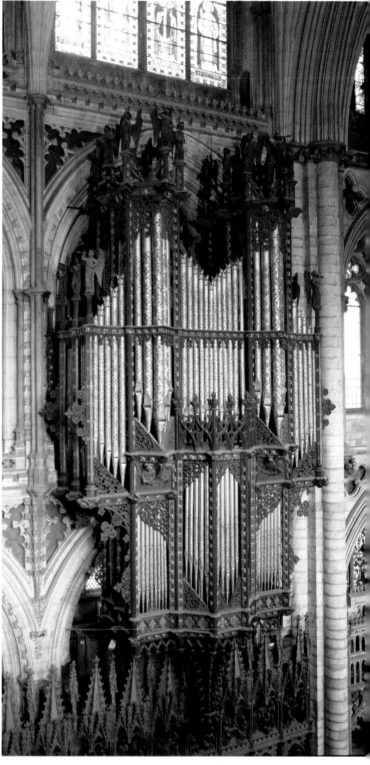

165   Minster, York, William Hill, 1829–32
Great Organ, Choir Organ (each with a compass of sixty notes), Swell Organ (forty-nine notes) and Pedal (nineteen keys). Neo-Gothic case by Thomas Elliot with wooden tracery gripping the different groups of pipes, and sometimes even individual pipes. Repeatedly rebuilt and restored (1859, 1903, 1931 and 1960), the organ now has four manuals and a pedal division, comprising in all seventy-eight speaking stops. Although the south transept of the minster was destroyed by lightning during the night of July 9, 1984, the organ appears to have suffered only slight damage from water.

166   Cathedral, Ely, Hill & Son, 1851; rebuilding and enlargement of the 1831 organ of Elliot & Hill
Great Organ, Choir, Swell and Pedal (forty-two stops). The organ case was designed by Sir Gilbert Scott "in imitation of the one in Strasbourg Cathedral." Additions and alterations in 1867 and 1884. In 1908 the firm of Harrison & Harrison built a four-manual organ (Great, Choir, Swell and Solo) with a Pedal division, comprising in all sixty-nine stops. Minor modifications were made to this instrument in 1956 and 1962. In 1974–5 the same firm added a fifth manual (Positive Organ), bringing the total number of speaking stops to seventy-eight.

167   Upper Chapel, Eton College, Eton, Dr Arthur George Hill, 1886; case and decorations by J.L. Pearson
Hill was one of the last great Victorian organ builders. Frequently modified, notably by Hill himself in 1902, this impressive organ, with its 32′ case pipes, now has five manuals (Great, Swell, Choir, Positif and Solo) and a Pedal division comprising sixty-four speaking stops.

168   Blenheim Palace Chapel, Woodstock, "Father" Henry Willis, 1891
This sumptuous instrument in the Long Library at Blenheim has four manuals (Great, Swell, Choir and Solo, each with a compass of fifty-eight notes) and Pedal (thirty keys), with a total of fifty-two speaking stops. In 1931 Henry Willis III installed a Welte System, enabling the instrument to play cylinders recorded by the great organists of the day. The organ was restored in 1949 by Henry Willis & Sons, and in 1978–9 by Wood, Wordsworth & Company.

169   Abbey, Selby, William Hill, 1909
Case by John Oldrid Scott to a design inspired by German and Spanish organ cases of the Gothic period, a style which asserts itself more clearly here than in the cases designed by his father. The instrument was altered and enlarged in 1930, again in 1947–50 and finally in 1975 by John T. Jackson & Son. It now has four manuals and a Pedal division, with a total of seventy-two stops.

VI Organce Music in France

FROM ITS ORIGINS TO THE BEGINNING OF THE NINETEENTH CENTURY

Although there are no specifically French documents before the sixteenth century, a remarkable flowering of medieval music was associated with the Notre-Dame school in Paris between 1150 and 1250. Under the cathedral's two organists Leoninus and Perotinus, this school produced works juxtaposing two, three and even four voices, and established by pragmatic means a number of the rules governing this early period of polyphony. The compositions in question, known as *organa* (*organum duplum*, *triplum* and *quadruplum*), although largely vocal in style, were almost certainly intended to be played on the organ, or on instrumental ensembles which included an organ.

The first tangible evidence of an organ repertory in France is the publication of seven volumes transcribed "en tablature d'Orgues Espinettes et Manicordions," published in 1531 by the Paris printer and music publisher Pierre Attaingnant. Four of these compilations contain secular music, including chansons and dances, and require an instrument in which the strings were either plucked or struck (although the works in question could certainly have been played on a portative, or court positive, or on a regal). The three remaining volumes, however, were intended specifically for use in religious services, and address themselves in effect to the organists of the day. The first of these brief volumes contains versets, intended to be performed *alternatim* with the choir, for the *Kyrie fons bonitatis* and *Cunctipotens*, two complete organ masses which postdate that of Hans Buchner by a number of years. The second volume comprises two preludes, versets for the Magnificat in all eight modes, and versets for the Te Deum. The final volume contains a prelude and transcriptions of two Italian songs, and polyphonic motets by a number of famous composers including Obrecht, Févin, Loyset Compère, Brumel, Lafage, Pierre Moulu, Claudin de Sermisy and Mathieu Gascongne. They are described as reduced "to organ tablature." None of these three tablatures, it must be said, contains works of any great merit: it appears that the publisher's intention was to provide contemporary organists with useful functional pieces capable of supplementing the somewhat limited repertory that existed at the time. Attaingnant's work was that of a compiler, who brought together works from the beginning of the sixteenth century and the very end of the fifteenth.

All these works, which are inferior to Italian or German compositions of that period and generally in two or three voices, are written on two staffs of five lines each. The three preludes, together with the versets in the first volume and some of the Magnificat and Te Deum versets, are original works; nor are the motet adaptations for choir, contained in the final volume, simply transcriptions of existing works. Certain of them are stylistically close to the fantasia. Many of them, moreover, involve finely-wrought imitations, in which the superius is particularly well developed.

Prior to the publication of Titelouze's two collections, French organ music of the sixteenth century was typified by popular dances such as the pavan, galliard and branle, and by fantaisies generally intended to be performed by an ensemble of keyboard instruments including organ, spinet and manicordion, or else by viols. The most important of these works are the *Fantazie sus Orgue ou Espinette* [Fantasia for Organ or Spinet] by Guillaume Costeley (1531–1606), organist to three kings, Henri II, Charles IX and Henri III; the three *Fantaisies instrumentales* [Instrumental Fantasias] (1612) by the Protestant composer Claude Le Jeune (*c*.1530–1600), based chiefly on secular themes; the forty-two *Fantaisies à III, IIII, V, et VI, Parties* [Fantasias in 3, 4, 5 and 6 Voices] published in separate voices in 1610 by Eustache Du Caurroy (1549–1609), for whom Henri IV created the post of Surintendant de la Musique du Roi in 1599; and the twenty-four *Fantaisies* "for viols or organ" by the Flemish composer Karel Guillet (d. 1654).

What makes these works interesting is, above all, the clear distinction between instrumental music on the one hand and vocal music on the other, together with the development of a style which, based on the ricercare form and the device of imitation, led to a type of writing unmistakably associated with the organ. It was a development encouraged first and foremost by Jehan Titelouze (1563–1633), who may be regarded as the founder of a style of music specific to the organ in seventeenth-century France.

Organist at the Cathedral of Notre-Dame in Rouen, where he succeeded François Josseline in 1588, Titelouze was also an erudite theorist, a friend of Marin Mersenne, a poet, a practising musician whom numerous other organists came to hear, an expert in organ building, and a teacher. His collected works were published by Ballard in Paris in two volumes: *Hymnes de l'Eglise pour Toucher sur l'Orgue, avec les Fugues et Recherches sur Leur Plain Chant* [Church Hymns to be Performed on the Organ, with Plainchant Fugues and Ricercari] appeared in 1623, followed in 1626 by *Le Magnificat, ou Cantique de la Vierge pour Toucher sur l'Orgue, Suivant les Huit Tons de l'Eglise* [The Magnificat, or Hymn to the Virgin, to be Performed on the Organ, following the Eight Ecclesiastical Modes]. The first volume contains twelve Latin hymns, each of three or four versets, while the second includes a group of seven versets for each of the eight Magnificats. In all, there are ninety-five pieces printed on two staffs of five lines each. Although the author is clearly in error when he informs the reader in his 1623 preface that "No organ tablature has been printed in France within living memory," his remark nevertheless reveals how poorly disseminated organ music must have been in seventeenth-century France. We may also mention here the instructions which Titelouze gives for performing his works: the instrument which he used (rebuilt and enlarged in 1600/1 by Crespin Carlier) was fitted with two manual keyboards, and with pedals with a compass of thirty notes "in order to be able to play the bass separately, without using the hands, the tenor on the second manual, the alto and treble on the third" ("pour y toucher la Basse contre à part, sans toucher de la main, la taille sur le second clavier, la Haute contre et le Dessus sur le troisième"). Titelouze's writing is based upon the principle of imitation applied to plainchant melodies in four (exceptionally, three) voices. Faithful to the church modes at a time when they were already giving way in secular music to the contrasting duality of major/minor tonalities, and attached to the idea of simple rhythms, Titelouze advises the performer to decorate the different lines with a variety of ornaments, although the printer's lack of the necessary characters prevented him from indicating any ornamentation in his scores (an omission which gives his writing the impression of bareness and austerity). Titelouze also indulges a refined predilection for dissonances and other unusual harmonic effects, and uses chromaticism, although sparingly, notably in his Magnificats. Most of his works adopt the form of the ricercare, which he himself calls a *recherche*, and are densely and even majestically polyphonic.

These works by the organist from Rouen are exceptional and, indeed, unique in the first half of the seventeenth century. They foreshadow a style of organ music which was to be typical of the age of Louis XIV. At the same time, Titelouze marks the culmination of a type of writing which, in the years following his death, was to undergo a spectacular transformation – a culmination, moreover, which finds a somewhat different expression in the works of Charles Racquet (1590–1664), organist at Notre-Dame in Paris and a collaborator of Mersenne. His *Fantaisie*, which is of impressive dimensions, belongs to the polyphonic and modal tradition of the earlier period, and displays an immense freedom of style.

It is impossible to do more than list the names of the Paris organists who were contemporaries or successors of Titelouze, and who have left at most a handful of keyboard works. They include Florent Bienvenu, Jean Lesecq, Marin Deslions, Etienne Richard (*c.* 1621–69), Pierre Chabanceau de La Barre (1592–1656) and his son Joseph Chabanceau de La Barre (1633–78), Charles Couperin (1638–79), the brother of Louis and father of François "le Grand," Jacques-Denis Thomelin (*c.* 1640–93), who taught François Couperin, and, finally, Henry Du Mont from the Liège region.

It is, however, François Roberday (1624–80), organist at Notre-Dame-des-Victoires and *valet de chambre* to Anne of Austria and Marie-Thérèse of Spain, whose works are best able to stand comparison with those of Titelouze. As he explains in his *Advertissement* of 1660, his *Fugues et Caprices, à Quatre Parties Mises en Partition pour l'Orgue* [Fugues and Caprices in Four Voices, printed in Full Score for the Organ] (transcribed for the organ but equally suited to performance on the viols) remain indebted to the polyphonic style of Titelouze, but also show the liberating influence of Frescobaldi and the latter's pupil Froberger. Borrowing freely from contemporary musicians such as de La Barre, Couperin, Robert Cambert, D'Anglebert, and even Froberger, Cavalli and Bertani (for the period, after all, was dominated by the musical taste of Cardinal Mazarin), Roberday wrote fugues and caprices with all the skill of an accomplished contrapuntalist. This collection, graced by the addition of three fugues by Frescobaldi, Ebner and Froberger, may be seen above all as evidence of the influence in France of the Italian Renaissance and of the Italianate composers of southern Germany.

By 1650, the erudite austerity of Titelouze had become little more than a distant memory. It was no longer the Italy of Frescobaldi which conditioned the musical taste of the period, but that of opera, as the world of French music grew increasingly fascinated by the luminous simplicity of a melodic line whose most eminent exponents in Paris were Cavalli and Lully. In this way the organ set out on the secular path which had already been traveled by more popular instruments such as the lute and, above all, the harpsichord. It was a development encouraged by the fact that the majority of organists were themselves *clavecinistes*: notably Etienne Richard, "maître d'épinette du Roi"; Jean Denis, the author of a *Traité de l'accord de l'Espinette* [Treatise on Tuning a Spinet] and a famous *Prélude pour sonder si l'accord est bon partout* [Prelude to Determine whether the Instrument is Accurately Tuned throughout its Compass]; Du Mont; Cambert; and, of course, Jacques Champion, Sieur de Chambonnières, organist and harpsichordist to the Chapelle royale. It was thus to be expected that French organists should borrow the form of the "suite" from the harpsichord, while from the theater they took its effects and *récit* and from the century as a whole its taste for a certain *préciosité* in music. This intrusion of elements and forms typical of secular music had a profound effect on the style of writing for the organ, although the pieces concerned continued to be based upon plainchant melodies. In 1662, moreover, the *Ceremoniale parisiense* defined the role of the organ in religious services: it was to give the choir its entry by means of a brief prelude; it alternated with the choir in the Kyrie, Gloria, Sanctus and Agnus Dei, and it functioned as a solo instrument in the Offertory, Elevation, and at the end of the mass. Respect for the old ecclesiastical modes, as shown by composers such as Nicolas Gigault (1625–1707), Nicolas-Antoine Lebègue (*c.* 1631–1702), Guillaume-Gabriel Nivers (1632–1714) and François Couperin (1668–1733), could not, however, resist either the assaults of the new tonality or the advent of more popular themes. It was a phenomenon already embodied in the works of Gigault and Lebègue, which was to culminate at the end of the eighteenth century and beginning of the nineteenth in the *noëls* of Pierre Dandrieu (d. 1733), Louis-Claude Daquin (1614–1772), Michel Corrette (1709–95) and Claude-Bénigne Balbastre (1727–99).

At a time of brilliant pomp and sumptuous display, it was inevitable that organ writing should rely heavily upon the art of improvisation – an art in which the organists of the day were past masters. Their aim was to seduce their listeners by melodic and sonorous means, and primarily by the first of these devices. With few exceptions, musicians were happy to abandon the more elaborate large-scale structures, preserving only a prelude by way of an overture, and delighting in writing *cantabile* lines for solo voice (*récit*) – in the soprano, tenor or bass – with discreet and simple support being provided by the remaining voices; or else they devised elegant antiphonal effects in duos, trios, echos and dialogs. The listener was also to be seduced by the new sonorities of the instrument, inasmuch as the pieces in question allowed the organist to show off the tonal colors of an instrument fitted with a third and, later, with a fourth manual – foundation voices, *pleins jeux, Dialogues sur les Grands Jeux*, and solo stops.

Following the example of Mersenne who, in his *Harmonie universelle* of 1636, has given us one of the earliest descriptions of French organ stops for the first part of the classical period, the majority of seventeenth-century composers wrote prefaces in which to set forth their intentions, often specifying the registrations which they required. To the later text by Dom Bédos de Celles (Part III, Chapter IV, "Les principaux mélanges ordinaires des Jeux de l'Orgue, lus, examinés, corrigés & approuvés par les plus habiles & les plus célèbres Organistes de Paris, tels que Messieurs Calviere, Fouquet, Couperin, Balbâtre, & autres," 1766–78), may be added prefaces by Nivers (*Premier Livre d'orgue*, 1665), Lebègue (*Premier Livre d'orgue*, 1676; anonymous text to the *Second Livre d'orgue*, 1678), Nicolas Gigault (*Livre de musique pour l'orgue*, 1685), André Raison (*Livre d'orgue*, 1688), Jacques Boyvin (*Premier Livre d'orgue*, 1689), Gilles Jullien (*Livre d'orgue*, 1689), Lambert Chaumont (*Livre d'orgue*, 1695), Gaspard Corrette (*Messe du 8e ton*, 1703), Michel Corrette (*Premier Livre d'orgue*, 1737), and two anonymous manuscripts dating from *c.* 1713 (Anonyme de Tours) and 1746 (Anonyme de Caen, *La Manière très facile pour apprendre la facture d'orgue* [A Most Simple Method for Learning Organ Building]).

Anxious to ensure an accurate interpretation of his works, and meticulous in his description of the sounds to be produced, the French organist of the seventeenth century may certainly be described, like the Provençal organist Luis de Aranda, as a "charming nightingale," both for his gift as an improviser and his talents as a *coloriste*.

The spectacular rise of the "melodic" organ under Louis XIV began with Louis Couperin (*c.* 1626–61), who in 1653 became organist of St. Gervais in Paris, a post which was to remain in the Couperin family for the next 175 years. Of his two hundred or so surviving works, the majority are clearly written for the harpsichord, although a number of them may be performed on the organ to excellent effect. The rich harmonic writing of his allemandes, sarabandes, chaconnes *en rondeau*, fantaisies, and dances such as pavans, galliards and branles, makes lavish use of extensive chromaticisms and splendid dissonances. From among Couperin's works we may single out for particular mention a Passacaglia with thirty-nine variations, and his *Carillon de Paris*, which tradition asserts was regularly played at St. Gervais between vespers on All Saints' Day and vespers on All Souls' Day. We may finally note that Louis Couperin was the creator of a genre which was to grace the great school of French organ music, namely the *Basse de trompette*.

Following Couperin's death, the names which stand out along the road leading to the golden age of French organ music are those of Louis Marchand (1669–1732), François Couperin and Nicolas de Grigny (1672–1702). There are, however, numerous other organist-composers of the time whose works seem constantly to hesitate between the demands of the liturgy on the one hand and the temptations of the concert organ on the other. Nivers, organist at St. Sulpice in Paris and a pupil of Du Mont and perhaps also of Chambonnières, was without doubt the first composer to define the new melodic style: in this way the polyphonic style, advocated in France by Titelouze and Roberday, finally succumbed to the seductions of accompanied monody. Nivers added new forms to the existing repertory, taking full advantage of the sonorous possibilities and the most varied tonal colors which his instrument had to offer. His three *Livres d'orgue*, published in 1665, 1667 and 1675, comprise works which are at once concise and varied.

A more traditional contribution is that of Jean-Henri D'Anglebert (1628–91), who published, in 1689, a volume of harpsichord works including *Cinq fugues pour l'orgue sur un même sujet* [Five Fugues for Organ, on the Same Subject], and a Quatuor on the Kyrie whose strict counterpoint is in the spirit of the ricercare, and reminiscent in style of the works of Titelouze. A native of Laon, Lebègue was organist at St. Merry in Paris. A recognized expert in organ building and an eminent teacher, whose pupils included Grigny, Lebègue was one of the most prolific composers of his day. He published four volumes of organ works in the dozen years beginning in 1676. Following Nivers's example, he paid tribute to the ecclesiastical modes, and grouped the versets of his Masses and Magnificats in the form of suites. There is a facility about his *concertante* writing for the *Récit*, including Cornet, Cromorne and Trompette solos, as well as Duos, Trios and so on. At the same time he is occasionally innovatory in the matter of registrations. His at times somewhat fashionable style is particularly impressive when he allows himself to be influenced by Lully, as in his symphonies, published in his *Troisième Livre d'Orgue* of 1685, which contains in addition some fine *noëls*.

Gigault, the incumbent of several Paris organs, has left us two volumes of works, a *Livre de Musique* dedicated to the Blessed Virgin Mary and published in 1683, and a *Livre de Musique pour l'orgue*, dated 1685. The first of these collections contains, most notably, a number of *noëls variés*. Like Lebègue, Gigault was to open the way in France to this new genre of variation on popular themes, a genre which continued to enjoy a lively success until as late as the early nineteenth century. Gigault's second volume contains upwards of 180 short pieces grouped into three Masses structured around the church modes, and a Te Deum.

André Raison (*c.* 1640–1719), organist at Ste. Geneviève-du-Mont in Paris, and Clérambault's teacher, published two sets of organ Masses. The first, dated 1688, contains *Cinq Messes suffisantes pour tous les tons de l'Eglise* [Five Masses Sufficient for all the Church Models], which the composer invites the organist to perform "in the same manner as on a harpsichord," but more slowly "because of the solemnity of the place." Also included here is an *Offerte du Vᵉ ton* [Offertory in the Fifth Mode] on *Vive le Roy* [Long Live the King], written for the entry of Louis XIV to the Hôtel-de-Ville on January 30, 1687, following the king's return to health. We may also note that in his *Messe du IIᵉ ton*, Raison has included a *Trio en passacaille* for the *Christe*, the theme of which almost certainly inspired Johann Sebastian Bach since it forms the first part of the theme of Bach's Passacaglia in C minor. Raison's second volume of 1714, published "to acclaim the much-desired peace" [of Utrecht], contains a number of *noëls variés*. Raison, who was a secular composer to the extent that he chose never to use plainchant melodies, remains interesting above all for his sense of improvisation, tonal color and brilliance.

Having studied in Paris under the above-mentioned organists, Jean-Nicolas Geoffroy (1633–94), Gilles Jullien (*c.* 1650–1703) and Jacques Boyvin (1653–1706) took with them to the provinces the lessons which they had learned in the capital. A pupil of Lebègue, Geoffroy was organist at St. Nicolas-du-Chardonnet in Paris until 1690, when he took up an appointment as cathedral organist in Perpignan. He appears to be the author of an unpublished *Livre d'orgue* preserved in the Bibliothèque du Conservatoire in Paris containing *noëls variés* and transcriptions of instrumental works by Lully.

Possibly a pupil of Gigault's, Jullien was organist at Chartres Cathedral from 1668 onwards. His *Livre d'orgue* of 1689 follows the church modes and comprises eight suites of ten works each. Boyvin, who probably studied under Lebègue, was appointed organist of Rouen Cathedral in 1674. His two *Livres d'orgue* of 1689 and 1700 comprise suites "in the eight Modes for ordinary use in Churches," and reveal Boyvin as an inspired composer both in respect of his rich harmonic writing and his taste for polyphony; his fugues owe much to the influence of Titelouze. Equally striking is his handling of tonal color, for, as he informed the reader of his *Avis au public* [Foreword] in 1689, "one of the finest of pleasures [. . .] is knowing how properly to handle the stops."

As the seventeenth century drew to a close, it was, however, François Couperin and especially Grigny who were left to complete the task which their predecessors had begun. These composers had progressively given a precise framework to the organ mass, according to the norms defined by the *Ceremoniale parisiense* of 1662: twenty-one versets allowed the organist to alternate with the choir during the four major prayers sung in plainchant. In addition to these interventions, the Offertory, and sometimes the Elevation and the Deo Gratias at the end of the mass, gave the organist an opportunity to express himself more freely. Two further characteristics gave an additional profile to this framework: a more precise definition of the formal structures of the versets and also of the registrations. Thus, the first verset of each section of the mass was conceived in the form of a *Grand Plein Jeu*, generally constructed on the *cantus firmus* of the plainchant melody played on the pedals in long note-values. The second verset of the Kyrie and Gloria was frequently a fugue; and the Gloria would also contain six "couplets" intended for the most part to be played on solo stops. The final versets of the Kyrie and Gloria often took the form of a *Dialogue sur les Grands Jeux.*

Louis Couperin's nephew, François Couperin (II) was born on November 10, 1668 in Paris, where his teachers included Jacques-Denis Thomelin and probably also Michel-Richard de Lalande. He was seventeen when, in 1685, he officially took possession of the "paternal" organ at St. Gervais. It had been held in reserve for him since the death of his father six years previously and maintained in the meantime by de Lalande, who was a friend of the family. It was soon after this, in 1690, that Couperin wrote his only volume of organ music, *Pièces d'orgue consistantes en deux Messes, l'une à l'usage ordinaire des Paroisses pour les Festes Solemnelles, l'Autre propre pour les Convents de Religieux et Religieuses* [Organ Works, consisting of Two Masses, the First for Ordinary Use in Parish Churches on Solemn Occasions, the Second appropriate for Use in Monasteries and Convents]. It was a precocious masterpiece by a composer who was soon to be appointed *maître de clavecin* to the Duc de Bourgogne, and later composer in ordinary to the king, and who subsequently wrote nothing but instrumental and vocal music. The *Messe des Paroisses* [Parish-church Mass] emerges as the more elaborate of the two masses: based on the Gregorian melodies of Mass IV, it contains some excellent pieces, albeit somewhat immature in style. As an example of exceptional spaciousness in French organ writing, we may single out the *Offertoire sur les Grands Jeux* [Offertory on the *Grands Jeux*], a vast triptych in which a solemn prelude, reminiscent of Lully, and a *fugato* gigue frame a splendid movement in three, and then four, voices, enlivened by dissonances and chromatic writing. Whereas the *Messe des Paroisses* is written for a large organ with independent pedals such as the one at St. Gervais, the *Messe des Couvents* is suited to a more modest instrument fitted with pedals of the "pull-down" variety. Written in the single key of G, this work is not based on any known plainchant melody.

In Grigny the school of French organ music produced a genius whose works for the instrument are without equal: works which are brief but dense, vital yet all too quickly forgotten by organists and composers who preferred the decorative impulses of the moment to the grandeur of rational intellect. Born in Rheims, Grigny was a pupil of Lebègue and organist at the abbey of St. Denis in Paris before he took up an appointment, probably in 1696, as organist of the cathedral in his native Rheims. Published in 1699, his *Premier Livre d'orgue* reveals him as the most demanding of composers and the most eminent not only of Titelouze's disciples but of the whole line of French organists who conformed to the newer style. Grigny represents a perfect synthesis of these two complementary trends. His superior intellect enabled him to achieve that rare combination of form and content which is indispensible to lasting merit and in which his only rival is Bach. His modernity is sustained by the most authentic of traditions: at a time when accompanied *récit* was the current fashion, he wrote fastidiously polyphonic textures of five voices displaying an elegant and lucid counterpoint, while at the same time reveling in the most skillful of dissonances and developing erudite fugues without the least signs of inflexibility, but, on the contrary, investing the writing with a hitherto unknown freedom of expression and clothing it with a rich profusion of ornaments. The works in question, a large-scale mass and five hymns, are stupendous pieces, unremittingly original and revealing an outstanding compositional technique and constant freshness of inspiration. They are imbued, moreover, with a profound sense of meditation: the hymns and *récits* – especially the one on the *Pange lingua*, which is the only ornamental chorale in the whole of French organ music – are veritable confessions of faith, comparable only to the works of

Johann Sebastian Bach himself. Indeed, it is worth remembering that in 1703, at Lüneburg, Bach copied out almost every page of Grigny's *Livre d'orgue*, omitting only the *pleins jeux*, an act of supreme homage to a genius whom the Thomascantor considered the equal of Frescobaldi.

The French organ had now reached its highest pinnacle of achievement; but, as the new century dawned, had not its example come too late? The liturgical organ would be forced, irremediably, to yield to the concert organ, although for a further fifteen years or so a number of practising composers continued steadfastly to maintain the older tradition.

Among the contemporaries of Couperin and Grigny, the most eminent was undoubtedly Marchand. A native of Lyons, Marchand held appointments as organist in Nevers, Auxerre, and, from 1689 onwards, in Paris where he officiated in several churches, as well as in the Chapelle royale at Versailles. He led a turbulent life in which charges of unscrupulous ambition and irascibility threatened his preeminence as a harpsichord virtuoso. His works for the organ, not published during his lifetime, have been grouped together in five volumes. The first, containing *Pièces choisies* [Selected Works] and published by his daughter in the year her father died, reveals a more accomplished style than the remaining volumes, in which many of the brief works appear to be pedagogical in character and intended as a basis for improvisations. This first volume of Marchand's works, in which many excellent things are to be found side by side with more trivial works, is at one with its period, both in its grandiose and archaic beauty and in its rather more galant elegance. His best work reveals an harmonic language which is always imaginative and sometimes bold, together with powerful tonal structures in which the composer demands the use of double pedals, notably in his splendid *Grand Dialogue* in C major, dating from 1696, and the *Plein Jeu* in six voices from the first volume of *Pièces choisies*. There is, finally, an inner sense of lyricism about these works – one thinks of the Quatuor in the same volume – while melodic phrases are given their due value by the virtuosity of this great *claveciniste*, whose abundant riches are unfortunately less well known than the comparatively minor episode of his unsuccessful contest with Bach in Dresden in 1717.

The great school of French organ music came to an end with the final generation of seventeenth-century composers, born around 1680, organists who were for the most part *clavecinistes* and who continued to show a willing respect for the church organ while adapting their own virtuosity and the charm of the age to suit its demands.

Marchand's deputy and almost certainly one of his pupils was Jean Adam Guillaume Guilain (fl. 1702–39), who was originally called Freinsberg and therefore presumably of German extraction. His most important work was a collection of *Pièces d'orgue pour le Magnificat* on the eight church modes (1706) in which the composer, in spite of the work's title, includes only four suites of seven pieces each (six versets alternating with the choir, and a concluding Amen), on the first four modes. These works bear the imprint of the style of their dedicatee, Louis Marchand (e.g. the Quatuor of the *Suite du IIIe ton*), together with a *sensibilité* influenced by Italianate models. An additional composer anxious to "write according to the learned school and the taste of the illustrious Monsieur Marchand" was another of Marchand's pupils, Pierre Du Mage (c. 1676–1751), a native of Beauvais and organist at the collegiate church of St. Quentin. Published in 1708, his *Premier Livre d'Orgue* contains a *Suite du Ier ton* comprising eight very fine pieces. Jean-François Dandrieu (or d'Andrieu) (c. 1682–1738), organist at St. Merry in Paris and later at the Chapelle royale, wrote a *Livre de Noëls* together with a *Premier Livre de Pièces d'Orgue* published in the year after his death. Dandrieu, who may have been a pupil of Lebègue's and who was also a *claveciniste*, is the author of an interesting work on the *Principes de l'accompagnement du clavecin* [Principles of Harpsichord Accompaniment]. His compositions are written in three tonalities, each in the minor and the major, and are stylistically agreeable pieces which draw from time to time on liturgical themes. Dandrieu was the last composer to tackle the genre of the large-scale Offertory.

With Louis-Nicolas Clérambault (1676–1749), organist at various churches, including St. Cyr and St. Sulpice where he succeeded Nivers, the organ addresses itself consciously and grandiloquently to its own age. Clérambault was descended from a family which had been in the service of the kings of France since the end of the fifteenth century. Dedicated to his teacher André Raison, his *Premier Livre d'orgue*, containing two *Suites du Ier et IIe ton* and dating from 1710, while conceived within the formal tradition of French polyphony, draws its inspiration from the lyric expressiveness of the Italian style and from the spirit of the dance. These works are among the most charming and most often performed in the French organ repertory. The final organ mass written in France was published in 1703 under the title *Messe du 8e ton pour l'orgue, à l'usage des Dames Religieuses et utile à ceux qui touchent l'orgue* [Organ Mass in the Eighth Mode, for Use in Nunneries and for All who Play the Organ], and was the work of the Rouen organist Gaspard Corrette, a native of Delft, who probably studied under Boyvin. Later composers whose names deserve to be mentioned include François D'Agincour (1684–1758), a pupil of Lebègue and organist in Paris and Rouen, who wrote six *Suites pour orgue*; Louis-Antoine Dornel (*c.* 1685–1765), organist in Paris; Nicolas Siret (d. 1754), a pupil of François Couperin and organist at Troyes Cathedral; and Charles Piroye (1668/72–1717/30), organist in Amiens and Paris.

The *noëlistes*

At a time when organ music was capitulating to the art of the *clavecinistes* and, more generally, to the new demands which were being made by the general public, French organists turned with enthusiasm to a type of melodic variation radically different from the genres previously associated with the instrument. The *Variations sur les "timbres" de Noël* drew on both the art of diminution as practised by the English virginalists and that of the "double," a genre in which the lutanists, violists and harpsichordists of the period all excelled. The extraordinary infatuation which ordinary folk felt for this new genre seems to be due to the semi-popular nature of these melodies, some of which date back to the sixteenth century, to their rustic and picturesque charms and to the engaging simplicity of their emotional impact. Additionally, and perhaps crucially, there was the attraction exerted by the digital dexterity of musicians giving free rein to a virtuosity which bubbled over with exuberance, and to the most imaginative use of the tonal and technical possibilities of their instrument, including echo effects, dialogs on the solo stops, and a profusion of ornaments. At the same time, the prodigious success of the *noël varié* may be the unconscious expression of a sense of nostalgia for an age which by the eighteenth century had ceased to exist, a regret for free and simple rhythms and for the particular flavor of a tonal coloring which was still mode-conscious. For these variations have an earthiness to them, a bitter taste of youthful immaturity typical of these regional products, which were slowly being destroyed in the process of cultural centralization. They include *noëls* from Provence, Burgundy, Poitou, Gascony, Lorraine and even from Switzerland.

Between the end of the seventeenth century and the beginning of the nineteenth, the genre of the *noël varié* was cultivated successively by Lebègue in his second and third *Livres d'orgue*, dating from 1678 and 1682; by Gigault, who published the first *Livre de Noëls variés* in 1682; and later by the abbé Pierre Dandrieu, the uncle of Jean-François Dandrieu and organist at St. Barthélémy in Paris, whose *Livre de Noëls: O filii, Chansons de Saint-Jacques, Stabat Mater et Carillons* appeared in 1714; and by André Raison in his *Second Livre d'Orgue* of 1714. A generation later are the *noëls* of Jean-François Dandrieu, who for the most part took up his uncle's works, publishing them under the same title and adapting them to the taste of the 1730s. Other collections are those by Dornel and, above all, Daquin, whose sole surviving work is his *Nouveau Livre de Noëls pour l'orgue et le clavecin, dont la pluspart peuvent s'exécuter sur les Violons, Flûtes, Hautbois, etc.* [New Book of Noëls for Organ & Harpsichord, the Majority of which may be Performed on Violins, Flutes, Oboes, etc]. There followed Michel Corrette, whose *Nouveau Livre de Noëls avec un Carillon* dates from 1733; and Balbastre and his *Recueil de Noëls formant quatre Suites avec des variations* [Collection of Noëls forming Four Suites with Variations]. Jean-Jacques Beauvarlet-Charpentier

(1734–94), Guillaume Lasceux (1740–1831) and Nicolas Séjan (1745–1819) showed little effectiveness or enthusiasm in continuing an art that was already decadent.

There are few works meriting attention in a century in which the French organ sought to satisfy the inordinate adulation of the masses, dazzled by the virtuoso performances they had come to hear. Indeed, there were times when the church authorities had to organize a police contingent to contain the crowds of admirers: they turned up in such force that their carriages blocked the streets around the church, so that the authorities were panicked into banning midnight mass to avoid further disorders.

Capitulating to public taste, composers of the period wrote their *noëls variés* interchangeably for the organ, harpsichord, fortepiano, or other melodic instruments. Among the few composers who wrote works of merit specifically for the organ are the following: Michel Corrette of Rouen, probably the son of Gaspard Corrette and organist in Paris, whose three *Livres de Pièces d'Orgue* and a collection of *Offertoires* contain a handful of pleasant surprises in addition to a number of highly trivial evocations of nature; Balbastre of Dijon, who also held a post as organist in Paris and who amused himself transcribing Rameau's *Ouvertures* for the organ; Séjan of Paris, a nephew and pupil of Forqueray, and, like Daquin and Balbastre, organist at Notre-Dame, who wrote a number of attractive Fugues, as did Lasceux and Jean-Jacques Beauvarlet-Charpentier, organist at Lyons and Paris and a specialist in imitating such climatic conditions as gales, thunder and storms. We may finally list Guillaume-Antoine Calvière (*c.* 1695–1755) of Paris, Christophe Moyreau of Orléans, Michel Corrette (II), son of the foregoing, who published his *Pièces pour l'orgue d'un genre nouveau* [Organ Works in a New Genre] in 1786, Jacques-Marie Beauvarlet-Charpentier (1766–1834), the son of Jean-Jacques, Pierre Février (1715–80), Eloi-Nicolas-Marie Miroir (1746–1815) and Jean-Nicolas Marrigues (1757–1834).

Thus we find the Revolution, Empire and Restoration taking pleasure in uninspired fugues, descriptive improvisations of uncertain taste, including storms, pastorals, carillons, marches and hunts, in addition to overtures and symphonies which for all their charm are unworthy of the church organ, and countless paraphrases of symphonies by Mozart and Haydn (for which Guillaume Lasceux wrote a performing guide, *Essai théorique et pratique sur l'art de l'orgue* [Theoretical and Practical Essay on the Art of the Organ]), not to mention transcriptions of operatic *scenas*, arias and choruses, piano works, and so on. There is only one exception to this flood of mediocrity, namely the improvisations which were performed on the *Ça ira* and *Marseillaise* and which, when played on the organ, saved the instrument from the turmoil of the Revolution.

In France, as in Italy, Germany and England at this time, the organ fell momentarily silent, holding its breath in anticipation of the arrival of Boëly and César Franck.

FRENCH ORGAN MUSIC IN THE NINETEENTH CENTURY

At the beginning of the nineteenth century there is only one musician whose contribution to French organ music could be described in any way as significant: Alexandre-Pierre-François Boëly (1785–1858). The son of one of the Chapelle royale musicians at Versailles, Boëly discovered the works of Bach and Beethoven through the intermediacy of Ignaz Anton Ladurner, his Austrian teacher of composition at the Paris Conservatoire. Organist at St. Germain-l'Auxerrois, where he had a German pedalboard installed, Boëly revealed to the new generation of French organ composers, including Gigout and Franck, as well as to his pupil Saint-Saëns, the polyphonic riches not only of Bach, Walther and Kirnberger, but also of Frescobaldi and Couperin. A prolific composer, Boëly left a significant number of works for the organ. They are characterized by their solid grasp of counterpoint, as illustrated by his preludes, fugues and canons, and by a new harmonic perception which may allow us to regard him as the precursor of a later generation. In his attempts to find a synthesis of opposing styles, he was to give the French organ a sense of originality which it had not enjoyed since the days of Grigny. By transcribing and publishing works by eighteenth-century French and German composers, he supplemented the existing repertory, adding to it, on the one hand, works which are thoroughly French in conception and which include *cantus firmus* versets, *Tierces en taille*, *Pleins Jeux*, dialogs, duos, trios, quatuors and *noëls*, and, on the other hand, German-type compositions such as preludes and fugues, and fantasias and fugues, of which he was the earliest exponent in France. His works, it may be added, are addressed not only to the organ, but also to the pedal piano and piano for three hands.

The direction which Boëly took was much to be welcomed and one in which he was followed – in spite of a general lack of interest on the part of the public at large – by the eminent composers of his day, including François Benoist (1794–1878), who in 1819 was appointed professor of the organ at the Paris Conservatoire, Clément Loret (1833–1909), and music publishers such as Louis Niedermeyer and Joseph d'Ortigue, who played a leading part in the plainchant revival by means of their Ecole de musique religieuse classique [School of Classical Religious Music] and, from 1857, the periodical *La Maîtrise*. When we recall that Reicha was appointed professor of counterpoint and fugue at the Conservatoire in 1818, that some of the great German organists gave a number of recitals in Paris at this time, that in 1840 Félix Danjou published his *Répertoire complet de l'organiste*, setting out the classical organ repertory, and that in 1843 the Benedictine abbot of Solesmes, Dom Prosper Guéranger, undertook a reform of plainchant in France, we can see that French organ music was now embarked on a profitable course.

A momentary lull ensued prior to the appearance of the major works of César Franck, whose *Six pièces* date from 1862. The interval was filled by the fashionable, and indeed unashamedly popular, works of two organists who were idolized by the masses at a time when Offenbach was all the rage – Antoine-Edouard Batiste (1820–76) and, above all, Louis James Alfred Lefébure-Wély (1817–69). It was to the latter that the honor fell of inaugurating the major Paris organs of Cavaillé-Coll: a somewhat tasteless joke on the part of destiny allowed this eminent creator of storm scenes and Last Judgements to perform on instruments intended for a totally different kind of music. The works of Lefébure-Wély, who was organist at St. Roch, La Madeleine and St. Sulpice, and who was acclaimed as a brilliant improviser, are by no means totally lacking in charm, as long as the listener does not take them too seriously.

We have noted that conditions now existed in France for a revival of organ music. The man to whom it fell to renew the language of organ music was César Franck, a composer of German extraction who was born in Liège and who studied in Paris, where he was a pupil of Benoist. The posts which he held in the French capital include *maître de chapelle* and organist at Ste. Clotilde, an appointment which he took up in 1858. His profound knowledge of the classical repertory of Mozart, Beethoven, Schubert, Mendelssohn and Bach, to whose works he was introduced by Boëly at a somewhat later date, was complemented by a thorough understanding of the symphonic aesthetic of the newer type of organ being built at this time by Cavaillé-Coll. An excellent improviser trained in the school of pianistic technique, Franck was forty years old when he began writing for the organ; he produced about a dozen works of importance.

Considered by Liszt as "l'égal de notre maître à tous, le grand Jean-Sébastien Bach," Franck returned afresh to the classical forms of the sonata and fugue, which he proceeded to subject to his own particular aesthetic. He essayed, albeit timidly, the "cyclical" use of themes in some of his large-scale compositions, a process to which Liszt himself was to lend the glory of his name, as, more systematically, did Wagner. Conceived for the most part in tripartite form, his works develop along vast and spacious lines, and are imbued with a highly personal lyricism. Although Franck wrote a number of more circumscribed works for harmonium and organ, including the fifty-nine short pieces of *L'Organiste*, his first major work for the "Grand Orgue" was his *Six pièces* (Opus 16–21), of 1862. These six pieces are a *Fantaisie* in C major; a *Grande Pièce symphonique* which is sufficiently important to be regarded as the earliest organ symphony before those of Widor; a *Prélude, fugue et variation* dedicated to the great technician of the age, Camille Saint-Saëns; a *Pastorale* dedicated to Cavaillé-Coll; a splendid *Prière*; and, last of all, a brilliant *Finale* which the organist of Ste. Clotilde could not but dedicate to Lefébure-Wély. Written for the inauguration of the organ of the Palais du Trocadéro in 1877 and published the following year, the *Trois Pièces* offer yet another triptych comprising a *Fantaisie* in A, a *Cantabile* and a *Pièce héroïque*. The *Trois chorals* of 1890, in E major, G minor and A minor, were described by Vincent d'Indy as Franck's "musical testament": with their message of absolute sincerity, these works form a kind of prayer or meditation in which the writing, lacking any liturgical theme, expresses itself simply and freely in the spirit of the *lied*, broken by sections of a more rhapsodical nature.

The generation of leading French composers who, from the 1870s onwards, devoted a significant part of their output to the organ, clearly inherited many of Franck's ideas; yet they were also part of the great German tradition, an essential influence which we should do well to bear in mind. It was a tradition perpetuated by the Belgian organist Nicolas Jacques Lemmens (1823–81), who boasted a direct line of descent from Bach himself, through his teacher Adolf Friedrich Hesse (1809–1863). Hesse was a pupil of Friedrich Wilhelm Berner and Ernst Köhler; both of them had known the musicologist Johann Nicolaus Forkel, who was a pupil of Carl Philipp Emanuel Bach. Thus French culture gained a knowledge of the works of Bach, of which Lemmens in Brussels was to make himself the leading voice, together with his pupil Clément Loret, who later taught Eugène Gigout (1884–1925), and together, also, with Widor and Alexandre Guilmant (1837–1911). Gigout, in turn, taught Léon Boëllmann (1862–97), and Guilmant was the mentor of Marcel Dupré, while Widor taught the founder of the *Orgelbewegung*, Albert Schweitzer, in addition to Louis Vierne (1870–1937) and Charles Arnould Tournemire (1870–1939), the last two major representatives of the French school of the symphonic organ.

This twofold heritage from France and Germany, involving an understanding not only of learned counterpoint but of structures and an architectural sense characteristic of German writing such as may be found in the chorale, sonata, symphony and symphonic poem, encouraged the rise of the symphonic organ in France, where it was to reach the climax of its technical and tonal possibilities. Technical advance came with a greater degree of virtuosity in fingerwork, with the independence of the pedals, and with the technical complementarity of *legato* and *staccato* phrasing, while the tonal potential of the organ was realized through the richer sounds of the foundation voices, increased power of the reed batteries, a new range of Gamba stops, a luminous brightness to the new Mixtures and an increased sensitivity of the swell box. It was a remarkable development, both musically and tonally, made possible by one of those rare coincidences in the history of the organ when a fully developed tradition in music coincided with a period of advance in techniques of organ building. These two factors retained their vitality for only a few decades, the former being destroyed by excessive formalism and an overindulgent use of modulations and chromaticism, while the latter fell victim to tonal excesses and to mediocre techniques in organ manufacture. As decadence set in on both fronts, a third – and crucial – factor hastened the decline of the symphonic organ, namely the isolation of composers who appeared unwilling to take account of the significant revolution that was taking place in music at the beginning of the twentieth century.

But we must return to the earlier generation of composers who devoted their prolific endeavors to the symphonic organ. The list is headed by Widor, organist at St. Sulpice, whom we may justifiably regard as the father of the orchestral organ. In his classes at the Conservatoire in Paris, where he succeeded Franck as professor of the organ, Widor applied himself to reforming the style of playing the instrument, believing that "the new instrument requires a new language [. . .] It is no longer the Bach of the fugue to whom we should appeal, it is the melodist of emotion and the master of expression" (Preface to his first four symphonies, 1879). Accordingly, he set out to redefine such questions as articulation, breathing, phrasing and the crucial importance of *legato* playing, which it was permissible and effective to interrupt by brilliant *staccato* passages; at the same time Widor dealt with the matter of pedal technique and the art of registration. A remarkable theoretician, to whom we owe a *Technique de l'orchestre moderne* (1904), Widor made an important contribution to the art of keyboard technique. He established a striking synthesis between the dexterous fingerwork of the French school and the Germans' facility of touch on the pedals. Rigorous in his style of writing, and less emotive a composer than Franck, Widor wrote ten organ symphonies between 1876 and 1900; the best known are the last two, based on liturgical themes, the *Symphonie gothique* of 1895 (No. 9) and the *Symphonie romane* of 1900 (No. 10). These are works which exploit to the full the contrastive possibilities presented by the tonal forces at Widor's disposal, and which reveal a style of writing which is both dynamic and decorative. We may note, finally, that Widor is also the author of a *Sinfonia Sacra* (Opus 81) for organ and orchestra, based on the German chorale tune "Nun komm' der Heiden Heiland."

Another of Lemmens's pupils, Guilmant, organist at La Trinité, followed up the leading options of Widor's teaching when he succeeded the latter at the Paris Conservatoire in 1906. A brilliant concert performer and celebrated recitalist, most notably in the United States, Guilmant possessed a profound knowledge of the history of organ music, and edited two vast anthologies on the subject. The first, which was devoted to French composers and published in ten volumes between 1898 and 1914, was entitled *Archives des maîtres de l'orgue* [Archives of the Great Masters of Organ Music] and included contributions by the eminent musicologist André Pirro. The second dealt with foreign organists and comprised twenty-five volumes, published between 1898 and 1903 under the title *Ecole classique de l'orgue* [Classical School of Organ Music]. Together with Charles Bordes and Vincent d'Indy (1851–1931), Guilmant founded the Schola Cantorum in 1894, and wrote a considerable number of works for the organ, many of which are based on plainchant melodies. They include eight Sonatas, or "symphonies," written between 1874 and 1907, whose language, while close to the virtuoso writing of Widor, is occasionally somewhat labored. A sizeable number of his compositions are collected together under the titles *L'Organiste pratique* [The Practical Organist], *L'Organiste liturgique* [The Liturgical Organist], *Soixante interludes dans la tonalité grégorienne* [Sixty Interludes in the Gregorian Mode], *Pièces d'orgue dans différents styles* [Organ Works in Different Styles], and *Noëls*.

While the great symphonic school went on its way, a parallel course was being followed by a number of more classically inspired composers, including Alexis Chauvet (1837–71), Camille Saint-Saëns (1835–1921) and Eugène Gigout. Organist at La Madeleine, Saint-Saëns, who studied under Benoist, expressed himself by preference in a proud and strictly contrapuntal language, using traditional forms in his preludes and fugues, fantasias and "improvisations." Gigout, who succeeded Guilmant at the Conservatoire and who was organist at St. Augustin, was concerned, like Saint-Saëns, to invest his toccatas and preludes and fugues with an elegance of form and clarity of language. He was additionally interested in plainchant and wrote several hundred pieces in Gregorian modes. A close friend of Gigout's, in addition to being his pupil, the Alsatian organist Boëllmann wrote works which bear the marks of the twofold influence of the symphonic school of Widor and the liturgical spirit inherited from his teacher, Gigout. Among these works we may single out for brief mention a *Fantaisie*, two Suites, including the celebrated *Suite gothique* [Gothic Suite], an *Offertoire* [Offertory] on two *noëls*, a *Fantaisie dialoguée pour orgue et orchestre* [Fantasia in Dialog Form for Organ and Orchestra], and a collection of some hundred works for harmonium or organ *manualiter*, *Heures mystiques* [Mystical Hours].

Other organists of this period who deserve mention here include Marie-Joseph Erb (1858–1944), whose *Trois Sonates* are reminiscent of Boëllmann in their liturgical mood; in the wake of César Franck came Théodore Dubois (1837–1924), Henri Dallier (1849–1934), d'Indy, Gabriel Pierné (1863–1937), and Guy Ropartz (1864–1955); and, finally, in the virtuoso spirit of Widor, Henri Nibelle (1883–1967).

The symphonic organ reached the pinnacle of its success in the works of two exact contemporaries, who embodied the two major options of this typically French school of organ playing, a school which they brought to an unparalleled pitch of achievement:

Vierne, who favored the concert organ, and Tournemire, who achieved an ideal fusion between the "Romantic" organ and its liturgical counterpart.

Born in Poitiers, Louis Vierne was deeply influenced by the art of Widor as much as by that of Franck and Guilmant. He was noted above all for his improvisations and celebrated for the recitals which he gave in Germany, Holland, Spain and, especially, in England and the United States, where he discovered the immense potential of electric traction and adjustable pistons. He was appointed organist at Notre-Dame in 1900, and it was at the console of that instrument that he died in 1937, just as he was beginning the final improvisation of his 1,750[th] recital, a long pedal note which symbolically intoned the death knell of the symphonic era.

Vierne's organ works are rigorously structured in conception, enriched by a wealth of harmonic detail, and both stylistically elegant and melodically imaginative. They resolutely exploit a contrastive opposition between tonal structures which the generous cathedral acoustics were able to highlight to exemplary effect. As a reflection of his own intense *sensibilité* and profound spiritual torment, his writing is often cyclical in structure, especially in his symphonies, where it is typified by a rich chromaticism of language and an attention to sharply contrasting themes. All his works are the expression of a profound mysticism, unfolding majestically and revealing a spirit of improvisation in their slow movements, which Vierne described as "cantilène," "romance," "méditation" or "adagio." His character pieces breathe a lighter spirit of virtuosity, as in his two collections of *Vingt-Quatre Pièces en style libre* [Twenty-Four Pieces in a Free Style] of 1913, and four Suites of *Pièces de fantaisie* of 1926/7. Apart from a *Triptyque* and two *Messes basses* [Low Masses] for organ or harmonium, we may draw attention to his six Symphonies dating from 1898 to 1930 and generally comprising five movements each. The most accomplished of these is the Third Symphony of 1911 (Opus 28), dedicated to Marcel Dupré.

A native of Bordeaux, Tournemire was organist at St. Médard and St. Nicolas-du-Chardonnet before moving to Ste. Clotilde in 1898. Influenced by the aesthetic outlook of César Franck and fascinated by the musical changes of his own day, Tournemire was above all else a liturgical organist whose mysticism perpetuated the tradition of Titelouze, Couperin and Grigny. In this way Tournemire, who was a frequent visitor to the Abbey of Solemnes, contributed to the plainsong revival by means of his large-scale paraphrases of Gregorian melodies. He created a type of music which was appropriate to the Catholic liturgy and respected the flexible freedom typical of the untexted melismas and phrasing of plainchant. Tournemire's style, which owes more to the *coloristes* than to the symphonists, derives its strength from its harmonic refinements, the flexibility of its melodic lines, and the subtle coloring of its halftones. There is frequently a boldness in his use of dissonances and in his handling of high-pitched sonorities and of the newer, brighter Mixtures. Tournemire was concerned above all with the art of feeling and of impressionism. Although he remains firmly within the concerto tradition with such works as his *Fantaisie symphonique* [Symphonic Fantasia], *Symphonie sacrée* [Sacred Symphony], *Symphonie-Choral* [Chorale Symphony], *Suite évocatrice* [Evocative Suite] and the two *Fresques symphoniques sacrées* [Sacred Symphonic Frescoes], it is in the art of the liturgical paraphrase that Tournemire finds his most admirable expression. His genius is illustrated by his *Postludes libres pour les antiennes de Magnificat* [Free Postludes for the Magnificat Antiphons], his *Sept Chorals-poèmes pour les sept paroles du Christ* [Seven Chorale Poems for the Seven Last Words], and above all the 255 pieces contained in *L'Orgue mystique* [The Mystical Organ], in which four or five alternatives are suggested for the fifty-one services of the liturgical year, the works in question being designed to suit the particular moments during the service when the organ might be required to play: *Prélude à l'Introït, Offertoire, Elévation, Communion*, and, at the end of the mass, a *Postlude, Fantaisie* and a *Carillon*.

Countless other composers shared this same perspective, regarding the organ as an "enlarged" orchestral instrument. For the most part they were pupils of Widor, Guilmant, Vierne, Tournemire and Dupré. They include Jules-Aimable Roger-Ducasse (1874–1954), Georges Jacob (1877–1950), Henri Mulet (1878–1967), Ermend

Bonnal (1880–1944), a descriptive poet of the Basque country, Augustin Barié (1883–1915), who wrote a *Symphonie cyclique*, Alexandre-Eugène Cellier (1883–1968), Joseph Bonnet (1884–1944), Léonce de Saint-Martin (1886–1954), André Fleury (b. 1903), Daniel-Jean-Yves Lesur (b. 1908), Henriette Puig-Roget (b. 1910), Jeanne Demessieux (1921–68), and above all Maurice Duruflé (b. 1902), the author of a *Prélude, Adagio et Choral varié sur le Veni Creator*, a *Prélude et fugue sur le nom d'ALAIN* and, most notably, an imposing *Suite*. His style is characterized by subtle registrations and impressionistic harmonies. The organ works of Jean Langlais (b. 1907) are often of a religious nature, their mood enhanced by brilliant registrations, rich harmonies, differentiated rhythms and the use of bitonality. Worth singling out from among Langlais's works, some of them based on plainchant melodies, are *Trois Poèmes Evangéliques*, three *Paraphrases grégoriennes*, a *Symphonie*, a *Suite médiévale*, an *Hommage à Frescobaldi* and *Huit Pièces modales*. Gaston Litaize (b. 1909) is the author of a *Grande Messe de tous les temps*, a *Suite*, a *Thème et Variations sur le nom de Victor Gonzales* and a *Passacaille* for organ and orchestra. Jean-Jacques Grunenwald (1911–82), whose melodic and colorful style is reminiscent of the works of Jehan Alain (1911–40), has written a number of memorable pieces including *Deux suites, Hommage à Josquin des Prés, Hymne à la splendeur des étoiles, Quatre élévations*, and *Fantaisie en dialogue pour orgue et orchestre*. Most important of all in this context is Jean-Pierre Leguay (b. 1939), a pupil of Jean Langlais and Olivier Messiaen (b. 1908) among others, whose *Dix-neuf préludes, Péan III* and *Sonate* are characterized above all by their vital intensity and denseness of color, as well as by their impassioned outbursts.

But throughout this period the French school has remained dominated by three important names: Marcel Dupré (1886–1971), Jehan Alain and Olivier Messiaen. A pupil of Guilmant, Widor and Vierne, the Rouen composer Marcel Dupré, who was organist at St. Sulpice in Paris, was without doubt the most famous virtuoso performer of his generation and the last major advocate of the symphonic organ. He was also an eminent teacher and the author of a famous *Méthode d'orgue*. His best known pupils include Messiaen, Langlais, Litaize, Grunenwald, Jehan Alain, Marie-Claire Alain, Pierre Cochereau and Jean Guillou. Dupré was the first organist to perform the entire corpus of Bach's organ works in a series of ten concerts given at the Paris Conservatoire, an event which was clearly destined to have profound repercussions on the world of music. His numerous works for the organ are austere in style and include the *Préludes et fugues* (Opus 7 and 36), a *Symphonie-Passion* (Opus 23) in four movements, the fourteen parts of the *Chemin de la Choix* (Opus 29), the *Tombeau de Titelouze* (Opus 38), and a Concerto for organ and orchestra (Opus 31).

The organ works of Jehan Alain, whose life was tragically cut short at the age of twenty-nine, remain unique for their inner refinement and rhythmic outbursts, as well as for a typically Romantic tonal exuberance and a rich diversity of harmonic colors. Alain's numerous works reflect an original mind constantly striving to break away from the course which his predecessors had taken. He prefigured Messiaen in his handling of a polymodal language and occasionally approached the boundaries of serialism. Aware of the multiple possibilities inherent in ethnic and oriental music (*cf.* his *Deux Danses à Agni Yavishta*), he was also fond of rediscovering the inflexions and flavor of older melodies, as in his *Variations sur un thème de Clément Jannequin* and *Deux Chorals*. His works, which exploit the rich possibilities of polyrhythm (e.g. the *Trois Danses*), reveal a constant flood of powerful lyricism, as expressed in his *Litanies* and *Suite*, and a colorful elegance whose impressionistic nature and constantly renewed imagination are expressive of an infinite *sensibilité* of character.

Organist at La Trinité in Paris, Messiaen has always regarded any form of musical creation as an act of faith to be expressed in a new language. Conscious of being the vehicle of theological truths, he has indeed developed a personal language governed by certain essential principles, the chief of which is a profound spiritual need to which the listener must fully submit. Although influenced by Tournemire and the latter's example of contemplative spirituality and subtle harmonic expressiveness, Messiaen has refused to espouse the polyphonic tradition and many of the formal options typical of Western music, including the notion of classical development. Instead, he has created a new, expressive art, revolutionary in its treatment of both the instrument's tonal possibilities and its forms. His style, which may be described as a symbolical exaltation of God, the Church, and of Glory and Light, is instinct with a constant freedom of movement, divorced from time and fixed tempi. Vast structures of chords and series of durations, added note-values, bold aggregates, rhythmic complexities, sensuous and refined harmonies and infinite melodies – these are the impressions, revelatory in their handling of color, produced by Messiaen's long meditation on the idea of constantly mobile rhythms ("non-retrogradable"), on modality ("modes of limited transposition") and on form ("structures which are fixed, juxtaposed, repeated, alternated or superimposed"). It is a science which Messiaen has refined by his analysis of non-European music, by his exploitation of Gregorian melodies, and, finally, by his scientific study of birdsong. Messiaen's music is thus at the focal point of diverse traditions; it absorbs their vital strengths in order to transcend them in a vision of profoundly mystical contemplation.

His œuvre is immense – forty-five works in all, including four separate pieces, the remainder being collected together in six anthologies; the majority of them are intended for liturgical purposes. The early works, which are traditional in their rhythmic and harmonic conception, include *Le Banquet céleste* (1926), *Diptyque* (1930) and *Apparition de l'Eglise éternelle* (1932), followed between 1933 and 1939 by three major cycles, *L'Ascension*, *La Nativité du Seigneur* and *Les Corps glorieux*. The *Messe de la Pentecôte* (1950) heralded the most accomplished of Messiaen's works, which include the *Livre d'orgue* (1951) and the vast *Méditations sur le Mystère de la Sainte-Trinité* (1972). Other French composers of note who were not themselves professional organists include Erik Satie (1866–1925), whose *Messe des pauvres* for organ or piano dates from 1895; Darius Milhaud (1892–1974), the composer of a number of organ preludes and a sonata; Francis Poulenc (1899–1963), famous for his Organ Concerto in G minor; and, finally, Charles Chaynes (b. 1925), who is also the author of an organ concerto of some interest. The Swiss Arthur Honegger (1892–1955) wrote organ works which include a fugue and a chorale.

170 Cathedral of St. Jean-Baptiste, Perpignan, 1490–1505
A striking organ case in the flamboyant Gothic style, flat, with double stories and decorated with a *cul-de-lampe* in the shape of a Moor's head with moving parts, the Perpignan case originally had two painted shutters, but these were removed in 1843 and are now stored elsewhere in the building. The pipework was Spanish. A *Rp* was added in the sixteenth century, bringing the total number of stops to twenty-one (two manuals and *Péd*). This instrument was restored by the brothers D. and G. Eustache in 1682: the display pipes were originally no doubt V-shaped and it was the Eustache brothers who were responsible for the present miter arrangement. In 1688 Jean de Joyeuse built a three-manual instrument with *Péd* (twenty-eight stops), which was restored by Claude Moucherel in 1744 and by Jean Pujol in 1786. Unfortunate alterations were made in 1844, but between 1854 and 1857 Aristide Cavaillé-Coll transformed the instrument, removing the *Pos* and rebuilding an organ with four manuals and *Péd*, with a total of fifty-seven stops. This instrument was rebuilt by Maurice Puget in 1928 when a further seventeen stops were added.

171 Minster of Notre-Dame, Strasbourg, Frederik Krebs, 1489
The colorful Gothic case, originally fitted with shutters, is perched on a swallow's nest whose *cul-de-lampe* base is adorned with the so-called *Roraffe*, a group of figures including two musicians with moving parts and Samson opening the jaws of a lion. The original instrument had three manuals (*Hw, Pos, Bw*) and *Ped*, and numbered 2,136 pipes. It was transformed by the Bavarian builder Neuknecht in 1608 and by Mathias Tretzscher and his follower Tobias Dressel in 1658–60. Andreas Silbermann built a new 39-stop instrument in 1714–16, using some of the old stops. He removed the shutters and replaced them with the present side panels of foliage. Changes were made to this instrument in 1833 by Georg Wegmann, who extended the compass of the keyboards and in 1840 added further stops to the *Réc*. In 1870 the organ, severely damaged by the bombardment of the city, was repaired by Martin Wetzel; and finally, in 1896, Henri Koulen built a fashionable instrument in keeping with the times. It was rebuilt by Roethinger in 1934–5 and now numbered thirty-nine stops (*GO, Pos* and *Réc*, each with a compass of fifty-six notes, and *Péd* with thirty-two keys). Tracker action was used. In 1958–9 a complete overhaul of the tracker action was undertaken by Roethinger, who also restructured the Mixtures. In 1980–1 Alfred Kern rebuilt the instrument, retaining around three hundred of Silbermann's pipes and reusing some of the 1935 stops. The instrument now comprises *Pos, GO, Réc* (all of fifty-four notes) and *Péd* (thirty keys), and has forty-six speaking stops.

172 Cathedral of Notre-Dame, Saint-Bertrand-de-Comminges, 1535–50
A notable example of the work of the wood-carver and architect Nicolas
Bachelier, this sixteenth-century case is all the more remarkable for being
built at a right angle. Nothing is known of the original instrument, although
there is a suggestion that it may have had twenty stops. In the seventeenth
century the organ had an *Echo* manual. Around 1760 Jean-François Lépine
the Elder added a *Pos*, bringing the total of speaking stops to about thirty.
Severely damaged in 1793, the instrument was rebuilt in 1835 by Daublaine,
who removed the *Pos* and added a forty-two-note *Réc* using the stops from
the *Pos*. It was again rebuilt in 1901, this time by the Magen brothers who
replaced the display pipes which had been melted down at the time of the
Revolution. This instrument had a *GO, Réc* (fifty-four notes each) and *Péd*
(twenty-five keys), and included the former *GO* wind-chests and a number of
the old stops. Some of these stops were reused by Chauvin & Swiderski
when they rebuilt the instrument in 1976, restoring to it the character of a
classical eighteenth-century French organ: *GO, Pos, Echo* (fifty-four notes)
and *Péd* (thirty keys), with thirty-nine speaking stops.

173 Notre-Dame, Caudebec-en-Caux, Antoine Josseline and Gilbert
Cocquerel, 1542–3
The turreted case is Norman in style (see St. Maclou and Le Grand Andely),
and is one of the most beautiful Renaissance cases in France. The organ was
rebuilt in 1738–40 by the brothers Jean-Baptiste and Louis Lefebvre who
added a *Pos*, with the result that the instrument now had four manuals and
Péd (twenty-five keys), and some forty speaking stops. Restored in 1930, the
organ was damaged during the Second World War and rebuilt between 1956
and 1959 by Chéron: *Pos, GO, Réc* (fifty-six notes) and *Péd* (thirty keys), with
a total of forty stops.

174 Notre-Dame-des-Marais, La Ferté-Bernard, 1536
The heptagonal case of 1536 is the work of the local joiner Sainctot-Chemin and erected on top of the flamboyant *cul-de-lampe* which the Lorrainese carpenter Evrard Baudot had built in 1501. It bears a similarity in design to the Strasbourg case of some years earlier. The 1536 organ, which replaced the earlier instrument of 1501, was the work of Pierre Bert or perhaps Evrard Baudot, who was an organ builder as well as a joiner. Nothing is known about this instrument except that in the eighteenth century it had two manuals, a *GO* (twelve stops) and *Pos.* Unfortunate alterations were made in the nineteenth century. The instrument was rebuilt by Paul Bertin in 1938.

175 St. Maclou, Rouen, Antoine Josseline, 1541
Organ case carvings by Martin Guilbert. The two pillars and stairs leading to the organ gallery are the work of Jean Goujon who also painted the case and may even have been responsible for designing it. Numerous transformations and additions have taken place, including restoration by Nicolas Dabenest in 1572, and the building of a *Pos* in 1631. By 1732, following rebuilding by Charles Lefebvre, the organ had four manuals (*Pos* = eleven stops; *GO* = sixteen; *Réc* = two, *Echo* = seven), plus *Péd* (four), a total of forty stops, of which no fewer than three were Voix humaine stops. In 1771, this number was reduced to thirty-eight by Jean-Baptiste-Nicolas Lefebvre, after which the organ was left to decay until 1866 when it was rebuilt by Merklin & Schütze. They removed the *Pos*, leaving two manuals and twenty-five stops. This instrument was overhauled in 1881 and 1924, dismantled following the bombing of Rouen in 1944, and rebuilt between 1959 and 1966 by Haerpfer-Erman who restored the *Pos* and added five stops.

176 Notre-Dame, Caudebec-en-Caux, 1542–3; detail of the main case front

177 Cathedral of Notre-Dame, Chartres, Antoine Josseline and Gilbert Cocquerel, 1545–51
Case built by the carpenters R. Foubert and Jacques Bely, who used elements from the earlier case of 1475 built by Brother Gombault Rogerie and notable for its flamboyant spurs, balustrades, pinnacles and *culs-de-lampe*.

The *Pos* was restored in 1596; additional changes were made by Gadault in 1846 and a general overhaul was undertaken by Abbey in 1911. There were now three manuals (fifty-six notes) and *Péd* (thirty keys) with thirty-nine speaking stops. This instrument was repaired by Gouault in 1950–1. It was completely rebuilt between 1965 and 1971 by the firm of Danion-Gonzalez who restored the 32′ pipe towers. There are now four manuals (*GO, Pos, Réc* and *Echo*, each of fifty-six notes) and *Péd* (thirty-two keys), with a total of sixty-seven stops.

178 St. Pierre, Dreux; case by Toussaint Fortier, 1614
The first instrument, by an unknown builder, was restored by Louis-Alexandre Clicquot in 1750. Various alterations took place during the course of the following century, until the instrument was rebuilt in 1867 by Aristide Cavaillé-Coll. It was overhauled in 1902 and 1952 by the firm of Gutschenritter and now comprises a *GO, Réc* and *Péd* with twenty-two speaking stops.

179 St. Etienne-du-Mont, Paris, Pierre Le Pescheur, 1631–6
Pos, GO (each of forty-eight notes), *Réc* (thirty-three notes) and separate *Péd* (thirty-two keys), with a total of thirty-four stops. Case by Jehan Buron. This instrument was restored and enlarged by Jacques Carouge in 1679, by Julien Tribuot in 1714 and, following the fire of 1760, by Nicolas Somer and, later, François-Henri Clicquot who rebuilt all the reed voices (1766–72). In the nineteenth century repairs were undertaken by Pierre-François Dallery and John Abbey, and, in 1873, by Aristide Cavaillé-Coll who built a new *Réc* but kept the old stops. There were now three manuals. Substantial changes were made in 1911 by Théodore Puget (thirty-nine stops) and in 1932 (fifty-two stops). Between 1938 and 1956 the instrument was rebuilt by the firm of Gloton (now Beuchet-Debierre). It currently comprises a *GO, Pos, Réc* and *Echo* (sixty-one notes each) and *Péd* (thirty-two keys), with eighty-three stops.

180 Military Chapel of St. Louis, La Flèche, organ attributed variously to Ambroise Levasseur, Jacques Nadreau and Jousse, 1639–40
Restored by the Dutch Jesuit priest G. Hermans between 1655 and 1658, the instrument appears at that stage to have had around forty stops (*Pos, GO, Réc, Echo* and *Péd*), with Tremulants and Rossignol. It was rebuilt by Victor Gonzalez in 1936, 1937 and 1947, and overhauled in 1962, bringing the total number of stops to forty-four (*Pos, GO, Réc, Echo* and *Péd*). The magnificent Louis XIII case recalls the art of the Renaissance. Tradition has it that the head of the caryatid beside the substructure of the instrument represents a likeness of Louis XIII.

181 Military Chapel of St. Louis, La Flèche, 1639–40; detail from the Louis XIII case front showing the balusters of the *Pos* towers and winged angels supporting the central tower of the main case.

182 Collegiate church of Notre-Dame, Le Grand Andely, Nicolas
Dabenest, 1573
All that remains of the original instrument is its superb case. It was restored
in 1641 by Guillaume Lesselier (or William Lesselie, a citizen of Aberdeen in
Scotland who settled in Rouen), and again in 1778 and 1861. In 1891 Aristide
Cavaillé-Coll built a new instrument inside the old case: two manuals and
Péd, with twenty-four stops. Electric bellows were installed in 1922.

183 Notre-Dame, Valréas
The first organ of 1506 by Antoine Milani was replaced a century later by a single-manual instrument built between 1602 and 1614 by Jean Duvivier, a native of Langres. It had eleven stops. A *Pos* was added in 1648 by Pierre Valon, bringing the total number of stops to sixteen. The Provençal case, designed by Duvivier, assumed its present form in 1667 when the *Pos* was removed by Nicolas Béraud and the main front extended sideways. An eight-key pedalboard was installed, together with two Rossignol stops. In 1723–4 Jean Eustache rebuilt the instrument on a new gallery and restored it. A second keyboard (*Réc*) was added in the nineteenth century, retaining some of the *GO* stops. Restored by Ernst Muhleisen in 1966, the instrument now comprises a *GO, Pos* (fifty-four notes each) and *Péd* (thirty keys), and has twenty-five stops.

184 St. Gervais, Paris, the organ of the Couperin family from 1653 (Louis, uncle of François le Grand) to 1826 (death of Gervais-François, who saved the instrument from destruction at the time of the Revolution)
The Flemish builder Matthieu Langhedul was responsible for the first organ at St. Gervais in 1601. It was built on the gallery of the south crossing and had two manuals (*Pos* and *GO* of forty-five notes each) and *Péd* (nine keys), with twenty-two speaking stops. In 1628–9 this instrument was resited on the west gallery by Pierre Le Pescheur who extended the manuals to a compass of forty-eight notes and the *Péd* to twenty-five, and added a *Cornet à double effet* with a compass of twenty-five notes. In 1649 Pierre Thierry added a 4′ stop to the *Péd* and in 1659 a *Jeu de tierce* to the *Pos*, together with a fourth *Echo*

manual with seven stops. The latter had been requested by Louis Couperin. In 1661, at the request of Charles Couperin, Alexandre Thierry added a large Cornet, then, between 1676 and 1684, at the insistence of the temporary organist Michel-Richard de Lalande, altered the main wind-chest and added a Bourdon 16′ and Trompette to the *Péd*. By 1685, when François Couperin took possession of the instrument, it was fully complete with four manuals and pedals: *Pos* (forty-nine notes, ten stops), *GO* (forty-nine notes, sixteen stops, including a Treble Cornet with a compass of twenty-five notes), a separate Cornet (twenty-five or thirty-two notes), Echo (thirty-seven notes, seven stops) and *Péd* coupled to *GO* (twenty-eight notes and three stops). Various changes and additions were made in 1714 by François Thierry; and in 1758–9 when the main case was rebuilt by the carpenter Pierre-Claude Thiessé; in 1762–3 when similar work was completed on the *Pos* case by Nicolas Rébillé, and the organ builder Louis Bessard added a fifth keyboard and various solo stops in addition to overhauling the action, wind-chests and keyboards (which now comprised fifty-one notes). This task was completed in 1767–8 by François-Henri Clicquot who replaced the *Péd* and added some new stops. Further changes were made in 1812 by Pierre-François Dallery, and in 1842 by Louis-Paul Dallery who overhauled the instrument and restored the *Pleins Jeux* which his father had removed. Having narrowly escaped destruction when a shell from "Big Bertha" fell on the church on Good Friday 1918, the organ was repaired between 1921 and 1924 by Béasse who fitted a modern pedalboard and electric bellows. The instrument was returned more or less to its 1769 condition by Gonzalez between 1967 and 1974. (For the stoplist in Couperin's day, see Appendix.)

185   Cathedral of St. Théodoric, Uzès, unknown builder, 1660–85 (?)
The case was gilded by de Pouville, a craftsman from Montpellier, and is the
only one in France to have retained its movable shutters. In the eighteenth
century there must have been thirty-four stops (*GO, Pos, Réc* and *Péd*). The
instrument was rebuilt and restored by Daublaine & Callinet between 1841
and 1843 and now had three manuals of fifty-four notes and a pedal department of twenty-five keys, totalling forty-six stops. Between 1961 and 1964 the
organ was restored by Alfred Kern who reused around twenty of the stops
from the eighteenth-century instrument and some of Callinet's stops, reducing the total to forty-four. A Grosse Tierce 3 1/5' was later added.

186   St. Louis-des-Invalides, Paris, Alexandre Thierry, 1679–86
Case designed by Jules Hardouin-Mansart and built by Germain Pillon. *Pos,
GO, Réc, Echo* and *Péd*: thirty-seven stops. Various repairs and additions were

carried out prior to the restoration by Jean Somer in 1806, when the manuals
were extended. Rebuilt by Charles Gadault in 1852, the instrument now had
three manuals and *Péd*, with forty stops. The organ was again rebuilt in 1957,
by Beuchet-Debierre, and now has sixty-one stops.

187   St. Sauveur, Le Petit Andely, Robert Ingout (born in Cherbourg but a
citizen of Caen) and Philippe Quesnel, 1674; case by Quesnel's brother
The organ was originally built for the Abbaye du Trésor-Notre-Dame and
removed to St. Sauveur in 1792. It was overhauled by Charles Reinburg in
1926, and inaugurated by Charles-Marie Widor; further work was done by
Gonzalez between 1963 and 1969. The organ now has thirty-five speaking
stops, *Pos* and *GO* (forty-eight notes each), *Echo* (thirty-seven notes) and *Péd*
(initially seventeen keys and two stops; since 1926 there have been twenty-
nine keys and three stops), Tremblant doux and Rossignol.

188 Cathedral of Ste. Marie, Auch, Jean de Joyeuse, 1688–95
Born in the Ardennes, de Joyeuse lived in Paris for some fifteen years before
moving to the South of France where he introduced habits of Parisian organ
building, notably at Rodez and Auch. There are four manuals and *Péd*, with
thirty-seven stops including a *jeu de brode* or Grosse Tierce 3 1/5′. One of the
finest of Louis XIV cases in France, the Auch case is the work of the joiner
Payerle. The instrument was rebuilt between 1954 and 1958 by Gonzalez and
Danion, who increased the number of stops to forty-three (four manuals and
Péd).

189 Collegiate Church, Saint-Quentin, Robert Clicquot, 1699–1703
Four manuals and *Péd*, fifty stops. Case *de style royal* designed by Jean
Bérain and built by Pierre Vaideau. The royal crown which originally surmounted the central dome was replaced by a lantern and cross at the time of
the Revolution. Repaired by Clicquot in 1718, by Boudos in 1727 and by
François Thierry in 1737, the organ was rebuilt in 1850 by Antoine Sauvage, a
follower of Aristide Cavaillé-Coll. It now had three manuals and *Péd*, with
fifty-two stops. Overhauled in 1888 by Augustin Brisset, the instrument was
destroyed in 1917. Only the case survived. A new organ was built between
1961 and 1967 by Haerpfer-Ernan with four manuals and *Péd*, and seventy-
five stops.

**190 Abteikirche (Abbey church), Marmoutier (Maursmünster), Andreas
Silbermann, 1709–10**
Silbermann, from Kleinbobritzsch near Frauenstein in Saxony, did not complete the instrument and it was not until 1746, twelve years after his death,
that his sons Johann A. and Jean Daniel finished off his work, adding a
Cromorne, Echo manual and *Péd* reeds, bringing the total number of speaking
stops to twenty-nine: *GO, Pos* (forty-nine notes each), *Réc* (twenty-five notes)
and *Péd* (twenty-five keys), two Tremulants, *Pos/GO*, no pedal coupler. A
number of repairs and modifications were made in the nineteenth century. In
1955 Muhleisen & Kern restored the instrument to something near its original condition (including a pedal department of twenty-seven keys).

191 Cathedral of Ste. Cécile, Albi, Christophe Moucherel, 1734–6
Moucherel learned the art of organ building with the Legros family, who had
themselves been apprenticed to Alexandre Thierry. He was particularly fond
of building large instruments: the Albi organ had four manuals (*GO, Pos, Réc,
Echo*) and *Péd*, with forty-three speaking stops. Alterations were made to this
instrument by François Lépine and his son Jean-François in 1747, by Joseph
Isnard in 1781, when a fifth, Bombarde, manual was added, with horizontal
reeds, and by Antoine Peyroulous in 1825. By 1868 this number had been
increased to fifty-two. The organ was rebuilt in 1903 by Maurice Puget, who
retained some of the old pipework and installed pneumatic action. The result
was a 74-stop, four-manual organ with *Péd*. In 1977 Bartolomeo Formentelli
restored the instrument to its original state, while taking account of the work
carried out by Lépine, Isnard and Peyroulous: its five manuals (*GO, Pos,
Bombarde, Réc* and *Echo*) and *Péd* comprise a total of fifty-five speaking
stops.

192 Benediktinerabteikirche (Benedictine Abbey church), Ebersmünster,
Andreas Silbermann, 1730
GO and *Pos* (forty-nine notes each), *Réc* (from c¹) and *Péd* (twenty-five keys),
Pos/GO, Tremulant (*GO*), no pedal coupler: thirty stops. *Péd* draw-stops
beneath the manuals, *Pos* draw-stops behind the organist's back. The Ebersmünster organ is one of only two complete surviving instruments by Andreas
Silbermann, the other being at Marmoutier. Silbermann studied with Casparini at Görlitz, before adopting the French style of organ building first in
Strasbourg and later in Paris (*cf.* the Cornet V planted on an independent
chest behind the display pipes), a style enriched by the German tradition of a
16′ *Péd*.

193 Basilica, Saint-Maximin-la-Saint-Baume (Var départ.), Brother Jean-
Esprit Isnard, with assistance from Joseph Isnard, 1772–3
Rescued from certain destruction during the Revolution by its organist Fourcade, who played *hymnes à la Liberté* at opportune moments, the organ
makes a powerful impression by virtue of its numerous reed voices, of which
there are fourteen, including eleven from the Trompette family, and by the
fullness of its *Pleins Jeux* (twenty-two ranks of Principals). There were forty-
two stops and four keyboards (*Pos, GO, Réc* and *Résonance*) and *Péd* drawing
the Bombarde stops of the *Résonance* chest. Various changes were made in
1880, including new manuals, a German pedalboard, inverted-fold bellows
and equal temperament. A detailed overhaul was undertaken by Pierre Chéron between 1953 and 1957.

194 St. Sulpice, Paris, François-Henri Clicquot, 1781
An impressive organ for its period, having sixty-four stops and five manuals of fifty-six notes each (*Pos, GO, Bombarde, Réc* and *Écho*) and *Péd* (F¹–e¹, thirty-six keys), fed by fourteen wedge-bellows. The case, in the form of a Greek temple, was designed by Chalgrin and built by Jadot, with carvings by Duret. Inaugurated by Armand-Louis Couperin, Claude-Bénigne Balbastre, Nicolas Séjan and Jean-Jacques Charpentier, the organ was modified by Nicolas Sommer in 1818, and by Callinet & Ducroquet in 1833–45, before being restored by Daublaine & Callinet in 1845, when forty-six of the old stops were preserved and twenty new ones added. Between 1857 and 1861 Aristide Cavaillé-Coll enlarged the instrument, while retaining the old stops. It now had five manuals and *Péd* (one hundred stops) and six Barker levers. This instrument was overhauled by Cavaillé-Coll in 1888; various changes were made by Charles Mutin in 1903, in 1922 when an electric fan was fitted, in 1934, in 1952 by Beuchet-Debierre, and in 1975. The instrument currently has 102 speaking stops, of which a third are by Clicquot.

195 St. Pierre-et-St. Paul (former Benedictine Priory), Souvigny (Allier départ.), François-Henri Clicquot, 1782–3
With its original French pedalboard, this instrument has twenty-eight stops and three manuals (*GO, Pos* [fifty notes], *Réc* [twenty-seven notes]) and *Péd* (twenty-eight keys, including F¹ and G¹ *en grand ravalement*), Tremblant fort, Tremblant doux (the latter a recent addition), and coupler *GO/Pos.* In 1887 Goydadin introduced modern pitch and replaced the wedge-bellows by inverted-fold bellows; in 1960 Merklin installed an electric fan; in 1963 Philippe Hartmann reintroduced unequal temperament, and in 1976–7 he rebuilt the wedge-bellows.

196 Cathedral of St. Pierre, Poitiers, François-Henri Clicquot, 1787–90; Louis XVI case by Berthou and Favre
This large 16′ organ is a rare example of French organ building at the end of the eighteenth century, notable for its numerous reed voices and XVI-rank *pleno.* In all it boasts forty-four stops, *GO, Pos* (fifty-three notes each), *Réc, Echo* (thirty-four notes each) and *Péd* (twenty-eight keys), *GO/Pos,* no pedal coupler. Subsequent modifications have done nothing to alter the originality of the instrument. These include changes by Pierre-François Dallery in 1813 and 1821, by Henry in 1835, and by Merklin and Schütze in 1871, when a German pedalboard was fitted and the wedge-bellows replaced by inverted-fold feeder-bellows. An electric fan was installed in 1925. (For the stoplist, see Appendix.)

197   Cathedral of Notre-Dame-des-Doms, Avignon, Piantanida, 1819
Piantanida, an organ builder of Lombard extraction, settled for a time in Milan, where he was responsible for a number of instruments. After a period in the army, he moved to Provence at the beginning of the nineteenth century, where the style of Italian organ building was making its mark. Piantanida built seven instruments in the region, including the organ at Notre-Dame-des-Doms. With its Corinthian case, the "gilt organ" was moved to its present position on the loft above the chancel in 1837. Although seventeenth-century display pipes from an earlier instrument were incorporated into the new organ, Piantanida's instrument is unequivocally Italian with its divided keyboard (b/c¹), *timbali ai pedali*, 17-note pedals, *ripieno* and twenty-six speaking stops. It was overhauled by Théodore and Eugène Puget in 1860 and 1881; and in 1939 Maurice Puget altered the pitch to conform with the *Chororgel* of Cavaillé-Coll and Charles Mutin. Piantanida's instrument was restored by Alain Sals in 1967.

198   Collegiate Church, L'Isle-sur-la-Sorgue, Mentasti, 1822–7
Mentasti, another native of Lombardy, completely rebuilt the organ which the Flemish builder Charles Le Royer had made for the Collegiate Church in 1648–9. Its twelve stops were part of the Renaissance case which now surmounts the front of the large double case of somewhat later date. Mentasti worked in Avignon, Cavaillon and Valréas. His organ for L'Isle-sur-la-Sorgue is resolutely Italianate in design, in spite of the French names given to its seventeen stops, some of which are divided. The *Réc* keyboard has a compass of thirty notes (starting from c¹) and the *GO* keyboard has a compass of fifty-two (starting from C). There is an Italian pedalboard with seventeen keys, and a *banda militare* comprising a Timballo and Chapeau chinois. Mentasti used part of the pipework from Le Royer's organ. The illustration shows the instrument before its most recent restoration of 1978–82 executed by Jean Deloye.

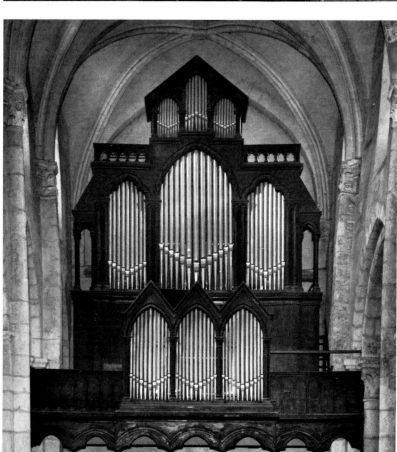

199   Notre-Dame, Saint-Etienne (Loire départ.), Joseph and Claude-Ignace Callinet, 1837
Thirty-six (?) stops: *GO, Rp, Réc* and *Péd.* The case front is of the "Mollau" type, with four *GO* towers and three *Rp* towers. The Callinets, like Riepp and Rabiny, were descended from the great French tradition of organ building, constructing around one hundred instruments between the end of the Clicquot era and that of Cavaillé-Coll. The Saint-Etienne organ was altered by Beaucourt in 1870–2 and by Merklin in 1964–5. It now has four manuals (*GO, Pos, Réc, Echo*) and *Péd*, with thirty-eight stops, of which fifteen are from the original instrument.

200   St. Denis, Paris, Aristide Cavaillé-Coll, 1837–41
Seventy stops and three manuals (C–f[111], 54 notes), plus *Péd* (C–f, 25 keys). Neo-Gothic case by the architect François Debret. This 32′ organ is without doubt Cavaillé-Coll's greatest achievement. In it he first used the pneumatic Barker lever, in addition to introducing harmonic stops and double pallet chests. Charles Mutin made a number of changes in 1901, extending the pedals to thirty keys, replacing three reed stops by *Jeux de tierce*, and adding a Voix céleste and Unda maris. The organ is currently out of action, although plans are in hand to restore it. It now has seventy stops: *Pos* (19), *GO* (20) and *Réc* (8), plus eleven stops on the *Bombarde* chest coupled to the second manual; the pedals have thirty keys and twelve stops. (For the original stoplist, see the Appendix.)

201   Abbey Church, Nantua, Nicolas-Antoine Lété, 1847
Forty-three stops: *GO, Pos, Réc, Péd.* A transitional builder faithful to the French tradition, Lété drew on contemporary devices such as isopneumic valves to lighten the touch of the instrument. Minor changes by Ruche in 1948 and by Hartmann in 1971.

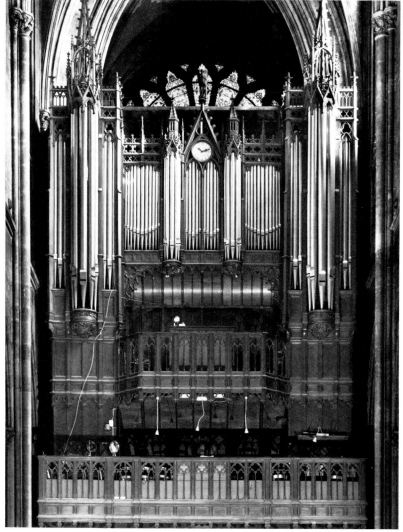

202   Cathedral of Notre-Dame, Luçon, Aristide Cavaillé-Coll, 1854–7
Whereas the case, completed in 1853, was intended for an earlier instrument which in the event was not made, the organ itself was originally designed for Carcassonne Cathedral. It comprised four manuals (*GO, Pos, Euphone* and *Réc* of fifty-four notes), *Péd* (twenty-seven keys), Thunder-stop, and Tremulant. There were forty speaking stops. The Euphone manual had neither a chest nor stops of its own. The instrument was overhauled in 1899 by Louis Debierre and rebuilt in 1967–8 by Schwenkedel, who extended the *Péd* to thirty-two keys, added a nine-stop Echo manual and introduced a number of other stops, notably in the pedal department.

203   Ste. Clotilde, Paris, Aristide Cavaillé-Coll, 1859
Three manuals (*GO, Pos, Réc* of fifty-four notes each) and *Péd* (twenty-seven keys), with forty-six stops. The case was designed by the architect Gau and carved by Pyanet and Lechesne. The first incumbent of this instrument was César Franck. It was enlarged around 1930 by Cavaillé-Coll's successors, and has been electrified.

VII Organ Music in the Iberian Peninsula

The earliest keyboard compositions to have survived in Spain or Portugal date back only as far as the second third of the sixteenth century, and were written interchangeably for the organ, harpsichord (*tecla* = keyboard), *vihuela* or harp.

Our knowledge of the origins of Iberian organ music in the sixteenth century derives from two works in particular, the *Declaración de instrumentos musicales* (1549 and 1555) by the Francisan monk Juan Bermudo (*c.* 1510–*c.* 1565) and the *Arte de tañer fantasia, assi para tecla como para vihuela, y todo instrumento* (1565) by the Dominican Tomás de Santa Maria. The first of these texts addresses itself more especially to organists who are just beginning to learn the organ – and who are informed by the author that it will take them some twenty years to master the instrument; but both works are veritable treatises on the subject of keyboard music. They describe the manner of playing, especially fingering, and the subtle art of ornamentation, and contain works treated imitatively in two, three and, most often, in four voices. Grouped in pairs, the voices reply to each other: this is a favorite device of Spanish organists.

The first collection of organ music to be printed in Spain was that of the Toledo organist Luis Venegas de Henestrosa in his *Libro de cifra nueva para tecla, harpa y vilhuela* (1557). Setting out the principles of figure notation (*cifra*), the author compiled transcriptions of vocal works by Josquin and Thomas Crecquillon and by the Spanish composer Cristóbal de Morales, together with Italian instrumental pieces by Julius de Modena (i. e. Giulio Segni) and keyboard works including *entradas de versos*, *tientos*, *ensaladas* and *glosadas* by some of the great Iberian composers: for example, Francisco Perez (Fernández) Paléro and Francisco de Soto, who were both organists in the royal chapel at Granada, Pedro Alberto Vila (1517–82), organist of Barcelona Cathedral, and "Antonio" (de Cabezón; *c.* 1500–66).

The keyboard repertory of the time, as listed by Bermudo and T. de Santa Maria, comprised a wide variety of works including transcriptions of motets, songs and dances, organ hymns and masses, versets (*versos*, *versillos* and *entradas de versos*), psalm tunes, versets on the Magnificat and Kyrie especially, and fauxbourdons. Two forms in particular flourished, the *tiento* (Portuguese: *tento*) and variation writing. The *tiento*, which generally comprised three or four distinct sections, elaborated motifs according to the principles of the ricercare or fantasia, while drawing on formal elements from the prelude or toccata; while the art of variation writing was enriched◁ by *glosas* or *glosadas*, figurative variations usually on a religious theme, and by *diferencias*, sets of variations on chanson- or dance-themes. These works are described either by the title of their theme, or by an indication as to their mode. After 1560/70 *tientos* might also be described as *medio registro*, a reference to the possibility of dividing the organ stops between the upper and lower halves of the keyboard (in Castile the division was between c^1 and c sharp^1). The term *tiento lleno* indicated a piece in which the same stops were drawn for the whole keyboard.

A major composer who merits attention is Antonio de Cabezón, whose works were published in two separate collections. Some forty or so appeared in the anthology of

204 St. François-de-Sales, Lyons, Aristide Cavaillé-Coll, 1880
Built at floor level, since Cavaillé-Coll considered "the instruments gain [...] from being placed in the lowest part" of the building, the organ comprises forty-five stops distributed over three manuals (*GO, Pos* and *Réc*, each of fifty-six notes) and *Péd* (thirty keys). The instrument is in its original state; only the mechanism of the three Barker levers is somewhat noisy. It was overhauled by Michel Merklin and Kuhn in 1964.

Fig. 72   Cathedral, Tarragona, Spain, 1559–67, Salvador Estrada and Perris Arrabassa. Engraving from A. G. Hill, London, 1883–91
Organ case by Jaime Amigo, wood carvings by Perris Ostris and Geroni Sanxo, and paintings by Père Pau. The instrument was renovated in 1863, and replaced by an electropneumatic organ.

Luis Venegas de Henestrosa mentioned above, while the greater part were published posthumously in 1578, edited by his son and successor in the royal chapel, Hernando. This collection, entitled *Obras de Musica para tecla, arpa y vihuela*, is clearly didactic in intent, and contains pieces not only by Antonio but by Hernando and by Antonio's brother Juan de Cabezón.

Harpsichordist and organist at the court of Charles V and Philip II, Cabezón accompanied his sovereign on his journeys to Italy, Germany, England and the Netherlands. His stay in England, which lasted from July 1554 to January 1556, had a profound influence on the works of the English virginalists of the later period. The art of keyboard variation, which undoubtedly originated in Spain where it rapidly attained a remarkable degree of perfection, also left its mark, of course, on the composers of the young Neapolitan school, including Maione and Trabaci. (Naples, we may remind ourselves, belonged to the Spanish crown from 1502 to 1707.) Nonetheless, the style of Iberian instrumental music appears to have developed a very individual personality, quite unlike that of Italian, German, French and Flemish music of the period.

Cabezón's *tientos* are conceived in one or more sections, each of which has a different theme. The counterpoint is sometimes embellished with ornamented passages which enliven the work's leisurely development. Cabezón also displays a rare skill in the art of variation writing, using themes which are generally well-known tunes such as *El canto lleno del caballero*, *Guardáme las vacas* and *La pavana italiana*. Spain produced a large number of works during the sixteenth century by countless organists, although comparatively few of these compositions are widely known: Juan Bermudo had already complained about the attitude of his country's organists who, he said, preferred to keep back their best works, rather than allow them to be published.

We have already mentioned Venegas de Henestrosa's *Libro de cifra nueva*, which contains two *tientos* each by Francisco de Soto and Pedro Alberto Vila. Other names which deserve to be listed here include Francisco de Peraza (1564–98), the first composer to write a *tiento de medio registro*; Bernardo Clavijo del Castillo (*c.* 1549–1626) and his son Francisco; and, of course, Sebastián Aguilera de Heredia (*c.* 1565–1627), whose style is close to that of Cabezón and who makes bold use of dissonances including intervals of a second, diminished fourth and seventh.

That we know so little about the sixteenth century is due to the fact that the majority of manuscripts are still hidden away in libraries and monasteries; and the same is true of the contribution which Portuguese composers made to the Iberian tradition. We may, however, single out the original fantasias and *tentos* of Antonio Carreira (*c.* 1520–87), organist in the royal chapel and later in the service of King Philip II of Spain. The municipal library in Oporto is noteworthy in particular for two important manuscripts. The first, compiled around 1600, includes contrapuntal works such as *concertados*, *tençãos* and a *concerto de meio registo* on secular or plainchant melodies, attributed to Gaspar dos Reis. The second, dating from 1695, is entitled *Livro de obras de orgão juntas pella curiosidade do P. P. Fr. Roque de Conçeicão* and includes works by the compiler himself, by Fr. Diego da Conçeição and by Pedro de Araujo. But the best known work, and one of the most fascinating in the whole history of Portuguese music, is that of Manuel Rodrigues Coelho (*c.* 1555–*c.* 1635), organist at Elvas and subsequently in the service of the royal chapel in Lisbon, who published his *Flores de musica pera o instrumento de tecla e harpa* in 1620. These pieces, which were the first to be published in Portugal, are stylistically related to the works of Aguilera de Heredia, and include twenty-four *tentos*, frequently based on more than one theme and divided into several sections.

Organ writing in Spain during the Baroque era reached its culmination in the works of Francisco Correa de Arauxo (*c.* 1575–1663), organist in Seville and the author of a work published in figure notation in 1626, *Libro de tientos y discursos de música practica, y theorica de organo intitulado Facultad organica*. A substantial preface is followed by seventy *tientos* and three sets of variations in which the author reveals himself as the incontestable master of the classical period of Spanish organ music. The works in question are written in four, and sometimes five, voices, and comprise *tientos llenos*, *medios registros* for the left and right hand, some of which include two solo voices, and some *glosadas* and settings of liturgical themes. Correa was an innovator in matters of harmony, following the example set by Cabezón and Aguilera, but his main contribution to the music of the period were his rhythmic innovations, including quintuple and septuple time. In the noble, poignant and often impassioned works of Correa de Arauxo, the organ music of the Iberian peninsula found one of its most eminent representatives.

We must not, however, forget the numerous other composers who wrote works which are formally related to those of their illustrious contemporary: Diego de Alvarado (d. 1643), Agostinho da Cruz (*c*. 1590-1633), Diego de Torrijos (d. 1691), Juan Pujol (1573-1626), Francisco Llissa (Llussa), Bartolomeo de Olague, Gabriel Menalt and, above all, Pablo (Pau) Bruna (1611-79), "the blind man of Daroca," where he was organist of the collegiate church. A favorite musician of King Philip IV, he merits attention for the quality and quantity of his organ works.

The end of the seventeenth century witnessed the appearance of a new characteristic in Spanish organs, one which was to have as important an influence on organ writing as the invention of the divided keyboard. A growing interest in reed pipes (initially regals, then pipes of actual length, as is indicated by their name Trompeta real) which organ builders began by placing at the back of the wind-chest before moving them to a position immediately behind the front of the case, paved the way for the triumphal entry of horizontal reeds, which dazzled the spectator with their clusters of gilt and multiform bells, and overwhelmed the listener with their strident bursts of penetrating sound. From now on these reeds *en chamade* were to contrast with the powerful and lower-pitched *lleno* and with the incisiveness of the Cornets and mutation voices, thus completing the rich symphony of sounds typical of the Iberian organ and its search for striking colors.

Italian influence began to leave its mark on Iberian organ writing at the beginning of the eighteenth century. The traditional forms increasingly adopted elements inherited from the compatriots of Frescobaldi, allowing new genres – including the toccata, fuga, sonatina, sonata and *paso* – to develop in the course of the eighteenth century.

Juan Bautista José Cabanilles (1644-1712), organist at Valencia Cathedral and a composer whose fame stretched as far as France even during his own lifetime, did not limit himself to traditional forms but borrowed characteristic features from other genres. His extensive œuvre contains examples of the canzone, passacaglia, galliard and *jácara*, not to mention the Frescobaldian passagework with which his *tientos* are freely interspersed. But Spain remained conservative: side by side with the foregoing are to be found works which could have been written 150 years previously.

If Cabanilles opened the way to a new conception of organ music, while continuing to respect the traditional structures of the Spanish school (just as his successors were later to do), his writing gave a greater emphasis to melody at the expense of harmonic experimentation, a development whose beginnings may be seen in the principle of the *medio registro*. Examples include works "entre el Antiguo y Moderno estilo" by José Elías (*c*. 1675–*c*. 1749), a pupil of Cabanilles and organist in Barcelona and Madrid, the *versos* (often written in half-stops) of Miguel López (1669-1723), and the *versos* of José Jiménez (d. 1672), who also wrote two celebrated battle pieces, a genre which enjoyed enormous popularity in Spain.

The dominating presence of Domenico Scarlatti, harpsichordist and organist to the courts of Portugal and Spain between 1720 and 1757, brought Iberian musicians into direct contact with the Italianate style: hence the toccatas of the Portuguese composer (José Antonio) Carlos Seixas (1704-42), organist and harpsichordist in Lisbon and Coimbra, works by Santo Elías and fugues by Joaquin Martínez Oxinagas, who was organist in the royal chapel. Italianate influence is also evident in the fugues of Juan Moreno y Polo, organist in Saragossa, Albarracín and in the royal chapel, in works by João de Sousa Carvalho (1745-98) and, of course, in those of "Padre" Antonio Soler (1729-83).

Organist and *maestro* at the monastery of the Escorial, Antonio Soler studied at the famous Montserrat choir school, as Elías had done before him, and may have been a pupil of Scarlatti. A prolific composer and the author of numerous keyboard works

205 Basilica (Basilica parroquial de Santa María de los Corporales), Daroca, Pascual de Mallén, 1488–98

The case, which appears to be earlier than 1488, has one of the most authentic Gothic fronts to be found in Spain. It is an open arrangement with the pipes divided into flat miters, unconnected with the bays and originally held in position by a decorated horizontal bar. It is reminiscent of the cases in the two cathedrals of Palma, Majorca (1497) and Saragossa (1444–69). Various changes were made to the organ in the course of the sixteenth century, notably by Juan de Córdoba (1511), Damián Puche (1547–64), maese Pierres (Perris Bordons [?], 1555) and, especially, Guillaume de Lupe. De Lupe, who was probably Flemish by birth and whose real name may have been Wilhelm Wolf, began a thorough restoration of the instrument in 1569, adding a number of new stops. Following extensions to the church in 1592, he rebuilt the organ adding a *Cadireta de espalda* or *Rückpositiv*. When Guillaume de Lupe died in 1607, his son Gaudioso completed the work for him. This instrument was repaired in 1701 by José de Longas, and in 1718 it was overhauled by Nicolás de Salanova and Thomás Grañera. Their work included new wind-chests, extending the manuals to forty-seven notes (CDE-c^{111}), adding two horizontal reed stops and building a swell box. In 1963–4 Gabriel Blancafort and Joan Capella rebuilt the instrument, recreating as closely as possible the 1718 instrument but with new wind-chests, a new console with tracker action, a 54-note compass (C-f^{111}), divided stops (c^1/c sharp^1) and a pedal department of thirty keys. There are now thirty-five half-stops: seventeen left-hand stops and eighteen right-hand stops on the *Organo Grande*, seven left-hand stops and eight right-hand stops on the *Cadireta*, and one stop on the Pedal.

including fugal works, sonatas and toccatas, Soler gave pride of place to the organ, as is clear from the role which the instrument plays in his vocal music, as well as from his six quintets for strings and organ, and, of course, his *Seis Conciertos para dos órganos obligados*. In each of the two or three movements of these six concertos, the two organs are required to play together, alternately or else in dialogs with each other. All six concertos end in a minuet with variations. Soler is also the author of a celebrated treatise, *Llave de la modulación y antigüedades de la música . . .* (Madrid, 1762) in which he not only propounds the most up-to-date theories on modulation and harmony, but also tabulates the most antiquated rules of music, some of which, like "coloration," had already gone out of fashion at the time of Cabezón and Santa Maria some two centuries previously.

With Soler, keyboard music achieved what might be described as a point of no return: while still bearing the imprint of the regional school, it was already moving in the direction of a more international concept, thus losing its intrinsic characteristics and hence its vital strength. It was a development which the whole of Europe was to undergo at the end of the eighteenth century.

It would be wrong, however, to conclude that Iberian music lost its entire personality, for it continued to cultivate certain privileged forms such as *phrases d'orgue* of a liturgical nature, but there was a noticeable lack of the rigor and firmness which had characterized the leading works of the golden age. The end of the eighteenth century and the whole of the nineteenth century produced a vast number of skillful but insipid works. We may pass quickly over the compositions of such men as José Lidón (1752–1827), organist in Malaga and at the royal chapel, his pupil Pedro Carrera Lanchares, organist at the Carmelite monastery in Madrid, and Miguel Hilarión Eslava y Elizondo (1807–78), chapelmaster in Burgo de Osma, Seville and Madrid, whose *Museo organico español* contains works by many composers of this period.

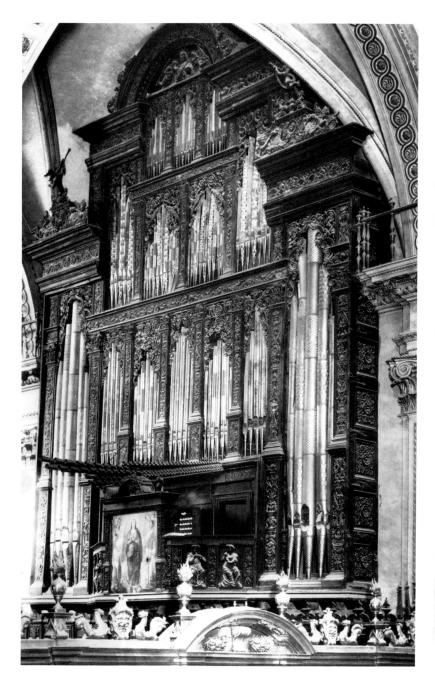

206 Cathedral, Valencia, Pedro Andrés Teixidor and Diego Ortiz, 1510–13. This instrument, of which Juan Cabanilles was the incumbent from 1665 to 1712, provides an example of one of the earliest Renaissance cases in Spain. The various miters are enclosed within an overall framework, the case front is flat and normally expresses a sense of vertical movement by means of highly ornamented pilasters. In this instance, however, it is the horizontals which predominate (cf. the organ in Perpignan Cathedral, 1504). Enlarged in 1575 by Salvador Estrada, the organ was rebuilt between 1631 and 1636 by Antonio Lloréns, a Franciscan friar, who was also responsible for the organ at Lérida Cathedral (1624). A number of new stops were added in 1693 by Roque Blasco, and in 1720 Nicolás de Salanova transformed the stops almost completely: the horizontal reeds presumably date from this period. The instrument was renovated by José Martínez y Alcarría in 1833, by Adolfo Ibach in 1860, and by Diego and Aquilino Amezua in 1888. At the beginning of the century, the organ comprised three manuals (4½ octaves) and Pedal (two octaves), with pneumatic action. Part of the case escaped destruction in 1936; the instrument has been dismantled.

207 Old Cathedral, "Salinas" realejo, Salamanca, Damián Luis (?), 1569 (?) At present in the diocesan museum in the cloisters of the catedral vieja, this small instrument must at one time have belonged to Francisco Salinas, music master at Salamanca University from 1567 until 1588. It is a single-manual instrument with a compass of forty-two notes (short octave) and has eight stops, divided into bass and treble. Many of the pipes have survived, as have all the essential parts of the instrument with the exception of the blowing mechanism.

208 *Organo del côro* (Epistle Organ), Real Basilica (Monasterio) de San Lorenzo del Escorial, El Escorial, Gillis Brebos and family, 1578–86
Born at Lierre near Antwerp and the son of Gommaar Brebos, Gillis Brebos settled in Antwerp around 1552 and soon established himself as one of the leading organ builders of his age. He was responsible among others for the organs at Notre-Dame, Antwerp (small organ on the rood screen, 1558; main organ, 1565–7, 1572), at St. Rombaut at Malines and at Averbode Abbey. None of these instruments has survived. Philip II of Spain invited him to build the organs for the Escorial, notably the four large organs for the Basilica de San Lorenzo.

Gillis Brebos was employed at the Escorial with other members of his family, including (presumably) his brothers Michiel (d. 1590) and Jasper (d. 1588). Although we know that a fourth brother, Hans, was organ builder to the Danish Court in Copenhagen in 1568 and that he probably died in Madrid in 1609, we have little information about Nicolas Brebos, another member of the family employed at the Escorial. When Gillis died in 1584, his brothers completed his work on the organs there. Designed by Juan de Herrera and built by the Italian wood-carver Giuseppe Flecha, the four gilded cases reveal a classicism of form which is remarkable in Spain at this time but which harmonizes well with the chill austerity of the basilica. The cases are arranged symmetrically in two groups of two identical frontages: two in the transept (*côro del prior*) and two on the north side of the altar. The Epistle Organs were two-manual instruments with pedals and a total of thirty-four stops each, whereas the two Gospel Organs were comparatively small, a single manual with thirteen stops, including four divided stops. A silent *Rp* gave a sense of proportion to the whole structure. It goes without saying that these instruments, being Flemish in conception, must have sounded strange to Spanish ears, particularly when we consider their 41-note compass and the eight pedal stops of the two transept organs. Iberian builders not unnaturally ignored them.

The Escorial organs were considerably modified in 1704 by Pedro de Liborna Echevarría who added ranks of horizontal reeds and a second manual to the single-manual Gospel Organs. Mention should also be made of later alterations by José Casas (at the time of Antonio Soler) and by José Verdalonga at the end of the eighteenth century. Of the two original Gospel Organs only the display pipes remain. The whole of the pipework was rebuilt by Eleizgaray in 1929 and by Organería española in 1964. The Epistle Organ has forty-two stops, the Gospel Organ nineteen.

209 Procession organ, apartments of the Infanta Isabella Clara Eugenia, El Escorial, Brebos, 1589 (?)
This portative organ is traditionally believed to have belonged to the Emperor Charles V. In reality it was probably built by a member of the Brebos family, either Gillis (?) or Hans. The decoration includes the arms of Philip II. The instrument was restored some fifteen years ago by Organería española using new pipework and electric blowing mechanism. It comprises six stops in an elegant case of sculpted wood. The single manual has a compass of thirty-eight notes, including a short octave.

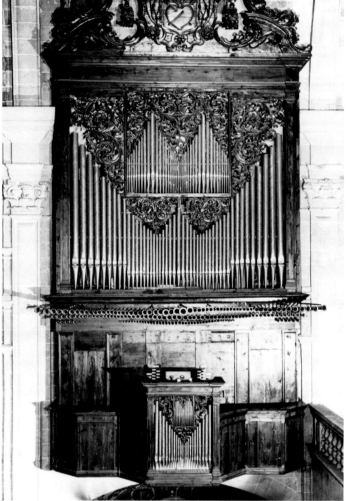

210 Cathedral, Seville, Antonio Pedro Faleiro, 1668–73
Faleiro was a Portuguese organ builder who settled in Valladolid. Enlarged in 1703, the Epistle Organ was the first organ in Spain to have four manuals (*Positivo* I facing the choir, *Organo Grande, Organo Segundo* and *Positivo* II facing the side-aisle) and 32′ reeds (Trompeta imperial on the Organo Grande, and Contras de Bombardas on the Pedal). An *Eco* keyboard was added later: it had three reed stops and was placed high up in the instrument. The organ was rebuilt in 1912 by Amézua and again in 1973 by Organería española. The two instruments, each of which has two Positives, form a vast ensemble in the *côro*.

211 Santa María del Socorró (Monastery of Sant Agusti), Palma de Mallorca, Caimari brothers, *c.* 1700; Jorge Bosch Bernat-Veri, end of the eighteenth century
Remarkable for the late dating of its Renaissance case, the Palma organ, perched on a swallow's nest, displays an impressive frontage of *guilloché* pipes. In contrast to the traditional Castilian organ, the tonal structures are here clearly differentiated and ordered in accordance with the *Werkprinzip*, with a main keyboard (*Organo Mayor*), separate Positive or *Cadireta*, and *Oberwerk* or *teclat d'alt*. The manuals, however, are not coupled to each other. Jorge Bosch Bernat-Veri added a battery of horizontal reeds and, hence, a new *GO* chest. There is no vertical trumpet (Trompeta real) in the case, an omission which is all the more striking in a Spanish organ. The Palma Cathedral instrument is an outstanding example of Majorcan organ building, which should not be confused with the Spanish school of organ building, which in turn is different from the Catalan school. All these regions were subject to powerful foreign influences, and German and Swiss influence was particularly keenly felt in the Balearic Islands. There is more than one organ by a Swiss builder both here (Minorca) and on the mainland (El Vendrell). The Palma organ was restored by Gerhard Grenzing in 1969–70.

212 Gospel Organ (choir side), Cathedral, Granada, Leonardo Fernández Dávila, 1744–6; case by Maestro de San Juan de Dios

Three manuals (*Órgano principal, Cadireta interior* and *Cadireta exterior*, C–c¹¹¹, 49 notes) and Pedal (eight keys). Dávila built the almost identical Epistle Organ between 1746 and 1749, and restored both instruments in 1765–6. Further restorations took place in 1811 and 1874, when Pedro Roqués altered the original stoplist and added some stops of his own, as well as a twelve-note pedal coupled to the manuals.

213 Epistle Organ, Cathedral, Toledo, Pedro de Liborna Echevarría, 1757–8

The wood carvings on the two sumptuous case fronts of this instrument are by Germán López, and the giltwork is by Próspero Martolo of Madrid. With its forty-odd divided stops, this organ by the so-called *Artifize de su Magestad* has three manuals (C–c¹¹¹, 51 notes, no short octave) and Pedal of thirteen keys. There are no couplers. An impressive *trompetería* enlivens each of the case fronts: the reeds of the *GO* (second manual) dominate the choir side, while those of the third manual look out over the side-aisle. The instrument was overhauled in 1971 by Organería española.

214 New Cathedral, Salamanca, Pedro de Liborna Echevarría, 1744

Salamanca's *catedral nueva* is endowed with three organs – a small sixteenth-century positive, a sixteenth-century organ notable for its large shutters and built on the gallery facing the third of the cathedral's organs, that of Echevarría. The latter surpasses the other two not only in its tonal qualities but also in the imposing size of its case and the sumptuous ornamentation of its case front, broken by the triple horizontal of its majestic *trompetería*. Typical of Spanish instruments are the two identical fronts, one of which faces the side-aisle, the other the *côro* (reproduced here). Only the first row of display pipes speaks, the other stories being made up of dummy pipes. Echevarría was a member of a long line of organ builders of Basque origin, although the links between them are not well defined. The builder who created the Salamanca organ was a man of genius, not least in his disposition of the *Jeux de tierce* and the *lleno* of the *Organo Grande*, which alone are placed flush with the chests, as if embedded in the instrument. They are dominated by the other ranks, positioned above them and conducted off from often remote chests.

The instrument has sixty-three half-stops (twenty-nine in the bass and thirty-four in the treble) and a pedal department of eleven notes. The end keys of the pedals operate a Drum-stop (two low-pitched pipes tuned a fifth apart), while the nine inner keys operate the Contras (16′ and 8′ together). The *Eco* ranks are positioned in the substructure behind the console. The organ was restored by Organería española, but without any great concern for authenticity. There is a modern keyboard and equal temperament. (See Appendix for the specification of this instrument.)

215 University, Salamanca, Pedro de Liborna Echevarría, 1709
Restored in 1975 by G.A.C. de Graaf, this charming organ has a single keyboard (C–c[III], 45 notes, short octave), controlling fifteen half-stops and Timbales.

216 Capilla del Palacio Real (de Oriente), Madrid, Jorge Bosch Bernat-Veri, 1778
It is said that this organ was designed by Padre Antonio Soler himself. It is one of the best preserved organs in Spain and has three manuals (C–d[III], 51 notes), with forty-two right-hand stops and thirty-four left-hand stops. The Pedal has twelve Contras (en 26 and en 13). There is also a Tambor and Timbal totaling four pipes. The first keyboard (*Organo principal*) has eighteen reed half-stops, eleven of which are *en chamade*. The latter include a half-stop of Viejos 8′ ("old men's voices") in the bass answering to a half-stop of Viejas 8′ ("old women's voices") in the treble. While paying homage to a certain mannerist elegance, the case front is splendidly classical in conception. It is a relatively plain style which began to leave its mark on Spanish organ building in the second half of the eighteenth century, the most notable exception being the four astonishing cases in the Escorial. One thinks in this context of the Gospel Organ built by José Verdalonga in 1797 at Toledo Cathedral. Two stylistic visions coexisted at this period, one of them classical, the other harking back to the Baroque and overladen with ornamentation and *putti*. In this respect, the case front of Pedro de Echevarría's Gospel Organ in Segovia Cathedral (1770) stands out as a skillful link between these two stylistic alternatives.

217 Emperor's Organ, Cathedral, Toledo, Valentín and José Verdalonga, 1798
Toledo Cathedral boasts no fewer than six organs, three large eighteenth-century instruments (the Emperor's Organ, and the two *Chororgeln*, namely Verdalonga's Gospel Organ of 1796–7 and Echevarría's Epistle Organ of 1757–8), and three positives housed in the side chapels. The Emperor's Organ is uniquely situated, high up on an imposing stone structure in the south transept of the cathedral. This *puerta de los Leones* was probably inherited from an earlier instrument built in the sixteenth century. Tradition has it that this instrument was built between 1543 and 1549 by Gonzalo Hernández de Córdoba and Juan Gaytán, and that the Emperor Charles V may even have heard it played on. Rebuilt by Valentín and José Verdalonga in 1798, this astonishing and exceptional instrument is one of the gems of Baroque organ building in Spain. It now has two manuals (C–e[III], 53 notes; prior to the 1922 rebuild by Albert Merklin, there was a compass of forty-five notes, with a short octave) and forty-five half-stops (22/23). The twelve-key double pedals have ten stops, making them the most richly endowed in Spain. The first series of half-keys operates the Flautados, while the second series operates the reeds, in addition to being coupled to the second manual. We may also draw attention to the fanciful battery of vertical reeds of the first manual, and the calm and sumptuous *fonds d'orgue* of the second (Flautado de 26 and 13, and Octava general). The builder has distinguished between the different tonal structures and, in the face of all tradition, separated the *lleno* from the horizontal *trompetería*: the *lleno* and the vertical reeds have been given to the first manual, the *fond d'orgue* and external reeds to the second manual, and the Contras (52, 26, 26 display pipe, and 13) and horizontal reeds to the Pedal. Another interesting feature is the existence of polyphonic pipes: the wood pipes covered with a layer of tin in the right-hand pipe-flat have a remarkable system of valves enabling each pipe to emit several different notes. The same is true of the Contras de 52 on the Pedal: two polyphonic pipes planted on the superstructure of the instrument and parallel to the case front each emits six notes. It may be that these polyphonic pipes derive their origins from the spirit of inventiveness shown by the instrument's sixteenth-century builders. It was restored in 1967 by Organería española. (See Appendix for the Specification of this instrument.)

218 Parish church, Andahuaylas, Peru, unknown builder, first half of seventeenth century

It is to Peru that we must turn to find the oldest surviving organs in Latin America. They are simple instruments, probably built locally and still to be found gracing the churches of Andean villages such as Pisac, Valle, Checacupe and Andahuaylas, the last two of which are situated near Cuzco. Like all these relatively large portatives, the Andahuaylas organ is primitively built and traditional in appearance, with a simple case painted to imitate the relief work of more costly stucco ornaments. Of interest is the radial (fan-shaped) disposition of the trackers, a feature characteristic of Iberian organ building.

219 Epistle Organ, Cathedral, Cuzco, Peru, unknown builder, first third of seventeenth century

Two organs face each other across the chancel of Cuzco Cathedral, one of them Flemish in design and possibly imported from Europe, the other built locally. Their position above the choir stalls is relatively rare in Latin America, although it was later to be exploited to an astonishing degree in the cathedrals at Mexico City and at Puebla. The Epistle Organ is a single-manual instrument (forty-four notes, short octave), divided into bass and treble, with a dozen half-stops at its disposal. Flemish influence is suggested by its disposition and the construction of its pipework, together with the absence of any decoration on the bodies of the pipes. Worth drawing attention to are two Faux-Bourdons in the left part of the case, and a Rossignol stop, recognizable by its water-container which can be seen on a level with the foot of the pipes of the left-hand pipe-flat. At the right-hand side of the case is a group of small pipes known as a *Lyre*.

220 Epistle Organ ("El Organo Carlos Quinto"), Cathedral, Puebla, Félix de Izaguirre, 1710

Designed by Esteban Gutiérrez de Villaseñor, the case of this instrument, viewed from the side-aisle, is probably descended from the case which Charles V bequeathed to the parish in 1560. Its formal variety makes it one of the most astonishing cases in the whole of Latin America: tierce-point towers are transformed into semicircular towers in their upper halves, while the semicircular central tower is surmounted by a tierce-point tower made up of two series of pipes arranged head to foot; the pipe-flats at either side are similarly inverted. The instrument originally had a *Cadireta* and around sixty-eight half-stops, but all that remains of it now are the case fronts.

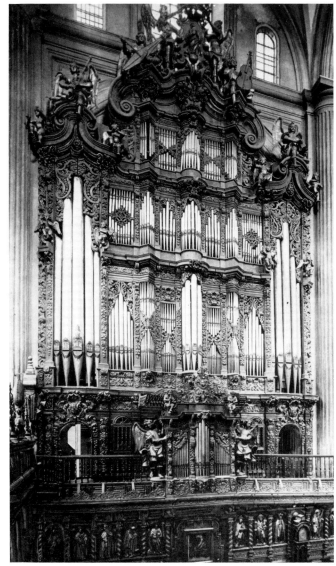

221, 222   Cathedral, Mexico City, Mexico

221: Epistle Organ, seen from the side-aisle, Jorge de Sesma Hacia, 1690, and José Nasarre, 1734

222: Gospel Organ, seen from the choir, José Nasarre, 1735; cases by Juan de Rojas

Inaugurated on October 23, 1736, the two magnificent organs of Mexico City's monumental cathedral face each other across the *côro*. They are similar to each other both in the structure of their case fronts and in their specifications. The Epistle Organ, built in Spain by Jorge de Sesma Hacia in 1690, was installed in the cathedral in 1695 by the Aragonese builder Tiburcio Sans. In 1734 it was rebuilt by José Nasarre who added a *Cadireta exterior*, a rarity in Latin America. Nasarre, a Mexican builder who had previously built the organ for Guadalajara Cathedral in 1730, was also responsible for the Gospel Organ at Mexico City. Completed in 1735, it was housed in a case which had been built at the same time as the Epistle Organ and which had remained empty during the intervening period. Each of the two organs has two manuals divided at c^1/c sharp[1]. The Epistle Organ has a compass of fifty-one notes ($C–d^{111}$), while the Gospel Organ has fifty ($CD–d^{111}$). The lower keyboard controls the stops of the *Cadireta exterior* – seven half-stops (3/4) on both instruments – and those of the *Cadireta interior*, of which the Epistle Organ has fourteen (7/7) and the Gospel Organ thirteen (7/6) half-stops. The upper keyboard controls the fifty-five (26/29) and fifty-eight (26/32) half-stops of the *Organo Principal*. The ten-key Pedal (CDEF–g) has three Flautados and three Bajoncillos. A notable, and exceptional, feature of the Gospel Organ is its twenty-seven-note *Solo* manual ($c^1–d^{111}$) fixed to the right of the upper keyboard and endowed with six stops. It may have been added by José Perez de Lara, who restored the instrument in 1817. Each of the cases, built of unwaxed cedarwood, has two fronts, decorated with dummy pipes and notable for the structure of their inverted miters. In 1967 a fire damaged the cases and the display pipes on the choir side. Both instruments were restored by Flentrop between 1975 and 1977. It may be observed that in Latin America, contrary to the European and North American tradition, the Epistle side is on the left and the Gospel side on the right of the altar.

223 Cathedral, Cuenca, Ecuador, António Estevan Cardoso, 1739
A single-manual instrument with a compass of fifty-five notes, and thirteen half-stops (seven in the left hand, and six in the right). Notable features of this instrument are the painted panels above the central pipe-flats, and the ten small figures with trumpets held to their lips. The classical motifs on the substructure are highlighted in gold and blue. The instrument, currently unplayable, was restored in 1924.

224 Parish church of Sta. Prisca, Taxco, Mexico, unknown builder, 1759 (?)
This single-manual instrument has fourteen half-stops in the bass and thirteen in the treble. It appears to have been built in two stages, probably in 1759 and in 1806, when it was enlarged by José António Sánchez de Ixmiquilpan. Attention may be drawn to the two lanterns on the balustrade, each of which contains a carillon operated by a simple iron crank-handle.

225 Sta. Rosa de Viterbo, Querétaro, Mexico, Ignacio Mariano de Las Casas, c. 1759
A single-manual organ (CDE–c^{111}) with twelve (6/6) half-stops. All that remains of it today are the pipes of the pipe-flats, beneath which can be seen the space formerly occupied by two rows of horizontal trumpets.

226 Parish church, Tiradentes, Brazil, unknown builder, mid-eighteenth century
This instrument is one of the most elegant in Latin America. Built to one side of the choir gallery, the case is richly decorated in a rococo style with stucco and paintings. Although the case front is clearly influenced by the Portuguese school of organ building, tradition has it that the pipes were built in Oporto and housed in a case of local origin.

227 Church of S. Felipe Neri, San Miguel de Allende, Mexico, Josefus Besar, 1775
This profusely ornamented instrument has a single manual with a compass of four octaves, and twenty-nine half-stops (13/16). Altered in 1869, it is currently unplayable.

228 Church of S. Martín (Convento franciscano), Texmelucán, Mexico, unknown builder, 1794
The disposition of the pipes in five large surface areas, each of them horizontally aligned, gives the case front of this instrument a characteristically squat appearance, accentuated by the sinuous lines around the pipe-mouths, decorated with masks and arabesques, and by the elegantly curving lines of two trumpet-playing sirens. The only concessions to verticality are the two bass pipes flanking the sides of the case. Beneath the gallery are busts of Tritons, each with a horizontal trumpet raised to his lips. The single manual of this instrument has a compass of forty-nine notes, and twenty-four half-stops (12/12) divided at c^1/c sharp[1]. The toy stops include a Tambores and Cimbales, operated by the same pedal, a Campanos and Pajaros Aqua (Vogelgesang). We may also note that the Sirena stop sounds the two large pipes on either side of the case, together with a reed pipe inside the case itself. The instrument was rebuilt in 1919.

229 Cabinet organ (formerly in the Museo José Luis Bello y González, Puebla, Mexico), Cathedral of S. Francisco, Tlaxcala, José Castro and his son, end of eighteenth or early nineteenth century
This instrument, built for the Convent of Sta. Rosa at Puebla, is housed in a silver-gilt cypresswood case. The display pipes are decorated with colorful motifs and highlighted in gold: the resonators are painted with arabesques, while masks enliven the pipe-mouths. The single, divided manual has sixteen half-stops (7/9) and a Sonido de pajaros, or Nightingale stop. The instrument was restored by Rubin S. Frels in 1973, when electric bellows were fitted.

230 Catholic Parish church of St. Joseph, Las Piñas, Manila, Philippines, Padre Diego Cera, 1824

Positioned high up under an arch between two pillars, the famous "bamboo organ" is noteworthy as one of the largest single-manual organs ever built by a Spanish organ builder. The rear side of the double-fronted case contains the pedal pipes. while the front is divided, straightforwardly, into seven pipe-flats. The bays and the other parts of the superstructure are painted with colorful *trompe-l'œil* effects. This instrument is one of three bamboo organs built by the Spanish monk Diego Cera who worked as a missionary in the Philippines from 1792 onwards. An ingenious craftsman, he has produced here an astonishing piece of work which for more than a century and a half has withstood a tropical climate where the level of humidity may reach as high as 98%. The pipes are made of bamboo previously treated with a salt solution. The mechanical parts are made of a variety of highly resistant types of wood. The horizontal reeds were imported from Spain.

The organ has a single manual, divided in the traditional way into treble and bass (c^1/c sharp^1). Its exceptional compass of sixty-one keys stretches from F^1 to f^{111}. There are twenty-one half-stops (10/11), in addition to a Pajaritos or Nightingale stop (seven metal pipes) and a Tambor (or Drum) of three pipes. The twelve-note Pedal has a single II-rank Contras stop. The *trompetería* comprises four half-stops, a Bajoncillo 4′ and Clarín compaña 2′ in the bass, and Clarín clara and Clarín campaña 8′ in the treble.

It was inevitable that such an exceptional instrument should require an exceptional form of restoration: Johannes Klais responded with a performance unique in the annals of organ building. The various parts of the instrument were transported to Bonn and placed in a building which recreated the climatic conditions of a tropical winter, with a temperature of 25°C and 85% humidity. The process of restoration was completed in 1975.

231 Cathedral, Evora, builder unknown; case probably 1562
Some few decades ago there were two identical sixteenth-century organs in Evora Cathedral, facing each other across the *côro alto*. Now only the Gospel Organ remains, the Epistle Organ having been carried off by a Dutch organ enthusiast, restored by Flentrop and sold to a buyer in Texas. A late Renaissance Italian influence is evident both in the general shape of the case and in the sonorities of certain of the stops. The case decoration is distinguished by a certain mannerism in its style, which may reveal Flemish influences. The draw-stop knobs are situated to the right of the performer, on a board at 90° to the case. The instrument was substantially altered in 1772 by Pascoal Caetano Oldovini, who added two half-stops of horizontal reeds (Trompeta and Clarim), and again in 1800. In 1966–7 the organ was restored by Flentrop. (See Appendix for stoplist.)

232 Convent of Santa Cruz, Coimbra
The original organ of 1532 by one Master João, restored in 1559 by Heitor Lobo, was housed in a case designed by the French master-joiner François Lorette. This case provided a base for a later case, probably built during the seventeenth century. Repaired in 1694 by the German organ builder Miguel Hensberg, the instrument was later repaired and renovated by the Spanish builder Benito Gomez de Herrera. It was again repaired in 1868, this time by José Joaquim da Fonseca; and in 1971 João Sampaio & Son began work on restoring it. The pipework on the balustrade is part of the *Eco* manual. There are twenty-eight half-stops (C–c[111], short octave).

233   Cathedral, Faro, "João Henriques Hulemcampo," 1715–16
The typically northern German structure of this organ may come as a surprise (*cf.* the case of the organ at Cappel, 1680): it is the work of the German organ builder Johann Heinrich Hulenkampf, a pupil of Arp Schnitger, who worked in Portugal at the beginning of the eighteenth century. He built at least two other instruments in Lisbon, at the Carmelite Monastery and at the Church of São Francisco, both of which were destroyed by the Lisbon earthquake of 1755. Built on a gallery next to the *côro alto*, the Faro Cathedral organ has twenty-six stops and two manuals of forty-five notes each. The lower keyboard is the *Orgão principal* or Great Organ, the upper keyboard the *Positivo de peito* or *Brustpositiv*, an arrangement attributable to the German origins of the builder. Certainly, such an ordering of the tonal structures is as exceptional in Portugal as it is in Spain, where the lower keyboard logically corresponds to the *Orgão do éco* and the upper manual to the *Orgão principal*. In 1767 the Italian builder Pascoal Caetano Oldovini completely rebuilt the wind-chest and added the horizontal Trompetas, the echo stops and pull-down pedals with a compass of eleven notes. Other notable instruments built by Oldovini include the *Chororgel* at Evora (1758) and the instrument at Elvas (1777). Like the organ in the University Chapel at Coimbra of some twenty years later, the Faro Cathedral organ case is decorated with sumptuous lacquerwork chinoiserie in which the dominant color is red. The instrument was restored by Flentrop in 1973–4.

234   Epistle Organ, Cathedral, Oporto, Lourenço da Conceição, 1727–33
Father Lourenço da Conceição built three instruments for Oporto Cathedral, a large organ on the gallery above the main door (1719–26, no longer extant), and the Epistle and Gospel Organs in the presbytery choir. Slightly different in design, the cases of these two instruments were the work of Luis Pereira da Costa. The Epistle Organ, which currently has two manuals (fifty-four notes), was completely rebuilt in 1869 by António José dos Santos, and altered again around 1945. Both instruments were replaced by Flentrop between 1969 and 1971, and are now only of interest for their case fronts.

235   Royal Chapel of São Miguel, University, Coimbra, Dom Manuel de São Bento Gomes, a Benedictine monk, 1732–3
Bracketed to the south wall of the chapel near the *côro alto*, this organ presents the beholder with a frenzied vision of ornate decoration, the work of Gabriel Ferreira da Cunha. Lacquerwork chinoiserie, attesting to Portugal's colonial power in the Orient, adorns the base of the case. A single manual (C–f^{111}, fifty-four notes) controls thirty half-stops of the *Organo Grande*, four complete stops of the *Eco* (swell), and seven half-stops of the upper *Eco* (not swell). The instrument was restored by Flentrop in 1971–2.

236   Sé (Cathedral), Braga, Brother Simão Fontanes, 1737   ▷
The two organs of Braga Cathedral are the work of the Galician builder Simão Fontanes, their monumental presence dominating the first bay of the central nave (Baroque *côro*). The identical cases were made by Marcelino de Araújo, and the paintings and gilding were carried out by Manuel Furtado de Porto. The Epistle Organ of 1738 has a single manual of forty-nine notes and twenty-eight half-stops, whereas the two-manual Gospel Organ, seen here, has a compass of forty-five notes (C–c^{111}, with a short octave). The upper keyboard controls the twenty-eight half-stops of the *Orgão Grande*, the lower keyboard controlling the eight half-stops of the *Orgão da cadeira* and the fourteen half-stops of the *Eco* situated on the floor of the gallery. The Pedal comprises ten iron keys, eight of which are coupled to the short octave of the *GO*, while the other two operate the arms of the angels stationed at either side of the *Cadireta* case. This system is known as *Carrancas*. The general disposition of the case front, with its tierce-point towers, and the decorative elements including the three statues of Faith, Hope and Charity at the very top of the case, and bearded satyrs supporting the gallery, left their mark on later cases, notably those built by Francisco António Solha and designed by the Benedictine friar José de Santo António Ferreira Vilaça at Tibães, Cabeceiras de Basto, and Guimarães. The Gospel Organ is currently being restored by L.A. Esteves Pereira.

237 Monastery of São Vicente de Fora, Lisbon, unknown builder, eighteenth century (the exact date is disputed)

This instrument, the largest in Portugal, has so far defied attempts to date it: if, as has been suggested, it was made by an unknown builder of great skill during the second quarter of the eighteenth century, it is a miracle that it survived the earthquake of 1755. At present all that restorers have been able to discover is an inscription on the wind-chest of the *Eco* organ which reads, "Remade in the year 1765 by João Fontanes de Maqueira." The instrument has fifty-nine half-stops and two manuals (*Orgão Grande* and *Eco* Organ including some stops in a swell box). The massive and imposing case towers over the choir, are structured symmetrically around a central tower of five 16′ pipes (Flautados de 24 palmos). Flanked at each side by towers of seven 16′ pipes, the lower level of the case front comprises 8′ pipes (Flautados de 12 palmos). The six upper stories are filled with dummy pipes. This organ has an impressive battery of horizontal trumpets, the ninety-eight pipes being divided into seven groups, to which must be added the ninety-four smaller pipes in two rows above the console. Also noteworthy is the progressive *lleno*, the biggest and most brilliant in the Iberian peninsula. Including the Flautado de 24 palmos (16′ Montre), it comprises twenty-one ranks of pipes at C, ascending to thirty-two ranks at c sharp[1]. The instrument was repaired by João Sampaio & Son in 1957, and the same firm is currently in the process of restoring it. (See Appendix for the specification of this instrument.)

238 Gospel Organ, Cathedral, Lamego, Francisco António Solha, 1756-7; double case by António Mendes Coutinho

Built on either side of the choir on a small gallery above the choir stalls, the two Lamego organs are the work of Francisco António Solha, a Spanish builder from Galicia who settled at Guimarães in Portugal. He was responsible for a number of organs, including those at São Miguel de Refóios at Cabeceiras de Basto (1770), at the convent of Santa Marinha da Costa at Guimarães (1788), and at the monastery of São Martinho de Tibães (1785). All that now remains of the Epistle Organ at Lamego, built in 1755, is an empty case and the display pipes. It was smaller than the Gospel Organ, having only a single manual and twenty-six half-stops. The Gospel Organ, seen here, has two manuals (*Orgão Principal* and *Orgão do éco*) with a compass of fifty-one notes; it currently has thirty-two half-stops. The stops of the *Eco* manual, operated from the lower keyboard, are traditionally located at ground level in the substructure of the instrument, only certain of them being placed in a swell box. It is worth noting the relatively modest dimensions of the instrument and the flatness of the case front, whose small upper stories are made up of dummy pipes or *cónegos*. The instrument has been altered many times in its history. It was restored between 1970 and 1974 by João Sampaio & Son.

239   Epistle Organ attributed to Brother Domingos de S. José Varella (1762–1834), i.e. end of the eighteenth century, São Bento da Vitória, Oporto.
This instrument, one of the most astonishing of Portuguese organs, comprises two manuals (*Orgão Principal* and *Orgão do éco*, C–f[111], 54 notes) and forty-four half-stops, including a Percussion stop and a Nightingale. The case, mannerist in inspiration, was built by Gabriel Rodrigues in 1719; the gilding, completed in 1761, must be contemporary with the panels at the base of the case, which is rococo in style. On the opposite side of the nave, with its back to the wall, stands a silent copy of the instrument just described. The Epistle Organ was rebuilt in 1880 by António José dos Santos and his son, and it was almost certainly they who installed the thirteen-key Pedal. Modest repairs were carried out between 1969 and 1971.

240   Monastery of Santa Clara, Vila do Conde, unknown builder (perhaps Francisco António Solha), 1775
The unified group of carvings, both on the gallery and on the case and its superstructure, forms a rococo framework of rare and complex richness. The case front, with its classical structure, is composed of a central tower framed by two double-story flats, while two tierce-point towers give a sense of proportion to the two sides of the case, which are themselves made up of two pipe-flats. This was a common design during the second half of the eighteenth century, especially in northern Portugal (*cf.* São Miguel de Refóios at Cabeceiras de Basto [1770], the monastery at São Martinho at Tibães [1785], and the monastery of São João de Tarouca [*c.* 1760]). The present instrument has two manuals (C–e[111], 52 notes, without a short octave) and seventeen half-stops in the left hand, nineteen in the right hand. It is currently in a state of disrepair and lacks its external reed pipes, but is due for restoration by the Department of Public Works as a historic monument.

241   Monastery Church of São Martinho, Tibães, Francisco António Solha, 1785
This two-manual organ is without doubt one of the finest in northern Portugal. Designed by the Benedictine friar José Vilaça, with carvings by Luis José de Sousa Neves de Santo Tirso, the case is comparable to those at São Miguel de Refóios at Cabeceiras de Basto (1770) and Santa Marinha de Costa at Guimarães (1788), two other instruments built by Solha and designed by José Vilaça. The case front is clearly influenced in design by that of the magnificent Braga organs: the general sense of movement is underlined by the outward thrust of the horizontal reeds.

242 King's Chapel, Boston (MA), engraving of the first music festival to be held in New England on January 10, 1786
The instrument depicted here was built in 1756 by the English organ builder Richard Bridge. It was unusual for its time, having three manuals (*Great, Swell, Choir*) and twenty stops. All that remains of it today is the case.

244 Christ Church, Philadelphia (PA), Philip Feyring, 1766
Feyring was a Lutheran organ builder, born at Arfeld in Germany. His twenty-seven-stop organ for Christ Church, Philadelphia, had three manuals and a pedal. It was replaced by a new instrument built by Henry Erben in 1837. The present Christ Church organ is by Ernest M. Skinner.

243 Congregational Church, South Dennis (MA), John Snetzler, 1762
Born in Switzerland in 1710, Snetzler worked with Christiaan Müller at St. Bavo in Haarlem before moving to England, where he became organ builder to King George III. Imported from England, the South Dennis organ has eight stops and two half-stops distributed between a single manual of fifty-seven notes (without G sharp) and a thirteen-key *Ped* coupled to the manual. The instrument was restored in 1959 by the Andover Organ Company.

245 Organ, Essex Institute, Salem (MA), George G. Hook, 1827
A pupil of William Goodrich, George G. Hook was twenty when he built this organ with its Empire-style case. The single manual (fifty-eight notes, without G sharp) has five stops. Electric bellows were fitted in 1945.

246 Unitarian Church, Nantucket (MA), William M. Goodrich, 1831
This two-manual instrument was substantially altered by George Peirce in 1883, and now has two manuals and a pedal, with thirteen stops. Most of the pipework is original.

247 St. Philip's Episcopal Chapel, Charleston (SC), Thomas Appleton, 1839
Originally in the Seamen's House at Charleston, this seven-stop instrument has a single manual (58 notes, without G sharp), and an eighteen-key pedal which appears to be of a later date than the rest of the organ.

248 Bates College, Lewiston (ME), Henry Erben, 1850
This is a good example of one of Erben's smaller organs. The single manual (56 notes) shares its four stops with a fifteen-key pedal. Restored by George Jardine & Son in 1861 and by the Andover Organ Company in 1978.

249 Music Hall, Boston (MA), Eberhard Friedrich Walcker, 1863 (Opus 200)
Walcker's organ arrived in the port of Boston on board the brig *Presto* after a stormy voyage lasting three months. Seven months later it was installed in the city's Great Hall. Concealed behind a large tapestry, it was revealed to the general public on October 31, and again on November 2, 1863: an act which might be taken to symbolize the dawn of a new era for American organ builders – the era of large-scale European (and specifically German) organ building. Following the foundation of the Boston Symphony Orchestra in 1881, Walcker's organ was dismantled to make room for the orchestra. It was placed in store for a time, and then auctioned off in 1884 for an absurdly low figure. In 1909 it was rebuilt by the Methuen Organ Company in a hall specially designed for the instrument by the architect and patron of the arts, Edward F. Searles. Walcker's eighty-nine-stop, four-manual instrument, with pedal and hydraulic bellows, was profoundly altered in 1947 by G. Donald Harrison of the Aeolian-Skinner Organ Company.

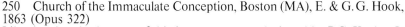

250 Church of the Immaculate Conception, Boston (MA), E. & G.G. Hook, 1863 (Opus 322)
Like the church, the case of this instrument was designed by P.C. Keeley. It originally had three manuals, but this number was increased to four by Hook & Hastings in 1902 (Opus 1959). The fifty-nine stops are distributed among a *Great, Swell, Choir, Solo* and *Pedal*.

251 Church of Jesus Christ of Latter-Day Saints (Mormon Tabernacle), Salt Lake City (UT)
The Mormon Tabernacle organ is without doubt the most famous instrument in the United States, its concerts being broadcast every Sunday on Mormon Radio. It is also the only organ in America to have been imported from Australia. Designed by Joseph H. Ridges, an English carpenter and cabinetmaker who converted to the Mormon faith and emigrated to Australia, the seven-stop organ was installed in 1857. Between 1866 and 1869 Ridges built a new twenty-seven-stop instrument with two manuals and pedal, with a case which appears to have been inspired by that of Walcker's organ in Boston Music Hall (1863). This instrument was enlarged in 1885 by Niels Johnson, in 1901 by the Kimball Organ Company, and in 1915–16, 1926 and 1940 by the Austin Organ Company. It was rebuilt between 1945 and 1948 by the Aeolian-Skinner Organ Company. All that remains today of Ridges' instrument is the case (extended sideways in 1915–16) and a handful of stops. The present Mormon Tabernacle organ has 154 stops distributed among five manuals (seven departments: *Great Organ, Choir Organ, Swell Organ, Positive Organ, Solo Organ, Bombarde Organ* and *Antiphonal Organ*) and a thirty-two-key *Pedal Organ*.

252 Holy Trinity Roman Catholic Church, Augusta (GA), George Jardine & Son, 1868
A native Englishman, George Jardine is noted for his barrel organs, and for his habit of adorning his instruments with unusual stops, many of which bore fantastic names such as the Boehmflute 4'. He was always interested in the latest inventions, notably the Barker Lever, which he employed in his own instruments. His organ for the Holy Trinity Church in Augusta has twenty-seven stops distributed among a *Great, Swell* and *Pedal*.

253 Church of Our Lady of Perpetual Help, Roxbury (MA), George S. Hutchings, 1896 (Opus 410)

254 Woolsey Hall, Yale University, New Haven (CT), Ernest M. Skinner Organ Company, 1928 (Opus 722)
This instrument, known as the Newberry Memorial Organ, incorporates elements from two earlier organs, one a seventy-six-stop instrument built in 1902 by the Hutchings-Votey Organ Company of Boston (Opus 1469), the other a 120-stop organ built in 1915 by the J.W. Steere & Son Organ Company of Springfield (Opus 682). The Newberry Memorial Organ is a good example of an orchestral organ, with 166 stops distributed among four manuals and pedal, with the following departments: *Great, Solo (Echo), Choir orchestral – Swell orchestral, String Ensemble, Swell, Pedal* and *Echo Pedal.*

VIII Organ Music
in the Twentieth Century

At a time when aspirations and affirmations of cultural autonomy were making themselves felt in countries such as those of Eastern Europe and Scandinavia, and also in Switzerland, which for centuries had been subject to foreign artistic domination – as well as in overseas territories which had been colonized – the spread of mass communications and the increasing facility of contact have tended in fact to undermine that autonomy, at least in the sphere of organ music, and to encourage a style which has grown increasingly international in outlook. The twentieth century, with the advent of the serial revolution and avant-garde forms of expression, has witnessed the triumph of this musical internationalism, which very few composers have sought to resist. Only in organ building has there been an increasingly militant awareness of national styles, although the necessary territorial and linguistic roots are lacking. It remains for us to discuss these areas, and the host of composers who are still with us or who have recently died.

Scandinavia

Long subject to northern German influences, the organ music of Denmark did not achieve any real degree of independence until the nineteenth century, when two composers may be said to have contributed to the formation of a recognizably Danish school: Johann Peter Emilius Hartmann (1805-1900) and Niels Wilhelm Gade (1817-90). Gade was the less ambitious of the two, being notable above all for his chorale preludes, whereas Hartmann, who was organist at the Garnisons-Kirke in Copenhagen, produced a number of fantasias, marches, character pieces and a Sonata in G minor (Opus 58). It was, however, Carl Nielsen (1865-1931) who was destined to make the most memorable contribution to Danish organ music with his *Commotio* (Opus 58), written in the year of his death. We may also list here Jens L. Emborg, Paul S. Rung-Keller, Niels Otto Raastad, Knud Jeppesen, Rued Langgaard, Otto Sandberg Nielsen, Bernhard Christensen and Finn Viderø, together with the serial compositions of Leif Kayser (b. 1919), Niels Viggo Bentzon (b. 1919) and Knud Høgenhaven (b. 1928). Also worthy of mention are the more contrapuntal and rhythmically freer works of Leif Thybo (b. 1922) and Svend-Ove Møller (1903-49), and, finally, the more complex compositions of Ib Nørholm (b. 1931) and Per Nørgaard (b. 1932).

Few Finnish, Swedish or Norwegian composers have written for the organ. In Finland, apart from two works (Opus 111) by Jean Sibelius (1865-1957), we may mention pieces by Oskar Merikanto (1868-1924), the doyen of Finnish organists, who was influenced by Max Reger; Sulo Salonen (1899–1976); Taneli Kuusisto (b. 1905); Einar Englund (b. 1916), whose *Passacaglia* is constructed along serial lines; Joonas Kokkonen (b. 1921); Jarmo Parviainen (b. 1928); Einojuhani Rautavaara (b. 1928), notable for his Concerto for organ, brass and wind band; Ilkka Kuusisto (b. 1933); Paavo Heininen (b. 1938) and Erkki Salmenhaara (b. 1941). Among Swedish composers whose works remain to be discovered are Johann G.E. Sjögren (1853–1918), Otto Emanuel Olsson (1879–1964), Harald Fryklöf (1882–1919), David Wilkander (1884–1955), Oskar Lindberg (1887–1955), Gottfried Berg (b. 1889), Hilding Rosenberg (b. 1892), Albert Runbäck (b. 1894), Daniel Olson (b. 1898), Gunnar Olof Thyrestam (b. 1900) and Valdemar Söderholm (b. 1909). As for the later generation of Swedish composers, we may note the new direction which has been given to organ music in Sweden by such composers as Bengt Hambraeus (b. 1928), Stig Gustav Schönberg (b. 1933) and Karl-Erik Welin (b. 1934). From Norway come the relatively conventional works of Knut Nystedt (b. 1915) and Conrad Baden (b. 1908).

Czechoslovakia and Hungary

Although arguably the greatest of Czech composers, Leoš Janáček (1854–1928) wrote only a handful of works for the organ, the chief of which is the Postlude to his Glagolithic Mass, the end of the nineteenth century in Bohemia is not without interest. Among Czech composers who were active at that time are Miloslav Krejči, Otto Albert Tichý, Josef Blatný, Bedřich Wiedermann (1883–1951) and František Michálek (1895–1951). The twentieth century produced a number of more elaborate pieces, including the Preludes of Karel Reiner (b. 1910), the free compositions of Klement Slavický (b. 1910), works by Milos Sokola (b. 1913) and Otmar Mácha (b. 1922), and especially the Preludes of Miloslav Kabeláč (b. 1908) and works by Petr Eben (b. 1929), whose *Laudes* are notable for their immense rhythmic complexity.

Hungary ensures a place for itself in the history of organ music with a number of works for chorus and organ by Zoltán Kodály (1882–1967), Josip Slavenski (1896–1955), Hidas Frigyes (b. 1928) and, above all, Erzsébet Szönyi (b. 1924), whose works include a Concerto for organ.

Switzerland

Poised between the French and German schools, and between the Romantic alternatives, traditional classical forms and a certain French impressionism, the leading Swiss composers may be categorized according to their regional background. Representatives of the French-speaking cantons include Otto Barblan (1860–1943) of Grisons (Graubünden), who worked in Geneva, a composer profoundly influenced by Reger, Henri Gagnebin (1886–1977), Frank Martin (1890–1974), whose *Passacaille* remains one of the key works in the organ repertory, and Bernard Reichel (b. 1901). The German-speaking cantons are represented by Rudolf Moser (1892–1960), Walther Geiser (1897–1970), Albert Moeschinger (b. 1897), Paul Müller-Zürich (b. 1898), Willy Burkhard (1900–55), a pupil of Karg-Elert, Adolf Brunner (b. 1901) and Armin Schibler (b. 1920), many of whom have written chorale settings.

The United States

The history of American organ music is closely bound up with the great periods in the country's colonization, and hence with the numerous religions which have found refuge there. In this context we may mention William Selby (1738–98), a composer of English extraction, who wrote voluntaries and a Concerto in the style of his compatriots, and James Hewitt (1770–1827), the author of a *Favorite Military Sonata*, *dedicated to General Washington*. Karl Theodor Pachelbel (1690–1750), the son of

Johann, was almost certainly the first German composer to settle in the United States (*c.* 1732). He was followed by a number of musicians who addressed themselves more directly to the larger type of organ which was now being built in America: Lowell Mason (1792–1872), John H. Willcox (1827–75), Dudley Buck (1839–1909), the first great organ virtuoso in America and the author, notably, of the *Concert Variations on the Star-Spangled Banner* (Opus 23), John Knowles Paine (1839–1906), who wrote *Variations on Austria*, Thomas Greene Bethune (1849–1908), a former slave known as "Blind Tom," George W. Chadwick (1854–1931), Horatio Parker (1863–1919) and James H. Rogers (1857–1940).

Following the Romantic experiments of the end of the nineteenth century, a constant exchange of musical ideas between Europe and the United States encouraged remarkable advances in American organ music, which openly espoused a variety of musical styles. Among examples of large-scale orchestral program works we may mention compositions by Eric DeLamarter (1880–1953), Harvey B. Gaul (1881–1945), Seth Bingham (1882–1972), Joseph Waddell Clokey (1890–1960), Leo Sowerby (1895–1968), Jaromir Weinberger (1896–1967), Robert Crandell (b. 1910) and Richard Purvis (b. 1917). Rather more traditional, and even conventional in their Romantic outlook, are Clarence Dickinson (1873–1969), H. Leroy Baumgartner (1891–1969), Carl McKinley (1895–1966), George Frederik McKay (1899–1970), G. Winston Cassler (b. 1906) and Myron Roberts (b. 1912). Other composers who have adopted a style related to that of Vierne or Widor include Bruce Simonds (b. 1895), Philip James (1890–1975) and Seth Bingham (1882–1972). Another group of composers, influenced by the *Orgelbewegung*, has returned to the traditional forms of the chorale, fugue and passacaglia: they include Douglas Moore (1893–1969), Virgil Thomson (b. 1896), Jan Bender (b. 1909), Robert Noehren (b. 1910), Wayne Barlow (b. 1912), Gardner Read (b. 1913), Cecil Effinger (b. 1914), Ludwig Lenel (b. 1914), Ellis B. Kohns (b. 1916), Homer Keller (b. 1917) and Paul Manz (b. 1919). More conventional are those composers whose style is modeled on that of English musicians of the period: Winfred Douglas (1867–1944), T. Tertius Noble (1867–1953), Everett Titcomb (1884–1968), T. Frederick H. Candlyn (1892–1964), Harold Friedell (1905–58), M. Searle Wright (b. 1918) and David N. Johnson (b. 1922).

The twentieth century, with its constant series of formal and tonal experiments, has witnessed a number of important organ compositions by American composers such as Charles Ives (1874–1954), memorable for his *Variations on "America"* of 1891, Richard F. Donovan (b. 1891) and Leo Sowerby (1895–1968), one of the most important of this century's composers and the author of hymn-tunes, preludes, toccatas, variations, and a Suite, Fantasia and Symphony in G major (1903) which are concerned to experiment with all the various possibilities of contemporary writing; further, Virgil Thomson (b. 1896), Samuel Barber (1910–81), Gardner Read (b. 1913), Jack C. Goode (b. 1921) and Gerald Near (b. 1942). While jazz rhythms have proved attractive to composers such as Robert Russell Bennett (b. 1894) and Robert Elmore (b. 1913), atonality has been espoused by other musicians such as Walter Piston (b. 1894), most notably in his *Chromatic Study on the Name of BACH*, Roger Sessions (b. 1896) and Vincent Persichetti (b. 1915).

Canada

The first major writer of religious music in Canada was the Anglo-Canadian composer Healey Willan (1880–1968), whose works include a number of hymn-tunes, preludes and fugues, passacaglias and fugues, all clearly related in style to those of English composers of the period. Among later composers are Lynwood Farnam (1885–1930), Kenneth Meek, Guy Ducharme, Eugene Hill and William France. A greater boldness in their treatment of a harmonic language which at times borders on atonality and in their rhythmic textures and handling of counterpoint characterizes the works of a number of Canadian composers born after 1900, including Keith Bissell, Maurice Boyvin, François Morel, Gerald Bales, Vernon Murgatroyd and Frederik Karam.

THE AVANT-GARDE

Recent years have witnessed an attempt on the part of organ composers to break away from historical and, later, national traditions – an attempt which has succeeded thanks to the boldness of musicians who have learned not to regard the organ as a keyboard instrument but to conceive of its sonorities as a mobile mass of malleable sounds. This change in attitude has been made possible, among other things, by contributions from composers outside the world of organ music and, indeed, from outside the confines of the church – men who have learnt fully to value the instrument's immense potential and who no longer consider it as an exclusively liturgical instrument, but quite simply as a means of creating the most extraordinary sonorities. For this change to take place it was necessary for composers such as Reger, Schoenberg and Messiaen to have shown the way ahead, even if their initial advances were not immediately understood. It was these factors which led to the emergence around 1960 of the avant-garde organ, an instrument whose tonal, technical and structural possibilities composers were not slow to exploit once, like György Ligeti (b. 1923), they had learned to regard the organ as a "giant prosthesis."

This reappraisal of the organ's function was conducted on three broad fronts: the first involved the new concepts of contemporary music, the second the optimal exploitation of the possibilities inherent in the keyboard and pipework, and the third a harnessing of the organ's mechanical elements. Hence the creation of "open" forms employing aleatory techniques which consciously destroyed the traditional framework of the score and which used the maximum resources at the performer's disposal, especially clusters and organ points; hence, too, the most astonishing sounds which were produced, including fifths without fundamentals, odd-numbered harmonics, the opposition of natural and tempered chords, the tonal collision of semitones, microtones, and a reduction in the wind supply to the pipes; and hence, finally, the discovery of new mechanical devices such as a reduction in the weight needed to depress the keys, variators to control the wind pressure in the chests, and greater attack produced by the draw-stop knobs. Nor have composers hesitated to supplement the organ's sonorous repertory with sounds and noises drawn from a variety of disparate sources, including wind and percussion instruments and prerecorded tapes. Parallel to musical experiments such as these are the attempts on the part of organ builders to adapt their instruments to the demands of the age. One thinks, for example, of the modifications to the Sinzig organ undertaken by the firm of Walcker in 1972, or the attempts by Jean Guillou to produce an "organ with variable structures."

The newer works written for this type of instrument continue to grow in number, and although still in their early stages, are already notable for their range and quality. The two leading experimental composers of this early period were Ligeti in his *Volumina* of 1961-2, *Etude No. 1 "Harmonies"* (1967) and *Etude No. 2 "Coulées"* (1969), and Mauricio Kagel (b. 1931) in his *Improvisation ajoutée* (1962) and *Phantasie*. Since then the way has been thrown open for other composers to follow. It is impossible to do more than cite the names of some of the composers whose works appear to us worthy of interest – a subjective list, since it is still too soon to stand back and assess their historical value: William Albright (*Organbook I* and *II*), Juan Allende-Blin (*Transformations; Echelons: Sonorités, Arrêtages, Sons brisés; Mein blaues Klavier*), Sven-Eric Bäck, Claude Baillif (*Quatre Sonates*), Peter Bares (*Kaleidoskop 1977 für zwei Spieler*), Günther Bialas, William Bolcom (*Black Host; Mysteries*), André Boucourechliev (*Anarchipel V*), J. Hartmut Brugmann (*Psalmus 84*), John Cage and his numerous Variations, Jacques Charpentier (*Livre d'Orgue; Hommage à Claude Daquin*), Xavier Darasse (*Organum I* and *II*), Guiseppe G. Englert (*Palestra 64; Vagans Animula*), Hans-Olaf Ericsson (*Orgelsimfoni*), Lucas Foss (*Etudes for Organ*), Henryk Mikolaj Gorecki (*Cantate pour orgue*), Jean Guillou, Cristobal Halffter (*Pinturas Negras*), Bengt Hambraeus (*Shogaku, Interferences*), Klaus Huber, Luis de Pablo (*Modulos V*), Enrique Raxach (*The Looking Glass*), Dietrich Schnebel (*Choralvorspiele I* and *II*), Marco Tomas (*Astrolabio*), Karl-Erik Welin, Yannis Xenakis (*Gmeeoorh*), Isang Yun (*Tuyaux sonores*) and Gerd Zacher (*Diferencias; Text; Das Gebet Jonas im Bauche des Fisches*).

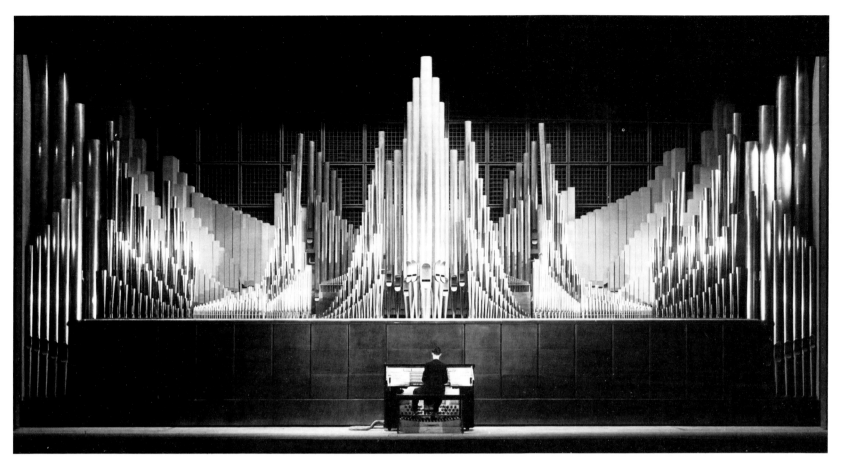

255 Auditorium Maurice Ravel, Lyons, France
This instrument was built by Aristide Cavaillé-Coll in 1878 for the concert
hall at the Palais du Trocadéro in Paris. It had sixty-six stops, four manuals
and a pedal department. In 1937–9 the instrument was rebuilt in an open
structure and enlarged by Victor and Fernand Gonzalez for the new concert
hall at the Palais de Chaillot, which was built on the site of the old Palais du
Trocadéro in 1937. In 1976–7 it was enlarged and transported to Lyons by
Georges Danion. It now has ninety-four stops, four manuals (*GO, Pos, Réc
expressif* and *Solo*) and *Péd*.

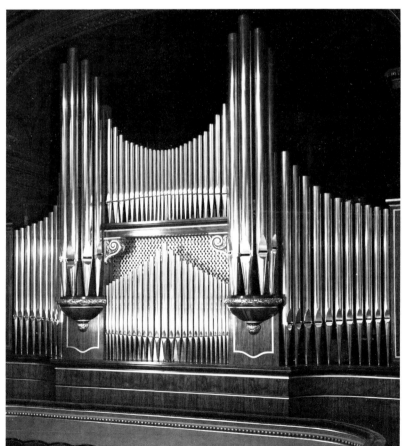

256 Victoria Hall, Geneva, Switzerland, Manufacture des Grands Orgues
de Genève, 1949
This instrument originally had eighty-two stops distributed among *GO, Pos,
Réc expressif, Solo expressif* and *Péd*. Two more stops were added in 1963,
including reeds *en chamade,* and an additional two in 1982, bringing the total
to eighty-six. The instrument was destroyed by fire on September 16, 1984.

257 Sct. Jakobikirke, Varde, Denmark, Marcussen & Søn, 1952
Hw, Rp, Bw and *Ped*, with thirty-four stops.

258 Evangelisch-Lutherische Marktkirche St. Georgi und Jacobi, Hanover, Federal Republic of Germany, Emil Hammer and Rudolf von Beckerath, 1952–4; case by Dieter Oesterlen
Hw, Rp, Bw, Ow and *Ped*, with fifty-seven stops.

259 Collegiate Church, Saint-Donat-sur-l'Herbasse, France, C. Schwenkedel, 1954
GO, Rp, Bp and *Péd*, with thirty-five stops.

260 Barfüsserkirche, Augsburg, Federal Republic of Germany, Rieger Orgelbau, 1958; case by Josef von Glatter-Götz
Hw, Bw, Ow and *Ped*, with thirty-five stops.

261 Grossmünster, Zurich, Switzerland, O. Metzler & Söhne, 1960
Chorpositiv, Hw, Réc, Schwellpositiv and *Ped*, with sixty-seven stops.

262 Protestant Chapel of the United States Air Force Academy Cadets, Colorado Springs (CO), Matthias P. Möller Inc., 1963 (Opus 9480); case designed by Walter Holtkamp
Great, Positive, Swell and *Pedal*, with sixty-seven stops.

263 Notre-Dame, Royan, France, Robert Boisseau and Jean-Loup Boisseau, 1964–80.
GO, Pos, Réc and *Péd*, with forty-seven stops.

264   Cathedral of St. Pierre, Geneva, Switzerland, A. Metzler & Fils, 1965; case by Poul-Gerhard Andersen
Pos, GO, Réc expressif, Echo and *Péd*, with sixty-seven stops.

265   Basilica Sta. Maria dei Servi, Bologna, Italy, Pontificia Fabbrica d'Organi Giovanni Tamburini, 1967 (Opus 544)
Positivo, Grand'Organo, Eco and *Pedale*, with fifty-eight stops, Nightingale and Campanelli.

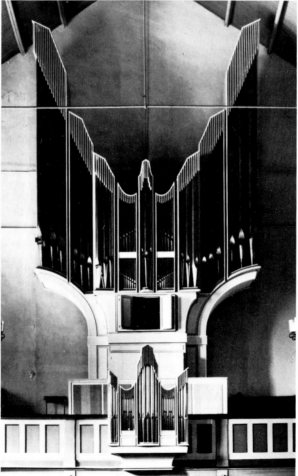

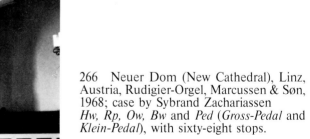
266   Neuer Dom (New Cathedral), Linz, Austria, Rudigier-Orgel, Marcussen & Søn, 1968; case by Sybrand Zachariassen
Hw, Rp, Ow, Bw and *Ped* (*Gross-Pedal* and *Klein-Pedal*), with sixty-eight stops.

267   Erlöserkirche, Witten-Annen, Federal Republic of Germany, Alfred Führer, 1968; case by Heinz Wolff
Hw, Rp, Bw and *Ped*, with thirty-one stops.

268 Sta. Maria Assunta, Merano, Italy, Bartolomeo Formentelli, 1968
Eco, Grand'Organo, Positivo and *Pedale*, with forty-four stops.

269 Concertgebouw "de Doelen," Rotterdam, Netherlands, D. A. Flentrop, 1968
Rechterwerk, Linkerwerk, Bovenwerk, Positief, Groot Pedaal/Klein Pedaal, with seventy stops.

270 Dom (Cathedral) of St. Kilian, Würzburg, Federal Republic of Germany, Johannes Klais, 1969
Rp, Hw, Pos, Schwellwerk and *Ped*, with eighty-five stops.

271 Agnes Flanagan Chapel, Lewis and Clark College, Portland (ME), Casavant Brothers, 1971
Sixty-eight stops, three manuals and pedal, with the following departments: *Great, Swell, Positive, Choral, Choral Pedal, Pedal, Continuo I* and *Continuo II*. The *Great, Positive* and one of the two *Pedal* departments are located in the suspended section.

272 Nostra Señora de la Encarnación, Marbella, Spain, Gabriel Blancafort, 1971–8
Cadireta, Organo Mayor, Espresivo, Corona and *Pedal*, with fifty-five stops and eight half-stops.

273 Islev Kirke, Copenhagen, Denmark, Th. Frobenius & Sønner, Orgel-byggeri A/S, 1971; case built in collaboration with the architects M.A.A. Inger and Johannes Exner
Hw I, Hw II, Rp and *Ped*, with twenty-one stops.

274 St. Peterskirche, Sinzig, Federal Republic of Germany, E.F. Walcker & Co, 1972; case built by Gebrüder Breitenfeld in 1879
Rp, Hw and *Bw* (61 notes, C–c^{1111}) and *Ped* (30 keys, C–f^1), with forty-eight stops. This instrument was built for performing a traditional repertory as well as more avant-garde works. Certain composers, including the present incumbent Peter Bares, wrote pieces especially for the Sinzig organ. The instrument exploits a number of new expressive possibilities, including hitherto unexplored odd-numbered partials in the highest ranks, various percussion stops with variable rhythms, an adjustable Tremulant, a *Mixturensetzer* which allows up to twelve notes to be grouped together under a single key, producing an agglomerate which can be transposed to the other notes, a *Register-manual* or control panel allowing stops to be changed during performance, and a *Tastenfessel* to hold down keys once they have been depressed. (See Appendix for the specification of this instrument.)

275 Parish church (zum guten Hirten), Nuremberg, Federal Republic of Germany, Orgelbau Sandtner, 1975
Hw (upper part of the case), *Rp* (lower part) and *Ped* (upper part), with sixteen stops; bellows beneath *Hw/Ped*; console on the gallery.

276 Vor Frue Kirke, Nyborg, Denmark, Poul-Gerhard Andersen, 1973
Rp, Hw, Crescendowerk and *Ped*, with thirty-six stops, including three dating from Hans Brebus's instrument of 1596.

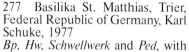

277 Basilika St. Matthias, Trier, Federal Republic of Germany, Karl Schuke, 1977
Bp, Hw, Schwellwerk and *Ped*, with thirty-nine stops.

278 Ned. Hervormde Kerk (Dutch Reformed Church), Joure, Netherlands, Jürgen Ahrend, 1978. *Hw, Rp, Bw* and *Ped*, with twenty-seven stops and two Zimbelsterne.

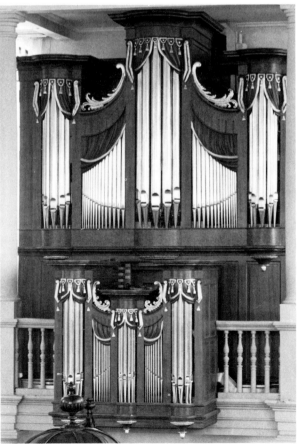

279 Cathedral, Ratzeburg near Lübeck, Federal Republic of Germany, Rieger Orgelbau, 1978
Rp, Hw, Schwellwerk, Bw and *Ped* (*Gross-Pedal* and *Klein-Pedal*), with sixty stops, Glockenspiel and Zimbelstern.

280 Temple de la Fusterie, Geneva, Switzerland, Pascal Quoirin, 1979
Pos, GO, Réc and *Péd*, with thirty-five stops. This instrument is designed in a classical French style and housed in the case of 1835.

281 Notre-Dame-des-Neiges, L'Alpe-d'Huez, France, Detlef Kleuker, 1978
GO, Réc and *Péd*, with twenty-three stops. The case was designed by the architect of the church, Jean Marol, in the form of a hand ("the hand of God"). The *Ped* 16' Flute pipes make up the fingers, the *GO* display pipes the thumb of the hand. The instrument was planned by Jean Guillou.

Glossary

Technical terms which are explained in full on their first appearance in the text are not included here. An asterisk indicates a reference elsewhere in the glossary to the word so marked.

For a complete list of stop names the reader is directed to the works of W L Sumner and Peter Williams listed in the bibliography.

Allemande is a "German" dance first appearing in written form in the mid-sixteenth century; it was in moderate duple time and often followed by a livelier dance in triple time.

Alternatim (from Latin *alternatus*, "alternately") is a term used to describe the practise whereby two or more performers, or groups of performers, play or sing in turn, as in antiphonal or responsorial psalmody. From the fifteenth century onwards the organ came to replace the vocal polyphony of the choir, a development which culminated in the organ works of François Couperin and Nicolas de Grigny in the seventeenth and eighteenth centuries.

Basse de Tierce is a classical French organ registration, usually based on the *Grand Orgue* 16′ and 8′ ranks and generally used for the bass line in duos and trios.

Bergamasca was originally a peasant dance or song from the Bergamo region of northern Italy; by the late sixteenth century the dance had acquired a fixed harmonic scheme for the accompanying instrument (usually a guitar).

Bicinium is an unaccompanied composition for two voices or instruments. In the seventeenth century Samuel Scheidt used the term to describe two-part organ *versets.

Blo[c]kwerk is the undivided chest of the medieval organ, an arrangement which precluded the possibility of separating off individual ranks. The term may be Dutch in origin.

Bombarde: in France the basic manual or pedal 16′ *reed, it was of considerable importance to the French classical organ, having a powerful tone and sometimes its own keyboard.

Borrowing or *duplexing* was made possible by the introduction of mechanical aids in the form of pneumatic or electrical transmission action, whereby each separate pipe could be individually brought into play; in this way a rank of pipes could be made playable in several pitches, one pipe serving, for example, as C^1, C and c in 2′, 4′ and 8′ pitches respectively. Duplexing enables manual 16′ stops to be played separately as pedal stops.

Bourdon is a word which first appears in England in the fifteenth century as a synonym for "bass"; applied to the organ it referred to the deepest bass pipes not played by manual keys but "latched" on so as to produce a sustained note (*cf.* the name for the low strings of a hurdy-gurdy, or the drones of the bagpipes). Since about 1820 the term Bourdon has been used to describe the basic pedal 16′ *rank in English organs. The most important use of the term is for the stopped pipes an octave below the main 8′ *rank in French organs, a usage first mentioned at Vannes in 1624: "*Fluste couverte, apelée*

bourdon," but known to have existed since the end of the sixteenth century. Of narrow *scale, the French classical Bourdon was constructed of wood for the lower octaves and metal for the upper ones.

Branle was a French rustic dance popular in the sixteenth century and later taken up by the court.

Brustwerk, literally the "breast department" of a German organ, is so called because its pipe chest is encased below the *Hauptwerk* or Great Organ. The *Brustwerk*, which originally resembled a *Regal in character, continued to be used as a chamber organ until the eighteenth century when it fell into desuetude.

Cantus firmus or "fixed melody" denotes a preexisting melody, usually of plainchant or secular origin, which is taken as the basis of a new polyphonic composition. The *cantus firmus* was generally "held" in long notes in the lower voice, hence the term "tenor" from the Latin verb *tenere*, "to hold." On the organ it was frequently given to the pedals at 8′ or 4′ pitch.

Canzone (plural *canzoni*) was initially an instrumental arrangement of a *chanson* by one of the French composers active between 1520 and 1550; the term was later applied indiscriminately to any contrapuntal piece conceived in instrumental terms and written for a string ensemble or for a keyboard instrument. The genre survived in Germany until the late seventeenth century, gradually giving way, as it had in Italy, to the sonata.

Capriccio (plural *capricci*), from the Italian word meaning "whim" or "fancy," is a term applied at random to any vocal or instrumental work of a capricious nature; though early seventeenth-century usage suggests keyboard pieces using fugal imitation, composers generally used the term interchangeably with *canzone* and other dance forms.

Carillon denotes various stops designed to imitate the sound of a bell. They were frequently real bells of 4′ or 2′ pitch, operated by trackers attached to small hammers which struck the bells. This effect was called the *Campanello* in nineteenth-century Italian organs. The term *Carillon* is also used to describe a late eighteenth-century German registration produced by certain flue stops, in addition to a three-rank treble *Tierce *mixture found on Dutch organs built during the period 1750–1850.

Chaconne (Italian *ciaconne*) was a dance in triple time taken up in the form of variations in Spain and Italy in the early seventeenth century, whence it spread progressively to France, Germany and England. The composers of such variations were confronted with a choice in their handling of the melody: either the same melody was repeated unchanged throughout the piece in the manner of a ground bass; or it was allowed to migrate to other parts; or else a series of different melodies might be used. The French *chaconne* was often written in rondo form, i.e. following the scheme ABACA.

Chair Organ is the English term for the small organ separate from the main organ and bracketed over the gallery edge behind the organist's bench or chair. It is the equivalent of the German *Rückpositiv* and the French *positif de dos*, and is also known, somewhat confusingly, as the Choir Organ. See also *Positif.*

Chorale is an anglicization of the German *Choral*, originally a plainchant melody sung chorally but, by the late sixteenth century, a term whose meaning had been extended to include vernacular hymns. Such chorale melodies were the basis of the chorale fantasias, fugues, *partitas, preludes and variations composed in Germany and elsewhere from the late seventeenth century onwards.

Chorus denotes the grouping together of stops, often in families.

Ciphering is the sounding of a note without pressure on the corresponding key.

Combination pedals and *pistons* allow stops to be controlled in groups. Initially operated by mechanical means, combination pedals were activated by the weight which a player could apply with one foot when seated at the console. With the advent of pneumatic power came the introduction of thumb pistons, small press-buttons placed between the keyboards, requiring a much lighter touch to operate them. Most modern actions are electromagnetic or electropneumatic.

Cori spezzati, literally "broken choirs," describes the custom popularized by Willaert and the two Gabrielis of dividing the church choir into two, or more, sections in order to produce the impression of a musical dialog, using echo effects and contrasting dynamics.

Cornet is a compound stop found especially, though by no means exclusively, in French classical organs of the period 1650 to 1850, and comprising five, four or three ranks of pipes. Its chief function is as a loud and colorful solo stop, reminiscent in timbre of a *reed *chorus. In order to make the sound more prominent, the stop is often planted on a soundboard of its own, and raised a few feet above the surrounding pipes: this arrangement is known as a "mounted Cornet." Since the tone color tends to break up into its constituent pitches below middle c, Cornets are short-compass stops seldom going below c^1.

Couplers are a device allowing the pedal or manual keys to pull down the corresponding keys of another manual, thus enabling the stops of one department to be played from the keyboard of another. Octave couplers, which sound the note an octave above, and sub-octave couplers, which sound the note an octave below the note struck, are operated by means of a series of levers picking up the key action at the appropriate point. Couplers are also a means of reuniting the instrument's different tonal structures which, following the development away from a single *Blockwerk*, had been fragmented into separate, contrasting divisions.

The *Crescendo Pedal* (sometimes called the Stop or Register Crescendo) is more widely used in North America and Germany than in the United Kingdom. When toe pressure is applied to the pedal, stops are brought on in a predetermined sequence, usually starting with the P.P. on each manual, and gradually building up to a comprehensive full organ. The German term is *Rollschweller.*

Cutup is a technical term used by organ builders to describe the height of the mouth of a *flue pipe expressed as a proportion of its width; thus a cutup of 1 in 4 means that the rectangle of the mouth is four times as wide as it is high. The smaller the cutup, the livelier the sound. Conversely, a large cutup will produce a somewhat dull sound.

Cymbale (German *Zimbel*) derives its name from the medieval *cymbala* (Greek *kymbala*), small tuned bells struck with a hammer. The classical French Cymbale was a high *Mixture of octaves and fifths, the ranks breaking twice per octave. Outside France, the precise contents of the Cymbale/Zimbel varied from period to period and from region to region. See also *Plein Jeu.*

Diapason, generally speaking, is an octave stop sounding an octave above the case pipes. In England in the early sixteenth century the term may have denoted a *Bourdon or *Trompe, but by 1613 it had assumed its present meaning of a Principal-*scaled open or stopped 8′ pipe. The French word *diapason* means "pitch," *diapason normal* having been fixed by the French Academy in 1858 at 435 vibrations per second for the note a^1.

Diminution is a melodic device, often found in fugal works, in which the time values of the notes are proportionally reduced, generally by half.

Divided stops are those in which the stop is made to draw in halves at middle c, thus enabling a solo to be played prominently with one hand, while the other hand performs a soft accompaniment.

Drum stop (German *Pauke* or *Trommel*, Spanish *Tambor*, Italian *Timballo*) is a toy stop consisting either of a real drum hit with drumsticks held by *putti* or angels, and activated by pedals or levers; or a stop which admitted wind to a palletless chest on which were planted two to four large-*scaled wooden pipes out of tune with each other so as to produce an imitative beat.

Duplexing see *Borrowing*

Durezza (Italian "dissonance") was a seventeenth-century style of keyboard writing involving the use of chromaticism and dissonances.

Echo: (i) a small-*scaled three- or four-rank *Cornet in many eighteenth-century German organs; (ii) a prefix denoting a soft color-stop in northern European organs of the eighteenth and nineteenth centuries; and (iii) the third or fourth manual of a French classical organ, originating as a subsidiary *Cornet chest below the *Grand Orgue. An Echo Box was a precursor of the Swell Organ in which the department in question was totally enclosed and fitted with shutters, thereby enabling it to achieve a wide variety of dynamic effects.

en chamade is a term coined by Aristide Cavaillé-Coll (1811–98) to describe *horizontal reeds. It is thought to derive from the Latin verb *clamare* and to refer to the trumpet calls which were sounded when parleys were summoned.

en ravalement denotes an extension of the pedal compass below C, a feature most notably of French classical organs.

Figural is a general term used to describe a florid polyphonic style of writing.

Flautados are the *Principal or *Diapason pipes in Iberian organs, 32′, 16′ or 8′ (52, 26 and 13 *palmos* respectively).

Flue is the windway in an organ pipe from the foothole to the mouth. A flue stop (American "labial voice") is distinct from a *reed stop in which the sound is produced by means of a beating reed.

Flute (Italian *Flauto*, German *Flöte*) was originally the generic term for organ pipes other than *Mixtures when the *Blockwerk was separated off into stops. The term was subsequently applied to stopped pipes of 8′ or 4′, or to color stops with prefixes indicative of their shape (*Spitzflöte*), sound (*Sifflöte*) or function (*Flûte majeure*). A *flûte à pavillon* was a large-*scaled metal 8′ *flue stop, its cylindrical resonator capped by an inverted conical bell.

Foundation stops are stops of 8′ pitch, so called because it takes a pipe of the speaking length of 8′ to produce the lowest note of the manuals at normal pitch.

Fourniture: according to the contract relating to Ste Geneviève-des-Ardents, Paris, in 1549, this basic French *Mixture was intended "pour fournir le plein jeu," i.e. to furnish the *pleno*. It originally included those ranks which had been separated off from the *Montres, acquiring a standard composition in Parisian organs of the late seventeenth century. See also *Plein Jeu.*

Frottola was a form of secular vocal music popular in Italy during the late fifteenth and early sixteenth centuries; the accompaniment was provided either by an ensemble of three instruments or by a solo lute.

Galliard (French *gaillarde*, Italian *gagliarda*) is a lively dance of Italian origin scored for keyboard or instrumental consort. It was popular from the late 1520s until the second half of the seventeenth century.

Glockenspiel is a toy stop consisting of a row of metal bars struck by hammers operated either by pedals or by the keys of a secondary manual.

Grand Jeu is the *reed *chorus of the classical French organ, reinforced by *Cornets, *Tierces and *Prestants 4′.

Grand Orgue is the main keyboard of a French organ, corresponding to the Great Organ in England and North America, and to the *Hauptwerk* in Germany.

Hauptwerk see *Grand Orgue*

Hexachord: from the Middle Ages onwards this term has been used to refer to any six notes with the intervallic pattern tone-tone-semitone-tone-tone, e.g. C-D-E-F-G-A.

Hintersatz denotes the ranks of pipes positioned behind the case pipes in a late medieval organ. These ranks contained the *Mixture remaining when the *Prestants had been separated off; as a result the terms *Mixtur* and *Hintersatz* became interchangeable.

Hocket (French *hocquet*) is a device of medieval polyphony in which the melody alternates rapidly between two contrapuntal voice parts, one of which rests while the other sings.

Horizontal reeds or *reeds *en chamade* are a feature of Iberian organs from the early seventeenth century onwards. The origins of this arrangement are not clear, though its advantages include penetrability of sound, accessibility (for easier cleaning), reliability, economy (replacing cathedral trumpeters) and their striking appearance.

Lleno is the *pleno* of Iberian organs.

Mixture (German *Mixtur*) is a term used to describe the highest pitched *ranks of the *Diapason- or *Principal-*scaled *choruses grouped together under a single stop control. The main advantage of such an arrangement apart from facility of operation is the control of balance between pitches. The Mixture always has two or more *ranks of pipes, their number being indicated in Roman numerals on the stop knob. *Tierces may be found in addition to the more usual octave and fifth *ranks.

Montres are the case pipes of a French organ, corresponding to the English Open *Diapason, the German *Prestant, and the Italian Principale.

Mutation (German *Aliquotstimmen*) is a word whose meaning varies according to time and place. In the nineteenth century the term described single or multi-rank stops introducing pitches other than unisons, suboctaves and superoctaves. It has now come to mean a single-rank overtone stop of flutelike character intended for use in solo writing rather than in chorus work. In the classical French organ *les mutations* were the ranks remaining when the *plein jeu*, *grand jeu* und solo *reeds had been separated off. In Spanish organs *mutaciones* were registrations, and in German *Mutationen* could be synonymous with the *Stimmen* or stops themselves.

Nachtigall see *Rossignol*

Oberwerk (Dutch *Bovenwerk*) or "upper work" was an extra division of the organ added above the *Blockwerk and containing stops which could be played separately from the undivided *Mixture of the *Blockwerk. This was an important structural development on the part of Netherlands organ builders in the sixteenth century, helping to create the special potential of the North German *Werkprinzip organ of the following century.

Organum is a term applied to polyphonic vocal music of the ninth to thirteenth centuries involving the addition of a second voice to a line of plainchant. It is not known whether the term contains an intentional allusion to the name of the instrument (the parallel octaves and fifths of the vocal line perhaps suggesting the sound of the organ), or whether it derives from a Latin verb *organare*, meaning "to organize" the new parts around the existing melody.

Orgelbewegung or "Organ Movement" was an organ reform movement in Germany during the early decades of the twentieth century. It advocated a return to pre-nineteenth-century principles of organ building, its chief requirements being a logical tonal structure based on *Diapason and *Flute manual *choruses of contrasting pitch, and the encasement of each department in a separate cabinet (see *Werkprinzip*). A return to mechanical tracker action was also felt to be desirable, in order to recreate the type of instrument for which the classical organ repertory had been written.

Ostinato is a form of ground bass repeated many times unchanged, to the accompaniment of melodic variations. See also *Chaconne* and *Passacaglia*.

Partita: in Italy in the late sixteenth and seventeenth centuries one of a set of variations; in Germany in the late seventeenth century an alternative title for a suite, hence any sort of instrumental piece in several movements.

Passacaglia (from Spanish *pasar*, "to walk," and *calle*, "street") was originally a Spanish serenade, but in the seventeenth century the term was transferred to instrumental *ritornellos* performed between the verses of a song. Such *ritornellos* were constructed over typical harmonic progressions which provided melodic formulas for instrumental variations. In Germany the term was normally restricted to keyboard compositions.

Passamezzo was an Italian dance of the sixteenth and seventeenth centuries.

Pauke see *Drum stop*

Pavan was a processional dance in duple time, probably originating in Padua in the early years of the sixteenth century; it was generally coupled (often thematically) with a quicker dance in triple time, such as a *galliard*.

Pipe flats are flat expanses of case pipes, often arranged in tiers or stories; *pipe towers* are groups of taller pipes (often pedal pipes) projecting from the main structure and framing the flats.

Plein Jeu denotes the combined *Fourniture* and *Cymbale* on a French classical organ. A typical scheme as formulated by Dom Bédos de Celles is as follows:

C	15.19.22.26.29	29.33.36
c		26.29.33
f	8.12.15.19.22	22.26.29
c¹		19.22.26
f¹	1.5.8.12.15	15.19.22
c¹¹		12.15.19
f¹¹		8.12.15

Pleno (or *organo pleno*) is a pseudo-Italian term describing the full *chorus, usually of *flue stops only, known in French as the *plein jeu*, in Italian as the *ripieno* and in Iberian organs as the *lleno*.

Point d'orgue is *either* a harmonic pedal point (i.e. a bass note sustained throughout a passage including chords of which it is not a part), *or* a cadenza in a concerto.

Positive (French *Positif*, German *Positiv*) was a small organ, such as a chamber organ, table organ or portable organ, which could be moved around the body of the church or else used domestically. As a result of the organist's desire to have control over both the main organ in the church gallery and the Positive on the floor of the building, the two divisions were incorporated into the *Blockwerk around the middle of the fifteenth century, either internally or else in the form of a *Chair Organ (or *Rückpositiv* or *Positif de dos*). Though based on the 4' *Principal, the *Chair Organ was a modification of the earlier Positive, inasmuch as an 8' *Flute was provided to give a bass to the *chorus.

Prestant (Dutch *Praestant*) is a term derived from the Latin *praestans* and refers to the case pipes which stand in front of the organ case. In France the term *Prestant* is normally used only of the 4' *Principal which, according to Dom Bédos de Celles, was the first stop to be tuned, the other pipes being tuned from it. In Holland and Germany the word was generally synonymous with *Principal.

Principal (German *Prinzipal*) was originally the *Diapason *chorus as a whole. In German organs the term has subsequently come to mean the open *Diapason or case pipes of 32', 16', 8', 4' or 2', and in the twentieth century may refer specifically to the basic 8' rank. In British and American organs the Principal is an open *Diapason of 4' length and pitch on the manuals, or 8' length and pitch on the pedals. In France the term Principal is generally replaced by other, more specific terms, including *Montre* and *Prestant*.

Pulldowns are pedal keys with no separate pipes. When the key is depressed, it pulls down the corresponding key on the manuals, thus providing a sustained note or *point d'orgue* and leaving the organist's hands free to add *figural textures above it.

Rank is a row or assembly of pipes having a single timbre.

Récit: the *clavier de récit* was originally a short-compass solo manual in French classical organs, generally incorporating a *Cornet and perhaps a Trumpet. In the nineteenth-century organs of Aristide Cavaillé-Coll the *Récit* became an "expressive" manual fitted with a swell box, and given a full range of soft *foundation, undulating and powerful *reed stops.

Reed is the part of a reed pipe which vibrates when subjected to a current of air entering the boot of the pipe; by extension, "reed" may refer to the pipe itself.

Regal is a *reed organ and, as such, the first known instrument to combine vibrating reeds with a keyboard. The Regal was in use from the middle of the fifteenth century until the end of the seventeenth century as a portable continuo instrument. Shortly after the invention of the instrument, the term Regal came to be used of a family of organ stops with small resonators similar to those of the instrument in question; they were incorporated into larger organs, usually in a subsidiary chest.

Ricercar[e] (plural *ricercari*) was a solo instrumental piece, originally improvisatory in style and possibly intended as a technical or virtuoso exercise. During the second half of the sixteenth century the term was often used to denote polyphonic instrumental works written for up to eight instruments, with flowing melodic lines organized by imitative points. By the early seventeenth century composers had begun to use the terms *ricercare* and *canzone* as if they were interchangeable.

Rossignol or *Nachtigall* is a toy stop, popular between 1450 and 1850, reproducing the sound of a nightingale by means of small open pipes suspended in a dish of water.

Rückpositiv see *Positive* and *Chair Organ*

Scale is a technical term used to define the comparative size of organ pipes measured in terms of the pipe's diameter. A narrow-scaled pipe will produce a bright sound rich in harmonics, with a relatively weak fundamental pitch. A wide-scaled pipe, conversely, will emphasize the fundamental pitch but produce comparatively few overtones. *Diapasons, which provide the organ's basic tone quality, are average-scaled.

Slider is *either* a medieval key mechanism which the player had to push in and then pull out again, thus aligning a hole in the slider with the foot of the corresponding pipe; *or* (in modern chests) the perforated strip of wood which controls the entry of air to a complete *rank of pipes.

Stile antico is an Italian term used in the seventeenth century to describe unaccompanied polyphonic church music written in the style of Palestrina, in contrast to the *stile moderno* or modern style, a type of music written for fewer voices and with continuo accompaniment.

Stretto is a fugal device in which subject entries follow each other in close succession.

Tablature is a system of musical notation using figures or letters in tabular form instead of, or in addition to, the conventional staff notation.

Tambor see *Drum stop*

Terza mano (literally "third hand") is the octave *coupler found on late eighteenth- and nineteenth-century organs in Italy.

Tiento (Portuguese *tento*) is the Spanish equivalent of the Italian *ricercare*.

Tierce (German *Terz* or *Tertia*) is the 1 3/5' *flute *mutation *rank of a French classical organ and is notable for its characteristic horn tone. Outside France this third-sounding stop is found as a single *mutation *rank only in the instruments of French-influenced builders such as those built by the Silbermann brothers in Saxony and the Rhineland.

Timballo see *Drum stop*

Tiratutti is a mechanical device found in Italian organs from the beginning of the eighteenth century, enabling the organist to draw all the *pleno *ranks at once.

Toccata is the past participle of the Italian verb *toccare*, meaning "to touch," and describes a piece, usually written for a keyboard instrument, designed to show off the player's touch by means of free and virtuoso passagework. The rhapsodic nature of such writing was further elaborated by Buxtehude and Bach, whose toccatas are long, sectional pieces with alternating passages of free and fugal writing.

Trommel see *Drum stop*

Trompes were the large open bass pipes placed on either side of the *Grand Orgue in some French and Dutch organs of the late fifteenth century. They varied in number from two to ten and were sometimes located as far as fifteen feet away from the main chest.

Untersatz describes the pipes planted on a chest below the main chest of large organs in northern and central Germany during the period 1575 to 1825. Since these were the pipes of the larger pedal stops, the term has come to denote open or stopped metal or wood pedal pipes of 16' or 32', and especially stopped wood 32' *ranks.

Verset is a piece of organ music designed to replace the verse of a hymn, psalm or other liturgical item which would otherwise have been sung by the choir. The genre found its greatest exponents in Italy and France in the seventeenth century, most notably in the figures of Girolamo Frescobaldi and François Couperin.

Vihuela is a plucked string instrument of the Spanish Renaissance, shaped like a guitar but tuned like a lute.

Voluntary was originally a sort of contrapuntal fantasia or *ricercare (*cf.* the Mulliner Book of *c.* 1560), but the term has subsequently come to describe any written or improvised piece performed before or after a church service.

Werkprinzip is a term coined by the adherents of the *Orgelbewegung during the 1920s to describe the system whereby each department or *Werk* has its own separate structure both tonally and architecturally. The basic pitches of each department are generally arranged an octave apart (Pedal 16', Great 8', *Positiv 4' and *Brustwerk 2' on a moderate-sized instrument); and each department has its own case, or a readily distinguishable part of the main case, with the *Principal of its basic pitch on display.

Zimbelstern was a toy stop popular in northern Europe during the period 1490 to 1790. It consisted of a revolving star near the top of the case driven by a wheel to which was attached a set of bells concealed from view.

Abbreviations

Bp Brustpositiv
Bw Brustwerk (Dutch: Bovenwerk, Borstwerk)
Fw Fernwerk
GO Grand Orgue *or* Great Organ
Hw Hauptwerk (Dutch: Hoofdwerk; Danish: Hovedvaerk)
Kp Kronwerk *or* Kronpositiv

Mw Mittelwerk
Ow Oberwerk (Danish: Overvaerk)
Ped Pedal (Dutch: Pedaal)
Péd Pédale
Pos Positif (German: Positiv)
Réc Récit
Rp Rückpositiv (Dutch: Rugpositief; Danish: Rygpositiv)
Rw Rugwerk (Dutch)
Sw Schwellwerk
Uw Unterwerk

Lexicon of Terms Used in Organ Building

action	mécanique	Mechanik
adjustable	réglable	einstellbar
adjustable combination	combinaison ajustable	Setzerkombination
backfall action	mécanique à balanciers	Wippenmechanik
Barker lever	machine Barker	Barkerhebel
beating or striking reed	anche battante	aufschlagende Zunge
bell	pavillon	Stürze
bellows	soufflet, soufflerie	Balg, Gebläse
block	noyau	Kopf
borrowing or, in case of pedals, duplexing	emprunt	Auszug, Transmission
cap	calotte	Spund oder Hut bei gedeckten Pfeifen
chimney	cheminée	Rohr, Röhrchen
Chororgel/Choir Organ	orgue de chœur positif (clavier)	Chororgel Positivmanual
ciphering	cornement	Heuler
concussion bellows, winker	régulateur	Stossbalg, Stossfänger
conductored off	posté	abgeführt, verführt
cone-valve chest (Kegellade)	sommier à pistons	Kegellade
cut to pitch length	coupé au ton	auf Ton geschnitten
detached console	console séparée	freistehender Spieltisch
diagonal/wedge/ hinged bellows	soufflet cunéiforme	Keilbalg
divided stop (bass/treble)	coupé, jeu (Basse/Dessus)	geteiltes Register (Bass/Diskant)
doubling of a rank	doublure	Verdoppelung eines Chores
dummy display pipes	chanoine (façade)	Blindpfeifen
ear, at side of pipe mouth	oreille	Seitenbart
even-numbered partials	harmoniques pairs	geradzahlige Partialtöne
extension	extension	Erweiterung
extension of the pedal compass/*ravalement*	ravalement	Pedalerweiterung unter Kontra-C
flue stops	bouche, jeux à	Labialregister
foot (labial, flue pipe);	pied (d'un tuyau)	Pfeifenfuss, Stiefel
foot (measure)	pied (mesure)	Fuss (Längenmass)
foundation voices	fonds, jeux de	Grundstimmen
free combination	combinaison libre	freie Kombination
free reed	anche libre	durchschlagende Zunge
fundamental	fondamental, son	Grundton
gallery organ	orgue de tribune	Emporenorgel
general cancel	annulateur	Abschalter

Great Organ, (*Grand Orgue* in French organs)	Grand-Orgue	Hauptwerk
harmonic, upper partial	harmonique, son	Aliquot, Teilton, Oberton
in the tenor	en taille (= au ténor)	im Tenor
key	touche	Taste
key action	traction (claviers)	Noten-Traktur
keyboard	clavier	Klaviatur
keyboard compass	étendue	Klaviatur, Ton-Umfang
keydesk, console	console	Spieltisch
languid	biseau	Kern
large/wide-scale	large (taille)	weitmensuriert
light, gentle	doux (dans le vent)	leicht
main organ	grand orgue	Hauptorgel
major	majeur	Dur
(manual) coupler	accouplement	Manualkoppel
master organ builder	facteur d'orgues	Orgelbaumeister
membrane	membrane	Tasche
membrane or pouch-pallet chest	sommier à membranes	Taschenlade
minor	mineur	Moll
Mixture V ranks	Fourniture 5 rangs	Mixtur 5 fach
Mixture/Fourniture	Fourniture	Mixtur
mouth	bouche	Labium
movable console	console mobile	fahrbarer Spieltisch
multi-rank mutation	mutation composée	mehrchörige Aliquot-Stimme
mutation voice	mutation, jeu de	Aliquot-Stimme
narrow/small-scale	étroit (taille)	engmensuriert
nick	entaille	Stimmschlitz
note channel	gravure	Tonkanzelle
odd-numbered partials	harmoniques impairs	ungeradzahlige Partialtöne
open-toe (voicing)	plein-vent	"auf vollem Wind"
organ	orgue	Orgel
organ building	facture d'orgues	Orgelbau
organ case	buffet	Gehäuse, Prospekt
organ gallery	tribune	Orgelempore
out-of-tune beats	battement	Schwebung
overblowing	harmonique	überblasend
pallet box	laye	Ventilkasten
parallel bellows	soufflet à plis parallèles	Parallel-Balg
pedal coupler	tirasse	Pedalkoppel
pedal key	marche	Pedaltaste
pedal keyboard	pédalier	Pedalklaviatur
pedal(s) (organ division)	Pédale	Pedal
pipe-flat	plate-face	Flachfeld im Prospekt
pipe scales	taille	Mensuren
pipe tower	tourelle	Pfeifenturm im Prospekt
pipe, tube	tuyau	Pfeife
(pipe) valve	soupape	(Pfeifen-)Ventil
pipe with direct wind supply	tuyau sur moteur	Pfeife mit direkter Windzufuhr
pipework	tuyauterie	Pfeifenwerk
piston	appel, piston	Einführungstritt, Kolben
positive	positif (instrument)	Positiv
push-pull coupler	accouplement à tiroir	Schiebekoppel
rackboard	faux-sommier	Halterbrett, Rasterbrett
radiating pedalboard	pédalier en éventail	Radial-Pedal
rank	rang (de tuyaux)	Reihe
recessed console	console en fenêtre	Spielschrank, eingebauter Spieltisch

reed	anche	Zunge
reed tongue	languette (anche)	Zungenblatt
reeds *en chamade*, horizontal reeds	chamade, anches en	Horizontalzungen, "Spanische Trompeten"
register, voice	jeu	Register, Stimme
reservoir	réservoir	(Magazin) Balg
roller	rouleau	Rollenbart, Abstraktenwelle
roller board	abrégé	Wellenbrett
rood loft	jubé	Lettner
Rückpositiv	Positif dorsal ou de dos	Rückpositiv
sheet iron	fer blanc	Eisenblech
single-rank mutation	mutation simple	Einzelaliquot
slider	registre	Schleife
stop knob, stop rod	tirant (registre)	Registerzug, Registerstange
stop-action mechanism	tirage (registres)	Registertraktur
stop-channel chest	sommier à cases	Registerkanzellenlade
stop-crescendo pedal or *Rollschweller*	crescendo, pédale de	Rollschweller
stoplist	composition	Disposition
strong, heavy	fort (à vent perdu)	stark
substructure	soubassement	Unterbau
suspended action	mécanique suspendue	aufgehängte Mechanik
swallow's nest	nid d'hirondelle	Schwalbennest
swell box	boîte expressive	Schwellkasten
swell pedal, expression pedal	expression, pédale d'	Schwelltritt
tilting tablet	domino	Registerwippe
tin	étain	Zinn
tin-lead alloy	étoffe	Zinn-Blei-Legierung
toeboard	chape	Pfeifenstück
tone color/timbre	timbre	Klangfarbe
tone-channel chest	sommier à gravures	Tonkanzellenlade
tracker	vergette	Abstrakte
tracker action	traction mécanique	mechanische Traktur
treble	dessus	Diskant
tremulant, tremolo	Tremblant	Tremulant
trompe	trompe	Basspfeifenturm im 15. und 16. Jhd.
tubular-pneumatic action	traction tubulaire	(Röhren)pneumatik
tuning	accord	Stimmung
tuning pitch	diapason	Stimmhöhe
tuning wire	rasette	Stimmkrücke
undulating, beating	ondulant	schwebend
voicing	harmonization	Intonation
wind	vent	Wind
wind-chest	sommier	Windlade
wind conductor	porte-vent	Windkanal
wind pressure	pression du vent	Winddruck
wind supply	alimentation	Windversorgung
windway, flue (flue pipe)	lumière	Kernspalte

Specifications

TOTENTANZORGEL (ORGAN IN THE CHAPEL OF THE DANCE OF DEATH), MARIENKIRCHE, LÜBECK, FEDERAL REPUBLIC OF GERMANY, BEFORE 1475

HAUPTWERK				
Quintadena	16	Hohlflöte	2	
Prinzipal	8	Quintflöte	1 $\frac{1}{3}$	
Spitzflöte	8	Scharf	IV	
Oktave	4	Krummhorn	8	
Nasat	2 $\frac{2}{3}$	Schalmei	4	
Rauschpfeife	II			
Mixtur	VIII–X	PEDAL		
Trompete	8	Prinzipal	16	
		Subbass	16	
RÜCKPOSITIV		Oktave	8	
Prinzipal	8	Gedackt	8	
Rohrflöte	8	Superoktave	4	
Quintatön	8	Quintatön	4	
Oktave	4	Oktave	2	
Rohrflöte	4	Nachthorn	1	
Sifflöte	1 $\frac{1}{3}$	Zimbel	II	
Sesqualtera	II	Mixtur	IV	
Scharf	VI–VIII	Posaune	16	
Dulzian	16	Dulzian	16	
Trichterregal	8	Trompete	8	
		Schalmei	4	
BRUSTPOSITIV		Kornett	2	
Gedackt	8			
Quintatön	4	Tremulant		

MAIN ORGAN, MARIENKIRCHE, LÜBECK, FEDERAL REPUBLIC OF GERMANY, 1516–18

HAUPTWERK		BRUSTPOSITIV	
Prinzipal	16	Prinzipal	8
Quintadena	16	Gedackt	8
Oktave	8	Oktave	4
Spitzflöte	8	Hohlflöte	4
Superoktave	4	Feldpfeife	2
Hohlflöte	4	Gemshorn	2
Nasat	2 $\frac{2}{3}$	Sesqualtera	II
Rauschquinte	II	Sifflöte	1 $\frac{1}{3}$
Mixtur	X–XV	Mixtur	VI–VIII
Scharf	IV	Zimbel	III
Trompete	16	Krummhorn	8
Tormpete	8	Regal	8
Zink	8		

RÜCKPOSITIV		PEDAL	
Bordun	16	Prinzipal	32
Prinzipal	8	Grosse Oktave	16
Quintadena	8	Sub-bass	16
Hohlpfeife	8	Kleine Oktave	8
Oktave	4	Gedackt	8
Blockflöte	4	Superoktave	4
Spielflöte	2	Bauerflöte	2
Sesqualtera	II	Mixtur	VI
Mixtur	V	Posaune	32
Scharf	V	Posaune	16
Zimbel	II	Dulzian	16
Dulzian	16	Trompete	8
Bärpfeife	8	Krummhorn	8
Trichterregal	8	Nachthorn	2
Vox humana	8	Kornett	2

2 Tremulants, 2 drum-stops, Zimbelsterne

DUOMO VECCHIO (OLD CATHEDRAL), BRESCIA, ITALY, 1536

Principale tutto intiero	Principal 8 (complete stop; the keyboard compass begins at F^1, i.e. F 12)
Principale spezzato	Principal 8 (the first twenty notes from F^1 to d are operated by the Pedal, the remainder by the manual)
Ottava	Octave 4
Quintadecima	Octave 2
Decima nona	Quinte 1 $\frac{1}{3}$
Vigesima seconda	Octave 1
Vigesima sesta	Quinte $\frac{2}{3}$
Vigesima nona	Octave $\frac{1}{2}$
Trigesima terza	Quinte $\frac{1}{3}$
Un' altra vigesima seconda (da concerto)	Octave 1 (wide, to give cornet effects)
Flauto in quinta decima	Flute 2
Flauto in ottava	Flute 4
Tremolo	Tremulant

CATHEDRAL, ÉVORA, PORTUGAL, SIXTEENTH CENTURY

Flautado de 24	16
Flautado de 12	8
Vox humana	8
Flauta de ponta da man esquerda	8
Corneta de 4 por ponto	IV
Octava real	4
Quinta real	2 $^2/_3$
Quinta e decima	II
Chejo de registros	IV

Trompeta real da man esquerda (added in about 1700)
Clarím da man direita
Tambor hen a (Drum stop: 2 8′ pipes in oak, sounding A and B)
Keyboard compass of forty-five notes, including short octave
Pedal of six keys (C, D, E, F, G, A)

ST. GERVAIS, PARIS, FRANCE 1653. Specification dating from the time of Couperin

First manual, Positif, AC - c^{111} (forty-nine notes)

Bourdon	8	Flûte	4
Montre	4	Nasard	2 $^2/_3$
Doublette	2	Tierce	1 $^3/_5$
Fourniture	III	Larigot	1 $^1/_3$
Cymbale	III	Cromorne	8

SECOND MANUAL, GRAND ORGUE, couplable (forty-nine notes)

Montre	16	Flûte	4
Bourdon	16	Nasard	2 $^2/_3$
Montre	8	Quarte	2
Bourdon	8	Tierce	1 $^3/_5$
Prestant	4	Cornet (two octaves)	V
Doublette	2	Trompette	8
Fourniture	IV	Clairon	4
Cymbale	III	Voix humaine	8

THIRD MANUAL, RÉCIT, g–c^{111} (twenty-five or thirty-two notes)

Cornet	V

FOURTH MANUAL, ECHO, c–c^{111} (thirty-seven notes)

Bourdon	8	Nasard	2 $^2/_3$
Flûte	4	Doublette	2
		Tierce	1 $^3/_5$
Cymbale	III	Cromorne	8

PÉDALE, A^{1}C–e (twenty-nine notes)

Flûte	8
Flûte	4
Trompette	8

Tremblant deux and *Tremblant fort*

SLOTSKIRKE (CASTLE CHURCH), FREDERIKSBORG, HILLERØD, DENMARK, 1610. Specification according to Praetorius

Upper manual		LOWER MANUAL	
Principal	8	Quintadena	8
Gedacktflöte	8	Klein Gedacktflöte	4
Klein Principal	4	Principal Diskant	4 (from f)
Gemshorn	4	Blockpfeife Diskant	4
Nachthorn	4	Super-Gemshörnlein	2
Blockpfeife	4	Nasat	1 $^1/_3$
Supergedackt	2	Klein Zimbel	I
Gedacktquint	2 $^2/_3$	Krummhorn	8
Rankett	16	Geigen Regal	4

PEDAL			
Grosser Gedacktflöte-Bass	16	Nachthorn-Bass	2
Gemshorn-Bass	8	Bauernflöte-Bass	16
Quintatön-Bass	8	Sordunnen-Bass	16
Querflöten-Bass	4	Jungfrauen-Regal-Bass	4
		Dolcian-Bass	8

DOM, FREIBERG, GERMAN DEMOCRATIC REPUBLIC, 1710–14. The specification is given in the original orthography, as it appears on the console

SECOND MANUAL, HAUPTWERK		FIRST MANUAL, BRUSTWERK	
Bourdon	16	Gedackt	8
Principal	8	Prinzipal	4
Viol di Gamba	8	Rohrflöte	4
Rohrflöte	8	Nassat	2 $^2/_3$ (3)
Octave	4	Octava	2
Quinta	2 $^2/_3$ (3)	Tertia	1 $^3/_5$
Super-Octave	2	Quinta	1 $^1/_3$
Tertia	1 $^3/_5$	Sufflöt	1
Cornet	V	Mixtur	III
Mixtur	IV		
Zimbeln	III	PEDAL	
Trompet	8	Untersatz	32*
Clarin	4	Prinzipal-Bass	16
		Octavbass	16*
THIRD MANUAL, OBERWERK		Sub-Bass	16
Quintaden	16	Octavbass	8
Principal	8	Octavbass	4
Gedackt	8	Mixtur	VI
Quintaden	8 (Jehmlich)	Posaunbass	16
Octava	8	Trompeten-Bass	8
Spitzflöte	4	Clarinbass	4
Super-Octave	2		
Flaschflöt	1		
Echo (Cornet)	V		
Mixtur	III		
Zimbeln	II		
Krumphorn	8		
Vox humana	8		

* a single stop,
speaking together
Tremulants: *fort* to *Hw* + *Ow* + *Bw* together *doux* (*Schwebung*) to
Ow Vox humana Hw/Ow Hw/Bw (no *Ped/Hw* coupler)

ST. GEORG, RÖTHA, GERMAN DEMOCRATIC REPUBLIC, 1718–21

HAUPTWERK		OBERWERK	
Prinzipal	8	Gedackt	8
Rohrflöte	8	Quintadena	8
Bordun	16	Prinzipal	4
Octava	4	Rohrflöte	4
Spitzfl.	4	Nasat	2 $^2/_3$
Quinta	2 $^2/_3$	Octava	2
Octava	2	Tertia	1 $^3/_5$
Cornett	III	Quinta	1 $^1/_3$
Zimbel	II	Sifflöt	1
Mixtur	III	Mixtur	III
		PEDAL	
		Prinzipal	16 (Bass)
		Posaune	16
		Trompete	8

MONASTERY OF SÃO VICENTE DE FORA, LISBON, PORTUGAL

ORGAO PRINCIPAL (UPPER KEYBOARD), C-d^{111}, forty-seven notes, short octave

Left hand		*Right hand*
	(Treble of Principal 16′)	Oitava magna
Flautado de 24	(Principal 16′)	Flautado de 24
Flautado de 12	(Principal 8′)	Flautado de 12
Oitava real	(Principal 4′)	Oitava real 2 filas
		(II ranks)
Quinzena	(Principal 2′)	
Contras de		
24 palmos	(Bass 16′, first octave)	
Flautado de		
12 tapado	(Bourdon 8′)	
Flautado de		
6 tapado	(Bourdon 4′)	
	(Flauto dolce 8′)	Flauta dolce
	(Flauto traverso)	Flauta travesiera
	(Undulating Principal)	Voz humana
Quinta real	(Quinte 2 ^{2}/$_3$′)	
	(Quinte 2 ^{2}/$_3$′ + 2′)	Quinta de 12 palmos
		2 filas
Requinta 2 filas	(Quinte 1 ^{1}/$_3$′, II ranks)	
	(2′, 2′, 1 ^{1}/$_3$′, 1 ^{1}/$_3$′)	Decimaquinta 4 filas
Vintedozena		
2–3 filas	(1′, II and III ranks)	
Mistura imperial		
5 filas	(Mixture)	Mistura imperial 6 filas
Cimbala 4 filas	(Cymbale)	Cimbala 4 filas
Subcimbala 4 filas	(Surcymbale)	Subcimbala 4 filas
Clarão 6 filas	(4′, 2′, 1 ^{1}/$_3$′, 1 ^{3}/$_5$′,	
	1′, ^{2}/$_3$′: Principal-	
	scaled, no breaks)	
	(4′, 2 ^{2}/$_3$′, 2′, 2′, 1 ^{1}/$_3$′,	Clarãozinho 7 filas
	1 ^{1}/$_3$′, 1′)	
	(Cornet VIII ranks: 8′	Corneta real 8 filas
	open, 8′ stopped, 4′,	
	2 ^{2}/$_3$′, 2′, 1 ^{3}/$_5$′,	
	1 ^{1}/$_3$′, 1′)	
Trombeta real	(Trumpet 8′ [internal])	Trombeta real
Tromba de batalha	(Trumpet 8′ [external])	Clarim
Baixãocilho	(4′ [external])	
	(8′ [external])	Trombeta marinha
Dulçaina	(Regal 8′ [external])	Dulçaina
Chirimía	(Chalumeau 4′	
	[external])	
	(Oboe 8′ [external])	Boé

ORGÃO DE ÉCO (LOWER KEYBOARD), forty-seven notes

Flautado de		
12 tapado		
Flautado violão	(Bourdon 8′)	Flautado de 12 tapado
	(Bourdon 8′)	
	(Flute 8′)	Flauta napolitana
	(Flute 4′)	Flauta de 6
Flautado de	(Bourdon 4′)	
6 tapado		
Quinzena	(Prestant 4′, II ranks)	Oitava 2 filas
1–2 filas	(Principal 2′, I–II ranks)	
	(Wide-scaled stop, 2′,	Pifaro 2 filas
	II ranks)	
Dezanovena	(Quinte 1 ^{1}/$_3$′,	
1–2 filas	I–II ranks)	
Vintedozena		
2 filas	(Principal 1′, II ranks)	Vintedozena 3 filas
Cheio claro	(Principal-scaled	Cheio claro 5 filas
5 filas	Mixture)	

Tolosana 3 filas	(Small cornet)	Cornetilha 3 filas
(^{4}/$_5$′, ^{2}/$_3$′, ^{2}/$_3$′)		(2′, 1 ^{3}/$_5$′, 1 ^{1}/$_3$′)
Nazardo éco	(Wide-scaled 2′, 1 ^{1}/$_3$′,	
3 filas	1′, in swell-box)	
	(Cornet VI ranks, swell)	Corneta 6 filas
	(Reed 8′, swell)	Clarim éco
Sacabucha	(Reed 8′)	

No Pedal. Drum stop operated by two pedals (four wood pipes, two metal pipes). Swell box operated by foot-lever

---

NEW CATHEDRAL, SALAMANCA, ECHEVARRÍA, SPAIN, 1744

ORGANO MAYOR (*GO*), SECOND MANUAL

Flautado de 26	(Montre 16′)	Bass/treble
Flautado de 13	(Montre 8′)	Bass/treble
		(choir side)
Flautado de 13	(Montre 8′)	Bass/treble
		(transept side)
Octava	(4′)	Bass/treble
Docena	(2 ^{2}/$_3$′)	Bass/treble
Quincena	(2′)	Bass/treble
Lleno	(Mixture)	Bass/treble
Zimbala	(Cymbale)	Bass/treble
Sobrezimbala	(Surcymbale)	Bass/treble
Violón	(Bourdon 8′)	Bass/treble
Tapadillo	(Bourdon 4′)	Bass/treble
Nasarte en 12a	(Nasard 2 ^{2}/$_3$′)	Bass/treble
Nasarte en 15a	(Quarte 2′)	Bass/treble
Nasarte en 17a	(Tierce)	Bass/treble
Nasarte en 19a	(Larigot)	Bass/treble
Corneta real	(Cornet)	Treble
Trompeta real	(Trumpet 8′)	Bass/treble
Trompeta magna	(Horizontal 16′)	Treble
Clarín 1	(Horizontal 8′)	Treble
Clarín 2	(Horizontal 8′)	Treble
Trompeta de batalla	(Horizontal)	Bass/treble
		(transept side)
Dulzayna	(Horizontal Regal 8′)	Bass/treble
Chirimía	(Horizontal 4′)	Bass
Trémolo		

CADIRETA (ECHO), FIRST MANUAL

Flautado de 13	(Principal 8′)	Bass/treble
Tapadillo	(Bourdon 4′)	Bass/treble
Nasarte en 12a	(Nasard 2 ^{2}/$_3$′)	Bass/treble
Nasarte en 15a	(Flute 2′)	Bass/treble
Nasarte en 17a	(Tierce in the bass; Tierce	
	+ Larigot in the treble)	
Nasarte en 19a	(Larigot)	Bass
Lleno	(Mixture)	Bass/treble
Zimbala	(Cymbale)	Bass/treble
Corneta real	(Cornet)	Treble
Trompeta real	(Trumpet 8′)	Bass/treble
Clarín	(Reed 8′)	Treble
Oboe	(Oboe 8′)	Treble
Bajoncello	(Reed 4′)	Bass

PEDAL

Tambores D, A	(Drum stop D, A)	
Contras 16 + 8	(Bass; C, D, E, F, G, A, B flat, B)	

CATHEDRAL OF ST. PIERRE, POITIERS, France, 1787-90

Grand Orgue (C–e¹¹¹)			Positif (C–e¹¹¹)		
Montre	16		Montre	8	
Montre	8		Prestant	4	
Prestant	4		Doublette	2	
Doublette	2		Plein Jeu	VII	
Fourniture	V		Bourdon	8	
Cymbale	IV		Flûte (in a)	8	
Bourdon	16		Nasard	2 ²/₃	
Bourdon	8		Tierce	1 ³/₅	
Flûte	8		Grand Cornet (in c¹)	V	
Grande Tierce	3 ¹/₅		Trompette	8	
Nasard	2 ¹/₃		Clairon	4	
Quarte	2		Cromorne	8	
Tierce	1 ³/₅				
Grand Cornet (in c¹)	V		Récit (in g)		
Bombarde	8–16		Flûte	8	
Trompette	8		Grand Cornet	V	
Clairon I	4		Trompette	8	
Clairon II	4		Hautbois	8	
Voix humaine	8				
			Pédale		
Echo (in g)			C–c¹		
Bourdon	8		Flûte (stopped)	16	
Flûte	4		Flûte (open)	8	
Trompette	8		Flûte (open)	4	
			a–c¹		
			Bombarde	16	
			Trompette	8	
			Clairon	4	

EMPEROR'S ORGAN, CATHEDRAL, TOLEDO, Spain, 1798

Reed battery of the second manual

Left hand			Right hand		
Trompeta real	8 (internal)		Trompeta real	8 (internal)	
Clarín clara	8 (external)		Clarín clara	8 (external)	
Clarín fuerte	8 (external)		Clarín brillante	8 (external)	
Bajoncillo	4 (external)		Clarín de campaña	4 (external)	
Clarín en octava	4 (external)		Chirimía	4 (external)	
Violeta	2 (external)				
			Trompeta magna	16 (external)	

Internal (vertical) reeds of the first manual

Left hand			Right hand		
Trompeta real	8		Trompeta real	8	
Bajoncillo	4				
			Clarín	8	
Clarín en 15a	2				
			Trompeta de 26	16	

Pedal reeds

Bombardas de 26	I (internal)	
Bombardas de 26	II (internal)	
Clarín	8 (external)	
Clarín octava	4 (external)	
Clarín en 15a	2 (external)	
Clarín en 22a	1 (external)	

It is important and of interest to note in this context how the different groupings of reeds are planned in an eighteeth-century Spanish organ. What we are dealing with in fact is a sort of reed Mixture based on a *Trompeta real* 8′ (normally internal), the other ranks raising the sonority to a pitch where it sounds most effective, namely the tenor or alto. The right hand plays the 8′ and 16′ stops, the left hand those of 4′ and 2′. Obviously, there are also technical reasons for this arrange-

ment: it is easier to suspend a 4′ Trumpet from the front of the case than a 16′ pipe, whereas in the treble the longest pipe of a 16′ stop (at c sharp¹) will be less than four feet in length.

ST. DENIS, PARIS, France, 1837-41

Grand Orgue II			Positif I		
Montre	32		Bourdon	16	
Montre	16		Bourdon	8	
Bourdon	16		Salicional	8	
Montre	8		Flûte	8	
Bourdon	8		Prestant	4	
Viole	8		Flûte	4	
Flûte traverse	8		Nasard	2 ²/₃	
Prestant	4		Doublette	2	
Flûte traverse	4		Flageolet	2	
Nasard	2 ²/₃		Tierce	1 ³/₅	
Doublette	2		Fourniture	IV	
Grande Fourniture	IV		Cymbale	IV	
Petite Fourniture	IV		Trompette	8	
Grande Cymbale	IV		Cor d'Harmonie	8 (bass?)	
Petite Cymbale	IV		Hautboy	8 (treble?)	
Cornet (mounted)	V		Cromorne	8	
Trompette	8		Clairon	4	
Trompette	8		Tremblant		
Basson	8 (bass)				
Cor anglais	8 (treble)		Récit IV		
Clairon	4		Bourdon	8	
			Flûte	8	
Bombarde III			Flûte	4	
Bourdon	16		Quinte	2 ²/₃	
Bourdon	8		Octavin	2	
Flûte	8		Trompette	8	
Prestant	4		Voix humaine	8	
Nasard ou Quinte	2 ²/₃		Clairon	4	
Doublette	2				
Cornet	VII		Pédale		
Bombarde	16		Flues C–f, eighteen notes		
Trompette	8		Reeds, F¹–f, twenty-five notes		
Trompette	8		Flûte ouverte	32	
Clairon	4		Flûte	16	
Clairon	4		Flûte	8	
			Nasard	5 ¹/₃	
			Flûte	4	
			Basse-contre	16 (24)	
			Bombarde	16 (24)	
			Basson	8 (12)	
			Trompette	8 (12)	
			Trompette	8 (12)	
			Clairon	4 (6)	
			Clairon	4 (6)	

Combination pedals and accessories (nine pedal-levers):
i swell pedal
ii IV/II coupler
iii III/II
iv II/II (*GO* stops could be drawn but did not sound until iv pressed)
v I/II
vi high-pressure trebles (lever working ventil to the special chest)
vii high-pressure basses
viii pedals coupled to all manuals
ix suboctave coupler to all manuals

ST. PETERSKIRCHE, SINZIG, Federal Republic of Germany, 1972. The specification of this instrument was designed by Peter Bares

Second manual, Hauptwerk
Pommer 16
Prinzipal 8
Spillpfeife 8
Hohlflöte 8
Oktave 4
Spitzgambe 4
Nasard 2 $\frac{2}{3}$
Schweizerpfeife 2
Mollterz $\frac{16}{19}$
Mixtur V (2 + 1 $\frac{1}{3}$ + $\frac{2}{3}$ + $\frac{1}{2}$)
Cymbel V ($\frac{1}{4}$ + $\frac{4}{21}$ + $\frac{2}{13}$ + $\frac{2}{17}$ + $\frac{1}{10}$)
Oberton II–IV
C = 3 $\frac{1}{5}$ + 1
G = 3 $\frac{1}{5}$ + 1 $\frac{7}{9}$ + 1
C^1 = 5 $\frac{1}{3}$ + 3 $\frac{1}{5}$ + 1 $\frac{7}{9}$ + 1
Französisches Krummhorn 16
Trompete 8
Röhrenglockenton 8

First manual, Rückpositiv
Quintade 8
Stillgedackt 8
Prinzipal 4
Flauto dolce 4
Nachthorn 2
Quinte 1 $\frac{1}{3}$
Fünfzehnte $\frac{8}{15}$
Scharff IV (1 + $\frac{2}{3}$ + $\frac{1}{2}$ + $\frac{1}{3}$)
Dulzianregal 8
Xylophon (*piano* or *forte*) 4
Tremulant

Third manual, Brustwerk (expressive)
Holzgedackt 8
Rohrflöte 4
Prinzipal 2
Terz 1 $\frac{3}{5}$
Blockflöte 1
Oberton II (1 $\frac{1}{7}$ + $\frac{8}{11}$)

Cymbel IV ($\frac{1}{2}$ + $\frac{1}{3}$ + $\frac{1}{4}$ + $\frac{1}{6}$)
Harfenregal 16
Schalmey 4
Psalterium[1]
Tremulant

Pedal
Prinzipal 16
Subbass 16
Oktavbass 8
Violoncello 8
Quintgedackt 5 $\frac{1}{3}$
Oktave 4
Gemshorn 2
Theorbe III (6 $\frac{2}{5}$ + 4 $\frac{4}{7}$ + 2 $\frac{2}{3}$)
Hintersatz III (2 + 1 $\frac{1}{3}$ + 1)
Dulzian 32
Bombarde 16
Fagott 8
Trompetenregal 4

Rp/Hw, Bw/Hw, Bw/Rp
Rp/Ped, Hw/Ped, Bw/Ped, Rp (upper octave)/*Ped*
Tutti
Nine individual reed cancel buttons
One general cancel

Registermanual
Mixturensetzer
Percussion
Tastenfessel
Cymbelstern
Three free combination pedals
Slider-chests and tone-channel chests
Mechanical action
Electric draw-stop action

(1) made of brass resonators struck with rapid frequency by small hammers so as to produce a rattling sound giving rise to high-pitched upper partials.

Bibliography

It will readily be understood that the following bibliography is not exhaustive. It will, however, enable the reader to explore in further detail the areas dealt with in the present work. For additional information, the reader is referred to the bibliographies by W.L. Sumner (*The Organ*), G.A.C. de Graaf (*Literatuur over het orgel*), P. Williams (*The European Organ*) and C.R. Arnold (*Organ Literature*). Published by the Scarecrow Press, Inc. (Metuchen, N.J.), the last-mentioned work also includes brief biographies of organ composers and, above all, references to editions of their works. (The dates of publication are normally those of the first edition.)

Adelung, W. (ed.), *Orgeln der Gegenwart*, Cassel, 1972
Adlung, J., *Anleitung zur musikalischen Gelahrtheit*, Erfurt, 1758
Alain, O., *L'œuvre d'orgue de Jean-Sébastien Bach*, Paris, 1968
Andersen, P.G., *Orglet*, Copenhagen, 1929
-, *Orgelbogen*, Copenhagen, 1955
-, *Organ Building and Design*, trans. by J. Curnett, New York, 1969
Antegnati, C., *L'Arte Organica*, Brescia, 1608; Mainz, 1958
Apel, W., *Geschichte der Orgel- und Klaviermusik bis 1700*, Cassel-Basle-Paris-London-New York, 1967
Arnold, C.R., *Organ Literature: A Comprehensive Survey*, Metuchen, 1973
Audsley, G.A., *The Art of Organ-Building*, New York, 1965
Azevedo, C. de, *Baroque Organ-Cases of Portugal*, Amsterdam, 1972

Banchieri, A., *Conclusioni del Suono dell'Organo*, Bologna, 1591
-, *L'Organo Suonarino*, Venice, 1605; Amsterdam, 1969
Barnes, W.H., *The Contemporary American Organ: Its Evolution, Design and Construction*, New York, 1925
Bédos de Celles, Dom F., *L'art du facteur d'orgues*, Paris, 1766-78; Cassel, 1973
Blanton, J.E., *The Revival of the Organ Case*, Albany, 1965
Bornefeld, H., *Orgelbau und Neue Orgelmusik*, Cassel-Basle, 1952
Bouvet, C., *Une dynastie de musiciens français: Les Couperin, organistes de l'église Saint-Gervais*, Paris, 1919
Buhle, E., *Die musikalischen Instrumente in den Miniaturen des frühen Mittelalters*, Leipzig, 1903
Burgemeister, L., *Der Orgelbau in Schlesien*, Strasbourg, 1925; Frankfurt am Main, 1973

Calahorra Martínez, P., *Música en Zaragoza, Siglos XVI-XVII*, Saragossa, 1977
Cantagrel, G. and Halbreich, H., *Le Livre d'or de l'orgue français*, Paris, 1976
Cavaillé-Coll, A., *De l'orgue et de son architecture*, Paris, 1872
Cavaillé-Coll, C. and E., *Aristide Cavaillé-Coll, ses origines, sa vie, ses oeuvres*, Paris, 1929
Cellier, A. and Bachelin, H., *L'orgue, ses éléments, son histoire, son esthétique*, Paris, 1933

Clicquot, F.H., *Théorie - pratique de la facture de l'orgue*, Poitiers, 1789; Cassel, 1969
Clutton, C. and Dixon, G., *The Organ. Its Tonal Structure and Registration*, London, 1950
Clutton, C. and Niland, A., *The British Organ*, London, 1963

David, W., *Johann Sebastian Bachs Orgeln*, Berlin, 1951
Diruta, G., *Il Transilvano*, Venice, 1593
Douglass, F., *The Language of the Classical French Organ: A Musical Tradition Before 1800*, New Haven, 1969
Dufourcq, N., *Esquisse d'une histoire de l'orgue en France, du XIIIe à la fin du XVIIIe siècle*, Paris, 1935
-, *La Musique d'orgue française de Jehan Titelouze à Jehan Alain*, Paris, 1941
-, *Le Livre de l'orgue français: 1589-1789*, 5 vols., Paris, 1969 -
-, *L'Orgue*, Paris, 1948

Eberstaller, O., *Orgeln und Orgelbauer in Österreich*, Graz-Cologne, 1955
Encyclopédie de la musique/Dictionnaire du conservatoire (Albert Lavignac and Lionel de la Laurencie); Pt. II: L'Orgue by C. Mutin; La Musique d'orgue by A. Guilmant; L'Art des organistes by A. Pirro
Erici, E., *Inventarium över bevarade äldre Kyrkorglar i Sverige*, Stockholm, 1965

Fellerer, K.G., *Studien zur Orgelmusik des ausgehenden 18. und frühen 19. Jahrhunderts*, Cassel, 1932
-, *Orgel und Orgelmusik: Ihre Geschichte*, Augsburg 1929
Fellot, J., *L'Orgue classique français*, suppl. issue of *Musique de tous les temps*, 1962
Ferrard, J., *Orgues du Brabant Wallon*, Brussels, 1981
Flade, E., *Der Orgelbauer Gottfried Silbermann*, Leipzig, 1926
Fleury, P. Comte de, *Dictionnaire biographique des facteurs d'orgues*, Paris, 1926
Fock, G., *Arp Schnitger und seine Schule*, ed. by Rudolf Reuter, Cassel, 1974
Forer, A., *Orgeln in Österreich*, Vienna-Munich, 1973
Friis, N., *Orgelbygning i Danmark*, Copenhagen, 1949
Frotscher, G. *Deutsche Orgeldispositionen aus fünf Jahrhunderten*, Wolfenbüttel-Berlin, 1939
-, *Geschichte des Orgelspiels und der Orgelkomposition*, Berlin 1934 and 1959

Gerber, E.L., *Historisch-Biographisches Lexicon der Tonkünstler*, Leipzig, 1790-2
Gerber, M., *De Cantu et Musica Sacra, a prima Ecclesiae aetate usque ad praesens tempus*, Sankt Blasien, 1774
-, *Scriptores ecclesiastici de Musica Sacra potissimum*, Sankt Blasien, 1784
Goléa, A., *Rencontres avec Olivier Messiaen*, Paris, 1960
Gołos, J., *Polskie Organy i Muzyka Organowa*, Warsaw, 1972

Goode, J. C., *Pipe Organ Registration*, New York, 1964
Graaf, G. A. C. de, *Literatuur over het orgel*, Amsterdam, 1957
Grabner, H., *Die Kunst des Orgelbaues*, Berlin, 1958
Grégoir, E. G. J., *Historique de la facture et des facteurs d'orgue . . . dans les Pays-Bas et dans les Provinces flamandes de la Belgique*, Antwerp, 1865 (Amsterdam, 1972)
Guédon, J., *Nouveau Manuel complet du facteur d'orgues*, Paris, 1903
Guillou, J., *L'Orgue, souvenir et avenir*, Paris, 1978

Haacke, W., *Orgeln*, Königstein, 1954
Hamel, P. M., *Nouveau Manuel complet du facteur d'orgues*, Paris, 1849
Hardmeyer, W., *Einführung in die schweizerische Orgelbaukunst*, Zurich, 1947
-, *Orgelbaukunst in der Schweiz*, Zurich, 1975
Hardouin, P., *Le Grand-Orgue de Saint-Gervais de Paris*, Paris, 1949
Haselböck, H., *Barocker Orgelschatz in Niederösterreich*, Vienna-Munich, 1972
Hill, A. G., *The Organ-Cases and Organs of the Middle Ages and Renaissance*, London, 1883–91; Buren, 1975
Hopkins E. J. and Rimbault, E. F., *The Organ, its History and Construction*, London, 1855; Amsterdam, 1972

Irwin, S., *Dictionary of Pipe Organ Stops*, New York, 1962

Jakob, F., *L'Orgue*, Lausanne, 1970
Jeppesen, K., *Die italienische Orgelmusik am Anfang des Cinquecento*, Copenhagen, 1943

Kaufmann, W., *Der Orgelprospekt in stilgeschichtlicher Entwicklung*, Mainz, 1949
Kelemen, P., *Baroque and Rococo in Latin-America*, New York, 1955
Keller, H., *Die Orgelwerke Bachs: Ein Beitrag zu ihrer Geschichte, Form, Deutung und Wiedergabe*, Leipzig, 1948
Kinkeldey, O., *Orgel und Klavier in der Musik des 16. Jahrhunderts*, Leipzig, 1910
Klotz, H., *Das Buch von der Orgel*, Cassel-Basle 1938; 6th rev. ed. Cassel-Basle, 1960
-, *Ueber die Orgelkunst der Gotik, der Renaissance und des Barock*, Cassel, 1931–4
Kruijs, M. H. van 't, *Verzameling van disposities der verschillende Orgels in Nederland*, Rotterdam, 1885; Hilversum, 1965

Libera, S. dalla, *L'Arte degli organi a Venezia*, Venice–Rome, 1962
Lindow, C.-W. and Blanchard, H. D., *Petit Lexique de l'orgue*, Delaware, OH, 1981
-, *Orgues historiques de France*, Maisons-Alfort, 1981
Lukas, V., *Orgelmusikführer*, Stuttgart, 1963
Lunelli, R., *Der Orgelbau in Italien in seinen Meisterwerken vom 14. Jahrhundert bis zur Gegenwart*, Mainz, 1956

Mahrenholz, C., *Die Orgelregister, ihre Geschichte und ihr Bau*, Cassel, 1930
-, *Die Berechnung der Orgelpfeifen-Mensuren*, Cassel, 1938
Mayer-Serra, O., *La Música y músicos de Latino-America*, Mexico City, 1947
Mellers, W., *François Couperin and the French Classical Tradition*, London, 1950; New York, 1968
Merklin, A., et alia, *Aus Spaniens altem Orgelbau*, Mainz, 1939
Mersenne, M., *L'Harmonie universelle* (vol. II), Paris, 1637 (1963)
Messiaen, O., *Technique de mon langage musical*, Paris, 1944
Metzler, W., *Romantischer Orgelbau in Deutschland*, Ludwigsburg, 1965
Meuren, F., van der, *Het Orgel in de Nederlanden*, Brussels-Amsterdam, 1931
Meyer-Siat, P., *Les Callinet . . .*, Paris, 1965
Moretti, C., *L'Organo italiano*, Milan, 1973
Moser, H. J., *Orgelromantik*, Ludwigsburg, 1961
Müller, W., *Auf den Spuren von Gottfried Silbermann*, Cassel-Basle, 1968

Münger, F., *Schweizer Orgeln von der Gotik bis zur Gegenwart. Ein Lebensbild des berühmten Orgelbauers*, Berne, 1961

Němec, V., *Pražské Varhany*, Prague, 1944
Niland, A., *Introduction to the Organ*. Foreword by F. Jackson, London, 1968

Ochse, O., *The History of the Organ in the United States*, Bloomington-London, 1975
"Orgues de France" in *Les Monuments historiques de la France* (new series, vol. VIII, fasc. 2–3), Paris, 1962

Peeters, F. and Vente, M. A., *L'Orgue et la musique d'orgue dans les Pays-Bas et la Principauté de Liège du 16e au 18e siècle*, Antwerp, 1971
Perrot, J., *L'Orgue de ses origines hellénistiques à la fin du XIIIe siècle*, Paris, 1965
Peschard, A., *Etudes sur l'orgue électrique*, Paris, 1896
Pole, W., *Musical Instruments in the Great Industrial Exhibition of 1851*, London, 1851
Pontécoulant, Comte A. de, *Organographie . . .*, Paris, 1861; Amsterdam, 1972
Praetorius, M., *Syntagma musicum*, Wolfenbüttel, 1619

Quoika, R., *Die altösterreichische Orgel der späten Gotik, der Renaissance und des Barock*, Cassel, 1953
-, *Das Positiv in Geschichte und Gegenwart*, Cassel, 1957
-, *Der Orgelbau in Böhmen und Mähren*, Cassel, 1968
-, *Vom Blockwerk zur Registerorgel*, Cassel, 1969

Raugel, F., *Les Organistes*, Paris, 1923
-, *Recherches sur les maîtres de l'ancienne facture française d'orgues*, Paris, 1925
-, *Les Grandes Orgues des églises de Paris et du Département de la Seine*, Paris, 1927
Ritter, A. G., *Zur Geschichte des Orgelspiels*, Leipzig, 1884
Robertson, F. E., *A Practical Treatise on Organ-Building*, London, 1897
Rokseth, Y., *La Musique d'orgue au XVe siècle et au début du XVIe*, Paris, 1930
Rupp, E., *Die Entwicklungsgeschichte der Orgelbaukunst*, Einsiedeln, 1929

Salmen, W., *Orgel und Orgelspiel im 16. Jahrhundert*, Neu Rum near Innsbruck, 1978
Schlick, A., *Spiegel der Orgelmacher und Organisten*, Speyer, 1511; ed. P. Smets, Cassel, 1959
Schweitzer, A., *Deutsche und französische Orgelbaukunst und Orgelkunst*, Leipzig, 1906
-, *J.S. Bach, le musicien-poète*. Foreword by C.-M. Widor, Paris, 1905, Leipzig, 1908
Serassi, G., *Sugli Organi Lettere*, Bergamo, 1816
Servières, G., *La Décoration artistique des buffets d'orgues*, Paris-Brussels, 1928
Skinner, E. M., *The Modern Organ*, New York, 1917
Smets, P., *Die Orgelregister, ihr Klang und Gebrauch*, Mainz, 1937; 7th ed. Mainz, 1958
-, *Neuzeitlicher Orgelbau*, Mainz, 1933; 8th ed. Mainz, 1949
Spitta, P., *Johann Sebastian Bach*, Leipzig, 1873–1880
Sumner, W. L., *The Organ, its Evolution, Principles of Construction and Use*, 2nd ed. London, 1952
-, *Father Henry Willis: Organ Builder and his Successors*, London, 1957
Supper, W., *Die Orgeldisposition. Eine Heranführung*, Cassel, 1950
-, (ed.), *Orgelbewegung und Historismus*, Berlin, 1958

Teulon, B., *De l'orgue*, Aix-en-Provence, 1981
Thornsby, F. W., *Dictionary of Organs and Organists*, Bournemouth, 1912–22
Tournemire, C.-A., *César Franck*, Paris, 1931

Utz, K., *Die Orgel in unserer Zeit*, Marburg, 1950

Vente, M. A., *Bouwstoffen tot de Geschiedenis van het Nederlandse Orgel in de 16e eeuw*, Amsterdam, 1942
-, *Die Brabanter Orgel: zur Geschichte der Orgelkunst in Belgien und Holland im Zeitalter der Gotik und der Renaissance*, Amsterdam, 1958
Villard, J.-A., *L'œuvre de François-Henri Clicquot*, Laval, 1973

Walcker, O., *Erinnerungen eines Orgelbauers*, Cassel, 1948
Walter, F. W., *Spiel und Kompositionen zu mehreren Orgeln vom 16. bis zum 19. Jahrhundert, vornehmlich in Oberitalien*, thesis, Berlin, 1923
Westblad, G., *Kyrkoorgeln*, Stockholm, 1936
Wester, B., *Gotisk Resning i svenska Orglar*, Stockholm, 1936
-, *Kyrkorglar i Sverige*, Stockholm, 1942–52
Williams, P. F., *The European Organ 1450–1850*, London, 1966
Wilson, M., *The English Chamber Organ; History and Development 1650–1850*. Foreword by W. L. Sumner, Oxford-Columbia, SC, 1968
Wörsching, J., *Der Orgelbauer Karl Riepp*, Mainz, 1939
-, *Der Orgelbauer Joseph Gabler*, Mainz, 1959
-, *Die Orgelbauerfamilie Silbermann in Strassburg im Elsass*, Mainz, 1941

In addition to innumerable monographs dealing with individual instruments, the reader will find valuable information in the various periodical publications edited by different societies of organ enthusiasts, as well as in pamphlets issued by organ builders and publishing houses. The following list gives only an indication of what is available:

France:
Bulletin des amis de l'orgue, Connaissance de l'orgue, Grand Jeu, Jeunesse et orgue, La flûte harmonique, L'orgue, Orgues méridionales, Renaissance de l'orgue and *Mélanges de la Casa Velazquez* (Paris, CNRS), in addition to the series *Orgues historiques* published by Harmonia Mundi, and the calendars *Organa Europae* published by Pierre Vallotton (Saint-Dié)

Switzerland:
La tribune de l'orgue, Musik und Gottesdienst, and the annual studies published by Kuhn (Männedorf) and edited by Friedrich Jakob

Germany:
Ars Organi and *Acta Organologica* (both published by the Gesellschaft der Orgelfreunde), *Musik und Kirche*, and the monographs on organs of historical interest published by Uwe Papc (Berlin), and the studies entitled *ISO-Information* published by the International Society of Organ Builders in Lauffen on the Neckar

Italy:
L'organo

Spain:
Anuario musical, Organos del Pais Valenciano, publications of the Associacion Cabanilles de Amigos del Organo, together with studies by G. A. C. Graaf and the Dutch organ builder Jacques Stinkens (Zeist)

Belgium:
L'organiste

Netherlands:
Organist en Eredienst, Het Orgel, De Praestant and the publications *The Organ Yearbook* and the reprints in the series *Bibliotheca Organologica*, edited by Fritz Knuf, under the general editorship of Peter Williams (Buren)

Scandinavia:
Orgelforum (Sweden), *Orglet* (Denmark) and *Organum* (Finland)

Great Britain:
The Organ, The Organ Club Journal, The Organists' Quarterly Journal, the journal of the British Institute of Organ Studies, and works published by Hinrichsen (London)

United States of America:
The Diapason, The American Organist, The Tracker, The Organ Institute Quarterly, The American Guild of Organists Quarterly and *Music / The A. G. O. and R. C. C. O. Magazine*

Index

The numbers in italics refer to the captions

Abbey, John *177, 179*
Abul Hasan El-Muchtar ben El-Hasan
  Fig. 54
Adam, Robert 175
Adams, Thomas 177
Adlington Hall *156*
Aebi, Christopher *122, 129*
Aeolian-Skinner Organ Company *249*
Agati 45
Agerwall, Johan *91*
Agincourt, François d' 192
Agoult, Marie d', Comtesse *137*
Agricola, Johannes 90
Agricola, Johann Friedrich 116
Aguilera de Heredia, Sebastián 218, 219
Ahle, Johann Gottfried 114
Ahle, Johann Rudolph 109
Ahrend, Jürgen *38, 40, 278*
Ahrend & Brunzema *60*
Ahrens, Joseph 124
Åkerman, Per Larsson 95
Alain, Jehan 198
Alain, Marie-Claire 198
Albarracín 219
Alberti, Johann Friedrich 109
Albertin, Alfons 75
Albi *191*
Albinoni, Tomaso 110
Ålborg *85*
Albrecht, Johann Christoph *126*
Albrechtsberger, Johann Georg 117, 119
Albright, William 246
Alessio, Giovanni d' *24*
Alexandria 10
Alkmaar *139*
Allende-Blin, Juan 246
Alpe-d'Huez, L' *281*
Altenbruch *47*
Altenburg 117; *73*
Altnikol 120
Alvarado, Diego de 219
Alwood, Richard 171, 173
Amerbach, Bonifacius 83
Amézua, Aquilino *206*
Amézua, Diego *206, 210*
Amiens 192; *10*
Amigo, Jaime Fig. 72

Ammann, Heinrich *133*
Ammerbach, Elias Nikolaus 84
Amorbach *55*
Amsterdam 161, 162
Andahuaylas *218*
Andersen, Poul-Gerhard *83, 264, 276*
Andover Organ Company *243, 248*
André, Julius 120
Andriessen the Elder, Hendrik 162
Angel, Jürgen Hinrichsen *80*
Anglebert, Jean-Henri d' 187, 188
Anjou 49
Anne of Austria 187
Anneessens, Charles *149*
Anneessens, Jules *152, 153*
Antegnati, Costanzo 55, 72; *26*
Antegnati, Gian Giacomo *26*
Antico, Andrea 73
Antwerp 160, 161; *150, 154, 208*
Appleton, Thomas *247*
Aranda (Rende), Louis de 188
Araújo, Marcelino de *236*
Araújo, Pedro de 218
Aresti, Giulio Cesare 77
Arfeld *244*
Arles *3*
Arlesheim *134*
Arne, Thomas Augustine 175
Arnell, Richard 177
Arnhem 162
Arnold, Johann August von *47*
Arnstadt 94, 109, 111, 112, 113, 115; *17*
Arrabassa, Perris Fig. 72
Aschbach 89
Attaingnant, Pierre 171, 185
Attwood, Thomas 121, 176
Auch Fig. 7; *188*
Audsley, George Ashdown *21*
Auffmann, Joseph Anton 119
Augsburg 86, 87; *33, 260*
Augusta *252*
Augustus III, King 119
Austin Organ Company *251*
Auxerre 191
Avery, John *157*
Avignon *197, 198*
Avison, Charles 175

Babell, William 174
Bach, Anna Magdalena 119f.

Bach, August Wilhelm 120
Bach, Carl Philipp Emanuel 75, 113, 118, 119, 195
Bach, Christoph 113
Bach, Georg Christoph 111, 113
Bach, Heinrich 109, 111, 113, 114
Bach, Johann 113
Bach, Johann Ambrosius 112, 113, 114
Bach, Johann Bernhard 89, 109, 111
Bach, Johann Christian 112f.
Bach, Johann Christoph (brother of Johann Michael) 109, 111
Bach, Johann Christoph (brother of Johann Ambrosius) 112, 113
Bach, Johann Christoph (brother of Johann Sebastian) 114
Bach, Johann Ernst 111
Bach, Johann Jacob 112, 113
Bach, Johann Ludwig 111
Bach, Johann Michael 89, 109, 111, 112
Bach, Johann Nicolaus 111, 112
Bach, Johann Sebastian 7, 60, 74, 75, 77, 85, 90, 91, 93, 94, 110, 111–20, 121, 123, 174, 177, 189, 191, 193, 194, 195, 198; *16, 17, 21, 51*
Bach, Lips 113
Bach, Maria Barbara 114, 120
Bach, Veit 112, 113
Bach, Wilhelm Friedemann 115
Bachelier, Nicolas *172*
Bäck, Sven-Eric 246
Baden, Conrad 244
Baden-Schlackenwerth, Margraves of 89
Badings, Henk 163
Baghdad Fig. 3
Baillif, Claude 246
Balbastre, Claude-Bénigne 187, 193; *194*
Bales, Gerald 245
Ballard 160, 186
Barber, Samuel 245
Barblan, Otto 244
Barcelona 219
Bares, Peter 246; *274*
Barié, Augustin 198
Barker, Charles Spackman 39, 59; Fig. 36; *200, 204, 252*
Barlow, Wayne 245
Bártfa 161
Bartholomäberg *74*
Bartolino da Padova 70

Basle 49, 83, 160; *135*
Batiste, Antoine-Edouard 194
Battiferri, Luigi 75
Bätz, Johan *141, 147*
Baucourt *199*
Baudot, Evrard *174*
Baumgartner, H. Leroy 245
Baurscheit, Jan Pieter van *154*
Bayreuth 88
Béasse *184*
Beaucourt *199*
Beauvais 191; *9*
Beauvarlet-Charpentier, Jacques-Marie 193
Beauvarlet-Charpentier, Jean-Jacques 192, 193
Becker, Gustav W. *91, 94*
Beckerath, Rudolf von *39, 47, 84, 258*
Beckwith, John Charles 175
Bédos de Celles, François, Dom 21, 28, 38, 188; Figs. 13, 24, 32, 54–60
Beethoven, Ludwig van 117, 118, 121, 193, 194
Beirut Fig. 3
Bellavere, Vincenzo 73
Bellini, Giuseppe 75, 77
Bely, Jacques *177*
Bencini, Giuseppe 71
Bender, Jan 245
Benevoli, Orazio 74
Bennett, John 176
Bennett, Robert Russell 245
Benoist, François 194, 196
Bentzon, Niels Viggo 243
Bérain, Jean *189*
Béraud, Nicolas *183*
Berg, Gottfried 244
Bergamo 39, 75; *32*
Bergöntzle, Josef *74*
Berlin 109, 116, 119, 120; *46*
Berlioz, Hector 74, 119
Bermudo, Juan 217
Bernardino della Ciaia, Azzolino 76
Bernat-Veri, Jorge Bosch *211, 216*
Berne 53
Berner, Friedrich Wilhelm 120, 195
Bert, Pierre *174*
Bertani 187
Bertin, Paul *174*
Besar, Josefus *227*
Bessard, Louis *184*
Best, William Thomas 177
Bethune, Thomas Greene 245
Beuchet-Debierre *186, 194*; see: Gloton
Beyer, C. F. *51*
Bialas, Günther 246
Bielfeldt, Erasmus *49*
Bienvenu, Florent 187
Biernacki, Dominik *104, 107*
Bihler *127*
Bijster, Jacob 163
Bingham, Seth 245
Bingsjö *94*
Bishop *159*
Bishop & Son *158*
Bissell, Keith 245
Biumi, Giacomo Filippo 74
Blancafort, Gabriel *205, 272*
Blanco, José 74
Blankenburg, Quirinus van 162

Blasco, Roque *206*
Blasi, Luca *28*
Blatný, Josef 244
Blitheman, William 172
Bloch, Konrad *131*
Blomfield, Sir Arthur *161*
Blow, John 173, 175; *159*
Bockelmann, Christian *35*
Böellmann, Léon 195, 196
Boëly, Alexandre-Pierre-François 193f.
Bohl, Joseph *33*
Böhm, Georg 92, 93, 94, 110, 112, 114, 115
Böhner, Johann Ludwig 120
Boisseau, Jean-Loup *263*
Boisseau, Robert *263*
Bolcom, William 246
Bologna 73, 74, 75; *23, 31, 265*
Bommer, Johann Jakob *130, 133*
Bonatti, Giuseppe *30*
Bonazzi, Ferdinando 75
Bonn *230*
Bonnal, Ermend 198
Bonnet, Joseph 198
Bordes, Charles 196
Bornefeld, Helmut 124
Borsetti 76
Boscoop, Cornelis 161
Bossard, Joseph *128, 131, 132*
Bossard, Victor Ferdinand Fig. 48; *131, 132*
Bossi, Marco Enrico 77
Bossinensis, Francescus 72
Boston 271; Fig. 45; *242, 249, 250*
Botzen, Johann *78*
Botzen, Peter Petersen *78*
Boucourechliev, André 246
Boudos *189*
Bourgogne, Duc de 190
Boxtel *148*
Boyce, William 174, 176
Boyvin, Jacques 188, 189, 192
Boyvin, Maurice 245
Brabant *34*
Braga *236*
Brahms, Johannes 121, 122, 123
Brandenburg *46*
Brassó 84
Bratislava 119
Brauner *75*
Brebos, family *208, 209, 276*
Brebos, Gillis *208, 209*
Brebos, Gommaar *208*
Brebos, Hans *209*
Brebos, Jasper *208*
Brebos, Michiel *208*
Brebos, Nicolaus *208*
Bredthaimer, Georg *68*
Breinbauer, Josef *67, 69*
Breinbauer, Leopold *72*
Breitenfeld, Brothers *274*
Breitkopf & Härtel 120
Bremen *35*
Brescia *26*
Breu the Elder, Jörg *33*
Bridge, Frank 177
Bridge, Richard 174; *242*
Briol, Maurus *126*
Brisset, Augustin *189*
Bristol 177
Britten, Benjamin 177
Brixi, František Xaver 119

Brno *109*
Brosig, Moritz 120
Bruckner, Anton 120, 122, 123; *71, 75*
Bruges 160; *152*
Brugmann, J. Hartmut 246
Bruhns, Nicolaus 92, 94, 115
Bruna, Pablo 219
Brunner, Adolf 244
Brunswick 92, 162
Brussels 87, 160, 172, 195
Buchau, Johann Conrad *41*
Buchner, Hans 83, 185
Buck, Dudley 245
Buckow, Carl Friedrich *75*
Buda 84
Budde, Jakob 16
Buffardin, P.G. 112
Bull, John 159, 160, 161, 172
Burgess the Younger, Henry 175
Burgo de Osma 220
Burkhard, Willy 244
Burney, Charles 176
Buron, Jehan *179*
Busch, Johann Daniel *80*
Busch, Johann Dietrich *80*
Busch, A. H. & Son *82*
Buttstedt, Johann Heinrich 89, 116
Buus, Jacob (or Jacques) 72, 73, 74, 159
Buxtehude, Anna Margrita 94
Buxtehude, Dietrich 43, 89, 92, 93, 94, 110, 112, 113, 115, 123, 173; Figs. 40, 66; *16, 79, 89*
Buxtehude, Johann *89*
Byrd, William 172
Byfield, John *158*

Cabanilles, Juan Bautista José 219; *206*
Cabeceiras de Basto *238, 240, 241*
Cabezón, Antonio de 172, 217, 218, 219, 220
Cage, John 246
Cahman, Hans Heinrich *81, 90, 93*
Cahman, Johan Niclas *93*
Caimari, Brothers *211*
Cairo Fig. 3
Caldara, Antonio 75, 119
Callaerts, Joseph 162
Callinet, Claude-Ignace *199*
Callinet, Joseph *199*
Callinet & Ducroquet *194*
Calvière, Guillaume-Antoine 193
Cambert, Robert 187
Cambridge 175; Figs. 20, 48; *157, 158, 161*
Candlyn, T. Frederick H. 245
Capella, Joan *205*
Cappel *39*; Fig. 13; *233*
Cara, Marchetto 73
Carcassonne *202*
Cardoso, António Estevan *223*
Carissimi, Giacomo 86, 87, 114
Carlier, Crespin 186
Carouge, Jacques *179*
Carré, Hendrik *144*
Carreira, Antonio 218
Carrera y Lanchares, Pedro 220
Cartaro, Mario *29*
Carvalho, João de Sousa 219
Casas, José *208*
Casavant, Brothers *271*
Casella, Alfredo 77
Casini, Giovanni Maria 77

Casparini, Adam-Horatius   41
Casparini, Dominik Adam   *116, 117, 118*
Casparini, Eugenio (Eugen Caspar)   59; *41, 118, 192*
Caspary, Reinerus   *84*
Cassel   117, 119
Cassler, G. Winston   245
Castile   *8*
Castro, José   *229*
Catarinozzi de Affile, Cesare II   *29*
Caudebec-en-Caux   *173, 176*
Cavaillé-Coll, Aristide   26, 27, 39, 59, 60, 177, 194, 195; Fig. 13; *77, 121, 170, 178, 179, 189, 194, 197, 199, 200, 201, 203, 204, 255*
Cavaillon   *198*
Cavalli, Pietro Francesco   187
Cavazzoni, Girolamo   72, 74
Cavazzoni, Marco Antonio   72
Celle   92, 115
Cellier, Alexandre-Eugène   198
Cellier, Jacques   48; *11–13*
Cera, Diego   *230*
Černohorský, Bohuslav Matěj   119
Cesti   114
Chadwick, George W.   245
Chalgrin, Jean   *194*
Chambonnières, Jacques Champion de   187, 188
Champion, Jacques   187
Chandos, Duke of   174
Chapman   *157*
Charles I, King   172
Charles II, King   87
Charles V, Emperor   83, 218; *209, 217*
Charles IX, King   186
Charleston   *247*
Charpentier, Jacques   246
Charpentier, Jean-Jacques   *194*
Chartres   55, 189; *177*
Chaumont, Lambert   161, 162, 188
Chauvet, Alexis   196
Chauvin & Swiderski   *172*
Chaynes, Charles   199
Checacupe   *218*
Chełmno   *101*
Chéron, Pierre   *173, 193*
Cherubini, Luigi   75
Chippendale, Thomas   175
Chrismann, Franz Xaver   *65, 71*
Christensen, Bernhard   243
Christian IV, King   *34, 77*
Christian Wilhelm of Brandenburg, Margrave   90
Ciaja, Azzolino Bernardino della   76
Ciconia, Johannes   82
Cima, Giovanni (Gian) Paolo   73
Cimino, Francesco   *26*
Cipri, Giovanni   *23*
Ciudad Rodrigo   74
Claesz, Allaert   *139*
Clausholm   *78*
Clavijo del Castillo, Bernardo   218
Clemens, Jacobus   85
Clement VIII, Pope   *28*
Clérambault, Louis-Nicolas   189, 191f.
Clercx, J. F.   *148*
Clérinx, Arnold   *149*
Clicquot, François-Henri   *22, 179, 184, 194–6, 199*
Clicquot, Louis-Alexandre   *178*

Clicquot, Robert   *189*
Clokey, Joseph Waddell   245
Cochereau, Pierre   198
Coci, Johannes   *47*
Cocquerel, Gilbert   *173, 176, 177*
Coelho, Manuel Rodrigues   218
Coimbra   219; *232, 233, 235*
Collet, Denis   Fig. 48
Colonna, Giovanni Paolo   *23*
Colorado Springs   *262*
Compenius, Esaias   27; *76, 77*
Compère, Loyset   185
Conceiçao, Fr. Diego da   218
Conceiçao, Lourenço da   *234*
Constance   83; *33*
Constantine V (Constantine Corpronymus)   12
Constantine VII   Fig. 3
Constantinople   112; Figs. 2, 3
Cooke, Benjamin   174
Copenhagen   89, 92, 94; *208*
Córdoba (Argentine)   76
Córdoba, Juan de   *205*
Corelli, Arcangelo   75, 112, 115
Cornet, Peeter   76, 159, 160
Correa de Arauxo, Francisco   218, 219
Corrette, Gaspard   188, 192, 193
Corrette, Michel   187, 188, 192, 193
Corrette, Michel II   193
Costeley, Guillaume   186
Cöthen   116, 117, 118, 119
Couperin, Armand-Louis   *194*
Couperin, Charles   187; *184*
Couperin, François I   43, 112, 113, 115, 187, 188, 189, 191, 193, 197
Couperin, François II   187, 188, 189, 190
Couperin, Gervais François   184
Couperin, Louis   187, 188; *184*
Courdrai the Younger, François   *52*
Covelens, Jan van   *139*
Coventry & Hollier   121, 173
Coxsun, Robert   171
Cracow   84; *106*
Crandell, Robert   245
Crecquillon, Josquin   217
Crecquillon, Thomas   217
Cremona   75
Croft, William   173
Cromwell, Oliver   172
Crotch, William   175, 176
Crüger, Johann   90
Cruz, Agostinho de   219
Császár   *115*
Ctesibius   10, 30, 59; Fig. 4
Cuenca   74
Cumming, Alexander   31
Cuzco   218; *219*

Dabenest, Nicolas   *175, 182*
Dalin, Eric   *93*
Dalitz, Friedrich Rudolf   *107*
Dallam, Thomas   Fig. 48; *157*
Dallery, Louis-Paul   *184*
Dallery, Pierre-François   *179, 184, 196*
Dallier, Henri   196
Dalza, Ambrosio   72
Dam, Lambertus van   *143*
Dandrieu, Jean-François   191, 192
Dandrieu, Pierre   187, 192
Danion, Georges   *177, 188, 255*

Danjou, Félix   194
Danzi, Franz   75
Danzig   89, 92, 120
Daquin, Louis-Claude   187, 192, 193
Darasse, Xavier   246
Darmstadt   120
Daroca   219; *205*
Daublaine & Callinet   45, *172, 185*
David, King   Figs. 50, 51; *72*
David, Johann Nepomuk   124
Davies, Walford   177
Dávila, Leonardo Fernández   *212*
Davis   *159*
Debierre, Louis   *202*
Debret, François   *200*
Decius, Nikolaus   90
DeLamarter, Eric   245
Delft   192
Delhaye, Jean-Joseph   *150, 154*
Deloye, Jean   *198*
Demessieux, Jeanne   198
Denis, Jean   187
Deslions, Marin   187
Desprez, Josquin   73
Deventer   161
Deventer, Matthijs van   *146*
D'Hondt, G.   *154*
Dickinson, Clarence   245
Dijon   54, 193; *56*
Dillens, Karel   *154*
Di Martino, Giovanni Domenico   27
Diruta   73
Distler, Hugo   124
Dobrau, Jan van   33
Doles, Johann Friedrich   116
Donovan, Richard F.   245
Dornel, Louis-Antoine   192
Douglas, Winfred   245
Dresden   84, 85, 87, 116, 117, 119, 121, 191; *52*
Dressel, Tobias   *171*
Dreux   *178*
Dropa, Matthias   *47*
Düben the Younger, Andreas   89
Dubois, Théodore   196
Du Caurroy, François Eustache   186
Ducharme, Guy   245
Duchenski, Roman   *103*
Ducroquet   *194*
Dufay, Guillaume   83, 159; *7*
Du Mage, Pierre   191
Du Mont, Henry   162, 187, 188
Dunstable, John   171
Dupré, Marcel   162, 195, 197, 198
Dupuis, Thomas Sanders   175
Durante, Francesco   77
Duret   *194*
Duruflé, Maurice   198
Duvivier, Jean   *183*
Duyschot, Jan   *139, 140, 142*

Eben, Petr   244
Eberlin, Johann Ernst   117, 118
Ebersmünster   *192*
Ebert, Jörg   *60*
Ebner, Wolfang   87, 187
Eccard, Johann   90
Echevarría, Pedro de Liborna   *208, 213, 214, 215, 216, 217*
Effinger, Cecil   245

Egedacher, Johann Christoph *66, 69*
Egedacher, Johann Ignaz *59, 69*
Eisenach 87, 109, 111, 112, 113, 114
Eisenbarth, Ludwig *59*
Eisenbarth, Wolfgang *59*
Eisenmenger, Philip *88*
Ekengren,Jonas *92*
Eleizgaray *208*
Elgar, Sir Edward William 177
Elías, José 219
Elías, Santo 219
Elizabeth I, Queen Fig. 69
Elliot, Thomas *165*
Elliot & Hill *166*
Elmore, Robert 245
Ely *166*
Emanuel, Carl Philipp 117, 119
Emborg, Jens L. 243
Englert, Giuseppe G. 246
Englund, Einar 243
Erb, Marie-Joseph 196
Erbach, Christian 85, 86
Erben, Henry *244, 248*
Erfurt 109, 110, 111, 112, 113, 116, 117, 119, 120; *57*
Ericsson, Hans-Olaf 246
Ernen *129*
Ernst August, Duke 116, 117
Eschwege *58*
Escorial, El *208, 209, 216*
Esslingen 120
Esterházy family 119
Esteves Pereira, L.A. *236*
Estrada, Salvador Fig. 72; *206*
Eton *164, 167*
Eule, Hermann *45, 51, 119*
Eustache, D. *170*
Eustache, G. *170*
Eustache, Jean *183*
Evers, Edo *40*
Evora *231, 233*
Exner, Johannes *273*
Eyck, Jan van *8*
Eynde, Jacob van *152*

Facchetti, Giovanni Battista *23, 25*
Faenza 70
Faleiro, Antonio Pedro *210*
Farnam, Lynwood 245
Faro *233*
Fasolo, Giovanni Battista 75
Felton, William 175
Ferdinando II de' Medici 76
Feroci, Francisco 74, 77
Ferreira da Cunha, Gabriel *235*
Fertörákos *114*
Février, Pierre 193
Feyring, Philipp *244*
Fiebig, Kurz 124
Figulus, Wolfgang 90
Fink, Christian 120
Fischer, Johann Kaspar Ferdinand 89, 110
Fischer, Michael Gotthard 117, 120
Flecha, Giuseppe *208*
Fleming, William B. *21*
Flensburg *34*
Flentrop Fig. 68; *119, 139, 144, 222, 233, 234, 235, 269*
Fleury, André 198
Flor, Christian 92, 94

Florence 73, 74; *6, 24*
Flügel, Gustav 120
Fogelberg, Sven *89*
Fogliano, Jacopo 72
Fonseca, José Joachim da *232*
Fontana, Fabrizio 75
Fontanes, Simaõ *236*
Forceville, Jean-Baptiste *150, 154*
Forkel, Johann Nikolaus 111, 177, 195
Formentelli, Bartolomeo *191, 268*
Förner, Christian 34
Forqueray 193
Fortier, Toussaint *178*
Förtsch, Johann Philipp 88
Foss, Lucas 246
Foubert, R. *177*
Fourcade 193
Framlingham *158*
France, William 245
Franck, César 119, 121, 162, 193, 194, 195, 196, 197; *203*
Franck, Johann 90; *21*
Frauenberg near Admont *65*
Frederick II the Great, King 116, 119
Frederiksborg (Hillerød) *76, 77*
Freiberg 60, 116; *42, 43*
Freiburg im Breisgau 83
Freinsberg: see Guilain
Freising *33*
Frels, Rubin S. *229*
Frescobaldi, Girolamo 73, 74, 75, 76, 85, 87, 94, 112, 114 115, 187, 191, 193, 219; *21*
Fresta *92*
Freundt, Johann Georg *64*
Fribourg 83; *137*
Friedell, Harold 245
Friedemann, Wilhelm 117, 119
Friedrichs (Friederici) *141*
Frigyes, Hidas 244
Fritzsche, Gottfried *47*
Fritzsche, Hans Christoph *47, 79, 90*
Frobenius *79, 81, 82, 85, 89*
Frobenius & Sønner, T. *78, 273*
Froberger, Johann Jakob 76, 86, 87, 110, 114, 187
Frombork *104*
Froment, Gustave 41
Frye, Walter 83
Fryklöf, Harald 244
Fugger family 85
Füglister, Hans-J. *123, 129*
Führer, Alfred 120; *267*
Furtado, Manuel *236*
Furtwängler & Hammer *40*
Furtwängler & Söhne *83*

Gabler, Joseph Figs. 48; *48, 50*
Gabrieli, Andrea 72, 73, 74, 85, 161
Gabrieli, Giovanni 72, 73, 74, 76, 86, 161
Gabry *141*
Gadault, Charles *177, 186*
Gade, Niels Wilhelm 243
Gagnebin, Henri 244
Galliera, Armando 75
Garrels, Rudolph *143*
Gartner, Antonin *111*
Gartner, Josef *108*
Gascongne, Mathieu 185
Gatto, Ignaz *67, 69*
Gattringer, Franz *74*

Gau 203
Gaul, Harvey B. 245
Gauntlett, Henry John 41, 177
Gaytán, Juan *217*
Gehren 109
Geiser, Walther 244
Geminiani, Francesco 175
Gemmelich, Georg *64*
Geneva 244, *256, 264, 280*
Geoffroy, Jean-Nicolas 189
George I, King 174
George III, King *164, 243*
Georgi, Johann Adam *42*
Gerardeschi, Giuseppe 77
Gerber, Heinrich Nicolaus 116
Gerhardt, Paul 90
German, Eric Mansson *92*
Gerritsz, Cornelius *138*
Gerritsz, Peter *138*
Gesualdo, Carlo 76
Geurts the Elder *150*
Gheyn, Matthias van den 161
Gibbons, Christopher 87, 173
Gibbons, Edward 173
Gibbons, Grinling Fig. 70; *159*
Gibbons, Orlando 172, 173
Giessen 120
Gigault, Nicolas 187, 188, 189, 192
Gigout, Eugène 193, 195, 196
Gisors 57
Giussani, Severo 75
Glatter-Götz, Josef von *260*
Gloton *179*
Głowacki, Błazej *106*
Głowiński, Jan *103*
Goebel, B. *102, 105*
Goebel, J. *107*
Goericke, Johann *51*
Goethe, Johann Wolfgang von 111
Goll, Friedrich *131*
Gombault Rogerie, Brother *177*
Gonzalez *177, 180, 184, 187, 188, 255*
Goode, Jack C. 245
Goodrich, William M. *246*
Gorecki, Henryk Mikolaj 246
Görlitz 59; *41, 192*
Gotha 87, 111, 113, 117
Gottfuss, Hans Fig. 68
Götz, Josef Matthias *59, 69*
Gouault *177*
Gouda *144*
Goujon, Jean *175*
Gounod, Charles 119
Graaf, G.A.C. de *215*
Grado Fig. 15
Gräfenroda 111, 116
Graindorge, Arnold *149*
Granada *212*
Grañera, Thomás *205*
Granlund, C. *97*
Grass, Johann Michael *74*
Graun, Carl Heinrich 119
Graz 74; *68*
Great Packington 174; *163*
Grefinger, Wolfgang 84
Green, Samuel 175
Greene, Maurice 175, 176
Greiter, Matthias 90
Gren, Jonas *95, 96*
Grenzing, Gerhard *211*

Grigny, Nicolas de 112, 115, 188, 189, 190, 191, 194, 197
Grob, Melchior *133*
Groningen 92
Grönlunds *88*
Grönvall, J. *92*
Grunenwald, Jean-Jacques 198
Grünpeck, Joseph 84
Guami, Giuseppe 73
Guéranger, Dom Prosper 194
Guest, George 176
Guilain, Jean Adam Guillaume 191
Guilbert, Martin *175*
Guillet Karel (Charles) 160
Guillou, Jean 198, 246; *281*
Guilmant, Alexandre 195, 196, 197, 198; *21*
Guimarães *236, 238, 241*
Gutiérrez, Esteban *220*
Gutschenritter *178*
Györ *112*

Haarlem 55, 161; Fig. 7; *141, 243*
Haas, Friedrich Fig. 25; *126, 127, 131, 137*
Hackl, Johann Joseph *52*
Haderslev *83*
Haeghen, Nicolaas van *150*
Haerpfer-Erman *175, 189*
Hagerbeer, Galtus & Germer Fig. 68; *141*
Hagerbeer, Jacobus Galtus van *139*
Hague, The 162
Halberstadt 30, 31, 54, 109; Figs. 23, 53
Halffter, Cristobal 246
Halle 89, 90, 92, 109, 116, 117, 174
Hällestad *91*
Hälsingborg 94; *89*
Hamburg 60, 82, 89, 91, 92, 114, 117, 119; Figs. 42, 43; *39, 83, 92*
Hambraeus, Bengt 244, 246
Hamilton, David 39
Hammarberg, Nils *97*
Hammer, Emil *258*
Hammerschmidt 114
Handel, Georg Frideric 75, 94, 109, 110, 116, 118, 173, 174, 176; *16, 21, 156, 163, 164*
Hanff, Johann Nicolaus 92, 93, 94
Hanover 89, *258*
Hansen, Emil *83*
Hardouin-Mansart, Jules *186*
Harris, Renatus 172; *157, 159*
Harrison, G. Donald *249*
Harrison & Harrison *157, 161, 166*
Hartmann, Johann Peter Emilius 243
Hartmann, Philippe *195, 201*
Hartop *157*
Harwood, Basil 177
Hasse *103*
Hasse, Karl 124
Hasselfelde 109
Hassler, Hans Leo 85, 86, 90
Hassler, Jacob 85
Hässler, Johann Wilhelm 117
Hassler, Kaspar 85
Haydn, (Franz) Joseph 77, 119, 193
Haydn, Johann Michael 119
Hayes, Philip 175
Heide, Johann *80, 81*
Heidelberg 85
Heiller, Anton 124
Heinemann Fig. 68
Heininen, Paavo 244

Heinrich Julius, Duke *77*
Hellwig, Johann *100*
Helsingborg 93
Helsingør (Elsinore) 93; *79*
Hencke, Johann *72, 73*
Henri II, King 186
Henri III, King 186
Henri IV, King 186
Henry *196*
Hensberg, Miguel *232*
Hereford 175
Hering, Berthold Fig. 66
Heringen 116
Herman, George *88*
Hermans, G. *180*
Hernández, Gonzalo *217*
Hero of Alexandria 10; Fig. 1
Herrera, Benito Gomez de *232*
Herrera, Juan de *208*
Herzogenburg *272*
Hesse, Adolf Friedrich 120, 195
Hestre, Oudin Fig. 48
Hewitt, James 244
Heymann (Neumann), Christian *101*
Hildebrandt, Zacharias *37, 45, 51, 52*
Hill, Arthur George Figs. 63, 64, 65, 66, 68, 72; *167*
Hill, Eugene 245
Hill, William 177; *157, 165, 169*
Hill & Son 166
Hillebrand, Harry Fig. 63
Hindelang *53*
Hindemith, Paul 124
Hinrichsen, Jürgen *83*
Hocqué the Elder, Floris *149*
Hocqué, Floris II Fig. 68
Hofer, Jörg *56*
Höfer, Matthäus *71*
Hoffmann, E. T. A. 120
Hofhaimer, Paul 83, 84, 85; Fig. 62
Høgenhaven, Knud 243
Hohenems *62*
Hökhuvud *97*
Holbein the Younger, Hans 49
Holtkamp, Walter *262*
Homilius, Gottfried August 116
Honegger, Arthur 199
Hooghuys, Louis *152*
Hook, George G. *245*
Hook & Hastings *250*
Hope-Jones, Robert 41
Horn, Karl Friedrich 177
Horst, Anthon van der *163*
Hötzel, Peter *65*
Howells, Herbert 177
Hradetzky, Gerhard *69*
Hradetzky, Gregor *72*
Huber, Klaus 246
Hulenkampf, Johann Heinrich *233*
Hummel, Johann Nepomuk 117, 120
Humpel, Caspar *60*
Hunter, Alfred *158*
Hurlebusch, Conrad Frederik 161
Husum 92, 94
Huss, Berendt *38, 49*
Hutchings, George S. *253*
Hutchings-Votey Organ Company *254*

Ibach, Adolfo *206*
Igra *110*

Ileborgh, Adam 82, 92
Indy, Vincent d' 195, 196
Inger, M. A. A. *273*
Ingout, Robert *187*
Innsbruck 84; *33, 60, 61*
Isaac, Heinrich 83, 85
Isnard, Jean-Esprit *193*
Isnard, Joseph *191, 193*
Ives, Charles 245
Izaguirre, Félix de *220*

Jackson, John T. & Son *169*
Jacob, Georges 197
Jacobsz, Jan *139*
Jacopo da Bologna 70
Jadot *194*
James I, King 172
James, Philip 245
Jan & Lublina 84
Janáček, Leoš 244
Janequin, Clément 85
Jardine, George 252
Jardine, George & Son *248, 252*
Jarlåsa *96*
Jedrzejów *19*
Jehmlich *52*
Jena 111
Jennens, Charles *163*
Jennings, Henry *157*
Jensen & Thomsen *82*
Jeppesen, Knud 243
Jiménez, José 219
João, Master *232*
Johann Ernst, Duke 115, 116
Johansen, Jasper *39*
Johnson, David N. 245
Johnson, Niels *251*
Jongen, Joseph 162
Jordan, Abraham 172, 174; *162*
Josquin Desprez 73, 85
Josseline, Antoine *173, 175, 176, 177*
Josseline, François 186
Joure *278*
Jousse *180*
Joyeuse, Jean de Fig. 7; *170, 188*
Julius III, Pope *61*
Jullien, Gilles 188, 189

Kabeláč, Miloslav 244
Kagel, Mauricio 246
Kaltschmidt, F. W. *107*
Kaltschmidt, Johann Christoph *16*
Kamiński, Heinrich 124
Kamiński, Zygmunt *104, 107*
Kampen 162
Kansas City *21*
Karam, Frederik 245
Karg-Elert, Sigfrid 123, 244
Karges, Wilhelm 109
Karlen, Felix *129*
Karow *46*
Karstensen, Peter *82, 83*
Kauffmann, Georg Friedrich 89, 109
Kauffmann, Johann M. *64, 73*
Kaunas 120
Kayser, Leif 243
Kazimierz Dolny *99*
Kee, Cor 163
Kee, Piet 163

Keeble, John 174
Keeley, P.C. 250
Keiser, Reinhard 115
Keller, Homer 245
Kellner, Johann Christoph 117
Kellner, Johann Peter 116
Kemper Figs. 63–6; 34
Kemper, Emanuel 104
Kemper, Karl 34, 47
Kemptcn 119
Kerckhoven, Abraham van den 160
Kerll, Johann Kaspar 86, 87, 89, 114
Kern, Alfred 171, 185
Khoffler, Jakob 64
Kimball Organ Company 251
Kindermann, Johann Erasmus 86, 87
Kircher, Athanasius 14
Kirchhoff, Gottfried 89
Kirnberger, Johann Philipp 116, 193
Kittel, Johann Christian 117, 120
Klais, Johannes Fig. 64; 230, 270
Klapmeyer, Johann Heinrich 47
Klapmeyer, Johann Werner 47
Klebe, Giselher 124
Kleber, Leonhard 83
Klemm, Johann 85, 86
Klengel, August Alexander 117
Klerk, Albert de 163
Kleuker, Detlef 281
Klosterneuburg 64
Knab, Armin 124
Knecht, Justin Heinrich 118, 120
Kneller, Andreas 92
Kodály, Zoltán 244
Koetsier, Jan 163
Köhler, Ernst 195
Kohns, Ellis B. 245
Kokkonen, Joonas 243 f.
Kolb, Karlmann 89
Konopka, Eduard 129
Körnelein, M. 139
Köster, Hans Fig. 65
Kotter, Hans 83, 84
Koulen, Henri 171
Kramer, Simpert 53
Kraśnik 84
Krebaum, Friedrich 58
Krebs, Frederik 171
Krebs, Johann Ludwig 117
Krebs, Johann Tobias 116, 117
Krejči, Miloslav 244
Krempe 47
Krenek, Ernst 124
Krenn, Brothers 65, 68
Kreutzbach, Urban 45
Krieger the Younger, Johann 88
Krieger the Elder, Johann Philipp 76, 88, 109
Kröger, Henning Fig. 67
Krüger, Hans 114; 101
Kruszewski, Czesla 105
Kuchař, Jan Křtitel 119
Kuhn, Theodor 50, 64, 122, 126, 127, 128, 129, 130, 136, 137, 204
Kuhnau, Johann 109 f., 112, 117; 45
Kuusisto, Ilkka 244
Kuusisto, Taneli 243
Kyburz, Louis 137

La Barre, Joseph Chabanceau de 187
La Barre, Pierre Chabanceau de 187

Ladegast, Friedrich 37, 51, 121
Ladurner, Ignaz Anton 193
La Ferté-Bernard 174
La Flèche 180, 181
Lalande, Micheal-Richard 190; 184
Lamann, Hermann 121
Lamego 20, 238
Lämmerhirt, Elisabeth 114
Landini, Francesco 70; 6
Lang 127
Langensalza 117
Langgaard, Rued 243
Langhedul, Matthieu 184
Langlais, Jean 198
Lantins, Arnold de 83
Laon 189
Larsson, Rolf 97
Las Casas, Ignacio Mariano de 225
Lasceux, Guillaume 193
Lasso, Orlando di 85, 114
Lauingen 84
Lebègue, Nicolas-Antoine 187, 188, 189, 190, 191, 192
Lechesne, T. 203
Ledou, Boudewijn 151
Leeuwen, W. van 140
Lefebre, Charles 175
Lefébure-Wély, Louis James Alfred 194, 195
Lefebvre, Jean-Baptiste Nicolas 173, 175
Lefebvre, Louis 173
Leffloth, Johann Matthias 174
Le Franc, Martin 7
Le Grand Andely 182
Legrant, Wilhelmus 82
Legrenzi, Giovanni 75, 112
Legros family 191
Leguay, Jean-Pierre 198
Leipzig 84, 109, 110, 111, 112, 113, 115, 116, 117, 118, 119, 120, 123
Le Jeune, Claude 186
Le Mire, Alphonse 10
Lemmens, Nicolas Jacques 162, 195, 197
Lenel, Ludwig 245
Leo, Hans 85
León 5
Leoninus 185
Leopold, Prince 116
Le Pescheur, Pierre 179, 184
Le Petit Andely 187
Le Picard, Antoine 153
Le Picard, Jean-Baptiste 145
Lépine, François 191
Lépine the Elder, Jean-François 172, 191
Lérida 206
Le Royer, Charles 198
Lesecq, Jean 187
Lesselier, Guillaume (Lesselie William) 182
Lesur, Daniel-Jean-Yves 198
Lété, Nicolas-Antoine 201
Leu, Johann Christoph 127
Levasseur, Ambroise 180
Lewiston 248
Leżajsk 49; 103
Lhôte, Georges 74, 135, 137
Lidón, José 220
Liège 57, 85, 161, 187, 194; 149
Ligeti, György 246
Lindau 81
Lindberg, Oskar 244

Lindner, Elias 42
Linek, Jiří Ignác 119
Lingiardi 77
Linköping 91
Linnell, John 175; Fig. 71
Linz 266
Lisbon 219; 233, 237
L-Isle-sur-la-Sorgue Fig. 40; 198
Lissewege 151
Liszt, Franz 7, 111, 119, 122, 162, 194; 37, 75, 119, 137
Litaize, Gaston 198
Liverpool 177
Llissa (Llussa), Francisco 219
Lloréns, Antonio 206
Lobenstein 116
Lobo, Heitor 232
Locke, Matthew 173
Löfvander, C.R. 96
Logteren, Jan van 141
Lohet, Simon 85, 160
London 41, 47, 87, 171, 172, 174, 175, 176, 177; Fig. 70; 159, 160
Longas, José de 205
Looser, Joseph 133
Looser, Wendelin 133
López, Germán 213
López, Miguel 219
Lorentz, Balthasar 34
Lorentz, Johann 34, 79, 82
Lorentzen, Boye 80
Lorenzo, Domenico di 24
Lorenzo di Giacomo da Prato 23
Lorenzo the Magnificent, Duke 83
Loret, Clément 194, 195
Lorette, François 232
Loret-Vermeersch, François Bernard 150
Louis XIII, King 180, 181
Louis XIV, King 186, 188, 189, 190; 188
Lövstabruk 93
Lübeck 60, 92, 93, 94, 115, 124, 173; Figs. 65–7; 16, 38
Lübeck, Vincent 92, 114; 34
Lucchinetti, Giovanni Bernardo 75
Luçon 202
Luis, Damián 207
Lully, Jean-Baptiste 88, 187, 189, 190
Lund, C.A. 98
Lund, Carl Johan 95
Lüneburg 92, 114, 191
Lupe, Gaudioso 205
Lupe, Guillaume de 205
Luscinius 83
Luther, Martin 90
Luython, Charles (Carl) 160
Luzzaschi, Luzzasco 72, 76
Lyons 191, 193; 204, 255

Maass, Nikolaus 34, 78, 82
Maastricht 162
Maccarinelli, Armando 26
Mácha, Otmar 244
Machaut, Guillaume de 7, 70
McKay, George Frederik 245
McKinley, Carl 245
Macque, Jean (Giovanni) de 73, 76, 159, 213, 216
Madrid 219, 220; 208
Magdeburg 90, 109, 120
Magen, Brothers 172

Maggenberg, Pierre 122
Mahns, Mathias (Meister Matze) *80*
Mahommed III, Sultan Fig. 69
Mailly, Alphonse 161
Mainz 83
Maione, Ascanio 72, 73, 218
Majorca 205
Malaga 220
Malamini, Baldassarre *23*
Maleingreau, Paul de 162
Malines *154, 208*
Mallén, Pascual de *205*
Mander, Noël Fig. 70; *156*
Manila 230
Mannheim 117, 119
Mantua 76
Manufacture des Grandes Orgues de Genève *256*
Manz, Paul 245
Marbella *272*
Marcellinus, Ammianus *4*
Marchand, Louis 115, 116, 188, 191
Marckhstainer, Leonhard *64*
Marcussen Fig. 65; *34, 44, 80, 141, 257, 266*
Marcussen, Jürgen *83*
Marcussen & Reuter *82*
Marcussen & Søn *80, 86, 93*
Mareschall, Samuel 160
Marie-Thérèse of Spain 187
Markull, Friedrich Wilhelm 111
Marmoutier Fig. 13; *190, 192*
Marol, Jean *281*
Marrigues, Jean-Nicolas 193
Marsh, John 176
Martin, Frank 244
Martin, Emil *119*
Martínez Oxinagas, Joaquin 200
Martínez y Alcarría, José *206*
Martini, Giovanni Battista 77, 119
Martino, Giovanni Domenico di *27*
Martolo, Próspero *213*
Marx, E. *54*
Marzola, Pietro 77
Mason, Lowell 245
Matteson, Johann 94, 173; *16*
Matthias Corvinus, King 84
Maucher *126, 127*
Maugars, André 76
Mauracher, Josef *66, 67*
Mauracher, Matthäus *68, 71*
Maurer, Ferdinand *72*
Maximilian I, Emperor 83; Fig. 62
Mazarin, Jules, Cardinal 187
Meckenem, I. van Fig 6
Meek, Kenneth 245
Megève 88
Meiningen 111
Melcher, Hans *131*
Memling, Hans *8*
Menalt, Gabriel 219
Mendelssohn-Bartholdy, Félix 111, 120, 121, 173, 176, 177, 194
Mendes Coutinho, António *238*
Mentasti Fig. 40; *198*
Merano *268*
Merckel *56*
Merikanto, Oskar 243
Merkel, Gustav Adolf 121, 122
Merklin, Albert *217*
Merklin, Joseph *137, 199*

Merklin, Michel *204*
Merklin & Schütze *175, 196*
Merseburg 109, 120, 122; *37*
Mersenne, Marin 55, 76, 186, 188
Merula, Tarquinio 75
Merulo, Claudio 72, 73, 74, 75, 161
Messiaen, Olivier 198f., 246
Metall, Matthias *73*
Methuen Organ Company *249*
Metzler, A. & Fils *264*
Metzler, O. *131, 132, 134*
Metzler, O. & Sons *161, 261*
Meun (or Meung), Jean de *8*
Mexico City *219, 221, 222*
Meyerbeer 122
Michálek, František 244
Micheelsen, Hans Friedrich 124
Michel, Merklin & Kuhn *121*
Middelburg *138, 140*
Mieck *44*
Mietke *104*
Mikolaj z Krakowa 84
Milan 73, 74, 75; *197*
Milani, Antoine *183*
Milhaud, Darius 199
Miroir, Eloi-Nicolas-Marie 193
Mizler, L.C. 120
Moberg, Brothers *90, 91*
Modena *25*
Modena, Julius de 217
Moeschinger, Albert 244
Møgeltønder *84*
Moitessier, Prosper-Antoine 41
Molins, Pierre de 70
Möller, Jacques *153*
Möller, Louis *153*
Möller, Matthias P. *262*
Møller, Svend-Ove 243
Mols 41
Moncel, Théodose, comte Du 41
Mondsee 82
Monnikendam, Marius 162
Montano, Giovanni Battista *28*
Monteverdi, Claudio 18, 72, 114
Montserrat 219
Moore, Douglas 245
Mooser, Aloys *137*
Morales, Cristóbal de 217
Morcote Fig. 7; *123*
Moreau, Jean (Jacob) François *144*
Morel, François 245
Moreno y Polo, Juan 219
Moretti, Felice (Padre Davide) 77
Morhardt, Peter 92
Morley, Thomas *172*
Moscow *121*
Mosengel, Johann Josua *41*
Moser, Rudolf 244
Moucherel, Christophe *191*
Moucherel, Claude 170
Moulu, Pierre 185
Moyreau, Christophe 193
Moyse, Johann *67*
Mozart, Wolfgang Amadeus 77, 111, 118, 119, 176, 193, 194; *66, 137*
Mudroch, Jan *109*
Muffat, Georg 76, 88, 89
Muffat, Gottlieb 89
Muhleisen, Ernst *183*
Muhleisen & Kern *190*

Mulet, Henri 197
Mühlhausen 109, 112, 115, 116
Mülisch, Gregor *82*
Müller, Christian (or Christiaan) Fig. 7; *141, 143, 243*
Müller, Christoph *111*
Müller, Hartvig Jochum *85*
Müller, Marian 75
Müller, Paul *88*
Müller, Pieter *139*
Müller-Zürich, Paul 244
Mulliner, Thomas 171
Munari, Pellegrino *25*
Mundt, Johannes *108*
Munich 82, 85, 87, 89, 121
Murgatroyd, Vernon 245
Muri 52; Fig. 48; *131, 132*
Murray M. Harris Organ Company *21*
Murrill, Herbert 177
Murschhauser, Franz Xaver Anton 89
Müthel, Johann Gottfried 116
Mutin, Charles *121, 194, 197, 200*

Naber, C.F.A. *139*
Nachtigall, Othmar: see Luscinius 83
Nadreau, Jacques *180*
Nantua *201*
Nantucket *246*
Naples 75; *27, 29*
Nares, James 174
Nasarre, José *221, 222*
Naumburg 119; *51*
Near, Gerald 245
Neidhardt & Lhôte *135, 137*
Nenning 1, 2
Nenninger, Leopold *53*
Neuberg on the Mürz *68*
Neuknecht *171*
Neumann, Christian; see: Heymann
Neumann, Hubert *61*
Nevers 191
Newcastle upon Tyne 175
New Haven *254*
New York *21*
Nibelle, Henri 196
Nicolai, Johann Georg 116f.
Niedermeyer, Louis 194
Niehoff family 57
Niehoff, Nicolaas *149*
Nielsen, Carl 243
Nijkerk *146*
Nikolai, Philipp 90
Nitrowski, Daniel *102, 104*
Nivers, Guillaume-Gabriel 187, 188, 189, 191
Noberg, Harry *94*
Noble, T. Tertius 245
Noehren, Robert 245
Noordt, Anthoni van 162
Norden Fig. 47; *40*
Nordström, Sven *98*
Nørgaard, Per 243
Nørholm, Ib 243
Nörmiger, August 84
Novello, Vincent 177
Nuremberg 85, 87, 174; *59, 275*
Nyborg *276*
Nylander, Jonas *94*
Nystedt, Knut 244

Obrecht, Jacob 159, 185

Ochsenhausen 49; *48, 53*
Odense *86*
Oesterlen, Dieter *258*
Offenbach, Jacques 194
Ohrdruf 111, 114, 116
Olague, Bartolomeo de 199
Oldovini, Pascoal Caetano *231, 233*
Old Radnor *155*
Oley, Johann Christoph 116
Oliwa (Gdańsk) *107*
Olson, Daniel 244
Olsson, Otto Emanuel 244
Oporto 218; *226, 234, 239*
Organería española *208–10, 213, 214, 217*
Orléans 193
Ortigue, Joseph d' 178
Ortiz, Diego 194; *206*
Ostris, Perris Fig. 72
Oswald von Wolkenstein 83
Ott, Paul *39, 40, 47, 49*
Ottobeuren 52; *18, 53, 56*
Ottoboni, Cardinal 116
Övertorneå *88*
Oxford 161, 171, 175, 176
Oxinagas, Joaquin Martinez 219

Pablo, Luis de 246
Pachelbel, Johann 82, 87, 88, 89, 109, 110, 111, 112, 114, 244; *21*
Pachelbel, Karl Theodor 244
Pachelbel, Wilhelm Hieronymus 82
Padova, Bartolino da 66
Padovano, Annibale 72, 73, 74
Padua 73, 161, 176
Paine, John Knowles 245
Paix, Jacob 84
Paléro, Francisco Perez (Fernández) 217
Palestrina, Giovanni Pierluigi da 85, 119
Palma de Mallorca *211*
Parabosco, Girolamo 72, 73
Paris 26, 45, 87, 88, 120, 160, 161, 171, 185, 186, 187, 188, 189, 190, 191, 192, 193, 194, 195, 198; Fig. 35; *121, 179, 184, 186, 188, 192, 194, 200, 203, 255*
Parker, Horatio 245
Parker, Thomas *163*
Parry, Sir (Charles) Hubert (Hastings) 177
Parviainen, Jarmo 244
Pasquini, Bernardo 75
Pasquini, Ercole 76
Passau 88; *59*
Pau, Père Fig. 72
Paumann, Conrad 82, 159
Paumgartner, Anton 82
Pearson, J.L. *167*
Pease, Lancelot Fig. 48; *157*
Pécs 84
Peeters, Flor 162
Peirce, George *246*
Pellegrini, Vincenzo 73
Pelplin 92; *102*
Pepin the Short, King 12
Pepping, Ernst 124
Pepusch, Johann Christoph 174, 176
Peraza, Francisco de 218
Perckhammer, Hans *60*
Pereboom *145*
Pereira da Costa, Luis 234
Perez de Lara, José *222*
Perotinus 185

Perpignan 189; *170, 206*
Persichetti, Vincent 245
Peruzzi, Baldassarre Fig. 47
Peschard, Albert 41
Peteghem the Elder, Pieter van *150*
Petershausen 75
Petrali, Vincenzo 77
Petrucci, Ottaviano de 72
Peyer, Max *64*
Peyroulous, Antoine *191*
Pfliegler, Anton *73*
Pforzheim 83
Philadelphia Fig. 45; *21, 244*
Philip II, King 218, 219; *208, 209*
Philips, Peter 76, 159, 160, 161, 172
Piantanida *197*
Piazza, Gaetano 74
Piccinelli, Alfredo *24*
Piccinelli, Emilio *31, 32*
Pierné, Gabriel 196
Piffero, Giovanni di Antonio Fig. 46
Pillon, Germain *186*
Pilotti, Gioacchino *31*
Pirchner, Johann *70*
Piroye, Charles 192
Pirro, André 196
Pisac *218*
Pistoia 45
Piston, Walter 245
Poffa, Giacomo 77
Poglietti, Alessandro 87
Poitiers 197; *21, 196*
Polaroli, Carlo Francesco 75
Polcyn, Robert *103, 106*
Polotsk *117*
Poltava 112
Pommersfelden Fig. 49
Portland *271*
Poulenc, Francis 199
Pouville *185*
Praetorius, Hieronymus 92
Praetorius the Elder, Jakob 92
Praetorius the Younger, Jakob 89, 92
Praetorius, Johann Stephanius 92
Praetorius, Michael 30, 54, 55, 90, 91, 92, 109; Figs. 22, 66; *77*
Prague 85, 88, 119, 160, 174; *108, 110*
Preston, Thomas 171, 172
Puche, Damián *205*
Puebla 219, 220, 229
Puget, Eugène *197*
Puget, Maurice *170, 191, 197*
Puget, Théodore *179, 197*
Puig-Roget, Henriette 198
Pujol, Jean *170*
Pujol, Juan 219
Purcell, Daniel 173
Purcell, Henry 173, 175; *159*
Pürro, Heinrich *137*
Purvis, Richard 245
Puteheim, Georg von 82
Pyanet *203*

Quantz, Johann Joachim 116
Quedlinburg 109
Quellin, Erasmus II *150*
Querétaro *225*
Quesnel, Philippe *187*
Quoirin, Pascal *280*

Raastad, Niels Otto 243
Rabiny 199
Racquet, Charles 186
Radavičius, Juozapas *116, 120*
Raison, André 188, 189, 192
Rameau, Jean-Philippe 193
Rathgeber, Valentin 89
Ratzeburg *279*
Rautavaara, Einujuhani 244
Raxach, Enrique 246
Read, Gardner 245
Reading, John 175
Rébillé, Nicolas *184*
Reda, Siegfried 124
Redford, John 171, 172, 173
Reger, Max 77, 123, 124, 243, 244, 246
Reicha, Antonín 119, 194
Reichardt, Georg Heinrich 116
Reichel, Bernard 244
Reimann, Aribert 124
Reina 70
Reinburg, Charles *187*
Reinburg, Félix 77
Reincken (Reinken), Johann Adam (Jan Adams) 92, 93, 112, 114, 115, 117
Reiner, Karel 244
Reiser *48*
Rembt, Johann Ernst 117
Rende: see Aranda
Rendsburg *44*
Respighi, Ottorino 77
Reubke, Julius 122, 162
Reutter the Elder, Georg 89
Rheims 48, 190; Fig. 48; *11, 12*
Rheinau *126, 127*
Rheinberger, Joseph Gabriel 121
Rhys, Philip ap 171
Ribe *81*
Richard, Etienne 187
Richborn, Joachim Fig. 65; *84*
Richborn, Otto Dietrich Fig. 66
Richter, Anton *109*
Ridges, Joseph H. *251*
Rieger Orgelbau *64, 73, 260, 279*
Riepp, Karl Joseph *18, 56, 199*
Riga 116, 117; *119*
Riga, Anton *109*
Rijnsburch, Jan Pieters van 162
Rinck, Christian Heinrich 117, 120
Ringerink, Henrich *34*
Rinkart, Martin 90
Rist, Johann 90
Ritter, August Gottfried 120
Roberday, François 187, 188
Roberts, Myron 245
Robertsbridge 54, 70, 171
Rodez *188*
Roermond *145*
Roethinger, Edmond *171*
Roger-Ducasse, Jules-Aimable 197
Rogers, Benjamin 173
Rogers, James H. 245
Roggenburg *53*
Rojas, Juan de *222*
Rolland, Romain 175
Rombaut, Walram *151*
Rome 75, 76, 86, 87, 88; Fig. 3; *28*
Roosevelt, Hilborne L. Fig. 45
Ropartz, Guy 196
Roqués, Pedro *212*

Roseingrave, Thomas   176
Rosenberg, Hilding   244
Rosenmüller   114
Roskilde   *82*
Rossi, Michelangelo   75
Rossini, Gioacchino Antonio   77
Rostock   *54*
Rötha   *45*
Rother, Paul   *44*
Rothwell   *159*
Rottensteen-Pock, Hermann Raphaëlis   *82*
Rotterdam   161; *269*
Rouen   57, 186, 189, 192; *175, 182*
Rousseau, Jean-Jacques   Fig. 1
Röver, Johann Heinrich   *38, 49*
Rovigo, Francesco   74
Roxbury   *253*
Royan   *263*
Ruche   *201*
Rudolfstadt   117
Ruffati, Brothers   *25*
Rühling, Johann   84
Runbäck, Albert   244
Rung-Keller, Paul S.   243
Russell, William   176
Rutland Psalter   Fig. 51
Rylander, C.   *91*

Sachs, Hans   90
Sachter, Simon   120
Sadkowski, Szymon   *106*
Sagan   82
Sainctot-Chemin   *174*
Saint-Bertrand-de-Comminges   *172*
Saint-Donat-sur-l'Herbasse   *259*
Saint-Etienne   *199*
Saint Gall   83
Saint-Hubert   *153*
Saint-Martin, Léonce de   198
Saint-Maximin-la-Sainte-Baume   *193*
Saint-Quentin   191; *189*
Saint-Saëns, Camille   193, 194, 196
Sankt Florian   *71*
Sankt Katharinental   *130*
Sankt Urban   *128*
Salamanca   54; *207, 214, 215*
Salanova, Nicolás de   *205, 206*
Salem   *245*
Salice, Walther de   82
Salieri, Antonio   119
Salinas, Francisco   *207*
Salling, Fredric   *94*
Salmenhaara, Erkki   244
Salonen, Sulo   243
Sals, Alain   *197*
Salt Lake City   *251*
Salzburg   74, 88, 117; *66, 69*
Salzburg, Hermann von   83
Samedan   *136*
Sampaio & Son, João   *232, 237, 238*
Sánchez, José António   *224*
Sand, George   *137*
Sandberg Nielsen, Otto   243
Sandtner Orgelbau   *275*
San Miguel de Allende   *227*
Sans, Tiburcio   *222*
Santa Maria, Tomas de   217, 220
Santini, Giuseppe Maria   77
Santos, António José dos   *234, 239*
Santucci, Marco   77

Sanxo, Geroni   Fig. 72
São Bento Gomes, Manuel de   *235*
Sapatski   *106*
Saragossa   219; *205*
Sarti, Giuseppe   74
Satie, Erik   199
Sauer, Wilhelm   *34, 46, 54, 59, 100, 121*
Sauvage, Antoine   *189*
Scarlatti, Alessandro   75, 176
Scarlatti, Domenico   75, 76, 116, 174, 176, 219
Schaab, Robert   120
Scheibbs   *67*
Scheibe, Johann Adolph   117
Scheidemann, Heinrich   89, 92, 161
Scheidt, Samuel   86, 89, 90, 91, 92, 109, 112, 161, 162; *21*
Schein, Johann Hermann   90
Scherer the Younger, Hans   Fig. 64
Scherer, Jakob   Fig. 67
Scherer, Jonas   *64*
Scherer, Sebastian Anton   87
Scherweit   *104*
Schibler, Armin   244
Schildt, Melchior   89, 92
Schlag   *103*
Schleswig   92
Schlick, Arnolt   28, 82, 83, 92; *33*
Schmahl, Georg Friedrich   *53*
Schmalkalden   111, 113
Schmid the Elder, Bernhard   84
Schmid the Younger, Bernhard   85
Schmidt, Bernhard   172, 175
Schmidt, Franz   123
Schmidt, J.   *141*
Schmidt, Konrad   *64*
Schmidt, Michael   *64*
Schmidt, Paul   *54*
Schmoele   41
Schnebel, Dietrich   246
Schneider, Friedrich   120
Schneider, Johann   116
Schneider, Johann Gottlob   120
Schnitger, Arp   34, 117; Figs. 13, 48; *34, 35, 38, 39, 40, 44, 47, 49, 92, 143, 233*
Schnyder, Jodokus   *131*
Schoenberg, Arnold   124, 246
Schönach, Alois   *74*
Schönberg, Stig Gustav   244
Schott, Thomas   Fig. 48; *131*
Schreider (Shrider), Christopher   *161*
Schroeder, Hermann   124
Schubert, Franz   194
Schübler, Johann Georg   114
Schuer, Theodorus van der   *141*
Schuke, A.   *116*
Schuke, Karl   *36, 44, 46, 277*
Schulze, Johann Friedrich   Fig. 64
Schumacher, Etienne   *149*
Schumann, Robert   111, 120, 121
Schuricht, K.F.   *107*
Schut, Jan Albertsz   *140*
Schütz, Heinrich   94, 109, 114
Schwan, Olof   *93, 97*
Schweinfurt   111
Schweitzer, Albert   60, 111, 195
Schwenkedel, Kurt   *202, 259*
Schwerin   116
Schysler, Gregor   Fig. 68
Scipione, Giovanni   75

Scott, Sir Gilbert   *166*
Scott, John Oldrid   *169*
Searles, Edward F.   *249*
Sechter, Simon   120
Seger, Josef   119
Segni, Giulio (Julio da Modena)   73
Segovia   *216*
Seibler, Franz   *109*
Seidl, Johann   *113*
Seixas, (José Antonio) Carlos de   219
Séjan, Nicolas   193, *194*
Selby   *169*
Selby, William   244
Selnecker, Nikolaus   90
Semrád, Bedřich   *110*
Senfl (Sänfli), Ludwig   84, 85, 92
Serassi family   74
Serassi, Giuseppe   39, 77; *26, 32*
Sermisy, Claudin de   185
Sesma Hacia, Jorge de   *221*
Sessions, Roger   245
Severijn, André   *149*
Seville   76, 218, 220; *210*
Shaw, Geoffrey   177
Shaw, Martin   177
's-Hertogenbosch   57; Fig. 68; *36*
Sibelius, Jean   243
Sicher, Fridolin   83
Siefert, Paul   89, 92
Siena   Fig. 47
Sigismund I, King   84
Sigmund, Duke   83
Silbermann, Andreas   Fig. 13; *41, 42, 56, 137, 171, 190, 192*
Silbermann, Gottfried   119; *41, 42, 43, 45, 46, 52, 107*
Silbermann, Johann Andreas   *134, 135, 190*
Silbermann, Johann Daniel   *52*
Simil   *121*
Simon, Ekkehard   *33*
Simonds, Bruce   245
Simons, Frans   Fig. 68
Sinzig   246, *274*
Sion   54; *122*
Siret, Nicolas   192
Sitarski, Józef   *19*
Sjögren, G.E.   244
Skinner, Ernest M. Organ Company   244, 254
Slavenski, Josip   244
Slavík, Jan   119
Slavický, Klement   244
Smend, Friedrich   113
Smith, ‹Father› (Bernard)   172; Fig. 70; *156, 159, 160, 161*
Smits, Franciscus Cornelius   *148*
Sneek   *143*
Snetzler, Johann   172, 175; *163, 243*
Söderholm, Valdemar   244
Soderini, Agostino   73
Söderling   *90*
Sokola, Milos   244
Solcito, Sebastiano   *27*
Soler, Antonio   74, 219, 220; *208, 216*
Solesmes   194
Solha, Francisco António   Fig. 48; *20, 236, 238, 240*
Somer, Jean   *186*
Somer, Nicolas   *179, 194*
Sommer, Michael   Fig. 64
Sondershausen   116

Sonneborn 117
Sopron *113*
Sorau *41*
Sorge, Andreas Georg 116, 117
Soto, Francisco de 217, 218
Soukup, Karl 75
South Dennis *243*
Souvigny *195*
Sowa, Jakub 84
Sowerby, Leo 245
Speisegger, Johann Conrad *126, 127, 133*
Spinacino, Francesco 72
Spitta, Philipp 111
Spring City Fig. 7
Springfield *254*
Spurden Rutt, R. & Company *162*
Stade 92; *38, 49*
Stahov 119
Stamic (Stamitz), Jan Václav 110
Stams *70*
Stanford, Sir Charles Villiers 177
Staniszewski, Jana *104*
Stanley, (Charles) John 175
Steck, János 84
Steenwijk, Gijsbert van 161
Steere, J. W. & Son Organ Company *254*
Steffani 114
Steibelt, Daniel 75
Steigleder, Adam 85
Steigleder, Johann Ulrich 86
Stein *67*
Stein, Georg Markus *33*
Stein the Elder, Johann Georg *57*
Steinmeyer, G. F. *33, 50, 55, 59*
Stellwagen, Friedrich Figs. 63, 64, 66, 67; *36*
Stephani, J. Fig. 67; *45*
Stettin 116
Stilpp, Karl *67*
Stockholm 89; *88, 92, 95*
Stråhle, Daniel *94*
Stråhle, Peter *95, 96*
Stralsund *36*
Strasbourg 49, 83, 85, 88; *42, 56, 166, 171, 174, 192*
Strategier, Hermann 163
Straube, Karl 123, 124
Studziński, Stanislav *103*
Strungk, Delphin 92
Strungk, Nicolaus Adam 109
Stumm, Johann Heinrich *55*
Stumm, Johann Philipp *55*
Sturgeon, William 41
Stuttgart 85, 86, 87, 160; Fig. 19
Suhl 111, 113, 117
Swahlberg, Mathias *88, 94, 97*
Swann, William 87
Sweelinck, Dirk 162
Sweelinck, Jan Pieterszoon 76, 85, 89, 91, 92, 112, 159ff.
Swieta Lipka *105*
Swybbertszoon, Pieter 161
Szoller, Maciej *102*
Szondi, János 84
Szönyi, Ersébet 244

Tallis, Thomas 171, 172
Tamburini, Giovanni Fig. 46; *23, 265*
Tannenberg, David Fig. 7
Taraschi, Giovanni *25*
Taraschi, Giulio *25*

Tarragona Fig. 72
Taverner, John 171
Taxco *224*
Taylor, John 120
Techelmann, Franz Mathias 89
Teixidor, Pedro Andrés *206*
Telemann, Georg Michael 108, 117
Telemann, Georg Philipp 110, 116, 117, 119
Tennstedt 117
Teplá *111*
Terlecki, Max *105*
Tertletzki, Brothers *102, 104*
Testa, Celestino *28*
Texmelucán *228*
Thamar, Thomas *157, 158, 161*
Thayssner, Zacharias 37; *51*
Theodosius Fig. 2
Theophilus, monk 53
Thiele, Ludwig 120
Thierry, Alexandre *184, 186, 191*
Thierry François *184, 189*
Thierry, Pierre *184*
Thiessé, Pierre-Claude *184*
Thomelin, Jacques-Denis 187, 190
Thomson, Virgil 245
Thorne, John 171
Thybo, Leif 243
Thyrestam, Gunnar Olof 244
Tibães Fig. 48; *236, 238, 241*
Tichý, Otto Albert 244
Tideman, Filip *140*
Tiradentes *226*
Titcomb, Everett 245
Titelouze, Jehan 57, 185, 186, 187, 188, 189, 197; *21*
Tlaxcala *229*
Toggenburg *133*
Toledo 45, 56, 57; *213, 216, 217*
Toller, Eberhard *44*
Tomas, Marco 246
Tomkins, Thomas 172
Tønder *80*
Töpfer, Johann Gottlob 120
Torelli, Giuseppe 110
Torrijos, Diego de 219
Torrlösa *89*
Toruń *100*
Tournemire, Charles Arnould 195, 197, 198
Trabaci, Giovanni Maria 72, 73, 76, 218
Traeri, Annibale *28*
Traeri, Francesco *23*
Trastevere 76
Travers, John 174
Trebel *57*
Tregian, Francis 172
Tretzscher, Mathias *171*
Tribuot, Julien *179*
Trier *277*
Trier, Johann 116
Trofeo, Ruggiero 74
Tromboncino, Bartolomeo 73
Tronci 45
Troyes 192
Tschupp, Anton Joseph *126*
Tunder, Franz 92, 93, 94; Fig. 66
Turin 74, 75
Tye, Christopher 171
Tyrannia, Julia *3*
Tytman *117*
Tytuvėnai *118*

Ulm 85, 87
Umbreit, Karl Gottlieb 117
Uppsala 161
Utrecht 53; Fig. 18; *138, 147*
Utrecht, Michael 161
Uzès *185*

Vaideau, Pierre *189*
Valencia 219, *206*
Valentinian III, Emperor *4*
Valentini, Giovanni 87
Valladolid 210
Valle *218*
Valon, Pierre *183*
Valréas *183, 198*
Vaňhal, Jan Křtitel 119
Van Vulpen *147*
Varde *257*
Västerlövsta *96*
Västra Eneby *98*
Växjo *90*
Venegas de Henestrosa, Luis 217, 218
Venice 49, 72, 73, 74, 75, 86, 94, 159, 161; *23, 32*
Verbruggen the Elder, Peter *150*
Verdalonga, José *208, 216, 217*
Verdalonga, Valentin *217*
Vermeersch, H. *154*
Vermeulen *145*
Verona *30*
Veronese, Paolo 49
Versailles 191, 193
Verschueren, Léon Fig. 68; *145*
Vesterlund, John *93*
Vetters, Andreas Nicolaus 89
Viderø, Finn 243
Vienna 83, 84, 85, 86, 87, 88, 89, 119, 120, 174; *41, 72, 75, 113*
Vierling, Johann Gottfried 117
Vierne, Louis 162, 195, 197, 198, 245
Vila, Pedro Alberto 217, 218
Vilaça, José *241*
Vila do Conde *240*
Vilnius *116, 117*
Vinnerstad *91*
Virestad *90*
Vitruvius Figs. 16, 18; *15*
Vivaldi, Antonio 75, 115, 116, 174
Vocelka *110*
Vogler, Georg Joseph 118, 120
Vogler, Johann Kaspar 116
Vogt, Jacques *137*
Vogt, Theodor *16*
Vulpius, Melchior 90

Wagenaar, Jasper *140*
Wagner, Joachim *46*
Wagner, Richard 194
Walcha, Helmut 124
Walcker, Eberhard Friedrich 47, 59, 120; Figs. 42, 43; *51, 58, 62, 249, 251*
Walcker & Company 45, 246; *48, 119*
Walker, J. W. & Sons *155*
Wallenström, Daniel *96*
Walmisley, Thomas (Attwood) 177
Walond, William 176
Walter, Johann 90
Walther, Johann Gottfried 89, 110, 115, 116, 174, 193
Wanamaker, Rodman *21*

Warwick, Thomas   172
Weber, Bernhard Christian   117
Wechmar   111, 113
Weck, Hans   83
Weckmann, Matthias   92, 93, 94
Wedrup, Bo   *93*
Wegmann, Georg   *171*
Weigle, Carl   *134*
Weigle, firm   50
Weimar   110, 115, 116, 117, 119, 120
Weinberger, Jaromir   245
Weingarten   50; Fig. 48; *50, 53*
Weissenfels   119
Weitz, Guy   162
Welin, Karl-Erik   244, 246
Wender, J.F.   *17*
Werckmeister, Andreas   109
Werner, Gregor Joseph   119
Werner of Brandenburg   *87*
Wernitzky, Heinrich   *80*
Wesley family   176
Wesley, Charles   175, 177
Wesley, John   177
Wesley, Samuel   175, 177
Wesley, Samuel Sebastian   177
Wetzel, Martin   *171*
Widor, Charles-Marie   121, 162, 194–8, 245; *121, 187*
Wiedermann, Bedřich Antonín   244
Wiest, Johann   *114*
Wiest, Josef   *114*
Wilhelm Ernst, Duke   115, 117

Wilhelmy, Georg Wilhelm   *49*
Wilhelmy, Johann Georg   *38, 39, 49*
Wilkander, David   244
Willaert, Adrian   72, 84, 159
Willan, Healey   245
Willcox, John H.   245
Willis, Henry   Fig. 70; *168*
Willis III, Henry   *168*
Willis, Henry & Sons   *168*; Fig. 71
Winchester   30, 176
Winsum   82
Wisniewski, J.B.   *107*
Wistenius, Jonas   *91*
Witt, Julius   *102*
Witte, C.G.F.   *141*
Witten-Annen   *267*
Wöckherl, Johann   *113*
Wolf, Wilhelm   *205*
Wolfenbüttel   89, 92
Wolff, Christian Michael   116
Wolff, Heinz   *267*
Wolff, Johann Georg   *102*
Wolf-Giusto, Henri   *137*
Wolz, Johann   85
Wood, Charles   177
Wordsworth & Company   *168*
Woodstock   *168*
Worm, Amdi   *83, 86*
Wren, Sir Christopher   Fig. 70
Wright, M. Searle   245
Wulf, Jan   *107*
Wulff, Hermann   *35*

Wulstand   30
Würzburg   *270*
Wybrański, M.   *100*
Wynyates, Compton   *160*

Xenakis, Yannis   246

York   *165*
Ypma, L.   *139*
Yun, Isang   246

Zaccara da Terama, Antonio   70
Zach, Jan   119
Zachariassen, Sybrand   *266*
Zacher, Gerd   246
Zachow, Friedrich Wilhelm   89, 109, 110, 116, 173
Zarlino, Gioseffo   160, 161
Zebrowski, Aleksander   *103, 106*
Zeitz   117
Zelter, Carl Friedrich   111
Zenolini, Carlo   74, 77
Zika, Wilhelm   *64, 71*
Zimmermann, Anton   119
Zipoli, Domenico   75, 76
Zisecke   113
Zittau   88, 109, 116
Zliten   *1*
Zurich   *261*
Zwettl   *69*
Zwickau   117
Zwolle, Arnaut de   54

Photo Credits

The author and publishers are grateful to photographers, museums and other institutions for providing the illustrations reproduced in this volume. The figures refer to the Plates.
The illustrations were compiled by Ingrid de Kalbermatten.

Aargauische Denkmalpflege, Aarau   131
A.C.L. Brusseles   8, 149, 152
Alinari, Florence   6, 29
Anderson   26, 28
W. Andraschek, Horn   73
Antikvarisk-Topografiska Arkivet, Stockholm   87, 90–4
Arch. Photo., Paris/S.P.A.D.E.M.   188, 189, 193, 198
Bärenreiter-Bild-Archiv, Cassel   260, 267
Ferdinando Barsotti   24
R. Bersier, Fribourg   Figs. 1, 2, 4, 10, 17, 18, 20, 21–3, 26, 32, 35, 42, 43, 50–2, 54–61
Klaus G. Beyer, Weimar   37, 42, 43
Bibliothèque nationale, Paris   4, 7, 10–13, 15; Fig. 62
Bildarchiv Foto Marburg   119
P. Boissonnas, Geneva   256
H. Bonde-Hansen   275
Boudot-Lamotte, Paris   1, 109
Erika Brande, Hanover   258
British Museum, London   Fig. 6
Bundesdenkmalamt, Vienna   64
Ottavio Clavuot, Samedan   136
G. Costa   82
Deutsche Fotothek, Dresden   17, 54
Deutscher Kunstverlag-Bavaria Gauting   52
Jean Dieuzaide, Toulouse   172, 217
Diözesanbildstelle, Linz   266
Essex Institute, Salem, MA   242, 244, 245
L.A. Esteves Pareira, Parede   20, 232
Cristina Fedele   123, 280
D.A. Flentrop, Zaandam   269
Fonds Mercator, Antwerp   138, 140, 144, 150, 151, 154 (photos De Schutter); 139, 141–3, 145, 146, 148, 153 (photos F. van Os)
Foto-Beleza, Oporto   234, 238, 239, 241
Fotofast, Bologna   31
Foto-Scholz, Rendsburg   44
Friebel AG, Sursee   128
Niels Fries, Copenhagen   77, 80, 84
Th. Frobenius & Sønner, Lyngby   79, 85, 89, 273
Hans-J. Füglister, Grimisuat   129
J.C. & S. Gabillet, St-Donat   259
Photo Gambetta, Poitiers   22
Pierre Ch. George, Geneva   264
Grønlund's Forlag, Copenhagen   78, 81
Dr. Dieter Grossmann, Marburg   58
Peter Heman, Basle   25, 30, 125, 134, 135, 170, 171, 173–84, 186, 187, 190–2, 194, 195, 197, 201–4
Historisches Museum, Basle   124
Gyula Holics, Budapest   112–14
Foto Holy, Innsbruck   60
Z. Hrubec   111
I.N.A.H., Mexico City   228
Institut d'Archéologie Méditerranéenne, Chéné-Foliot   3
Karl Jud, Zurich   53, 71
Kant. Hochbauamt, Zurich   126, 127
KAW, Warsaw   107
Johannes Klais, Bonn   230, 270
Klasztor OO. Cystersów, Jedrzejów   19
Pal Kelemen, Norfolk, CT   218, 219, 223–5 (photos Elisabeth Z. Kelemen); 221, 222, 226
Detlef Kleuker, Bielefeld   281

Atelier Krassel, Haderslev   83
Dorothy & Henry Kraus, Braziller, NY   9
Orgelbau Th. Kuhn AG, Männedorf   133
Lauros-Giraudon, Paris   185
Jim Lewis, Pasadena, CA   253; Fig. 45
Linda Color S.A., Petit-Lancy   122
Domenico Lucchetti, Bergamo   32
P. Stanislaus Mali, Stams   70
Mas, Barcelona   5, 206, 207, 210, 212, 213, 216
Mather Corporation, Portland, OR   271
Leonore Mau, Hamburg   76
MTI, Budapest   115
Willy Müller, Gottlieben   130
Ludwig von Münchow   86
Thomas Murray, Newbury, MA   243, 246, 250
Mario Novais, Lisbon   231, 233, 235–7, 240
Oronoz S.A., Madrid   208, 209, 214, 215
Osuna   220
Roman Pankofer, Herrsching   18, 33, 48, 50, 55, 56, 63, 66–9, 74, 75
Gregor Peda, Passau   59
Polska Akademia Nauk   99, 100, 104
Rapuzzi, Brescia   27
Michael Reckling, Marbella   272
Gerd Remmer, Flensburg   34
Rheinisches Landesmuseum, Trier   2
Christopher Ridley, London   155–69
Viktor Rihsé, Stade   38–40, 47, 49
Pete Rumo, Fribourg   137
Foto Saebens, Worpswede   35
Ernst Schäfer, Weimar   36, 41, 45, 46, 51
Schlossverwaltung, Innsbruck   61
Otto Schwarz, Barcelona   211
Albert Seeberger, Paris   255
Jean-Jacques Soin, Royan   196, 200, 263
Studio Guy, Saint-Etienne   199
Jarzy Szandomirakj   102
Giovanni Tamburini, Crema   265
R.A. Unnerbäck   88, 98
VAAP, Moscow   116, 117, 118, 120
William Van Pelt, Glen Allen, VA   247, 252, 254
A. Villani & Figli, Bologna   23
Vorarlberger Landesmuseum, Bregenz   62
Gösta Wiberg   97
Helmut Wilhelm   96
T. Zalewski   101
Figures 63–7, 68, 70 and 72 are taken from A. G. Hill, *Organ-Cases,* London, 1883–91 (Buren, 1975).

The technical drawings were made by François Delor

This book was printed in January 1985 by Paul Attinger S. A., Neuchâtel
Photolithographs: Schwitter AG, Basle
Setting: Typobauer Filmsatz GmbH, Ostfildern
Binding: Schumacher AG, Schmitten
Layout and production: Emma Staffelbach

Printed in Switzerland